1997

About Island Press

Island Press is the only nonprofit organization in the United States whose principal purpose is the publication of books on environmental issues and natural resource management. We provide solutions-oriented information to professionals, public officials, business and community leaders, and concerned citizens who are shaping responses to environmental problems.

In 1994, Island Press celebrated its tenth anniversary as the leading provider of timely and practical books that take a multidisciplinary approach to critical environmental concerns. Our growing list of titles reflects our commitment to bringing the best of an expanding body of literature to the environmental community throughout North America and the world.

Support for Island Press is provided by Apple Computer, Inc., The Bullitt Foundation, The Geraldine R. Dodge Foundation, The Energy Foundation, The Ford Foundation, The W. Alton Jones Foundation, The Lyndhurst Foundation, The John D. and Catherine T. MacArthur Foundation, The Andrew W. Mellon Foundation, The Joyce Mertz-Gilmore Foundation, The National Fish and Wildlife Foundation, The Pew Charitable Trusts, The Pew Global Stewardship Initiative, The Rockefeller Philanthropic Collaborative, Inc., and individual donors.

The Tallgrass Restoration Handbook

The Tallgrass Restoration Handbook

For Prairies, Savannas, and Woodlands

Edited by Stephen Packard and Cornelia F. Mutel

Foreword by William R. Jordan III

Society for Ecological Restoration

ISLAND PRESS

Washington, D.C. / Covelo, California

ISLAND PRESS is a trademark of the Center for Resource Economics.

No copyright claim is made in Chapter 14, "Conducting Burns," a work adapted from "How to Manage Small Prairie Fires," by Wayne Pauly, published by the Dane County Park Commission, Madison, WI, 1982, 1985.

Library of Congress Cataloging-in-Publication Data

The Tallgrass restoration handbook : for prairies, savannas, and
   woodlands / edited by Stephen Packard and Cornelia F. Mutel;
   foreword by William R. Jordon III.
       p.   cm.
     Papers presented at a two-day session at the Society for
   Ecological Restoration's Second Annual Conference in Chicago, 1990,
   and prepared for the 12th North American Prairie Conference, held at
   the University of Northern Iowa, Cedar Falls, summer 1990.
     Includes bibliographical references and index.
     ISBN 1-55963-319-0 (cloth). — ISBN 1-55963-320-4 (pbk.)
     1. Prairie plants—Middle West—Handbooks, manuals, etc.
   2. Restoration ecology—Middle West—Handbooks, manuals, etc.
   I. Packard, Stephen.   II. Mutel, Cornelia Fleischer.   III. Society
   for Ecological Restoration. Conference (2nd : 1990 : Chicago, Ill.)
   IV. North American Prairie Conference (12th : 1990 : University of
   Northern Iowa)
   SB434.3.T35   1997
   639.9'9—dc20   96-9763
                                                                CIP

Printed on recycled, acid-free paper ∞ ♻

Manufactured in the United States of America
10   9   8   7   6   5   4   3   2   1

This handbook is dedicated to the evolving plants, animals, and natural communities of the tallgrass region; to the people past, present, and future who inhabit and nurture them; and to all those who recognize our kinship and interdependence with all life on this planet.

Contents

Illustrations

Tables

Foreword

The prairies, as poet Vachel Lindsay wrote, have been "swept away by wheat." What, if any, is to be their future?

This book offers part of the answer to that question. It is, first and foremost, a state-of-the-art account of the craft of prairie restoration, a parts catalogue and repair manual for the tallgrass prairies and oak openings of the Midwest. But it is more than that. It is an account, if you read between the lines, of a new way of perceiving the natural landscape and of interacting with and inhabiting it; the acting out, in practical, hard-headed terms, of an idea about nature that many are coming to see as the basis for a new kind of environmentalism—and ultimately as the key to the survival of classic ecosystems such as the tallgrass prairie.

The prairies are not alone here. Restorationists now work with many other kinds of ecosystems, from alpine meadows to coral reefs. But the prairies of the Midwest have played a leading role in the development of the craft of restoration since its beginning, half a century ago. This being the case, it seems appropriate to begin by considering why our species first came up with the idea of ecological restoration on the tallgrass prairies, and what we have learned in the process.

Prairies provided the occasion for some of the earliest deliberate attempts at ecological restoration for a number of reasons. Of these, the most obvious was that when Americans began to care about prairie conservation, the old prairies were nearly gone. Besides this, and in contrast to some other kinds of ecosystems—notably the forests of the Northeast—prairies, once destroyed, did not come back on their own. If there were going to be any prairies of significant size in most parts of the vast prairie triangle reaching from Indiana south into Texas and north into Manitoba, they would have to be re-planted. Thus people interested in the conservation of prairies found themselves drawn into increasingly sophisticated and self-conscious attempts at the active re-creation—or restoration—of prairies.

What was distinctive here, of course, was not so much the prairies themselves as the cataclysmic change that had taken place on the prairies within the span of a single human lifetime. At no other time in history had an entire landscape been changed so dramatically and in so short a time. In a distinctively American drama, an Edenic landscape was gained and then lost, and our sense of that loss has undoubtedly been a driving force behind prairie restoration from the beginning.

The discovery and elimination of an Arcadian landscape goes a long way toward accounting for the single most distinctive aspect of restoration—the restorationist's commitment not just to rehabilitate or "heal" the land in an abstract sense, but actually to re-create a particular kind of ecosystem, returning it to the landscape and setting it in motion again. Perhaps ironically, the emergence of the notion of restoration in this sense was also encouraged by the fact that prairies have relatively little direct economic value and have never been afforded any kind of legal protection in the United States. Thus the early efforts to restore prairies have all been labors of love motivated by an interest in the ecosystem itself, rather than by laws or regulations or a desire to improve the landscape for some utilitarian purpose. This no doubt helps explain the emphasis on accuracy, as well as the concern about authenticity that has marked prairie restoration efforts almost from the beginning and that makes them a widely accepted paradigm for restoration in its purest and most ecologically ambitious form.

In any case, this emphasis on ecological accuracy (including attention to dynamic and functional as well as structural features of the system) is what distinguishes restoration from other forms of gardening, and from other merely restorative forms of land management. It is, moreover, a distinctively American or New World idea—the result in large part of the cataclysmic encounter of Old World peoples with the prairies and other native landscapes of North America. As Americans consider the form of garden that best reflects American experience, they should keep this in mind. Surely the American garden will include—and in fact may even be—a restored prairie.

In addition to these historical reasons for the emergence of restoration on the prairies, there were technical reasons as well. For one thing, remnants of the old prairies and degraded savannas still survived early in this century, when interest in their conservation began to grow. These served both as models and as inspiration, and as a source of seed, plants, and, more recently, insects and other animals—basically the DNA for restoration efforts.

For another, prairies lend themselves to restoration. This is not to say that prairie restoration is easy, but only that prairies are amenable to tinkering on a reasonable scale and over a reasonable period of time. Many prairie plants mature fairly rapidly. In fact, most will flower and set seed within five years—not overnight, certainly, but a lot faster than most trees. Prairie plants are also relatively small and easy to handle and lend themselves to manipulation by more or less traditional agricultural methods. And finally the prairie itself, though it once covered vast areas, is in many respects a small-featured, fine-textured community, so that it is possible to reproduce many—though certainly not all—of the attributes of a prairie in an area as small as an acre or even less.

These are some of the reasons that, right from the first, prairie emerged as a favorite restoration objective and a kind of exemplar for all restoration. This was true, for example, even in the case of the classic efforts at the University of Wisconsin at Madison Arboretum, where, despite a comprehensive effort to restore a wide variety of native community types, the prairies soon emerged as the centerpiece and in many ways the most successful projects.

All these considerations help explain why prairies have become the Kitty Hawk, as it were, for the craft of ecological restoration. And in the process they have produced a steady stream of lessons—about the prairies themselves, of course, but also about natural landscapes in general and the relationship of humans to them. Many of these lessons will emerge in due course in the chapters of this book. Here, however, it seems appropriate to summarize some of these "lessons of the prairie":

- "Nature" is resilient enough so that even major changes brought about by humans are sometimes reversible. Quite often, in fact, injury to ecosystems can be reversed if we are willing to pay the price in time and effort, though certain kinds of change—the loss of a species or the loss or severe degradation of soil, for example—probably are irreversible, at least for all practical purposes. In fact, one of the benefits of the work of restoration is that it helps us learn to discriminate between reversible and irreversible change—and to judge the difficulty and cost of various types of restoration.

- Restoration is an essential component of any comprehensive conservation program. Ordinarily, people think of ecological restoration in its most dramatic form, where damage is severe and it is necessary to reassemble the ecosystem wholesale, from the ground up. The experience of restorationists, however, makes it clear that significant influences on ecosystems are not necessarily obvious, that subtle influences can have profound effects, and that a program to compensate for those influences is essential if the ecosystem is to survive on its own terms. Consider for example the prairies and savannas of the Midwest, where a single act—a decrease in the frequency of fire at the time of European settlement—resulted in the conversion of millions of acres of rich, ancient prairie to depauperate, young forest.

• Restoration is a powerful way to learn, both about the ecosystem being restored and about our relationship with it. The reason for this is obvious: You can disassemble a thing (such as a prairie) without knowing much about it, but you can't put it back together—that is, restore it—without understanding it pretty well, and also without having a clear idea about how you have affected it. Thus, attempts to restore prairies, beginning with the early experiments at the UW–Madison Arboretum in the 1930s, have led to a constantly deepening understanding and awareness of them. More recently, new ideas about the nature of oak savannas, first put forward by restorationists, have been recognized by some as nothing less than a step toward the rediscovery of a forgotten ecosystem.

• Restoration is essential to conservation, and, although this concept may challenge commonly held ideas of "nature" and what is "natural," such a challenge is not a bad thing. In fact, modernist ideas of nature as radically distinct from humans are themselves destructive and should be challenged. Restoration gives humans a role in "nature's" work and creates artificial natural ecosystems that not only make nonsense of any radical distinction between humans and nature, but also provide a way of negotiating the differences between them.

• The hard work of restoration is not repellent drudgery that people will do only under pressure or for pay or in a spirit of ambivalence, as some have suggested, but is in fact engaging, deeply rewarding work that people seek out eagerly and that tends to become the occasion for rituals of celebration and festival. This is evident from the work of restorationists in many parts of the United States, in Canada, and throughout the world.

But it is perhaps most clearly evident in the emergence of community-based, volunteer-driven restoration projects, such as those in the Chicago area.

This may be the single most important realization that has yet emerged from the restoration community, since it offers nothing less than a warrant for the survival of the prairies and other classic ecosystems on a planet increasingly dominated by human beings.

Hence the importance of prairie restoration. There are good reasons for a new book on the subject. New restoration techniques have been developed, and the work of restorationists has led to clearer ideas about the nature of prairies and oak savannas. The craft of restoration has developed especially rapidly in recent years.

An example is the emergence of interseeding (chapter 11)—the deceptively simple practice of tossing seed of prairie species directly into an existing old-field sod. This development alone has profound implications for the practice of restoration. For one thing, it shows great promise for large areas of degraded woodland and prairie that formerly would have been dismissed as too good to be plowed but not good enough to be managed as a natural area. For another, it has important theoretical implications, raising basic questions about succession, establishment niches and strategies, and other aspects of the dynamics of prairies.

But of particular importance here, interseeding provides a whole new perspective on the process of prairie restoration. In the past, restorationists have commonly started by plowing down existing vegetation, the idea being to clear the way for the natives. That this is not necessary, and in fact is sometimes counterproductive, suggests a radically different approach to restoration of these ecosystems, one less like the traditional gardening practice of plowing followed by seeding or seedling transplant and then by intensive cultivation—or the use of herbicides—to control weeds. Interseeding instead resembles ecologically sophisticated approaches to forestry or range management, which are less intensive and rely more heavily on the ecology of the system itself to accomplish the desired result.

This book is an attempt to represent the "state of the art," but the reader should be aware that we do not thereby mean "the last word." In fact, very little about prairie restoration has achieved the status of the routine or even the commonly accepted. Rather than a mature craft, prairie restoration still, six decades after the first projects were undertaken, involves much of the ongoing experimentation and trial of ideas characteristic of a young, rapidly developing discipline. We hope that this is clearly reflected in this volume, and that many readers will be inspired to undertake the process of exploration and experimentation on their own.

The ongoing experimentation and rapid evolution of techniques account for what is perhaps the book's single most distinctive feature—that it is a compilation of reports from many restorationists, not just one or two, and that most of the authors are practicing restorationists whose primary work is actually the making of prairies. A few work in academic settings, but restorationists from outside the academy are well represented, reflecting both a commitment to get at the nuts and bolts of restoration in a practical, useful way, and also a belief that much of the best work has been done and continues to be done by practitioners directly involved in restoration either avocationally or professionally. While these people may be leaders in the development of new methods and ideas, they are often under-represented in the literature, simply because their work allows them little time—and often little incentive—to report their findings in print.

This book is at least a step toward remedying that deficiency.

William R. Jordan III
University of Wisconsin–Madison Arboretum

Perspective

Stephen Packard and Cornelia F. Mutel

Ecological restoration is a young discipline that takes many forms. Potential benefits range from the modest and immediate—improving the aesthetic appeal of a neighborhood—to the momentous and long-term: saving the atmosphere of the planet. In its present expression, restoration is critical to the recovery of many rare plants, animals, and natural communities.

The techniques of this young science are growing in number and evolving rapidly as restorationists experiment and learn in places as various as backyard garden plots, ten-acre prairies, and ten-thousand-acre landscapes. Restoration also is growing in the hearts of hundreds of thousands of people as they enjoy its products in their yards, on the corporate campuses of their workplaces, and in the forests, prairies, and wetlands where they spend their leisure hours.

As this discipline grows, its terminology evolves. Until recently, the word *restoration* meant something quite distinct from the words *natural area management*. The general rule was that degraded ecosystems were to be restored, but that pristine natural areas were to be largely left alone. Gradually, as managers realized that certain key species in natural areas required larger territories if these species were to reproduce successfully, the line blurred: low-quality land surrounding natural areas was restored, and these restored sites came to be seen as parts of natural areas.

At the same time, conservationists were looking for habitats to restore populations of endangered species in order to foster these species' recovery. For rare plants characteristic of the ancient prairies, the best habitat for reintroduction was often found in the protected natural areas. Thus species began to be restored to natural areas, and the dividing line between restored sites and natural areas blurred further.

Today the word *restoration,* as defined by the Society for Ecological

Figure A. Original tallgrass landscape

Restoration and as used in this book, includes natural area management as well as both *reconstruction* (e.g., planting prairie on plowed ground) and *rehabilitation* (e.g., nursing a degraded prairie back to good health). At many sites all three types of effort are proceeding simultaneously, each having borrowed techniques from the others, and all three contributing to the goal of creating a reintegrated and flourishing landscape where there was once a mixture of tiny remnants, pastures, cornfields, and woodlots.

Applying this expanded definition of restoration to the Midwest, which ecosystems are perceived as prime restoration candidates? Again ideas have changed, for although tallgrass prairies have been replanted and burned for over half a century, woodlands until recently were seen as distinctly different ecosystems that did not need fire (or, for that matter, reseeding or other restoration). Restorationists have come to realize that both our positive and our negative ideas about fire have been too simple minded. For example, we now know that excessive fire can be harmful to small prairies, in particular to their invertebrates. And most mid-western woodlands, as research cited in this volume has increasingly demonstrated, were historically fire-dependent, as were some wetlands. In fact, many of the species of the vast majority of the mid-continent's ecosystems had been fire-adapted for thousands or millions of years when the first Euroamericans (and even the first Native Americans) arrived. Thus today oak savannas and woodlands have become so degraded that they have surpassed even the prairies as prime restoration candidates. And modern restorationists, like the Potawatomi and Osage before them, use fire as a restoration technique on a wide range of midwestern eco-systems—wet to dry, prairie to closed woodland.

This handbook discusses all of these fire-dependent midwestern eco-systems. The region covered is outlined in figure B, a map of the extent of tallgrass prairies and allied woodlands before Euroamerican settlement. The book's initial focus is the prairie, the region's major natural landscape and the one for which restoration techniques are best understood. But, as noted above, the oak savannas and woodlands that mingled with the prairies (see figure C) are now seen as perhaps an even higher priority for conservation. Savannas and woods are discussed here in less detail than the prairies only because this handbook is based on restoration practice, and there has been relatively less restoration practice developed for these oak ecosystems. It should also be noted that prairies and woodlands fre-quently lacked delineation, prairies fading into savannas and savannas into woodlands. This lack of boundaries is often reflected in the overlap-ping use of terms, both in this publication and elsewhere.

Wetlands are a natural part of both grasslands and woods, and in this volume all references to prairie, savanna, and woodland should be un-derstood to include their wetland components unless the context indi-cates otherwise. Most restoration techniques described here apply equally well to fens, sedge meadows, marshes, ephemeral ponds, wet woodlands, and the like (see figure D), particularly to the intermittently wet components that burned regularly. The treatment of wetland restoration in this book focuses principally on the vegetation. There is an abundance of literature on wetland ecosystems elsewhere; refer to this literature especially on such topics as water quality and hydrologic restoration and for treatment of deep-water species of plants and animals. The handbook does not cover non-fire-dependent ecosystems located in this region, including maple-basswood forests and ponds, streams, and deep-water marshes.

This handbook spans the restoration process, from the planning which precedes it through monitoring, which may continue for decades. In addition, the appendixes include information on a variety of subjects (such as prairie plants, vertebrate animals, and literature) useful to anyone interested in the Midwest's natural landscape. Lists of references following the chapters are not intended to be comprehensive; rather, they provide a door that allows entry to the scientific or applied literature. To keep

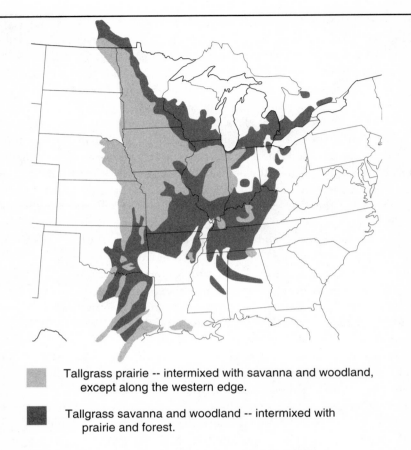

Tallgrass prairie -- intermixed with savanna and woodland, except along the western edge.

Tallgrass savanna and woodland -- intermixed with prairie and forest.

Figure B. Map of tallgrass prairie and oak woodland region

The above map highlights some of the areas of central North America where remnants of tallgrass prairie, savanna, and oak woodland communities may be sought and restoration considered. These communities developed over thousands of years prior to Euroamerican settlement, but today few large intact examples survive anywhere. Immense treeless prairie was once found from Manitoba to Texas to Indiana. East of this open prairie was a mosaic of scattered patches of smaller prairies amid oak savanna and woodland. To the south and southeast of the oak region lay vast pine savannas, which share many species and ecological processes with the oak grasslands. East and north of the oak region, in many places, were forests of fire-intolerant species, but islands of prairie and open woodland (not shown here) were once found in most eastern states. To the west of the tallgrass region were drier prairies—with well-watered grasslands and woodlands becoming widespread among the mountains and along the west coast.

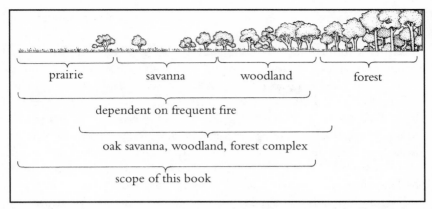

Figure C. *Prairie-forest continuum.* In the prairie region, natural communities are rarely discrete entities separated by sharp lines. Instead, they often blend into each other imperceptibly. Even so, named communities are useful abstractions that help us think and communicate about various parts of the landscape. Healthy savanna and woodland communities have almost disappeared, and the natural continuum as shown above rarely exists today.

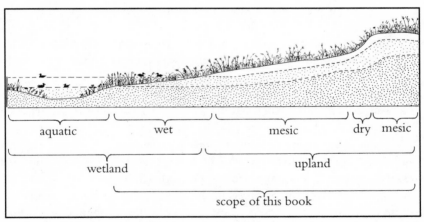

Figure D. *Wetland-upland continuum.* Ducks swim in spring where grasses will wave in the midsummer breeze; wetland restoration overlaps with prairie and woodland restoration.

current on all topics related to prairie restoration, readers are encouraged to follow the periodical publications that discuss this topic, namely the journals *Restoration and Management Notes, Conservation Biology, Natural Areas Journal,* and *Restoration Ecology,* and the proceedings of North American Prairie Conferences, savanna conferences, and wetland and wildlife conferences.

Restoration is a discipline of contrasts. Some restorationists use sophisticated global positioning systems to locate their monitoring plots; others stick to muscle–powered techniques not that different from those practiced by ancient hunter-gatherer civilizations. Some restorationists recommend only those techniques whose efficacy is objectively proven by scientific study; others experiment using their own intuitive inclinations. The latter approach is often the only route possible, for if a practitioner waits for orderly species-by-species, technique-by-technique studies to weigh the many factors involved before beginning restoration, the populations of species in question may in the meantime vanish from the landscape.

Restoration today is similar to battlefield medicine. We learn, by necessity, from attempts to revive torn and insulted ecosystems. The discipline profits much from watching the results of extreme measures taken in these emergency situations. As a result, practical knowledge is far ahead of hard science. We need as much scientific knowledge as we can get to inform restoration decisions, but restorationists must often act with imperfect knowledge if they are to act at all before the biodiversity they seek to preserve disappears. Thus, restoration relies on art and intuition as well as on objective knowledge.

From the outset, this book was intended to be written *by* practitioners, *for* practitioners. The intended reading audience encompasses the wide variety of practicing restorationists, from the backyard gardener to the professional manager of large landscapes, from the conservationist restoring endangered species habitat to the department of transportation landscaper planting protective roadside vegetation. Volunteers and professionals, scientists and consultants, teachers planting schoolyard prairies and researchers involved in biodiversity preservation, all who are restoring native ecosystems should find this book useful.

A similar diversity is reflected in the authors of this book. Academic researchers are among them, yes, but volunteers, agency staff, and restoration entrepreneurs and consultants are also represented. Authors were selected not because of their formal credentials, but because they are practical experts in their fields, people who are intimate with the material since they have tried and tested it on the ground. Practitioners who were adept at a particular component of restoration were solicited to describe that aspect. That person's writing then was sent to a variety of "coaches" who were asked to watch for errors, recommend alternative approaches, and contribute new material of their own. Some were very generous in their contributions, but most often it was left up to the principal chapter authors to decide which suggested revisions to make. While this handbook stresses action and application rather than theory, a few chapters are somewhat more academic in nature, often those on subjects for which an established practice has not yet been developed.

With such a variety of authors, the book naturally conveys a variety of points of view and even some disagreement—a fact that reflects not only the state of the art of restoration, but also the ingenuity and sturdy individualism of the current generation of restorationists, all of whom are in some measure pioneers and share the pioneer's independent spirit. Seeing this as a virtue, we encouraged the contributors to express their own ideas in their own voices. As a result, the chapters do not necessarily represent a consensus among restorationists and may at times contradict one another. But it is not possible to portray the richness of present-day restoration without incorporating these contradictions. Thus, instead of antagonistic, the variations in approaches can be thought of as similar to the products of six grandmas baking cookies in a single kitchen. They probably will never agree on one perfect recipe, but each knows a good method and can be expected to turn out a fine product.

In summary, what lies before you is a hands-on restoration manual for some of this continent's richest and rarest landscapes. It attempts to present a state-of-the-art compendium of this new craft and science. In doing so, it explores a myriad of restoration philosophies and techniques—and seeks to unite them all in a vision of restoring to health and integrity the ecosystems of North America's heartland.

Restorationists today are developing a wealth of information by testing various approaches and learning through trial and error. Their practical knowledge often is great, as is the need for that information among other restorationists. Restorationists are forging a history that is yet mostly unwritten. We hope that this book encourages future efforts and stimulates additional sharing of information, so that the fusing of hands-on knowledge with applied and basic scientific research will forge the foundation for a discipline worthy of playing a powerful role in the future of this planet.

How to Use This Book

A quick skim will familiarize you with the type of information included in this book. The first two chapters describe the ecosystems under consideration, both above and below the ground. These are followed by four chapters that outline factors to consider when planning a restoration. Chapter 3 takes a broad look at the many facets of the planning process, while chapter 4 looks more specifically at how to choose a target restoration community. The latter includes a glossary of important terms and a key to restoration options, both of which may be helpful references throughout your restoration deliberations. The key will lead you in step-wise fashion through a set of choices to a detailed set of instructions for restoring prairie, savanna, and woodland communities. Chapter 5 examines the process of nursing back to health remnants—degraded communities in which some components of natural character survive—while chapter 6 considers the restoration of rare plants to midwestern ecosystems. Included in chapter 5 is a listing of conservative plants that will help you identify degraded savanna and open woodland remnants.

Your planning may steer you next to the chapters on seeds and planting, burning, weed control, or monitoring; the restoration process can begin with any of these. Considerations of collecting or purchasing seed, processing and treating seed, and planning seed mixes that are specific to site are outlined in chapters 7 through 10. Before you sow seed, you will need to choose between the two very different techniques for doing so described in chapters 11 and 12. Generally speaking, interseeding (chapter 11) is chosen for remnant communities where some native species remain (although other types of sites also can be interseeded). In contrast, plowed-ground planting techniques, discussed in chapter 12, are usually applied to lands that have been cultivated for many years and thus have already lost most of their biodiversity. Chapter 13 presents a specialized technique for restoring small areas: the hand planting of seedlings. These seven chapters are supplemented by numerous tables which include a chart of seed collection dates, several specific types of seed mixes, and a summary of seed treatment and propagation techniques.

Management and monitoring is crucial to the restoration process. Chapters 14 through 16 describe prescribed burning and multiple techniques for controlling weedy invaders on a species-by-species basis. A good guide to the plants of your state or region will greatly aid weed identification; such a guide is imperative to most steps of the restoration process. Plant-monitoring techniques along with case studies constitute chapter 17. This chapter presents details of the floristic quality assessment (FQA), a technique for measuring changes in community quality that depends on coefficients of conservatism. (Chapter 5 also describes use of the FQA to assess remnant quality.) Coefficients of conservatism are assigned to native plants on a statewide or regional basis, reflecting the species' fidelity to high-quality ecosystems. Coefficients for those areas where they have been assigned are listed in appendix A for prairie plants, and in table 5.1 for selected savanna and woodland plants.

Restorations are aimed at the entire community of organisms, not just at plants. Chapters 18 through 21 present some of the current knowledge about restoring, managing, and monitoring populations of native insects, amphibians and reptiles, birds, and bison. Although restoration of animal populations is understood less well than that of plants, knowledge of animal restoration is crucial and growing.

The appendixes provide mechanisms for more deeply understanding the communities in question. Appendixes A and B consist of comprehensive lists of tallgrass prairie vascular plants (along with their distribution, status, and coefficients of wetness and conservatism) and of vertebrate animals, their habitats, and distribution. Appendix D lists publications that describe in detail, for each region or state, the communities that are the goals of restoration. Sources of seed for purchase and of equipment for the many steps of the restoration process—planting, seed collection, burning, and the like—are included in appendix E. The listing of restoration organizations and World Wide Web sites in appendix F opens the door to other sources of information, which can provide current knowledge on an ongoing basis.

Common rather than scientific names of plants have been used throughout the text, excluding the tables. Appendix C includes the scientific names of all plants mentioned in the text. These scientific names are included not only to assure correct plant recognition, but also to allow cross-referencing of the many tables in the book, which do include scientific names and are typically arranged alphabetically by genus. Scientific names generally follow the nomenclatural concepts of Kartesz (*A Synonymized Checklist of the Vascular Flora of the United States, Canada, and Greenland,* 2 vols., Timber Press, 1994)—the only authority covering the entire biome. Unless otherwise indicated, all trinomial scientific names refer to varieties. In the few instances when this book's nomenclature differs from that of Kartesz, the scientific name is followed by an asterisk (*). Since other plant guides may use names that differ from those in Kartesz, appendix C also provides a cross-referenced list of scientific names that are most likely to be encountered by the restorationist. Scientific names that have been cross-referenced in this appendix have been preceded by a dagger (†) throughout the book's tables.

While this manual focuses on the extensive tallgrass region as outlined in figure B, the applicability of parts of the text is sometimes broader and sometimes narrower. Certain principles and techniques apply to fire-adapted woodlands and grasslands beyond the midwestern United States. Other principles and techniques, as indicated in the text, apply most specifically to the region where the majority of prairie and savanna restoration has been performed: the east-central tallgrass region including northwestern Indiana, northern and central Illinois, southern Wisconsin, southeastern Minnesota, eastern and central Iowa, and northeastern Missouri. Toward the edges of and outside of this region, dates for planting and seed gathering, appropriate species for planting lists, problem species, and other factors vary, changing quickly as one moves from north to south and more gradually as one moves from east to west. Thus, outside of the east-central tallgrass region, timing of activities, techniques, and other specifics will need to be modified either through personal experience or by consulting local literature or practitioners.

Likewise, the reader will note that the plants listed vary from chapter to chapter and table to table. This variation springs not only from the differences in communities, types of sites, authors' experiences, and restoration techniques discussed in this book, but also from changes in the tables' coverage and applicability, which range from the entire tallgrass biome to much smaller, restricted areas. Often the scope is narrow, and has been indicated as such, when more widely applicable information was not available. Sometimes tables have been purposely limited to specific regions, or to areas toward the edge of the prairie region, to aid restorationists in those locales.

Whether you initially read certain sections or the handbook in its entirety, you are likely to cycle through this book again and again, flipping back and forth from chapter to chapter as your concerns and management activities change with the season. We encourage you to apply the concepts to your particular circumstances. Consider the manual a restoration tool, mark it up with information found to be useful in your area and, as you do so, initiate this book into the ranks of an old and faithful companion.

Acknowledgments

As ecologist Frank Egler put it, an ecosystem is more complicated than we think—and more complicated than we *can* think. It is not possible for any person to have read and retained all the ecological literature on the plants and animals of the tallgrass region. It is also impossible to know all facets of the rapidly developing discipline of ecosystem restoration—including both its literature and its practice. Thus, this book by necessity has resulted from the efforts of a great many people. The major contributors are listed here. Yet so many have contributed so much that the listing is only partial.

The handbook was originally the idea of William Jordan III, who enlisted Stephen Packard as editor. Packard invited some of the most widely respected and experienced practitioners and researchers from across the tallgrass region to present draft chapters during a two-day public session at the Society for Ecological Restoration's second annual conference in Chicago in 1990. Following the SER conference, many of the participants and some additional restorationists agreed to turn tapes of the presentations and audience responses into book chapters. Drafts of these were prepared in time for the Twelfth North American Prairie Conference at the University of Northern Iowa, Cedar Falls, held in the summer of 1990, and once again these were reviewed in a plenary session at that conference.

It soon became apparent that the multi-authored and participatory work that was planned would require major editing support, and Bill Jordan recruited Harold (Bud) Nelson to assist with this. Bud solicited, managed, and edited significant sections of the first manuscript draft. Sadly, although he invested several years of energy and intensive effort in this project, he did not live to see the fruits of his labor. Two years prior to his death in early 1996, Cornelia Mutel assumed co-editorship with

Packard. Although only a few of project's earliest efforts appear in their original form in the present volume, participants at the two conferences as well as Bud Nelson helped identify the issues and lay the foundation for the later work of authors and editors.

The project was greatly improved by the support and counsel of Barbara Dean and Barbara Youngblood at Island Press, which also solicited a crucial grant from the National Fish and Wildlife Foundation. Don Falk and others at the Society for Ecological Restoration administered the grant and sponsored the project.

The contributions of the many authors of book sections represented a difficult tradeoff for these authors, since effort invested in this project frequently wrenched them from businesses and professions that demand their attention. Although few of the authors write regularly as part of their work, they all went through the sometimes trying process of composition and multiple revisions with grace and patience. Principal credit for the substance of this book goes directly to the chapter authors, as well as to those earlier contributors whose writing and ideas enriched but did not appear in the final volume.

Many others contributed to various manuscript sections. Some who have been most central to the concept and realization of this book include: Pauline Drobney, William Jordan III, Virginia Kline, Doug Ladd, Ken McCarty, Harold (Bud) Nelson, Paul Nelson, Laurel Ross, and Bill McClain. Dave Egan, University of Wisconsin–Madison Arboretum, assumed editorship of chapters 7, 8, and 9 on seeds. Table 5.1 was prepared by Gerould Wilhelm of Conservation Design Forum, Illinois. Tables 7.1, 10.1, and 12.1 were prepared by Jim Steffen, with information for table 7.1 in part contributed by Jane and John Balaban and Bev Hansen of the North Branch Prairie Project near Chicago, and Tom Vanderpoel, Savanna Landscaping, Illinois. Table 9.1 was put together by Neil Diboll, Prairie Nursery, Wisconsin, and by Dave Egan. Tables 11.1 and 11.2 are sample seed-mix lists compiled by John and Jane Balaban and Stephen Packard for the North Branch Prairie Project. The regional seed lists in table 12.2 were compiled by Dave Egan, with assistance from Alan Wade, Prairie Moon Nursery, Minnesota; and Bill Whitney, Prairie/Plains Resource Institute, Nebraska. Sections of appendix B were substantially reviewed by Elmer C. Birney, Bell Museum of Natural History, Minnesota; Jim Herkert, Illinois Endangered Species Protection Board; and Ken Mierzwa, TAMS Consultants, Inc., Illinois. Appendix D was put together by Laurel M. Ross of the Nature Conservancy in Illinois and Gregory Mikkelson, University of Chicago, with assistance from the following: Dennis Albert, David Diamond, Pauline Drobney, Don Faber-Langendoen, Cloyce Hedge, Bruce Hoagland, Kelly Kincher, John Morgan, Dave Ode, Gregory J. Schneider, Jerry Steinauer, Chris Wilson, and Daniel Wovcha. Michael Ulrich, Intercoastal Ecological Services, Wisconsin, along with Katie Green and Dave Egan, produced appendix E. Dave Egan also compiled the list of World Wide Web sites included in appendix F. Other persons who gave special assistance with chapter 16 and appendix A are listed within those sections. Invaluable advice and assistance with questions of plant nomenclature were provided by Doug Ladd, Missouri Nature Conservancy, and Floyd Swink, Morton Arboretum. Editorial assistance was contributed by Rebecca Gee, Christine Mlot, Jennifer Page, Laurel Ross, and David Wachtel.

Paul W. Nelson went to great pains to achieve technical accuracy in his sketches and created the elegant illustrations that appear as figures A, C, D, and those in chapters 1, 3, 4, 5, 7, 11, and 16. John Norton prepared the fire sketches in chapter 14. Figure B was taken from a base map by A. W. Küchler (*Potential Natural Vegetation of the Coterminous United States,* American Geographical Society Special Publication No. 36, 1964), with modifications suggested by published and unpublished local maps from Dennis Albert, Wasyl Bakowsky, Tom Foti, Michael Homoya, Scott Simon, and Gerald Steinauer.

Reviewers made major contributions to most sections of the book. They corrected errors, provided additional information, and improved clarity, emphasis, and focus. Reviewers are listed here with the parts or chapters they coached: Brian J. Bader, University of Wisconsin-Madison Arboretum (table 7.1 and chapter 10); John and Jane Balaban, North Branch Prairie Project, Illinois (chapters 4, 7, and 17); Paul Christiansen, Cornell College, Iowa (chapters 4 and 11); Ed Collins, McHenry County Conservation District, Illinois (chapters 5 and 11); Pauline Drobney, Walnut Creek National Wildlife Refuge, Iowa (chapters 1-4, 11, and 17); Christopher Dunn, Morton Arboretum (chapter 17); Rich Henderson, Wisconsin Department of Natural Resources (chapters 4, 5, and 11); Jim Herkert, Illinois Endangered Species Protection Board (Chapter 20); Rich Hyerczyk, Palos Restoration Project, Illinois (chapter 4); Tom R. Johnson, Missouri Department of Conservation (chapter 19); Virginia Kline, University of Wisconsin-Madison Arboretum (chapters 4, 14, and 15); Douglas Ladd, Missouri Nature Conservancy (chapters 5 and 17); Larry Larson, Prairie State Park, Missouri (chapter 21); Mark Leach, University of Wisconsin-Madison Arboretum (chapter 7); Loren Lown, Polk County Conservation Board, Iowa (chapter 16); J. Kenneth McCarty, Missouri Department of Natural

Resources (chapters 1–5, 11, and 21); Bill McClain, Illinois Department of Conservation (chapters 2 and 12–15); John Morgan, Prairie Habitats, Manitoba (chapters 7–10); James Mundy, Hamilton County Park District, Ohio (tables 12.1 and 12.2); Dennis Nyberg, University of Illinois at Chicago (chapter 17); Ron Panzer, Northeastern Illinois University (chapter 18); John Pearson, Iowa Department of Natural Resources (chapter 17); Scott Robinson, Illinois Natural History Survey (figure 4.1); Laurel Ross, Illinois Nature Conservancy (chapters 4, 11, and 17); John Shuey, Indiana Nature Conservancy (chapter 18); Thomas Simpson, Morton Arboretum (chapter 17); David Sollenberger, Chicago Botanic Garden (tables 12.1 and 12.2); Tom Vanderpoel, Savanna Landscaping, Illinois (chapter 11); Alan Wade, Prairie Moon Nursery, Minnesota (tables 12.1 and 12.2); Gerould Wilhelm, Conservation Design Forum, Illinois (chapter 17); Brian Winter, Minnesota Nature Conservancy (chapters 14 and 15); and Joy Zedler, Pacific Estuarine Research Laboratory, California (chapter 17).

Thanks to the University of Wisconsin-Madison Arboretum for administrative and logistical support to Bud Nelson and others, to the Illinois chapter of the Nature Conservancy for support to Stephen Packard, and to the Iowa Institute of Hydraulic Research, the University of Iowa, for support to Cornelia Mutel.

A significant number of additional natural area managers, researchers, and restorationists contributed time, ideas, information, and productive criticism to segments of the book throughout its long gestation and birth. Although far too numerous to name, these individuals and their contributions were influential and appreciated.

It is all of these, the many who through the years have devoted their lives and dedicated their energies to the exploration, preservation, and restoration of disappearing ecosystems, who deserve ultimate credit for the insights and techniques outlined in this handbook.

Introduction

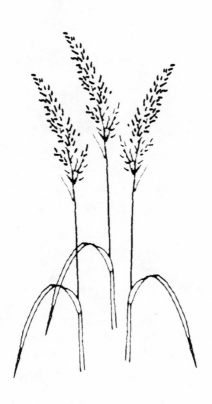

1
Orchards of Oak and a Sea of Grass

Virginia M. Kline

Grasslands developed in the midsection of the North American continent millions of years ago, sometime after the uplift of the Rocky Mountains created a wedge-shaped rain shadow extending from the mountains toward the east, which provided drier habitats favorable to grasses. Over the millennia, in response to climate changes, the size and the eastward extent of the grasslands have fluctuated. Figure B shows the configuration that the tallgrass prairies have assumed for roughly the past five thousand years. From west to east the height of the grasses and the frequency of trees increase, reflecting a gradient of increasing moisture.

The tallgrass prairie and the prairie-forest transition, which are the focus of this book, extend from Texas north into Canada and from central Nebraska east to Ohio, with major portions in Iowa and its adjacent states. The prairie-forest transition was most likely a shifting mosaic of prairie, oak savanna, and oak forest, the boundaries of each determined by recent fire history and short-term climate fluctuations, with frequent fires and dry periods favoring prairie and savanna over forest.

Early observers, seeing the tallgrass prairie for the first time and marveling at the phenomenon of wind-rippled grass stretching to the horizon, frequently compared the effect to that of the ocean. For example, in 1835, Lieutenant D. Ruggles, stationed at Fort Winnebago in south-central Wisconsin, described the surrounding prairies with these words:

> In some instances, prairies are found stretching for miles around, without a tree or shrub, so level as scarcely to present a single undulation; in others, those called "rolling prairies," appears in undulation upon undulation, as far as the eye can reach presenting a view of peculiar sublimity, especially to the beholder for the first time. It seems when in verdure, a real troubled ocean, wave upon wave, rolls before you, ever varying, ever swelling; even the breezes play around

to heighten the illusion; so that here at near two thousand miles from the ocean, we have a facsimile of sublimity, which no minia-ture imitation can approach. (Curtis 1959, p. 264)

At about the same time, W.R. Smith, traveling into Wisconsin Territory from Pennsylvania, was impressed with the view from Belmont Mound farther to the southwest, a view that included groves of oaks as well as open prairie:

The view . . . beggars all description. An ocean of prairie surrounds the spectator whose vision is not limited to less than thirty or forty miles. This great sea of verdure is interspersed with delightfully varying undulations, like the vast waves of the ocean, and every here and there, sinking in the hollows or cresting the swells, appears spots of trees, as if planted by the hand of art for the purpose of ornamenting this naturally splendid scene. (Curtis 1959, p. 264)

Exploring geologist D.D. Owens noted the flowers in his 1848 descrip-tion:

On the summit levels spreads the wide prairie, decked with flowers of the gayest hue; its long and undulating waves stretching away till sky and meadow mingle in the distant horizon. (Curtis 1959, p. 264)

In *My Antonia,* first published in 1918, prairie author Willa Cather has her character Jim Burden recall his reaction when he was a ten-year-old boy, newly arrived in Nebraska from Virginia, and seeing the prairie for the first time. Again the fascination with the ceaseless motion of the prairie:

As I looked about me I felt that the grass was the country, as the water is the sea. The red of the grass made all the great prairie the colour of wine-stains, or of certain seaweeds when they are first washed up. And there was so much motion in it; the whole country seemed, somehow, to be running.

The settlers soon learned firsthand of the often harsh environment that sustained the sea of grass. Winters were long, with fierce winds and life-threatening cold. Summers brought extreme heat, severe droughts, and more wind. Prairie fires, moving with the wind at frightening speed, could easily wipe out a wheat crop or a cabin.

The beauty and diversity of the landscape of prairies and savannas, noted by many, were not enough to save them from nearly total destruc-tion. Those on deep, well-drained soils were plowed, providing some of the richest agricultural soils in the world. Where soils were too dry or too wet to plow, grazing was a frequent agent of destruction. Prairies and savannas that were neither plowed nor grazed rapidly converted to oak forest in the absence of fire. Such conversions had taken place before settlement also but always in the context of a shifting, fire-maintained mosaic of prairie, savanna, and forest. Today the few remaining tallgrass prairies and savannas occupy less than 1 percent of the area once covered, and even these few remnants are threatened with degradation. This book is written in response to what we perceive as a new interest in restoring these once common, now rare communities, and a growing recognition of the need for ecologically sound, creative land stewardship. What better way to minister to abused land than to restore the soil-nurturing communities that once were there?

Like other institutions known for their work in prairie and savanna restoration, the University of Wisconsin–Madison Arboretum has been receiving increasing numbers of inquiries from people who would like to restore prairie or savanna but lack expertise and don't know where to find the information they need. Some typical inquiries: An urban property owner, concerned about the continual input of water, chemicals, and labor required to grow a lawn, wants to know how to turn lawn into prairie. A small local group organized to preserve and enhance a remnant prairie on a steep bluff would like to know how to proceed without damaging what is already there. Two thousand acres of abandoned farmland have been acquired by a public agency, and the land manager would like to know how to create a landscape of prairie, savanna, and woodland. Frequently the requests for help are accompanied by a comment such as, "This is what we would like to do, but we don't know much about prairies (or savannas)." A basic understanding of the ecology of prairies and savannas is indeed essential for those who wish to restore and manage these unique communities. Some important aspects of prairie-savanna ecology are briefly summarized here; the books by Weaver and Fitzpatrick, Costello, and Madson, listed in the references at the end of the chapter, are excellent sources of further information. Other more detailed regional references are listed in appendix D.

The Tallgrass Prairie

What Is a Prairie?
French explorers called it *prairie,* taken from a French word meaning "meadow," and early settlers adopted that name for this unfamiliar New World grassland, for which there seemed to be no appropriate word in English. Those who experienced the prairie firsthand had no need for a

precise definition of the term; that would come much later, after a fledgling science acquired its own new name: ecology. John T. Curtis, the first ecologist at the University of Wisconsin, undertook with his students the task of delineating and characterizing each of the major biotic communities of Wisconsin. Based on their extensive field studies, Curtis's book *The Vegetation of Wisconsin* was published in 1959. In it Curtis defined a prairie as an open community, dominated by grass, and having less than one tree per acre. In setting this limit, he cautioned that this was an arbitrary distinction for the convenience of those studying a continuum of vegetation. Nature seldom draws lines; one community is likely to blend into the next.

Plants of the Prairie Community

Prairies are rich in species, and the grasses, composites, and legumes are especially well represented. (See appendix A for a listing of tallgrass prairie vascular plants.) The particular group of species present depends on geographic location, since some species ranges are limited to certain areas within the prairie region; it also depends on local topography and soil. Prairies near the northern limits of the prairie region differ in composition from those farther south, while within the same geographic area, prairies on high rocky hill slopes, sand terraces, deep silt loam soils, and poorly drained lowlands also differ from one another. In Wisconsin, characteristic grasses of the drier prairies include little bluestem, prairie dropseed, and side-oats grama. Sites with deep silt loam soils are dominated by big bluestem and Indian grass, while wetter sites have blue joint grass and prairie cord grass. (See figure 1.1.) Disturbance and fire history influence composition as well; for example, some species require soil disturbance, such as that provided by bison wallows or animal burrows, to get started, and some species do best when fires are frequent or occur at a particular season.

   Prairie plants grow close together, sharing available resources in time and space. Some species flower early in the season, some in midsummer, some in fall. Thus not all the species have their most rapid growth phases at the same time; instead they take turns. Early growers tend to be short, and height tends to increase over the growing season, culminating in the tall grasses in early fall. However, some species that bloom later than the tall grasses, including goldenrods, asters, and gentians, are shorter than the grasses, taking advantage of the increased light levels as the grass leaves turn fall color. Beneath the ground surface, roots of different shapes, sizes, and depths divide the space.

Adaptations of the Plants

Each species is adapted to the extreme temperatures, drought, wind, high light intensity, fire, and grazing that are part of the prairie plant's environment. Some of the morphological adaptations easily observed on the prairie include finely divided or narrow vertical leaves to prevent overheating by the sun and offer less resistance to the wind, hairy surfaces to deflect sunlight and wind, and leathery or waxy leaves to reduce water loss. Unseen are the extensive root systems that make up two-thirds of the total plant biomass—an adaptation that helps maintain a favorable water balance and allows rapid regrowth after fire or grazing. Buds located at or below the ground surface are important for resprouting, as is the ability, in grasses, to regrow from nodes low on the plant.

Although we often consider wind and high light levels as factors that plants must withstand, wind and light are important resources as well. Many prairie species take advantage of wind for pollen or seed dispersal. Many have a large amount of leaf surface per plant or per unit of ground surface (even though individual leaves may be small) to take advantage of the high light intensity, thereby increasing productivity. Many of the plants, including the warm-season grasses, carry out photosynthesis using a distinctive chemical pathway that is advantageous under the hot and dry conditions frequently encountered in prairies. This C4 pathway (so named because the first product formed is a four-carbon molecule) allows a high rate of photosynthesis at high temperatures and a higher efficiency of water use. Tallgrass prairies are among the most productive vegetation types in the world.

Fire

Fire is an important process in prairies, where it is part of a positive feedback system, the growth of prairie grass providing excellent fuel for fire and fire in turn stimulating the growth of prairie grass. Lightning can ignite a prairie fire, but during the centuries preceding European settlement, fires set by Native Americans were much more important. These people used fire for a variety of reasons, which can perhaps be summarized as managing their habitat. They burned frequently, possibly as often as every year.

Where the climate is suitable for trees and shrubs, fire is critical to prevent woody invasion of prairie. Fire played a major role in maintaining the mosaic of prairie, oak savanna, and oak forest that characterized the eastern boundary of the prairie. Fire also increases the vigor of many prairie species, and the year of a burn is likely to be associated with taller plants, especially the grasses, and greater abundance of flowers. The

Figure 1.1. Prairie grasses.

(Note: There are as yet no popular guides to the identification of most prairie or woodland grasses and sedges. Yet these plants are crucial to restoration. The best way to learn them is to master the technical keys and to find local botanists who can coach you. The drawings and captions here will introduce a few of the most widespread species.)

a. Little bluestem (*Schizachyrium scoparium*): Seed heads throughout top half of the stems. Leaves folded ("v-shaped") in bud. Base of stem very flat. Mesic to dry soil. Thigh high.

b. June grass (*Koeleria macrantha*): Long, compact, erect seed heads. Dry, often sandy soil. Shin high.

c. Big bluestem (*Andropogon gerardii*): "Turkey-foot" seed heads. Stems often multicolored (with blue, purple, red, green, yellow, and orange). Base of stem roundish. Leaves rolled in bud. Mesic soil. Head high.

d. Indian grass (*Sorghastrum nutans*): Seed-head feather-like. Distinctive auricles (lobes that hug stem at base of leaf). Mesic soil. Head high.

e. Porcupine grass (*Stipa spartea*): Needle-sharp seeds measure five to eight inches long. Dry soil. Waist high.

f. Blue joint grass (*Calamagrostis canadensis*): Wispy seed heads on three- to four-foot stems. Papery ligule around stem at base of leaf. Forms solid stands in wetlands; spreads by runners. Waist high.

g. Switch grass (*Panicum virgatum*): Open seed heads. Hairy where leaf meets stem. Wet-mesic soil. Chest high.

h. Canada wild rye (*Elymus canadensis*): Plant is pale blue-green at flowering time. Nodding heads of bristly seeds, which spread and recurve as they dry. Wet-mesic soil and woods edges. Waist to chest high.

i. Prairie dropseed (*Sporobolus heterolepis*): Very narrow leaves in dense clumps. Spherical seeds in open heads that rise well above leaves. Strong scent of buttered popcorn or hot wax. Mesic to dry soil. Seed heads waist high.

j. Prairie cord grass (*Spartina pectinata*): Coarse, rough-edged leaves tapering to very fine tips. Rows of brush-like seed heads. Wet soil. Over head high.

stimulation is due to removal of the insulating litter of grass stems and leaves by the fire, which allows the soil to warm up earlier in the spring and thus increases the length of the growing season. Today managers of prairies often use carefully timed burns to help control unwanted exotic weeds as well.

Succession in Presettlement Prairies

Natural replacement of one group of species by another over time is a common phenomenon in nature and is known as natural succession. Succession is an important component of prairie dynamics, even in mature prairies. In the presettlement prairie, soil was exposed by animal activity, such as ant mound building, badger digging, and buffalo wallowing. The resulting disturbed areas were colonized by short-lived native weed species such as horseweed and fleabane that could invade quickly and stabilize the soil. When burned, these weeds would give way to prairie pioneers such as grey-headed coneflower, black-eyed Susan, and wild bergamot, and eventually to legumes, compass plant, and other conservative and long-lived species. As might be expected, plant species form a continuum along a gradient of disturbance tolerance, with weeds at one end and conservative species at the other. The sequential replacement of weeds by prairie pioneers and then by prairie conservatives is an example of natural succession. This sequence requires both fire and the availability of seeds of appropriate species. In the absence of fire, the usual presettlement successional sequence was open prairie to brushy prairie to oak woods.

In the presettlement situation, areas of disturbed soil were small compared with the rest of the prairie, but over long periods of time each part of the prairie was likely to experience soil disturbance, and at any point in time there were areas representing every stage of succession. Seeds of early and late successional species were readily available to fill gaps at any stage. A mature prairie was a dynamic system with changes taking place continually in response to small soil disturbances. This increased species diversity.

Effects of Settlement on Successional Processes

Changes after settlement profoundly affected this dynamic, self-healing system. A major impact was the introduction of exotic species, including herbaceous weeds and invasive trees and shrubs. Other changes were the tremendous increase in the amount of disturbed ground associated with agriculture and development, which greatly reduced native seed sources, and the cessation of fire. An all too common successional sequence on abandoned farm fields and overgrazed pastures starts with short-lived exotic weeds, which give way to long-lived perennial exotics and then to exotic trees and shrubs mixed with native trees such as box elder, American elm, and green ash, which were species limited to floodplains and swamps before settlement. Restorationists often must deal with such a situation.

Prairie Animals

With so much plant material available as food, plant-eating animals are abundant. (See appendix B for a comprehensive listing of tallgrass prairie terrestrial vertebrates.) Large ungulates, especially the bison, which roamed the prairies in huge herds, consumed the greatest amount of plant biomass. The herds moved on periodically to graze new areas, thus allowing the heavily grazed areas to recover. Their activities, including development of wallows with denuded and compacted soil, provided a disturbed habitat for pioneer plant species. Bison also played a role in suppressing invading shrubs and trees and influenced patterns of fire.

While large size, ability to run, and assembling in large herds provide protection for bison, a well-represented group of small prairie mammals, including the Franklin's ground squirrel, depend on sharp eyesight to detect danger and nearby tunnels for escape. The badger, an important predator of the small tunnel makers, is also a capable tunnel digger.

Harvest of plant material by crickets and grasshoppers is impressive in quantity—second only to that of the large ungulates. Other plant-eating insect groups, such as the hoppers, are well represented in terms of numbers of species. Many of these feed only on particular plant parts such as leaves, roots, pollen, or seeds. Some specialize in one or a few species of plants, while others, known as generalists, eat a wide variety of plant species. Some appear to be limited to the few remaining good-quality prairie remnants. Insects that eat other insects are common on the prairie as well; they too may be generalists or specialists depending on the selectivity of their diet.

The abundance of large insects, especially the grasshoppers, helps sustain an interesting guild of rather large birds capable of taking advantage of this food source. These include the upland sandpiper, eastern and western meadowlarks, prairie chicken, northern bobwhite, loggerhead shrike, and even a small falcon, the American kestrel. At one time the swallow-tailed kite and the long-billed curlew, now gone from the prairie, were part of this group.

Like the plants, the animals must be adapted to the prairie environment. The relatively large size of grasshoppers and some other prairie insects is an advantage in a hot, dry habitat because there is less body surface area (the interface where water is lost) per volume enclosed. Ants and many small mammals dig tunnels, which provide shelter from heat and desiccating winds in summer and from cold in winter. Tunnels also afford fire protection. Construction of the burrows creates small-scale disturbed habitat and microrelief, which benefit certain plants.

Some species of prairie birds, such as the bobolink, have adapted to the scarcity of woody perches in the prairie by performing their mating and territorial songs in flight. The American kestrel hovers in the air while scanning for prey, while the northern harrier hunts as it flies low over the grass. Certain grassland sparrows, such as the grasshopper sparrow and Henslow's sparrow, are so light in weight that they can perch on and eat the seeds of the tall swaying grasses without bending them to the ground.

Most prairie birds nest on or near the ground, and the incubating adults are well camouflaged to blend in with the grassy background. Although ground nests are vulnerable to predators, many ground-nesting birds have the extra insurance of being able to nest again if the first clutch of eggs is lost.

Many prairie birds escape the severe winters by migrating south. One insect, the monarch butterfly, also migrates, but most prairie insects spend the winter in the soil or the leaf litter, often as eggs or pupae. Most small mammals remain active or semi-active, using their underground tunnels and dens for shelter during severe weather; a few, including the Franklin's ground squirrel, are true hibernators.

Soil

The most striking feature of a prairie soil profile is the deep layer of top-soil—often 20–28 inches deep, with somewhat darkened subsoil beneath. Prairie soils contain as much as 120 tons of organic matter per acre, compared with 70 tons per acre for a forest soil. A dense network of grass roots fills the profile, most extending to a depth of 5 to 7 feet. Forb roots of various shapes and lengths are interspersed; some penetrate as deep as 20 feet. In contrast to forests, where organic matter enters the soil from the surface and must be "plowed in" by earthworms, the organic matter deeply incorporated in prairie soil comes from the roots as they decay in place. There is little input from litter at the surface. Mound-building ants play an important role in the development of prairie soils. They mix and aerate the soil as they build their tunnels, and bring up nutrients and clay particles from the subsoil. Their activities increase potassium and phosphorus levels in the topsoil. Mounds are periodically abandoned in one location and new ones built in another, so that over thousands of years all of the prairie benefits. Soil scientist Francis Hole estimates (personal communication) that in thirty-five hundred years, mound-building ants could have added a new 2-inch layer of subsoil to the land surface six or seven times.

When a prairie burns, nitrogen in the litter is oxidized and escapes from the prairie system. Nitrogen is returned to the system through nitrogen-fixing bacteria in the root nodules of the plentiful prairie legumes, and also through free-living nitrogen-fixing bacteria in the root zones of the prairie grasses. Within the system, most of the nitrogen is held in the tissues of living plants, especially the grasses.

It was the deep, rich prairie soils that eventually led to the nearly total conversion of tallgrass prairie to agricultural crops. The first crop was often wheat, but now the tallgrass prairie region has become the Corn Belt of the Midwest.

The Oak Savanna

Savanna comes from the Spanish *sabana* (earlier, *zabana*). It was adopted from a native language by sixteenth-century Spanish colonists in the Caribbean islands to describe the flat, grassy, treeless areas found there. By the end of the nineteenth century *savanna* had become a name widely used for tropical grasslands of many types, with or without trees and shrubs, and there was (and still is) considerable disagreement over precise definition of the term as applied to these tropical communities.

The less complex situation in the North American Midwest is described by R. Henderson in a 1995 publication of the Wisconsin Department of Natural Resources:

> Fortunately for us in the Midwest, the term "savanna" has a relatively narrow definition. Here it is generally used to describe an ecosystem that was historically part of a larger complex bordered by the prairies of the west and the deciduous forests of the east. This complex was a mosaic of community types that represented a continuum from prairie to forest. Savannas were the communities in the middle of this continuum. The mosaic was maintained by frequent fires and possibly by large ungulates such as bison and elk.

A number of systems have been proposed for dividing the continuum into four or more communities based on amount of tree canopy cover. Several of these savanna-woodland classification systems are compared in the Midwest Oak Ecosystems Recovery Plan edited by Leach and Ross (1995). Most include woodland and savanna categories, but there is currently no general consensus as to where woodland and savanna begin and end along the continuum.

The discussion on savanna in this book is applicable to the full range of fire-maintained oak communities along the continuum between prairies and closed-canopy forest, regardless of their classification. Pine savannas are not included.

Plants of the Oak Savanna Community

THE TREES   The tree species present depend, in part, on geographic location. The prairie-forest transition zone extends from northeastern Texas into Canada. Of the major savanna tree species, only bur oak grows nearly throughout that zone. Others are more limited; for example, blackjack oak and post oak are found only in the southern part of the transition zone, while northern pin oak is important in northern locations.

Within a geographic region, soil and topography influence the distribution of the savanna tree species. In Wisconsin, for example, mesic soils supported the much admired and now extremely rare "oak openings" with their groves of open-grown bur oaks. Bur oak can attain impressive girth and crown spread on such soil. Less frequently, there were open-grown white oaks. Mesic prairie grasses and forbs grew in the large openings between the groves of oaks.

A less common type of oak opening was found in wet areas, where the trees were swamp white oak and bur oak, with wet prairie species in the open spaces.

In sandy areas, the trees were likely to be black oak and/or northern pin oak, with some bur and white oak, and with sand prairie grasses and forbs between. "Oak barrens" is the name given to this community in Wisconsin; elsewhere *barrens* is often used as a more general term for savanna. In contrast to the oak openings, this savanna type can still be found in substantial blocks, sometimes with a fairly intact ground layer. A history of light grazing seems to have been beneficial in some cases.

On dry hillsides with shallow, rocky soil, bur oak was the most likely savanna tree. Bur oaks grown in such a setting were often stunted and gnarled and twisted in extremely picturesque shapes. Sunny areas once supported dry prairie species on these hills, but in recent years many have become overgrown with shrubs, even when prescribed burns have been carried out.

Savannas depend on fire for their continued existence, and the trees present must tolerate frequent fire. In general, only the oaks qualified; other species were seldom present. In the oaks, fire tolerance is conferred by fire-resistant form (thick bark, deep roots), by resprouting ability, or both. In bur oak, the most fire-resistant oak, thick corky bark protects all but the youngest shoots from fire. Furthermore, if the young shoots on a branch of a bur oak are killed by fire, adventitious buds along the branch will produce a vigorous row of new shoots the same season. Black oak is likely to be top-killed during a burn but will resprout with great vigor. White oak is moderately resistant to fire, and there is some evidence that it grows thicker bark when in exposed situations. Both bur and white oaks are good resprouters. Red oak is not very resistant to fire and is less able to resprout when top-killed. It was most likely to persist as a savanna tree on steep north slopes, where fires were less frequent and not as hot. North slopes may have also provided the better moisture conditions required by red oak. Although on a landscape scale the oaks were highly aggregated in groves, the trees within a grove were rather evenly spaced and were similar to each other in size, giving the grove the orchardlike aspect so frequently commented on in the early descriptions. In some areas, the trees in all the groves were similar in size, suggesting that all originated in response to a widespread factor—perhaps a period of reduced fire frequency.

The conspicuous trees of the savannas were the open-grown oaks, but another, less visible size class was well represented. The groves of large oaks were surrounded by and intermingled with large numbers of oaks of a different size class—multistemmed grubs, mostly white and black oak, that were annually top-killed by fire, but whose roots continued to increase in size. These were the nascent oak woodlands and oak forests of the future, awaiting a break in the fire regime that would release them and change that part of the mosaic from sparse to dense trees. The widespread cessation of fire accompanying settlement allowed large numbers of these grubs to grow into even-aged oak woods—the last instance of widespread oak forest regeneration to take place in the region. Regeneration of oak in these forests is problematic now because of the shade intolerance of the oaks, and there is no longer a bank of grubs on hold in widespread nearby savannas.

THE SHRUBS   Gray dogwood, hazelnut, and smooth sumac, all strong clone-formers that are common in oak woods, were well represented in the savannas, along with lead plant, New Jersey tea, and wild rose, which are common in prairies. While early observers seldom mentioned either shrubs or grubs and stressed the openness of the landscape, it is likely that these woody inhabitants, burned to the ground almost annually, were simply concealed from view by the taller grasses and forbs growing with them.

THE GROUND LAYER   Like the trees and shrubs, the ground-layer species must survive fire; in fact, as the response of the ground layer of degraded savannas to fire frequently shows, many not only survive fire but appear to benefit greatly from it.

The diversity of light environments in the savanna can meet the needs of ground-layer species with a broad range of light requirements, from full sun to continuous shade. In a 1995 publication, Henderson lists five categories of species based on light requirements. In addition to the full sun and shade groups, his categories include prairie-associated species that thrive in light shade, forest-associated species that thrive with moderate amounts of sunshine, and "true savanna species" that require a blend of shade and sun. Some of the true savanna species are fairly common today and may appear spontaneously or can be planted from seed when a savanna restoration is undertaken. Others have become quite rare and are no longer represented in the ground layer of disturbed remnant savannas. Some characteristic savanna and woodland grasses are shown in figure 1.2. In most regions, the earliest plant lists available were made after the savannas were already disturbed, and some species may have already disappeared. One exception is a list of plant species found in Illinois "barrens" in 1846, as described in a 1988 publication by Stephen Packard. Many are obscure, seldom seen species, but when used in restoration plantings beneath the oaks several have done remarkably well.

Conditions in any one part of a savanna change as groves of old trees deteriorate and younger groves spring up elsewhere. Seeds of true savanna species are likely to have specialized dispersal mechanisms, a reflection of the exacting light requirements of these species and of the great distance that often separates one grove from another.

Savanna Animals

Many of the mammals now associated with forest edges were probably common—perhaps even more common—in savannas, including the cottontail rabbit, fox squirrel, woodchuck, skunk, and white-tailed deer. The sloughing bark of savanna trees probably provided habitat for nursery colonies of the Indiana bat, currently a federally endangered species. Predators such as red fox have territories large enough to have included a variety of the communities in the prairie-savanna mosaic. Bison and elk used savannas as well as prairies.

The passenger pigeon, now extinct, once occurred in flocks so enormous that they blackened the sky over the midwestern savannas. Another acorn-eating bird, the wild turkey, has been successfully reestablished in savanna areas where it was extirpated. Acorns are also very important in the diet of the blue jay, which can carry five or more at a time in its specially adapted cheek pouches. Blue jays cache acorns in the ground and are at least as important as squirrels in their dispersal.

Savannas provide a variety of nesting habitats. Birds taking advantage of cavities in trees adjacent to open foraging areas are the northern flicker, red-headed woodpecker, great crested flycatcher, eastern bluebird, and American kestrel. Savanna species of conservation significance include the common barn owl, Cooper's hawk, sharp-tailed grouse, Bewick's wren, Bachman's sparrow, loggerhead shrike, and swallow-tailed kite. Shrub nesters include indigo bunting, American goldfinch, and chestnut-sided warbler, as well as several that have adapted well to the "savanna habitat" of the city suburb: American robin, gray catbird, cardinal, and blue jay. The rufous-sided towhee and brown thrasher build nests on the ground, taking advantage of the protection of shrubs overhead.

A rare butterfly, the Karner blue, requires substantial populations of lupine, a legume characteristic of oak barrens, for its larval stage. This savanna insect has been studied extensively, but there are others thought to be dependent upon savanna habitat about which little is known. Some may also be rare.

Soil

Savanna soils have been little studied. The patchy distribution of oaks probably results in patchy distribution of soil types, with areas presently or recently influenced by the oak trees and their leaves tending to have pod-solic soils, and open areas with prairie grasses tending toward mollisols. Such trends would be opposed, however, by the periodic burning of oak litter, which would slow the formation of a podsolic profile, and by the shifting location over time of the groves of oaks, which would tend to in-terrupt the long time period required for formation of a mollisol. Soil de-velopment in both situations could be slowed if the open areas lack mound-building ants and earthworms are not available under the trees.

The Challenges for Restorationists

Those who wish to bring together the multitude of species represented in a prairie—or any other natural community, for that matter—would seem to have a task exceeding that allotted to Noah, who after all was able to ignore plants (and, presumably, microscopic organisms, insects, and most soil dwellers as well). Prairie plants have not fared well in the floods of civilization, and for most restorationists the primary focus is to bring together the plant species that once shared the prairie sun. Even this can seem formidable; the oldest prairie restored from scratch, the

Figure 1.2. Savanna and woodland grasses and sedges.

a. Wood reed (*Cinna arundinacea*): Seed head feathery. Stems tall and erect with gray-green leaves. Middle leaves have distinctive strong, white midrib. Ligule (at leaf base) long and membranous. Spreads by runners (not clumped). Chest high.

b. Woodland brome (*Bromus pubescens*): Graceful, spreading seed head with well-separated, flattened clusters of seeds. Sheath enclosing stem from bottom of leaf is tubular (not split, except near top). Hairs on stem point slightly but clearly downward. Auricles do not cross (see silky wild rye). Waist high.

c. Broad-leaved panic grasses (*Panicum latifolium* and *boscii*): Leaves broad and short. Shin high. There are a great many smaller panic grasses.

d. Bottlebrush grass (*Elymus hystrix*): Long seeds spread perpendicular to stem (like bristles on a bottle brush). Auricles as in silky wild rye. Waist high.

e. Virginia wild rye (*Elymus virginicus*): Erect seed head often partly enclosed within leaf sheath. Leaves not hairy. Thickened, bowed structures (glumes) surround seed. Wet-mesic to mesic. Thigh high.

f. Silky wild rye (*Elymus villosus*): Seed head typically nodding, entirely outside leaf sheath. Upper surface of leaf softly downy, but leaf flips at base, so the hairs end up underneath. Auricles (lobes at base of leaf) criss-cross or "point past" each other. Mesic to dry mesic. Thigh high.

g. Long-awned wood grass (*Brachyelytrum erectum*): Large long-bristled seeds. Lower leaves short, triangular. White zone at base of leaf. Shin high.

(*Note on the sedges: The three species shown are examples of this large, important, difficult-to-identify genus. Most sedges have triangular stems (unlike most grasses, which have round stems). The male flower spikes are often separate from the (female) seed heads.*)

h. Bur sedge (*Carex grayi*): Seed heads large, spherical, inflated. Knee high.

i. Sedge (*Carex rosea*): Dense tufts of fine leaves. Seed clusters tiny, well separated. Ankle high.

j. Pennsylvania sedge (*Carex pensylvanica*): Red stems. Spreads by runners. Ankle high.

University of Wisconsin–Madison Arboretum's Curtis Prairie, contains over two hundred native species within its sixty acres, and a natural prairie of that size may well have had three hundred or more, many of them now rare or uncommon.

Whether you start your restoration by introducing ten species of plants or one hundred, it is important to remember that each one has become adapted to a set of conditions over a long period of evolutionary time. A restorationist cannot change the adaptations; rather, the plants must be put into appropriate locations where their adaptations will let them succeed. Matching community to site is critical.

Because of their interrelationships with other organisms, some species have more exacting requirements, such as animal disturbance, particular host plants, specific mycorrhizal fungi on the roots, or a special pollinating or seed-dispersing animal. Usually there is little practical advice for the restorationist about these species. Until more research (or trial and error by interested restorationists) adds to our knowledge, many of these species will remain uncommon in prairie and savanna restorations.

It is customary in restorations to establish plants and then wait for appropriate animals to take advantage of this new habitat. The success of this approach (assuming the habitat is indeed appropriate) will depend on whether such animals have persisted in the area despite agricultural and urban impacts or have viable populations elsewhere within travel range for the species. Some species are not likely to be present or not sufficiently mobile to move in without help. Restorationists may direct more attention to animal introductions in the future, as prairie and savanna plantings become more widespread and their dynamics better understood.

Like Noah, prairie restorationists usually assume the presence of a system of soil organisms effective enough to sustain the vital underground processes of the community. The many robust restorations existing today suggest that this is often the case, yet a better understanding of the underground realm and more consideration of its complex relationships might lead to improved techniques for the establishment of healthy, complex prairie and savanna ecosystems that are good representations of communities described by the early explorers.

REFERENCES

Allen, Durward L. 1967. *The Life of Prairies and Plains*. New York: McGraw-Hill.
Cather, Willa. 1918. *My Antonia*. Boston: Houghton Mifflin.

Costello, David F. 1969. *The Prairie World*. New York: Thomas Y. Crowell.

Curtis, J. 1959. *The Vegetation of Wisconsin*. Madison: University of Wisconsin Press.

Henderson, R. 1995. "Oak Savanna Communities." In *Wisconsin's Biodiversity as a Management Issue: A Report to Department of Natural Resources Managers*. Madison: Wisconsin Department of Natural Resources.

Leach, M.L., and L. Ross, eds. 1995. *Midwest Oak Ecosystems Recovery Plan: A Call to Action*. Chicago: Nature Conservancy, Illinois Field Office, and U.S. Environmental Protection Agency, Great Lakes National Program Office (available from EPA at 77 W. Jackson Blvd., Chicago, IL 60604–3590).

Madson, John. 1985. *Where the Sky Began: Land of the Tallgrass Prairie*. San Francisco: Sierra Club Books.

Packard, S. 1988. "Just a Few Oddball Species: Restoration and the Rediscovery of the Tallgrass Savanna." *Restoration and Management Notes* 6, no. 1:13–20.

Smith, D.D. 1981. "Iowa Prairie—Our Endangered Ecosystem." *Proceedings of the Iowa Academy of Science* 88:7–10.

Weaver, J.E., and T.J. Fitzpatrick. 1934. *The Prairie. Ecological Monographs* 4:109–295. (Reprinted in 1980 by the Prairie-Plains Resource Institute, 1219 16th St., Aurora, NE.)

2
Prairie Underground

R. Michael Miller

Restorationists spend most of their time working with the visible, above-ground part of the ecosystem, but an equally important component exists below ground. In fact, the below-ground component is an important part of virtually all terrestrial ecosystems. This is especially true of tallgrass prairies, where as much as 65 percent of the biomass is underground, even at the end of summer when above-ground biomass is at its peak.

So many important processes in the prairie ecosystem take place underground that ecologists frequently regard the prairie as a root-driven ecosystem. In fact, the majority of biological activities take place at the root-soil interface, a region referred to as the rhizosphere. The rhizosphere exists because photosynthetically derived, low-molecular-weight, energy-rich compounds are allocated to the roots. These compounds are then exuded by roots of prairie plants into the surrounding soil, where they serve as carbon sources and vitamins for microbial growth and the turnover of organic matter.

The abundance of microbes requiring simple carbon compounds for growth in rhizospheric soils suggests that these organisms utilize low-molecular-weight compounds. Such microbes are usually not abundant in nonrhizospheric soils, where the prevalent microbes can use the more complex substrates associated with plant debris and soil organic matter.

The rich diversity of organisms in the rhizosphere gives these soils a larger functional capacity than nonrhizospheric soils. Many microbially mediated processes found only in the rhizosphere are a direct consequence of the richness of organisms and their consortial nature (their tendency to work in teams). Many of the symbiotic associations between plants and microbes also occur in the rhizosphere. Two of the more important associations, discussed below, are mycorrhizae and the rhizobial-root nodules.

Most prairie plants have a symbiotic association with mycorrhizal fungi. Stated another way, the absence of mycorrhizal colonization of prairie plant root systems is unusual. The mycorrhizal fungi typically associated with prairie plants are referred to as being endophytic. That is, the obvious portion of their thallus is found within the cortex of roots. However, the majority of the fungus consists of hyphal threads growing from the root into the surrounding soil.

These fungi acquire all of their carbon from the plant. The carbon drain can be substantial (researchers have measured sink strengths of up to 20 percent of photosynthetic production), but the benefits to a host are considerable. The hyphae of mycorrhizal fungi basically act as an extension of the root system, transporting nutrients, especially phosphates, back to the root. Researchers have found that mycorrhizae are associated with increased nutrient uptake, tolerance to heavy metals, improved water relations, and disease resistance in host plants. Mycorrhizae are also associated with improved soil structure and cycling of organic matter.

The need for mycorrhizal fungi by prairie plants can vary. Most of the warm-season grasses, e.g., big bluestem and Indian grass, require the mycorrhizal association for optimal growth, while cool-season grasses like Canada wild rye and June grass do not. The needs of prairie forbs for mycorrhizal fungi, though, are more complicated and appear to be related to root morphology and phenology. For example, forbs like grey-headed coneflower, purple prairie clover, and round-headed bush clover are more obligate in their need for mycorrhizal fungi for optimal growth than stiff goldenrod and rough blazing star, which can do quite well without the fungus. The first group's roots are rather coarse, while the last group's roots are more fibrous. However, roots of both groups can be heavily colonized.

The second major microbe-based mutualism found in the prairie is the rhizobia-root nodule association of legumes. Symbiotically derived fixed nitrogen from legumes is not a major factor in the nitrogen economy of prairie remnants. Instead, this nutrient's economy is driven by symbiotically fixed nitrogen from blue-green algae and asymbiotically fixed nitrogen from rhizosphere microbes. Nevertheless, the contributions of legumes during prairie reconstruction can be important because reconstructions are usually on degraded soils.

The rhizosphere is also responsible for creating conditions conducive to forming soil aggregates or crumbs. The binding of soil particles into aggregated units creates structures that are relatively resistant to erosion. These structures can affect the physical accessibility of food, shelter, water, and oxygen to soil organisms. Furthermore, the process of packaging soil particles into aggregated units is a primary means by which soils accrue organic matter.

All these processes are crucial to the development of a healthy, properly functioning prairie. Much of the advice in this book—on soil preparation, for example, and on the care and handling of seedlings and transplant stock for prairie restoration work—reflects these peculiarities of prairie plants and the importance of the underground part of the prairie ecosystem. Fortunately, however, development of the below-ground system usually goes hand in hand with development of the above-ground system. If the above-ground portion of the developing community receives the correct treatment, the below-ground system will usually take care of itself.

My studies with J. Jastrow at the Fermilab prairie, an ongoing thousand-acre reconstruction just west of Chicago, are aimed at identifying the contributions of mycorrhizal fungi to the restoration process. The study areas consist of a chronosequence of tallgrass prairie restorations, adjacent cornfields, and ungrazed pastures. We have found the rowcrop soil's mycorrhizal fungal communities are made up of weedy species. After these soils are planted with prairie plants and a burn regime is initiated, a more diverse mycorrhizal fungal community develops, including more conservative mycorrhizal species. Hence, the changes underground are similar to those in the plant community above-ground. The difference is that the appropriate below-ground organisms seem to be present in most cases and do not need to be introduced. However, since the mycorrhizal fungal species concept is based on morphology rather than the ability to exchange genetic material, we have no way of knowing how much selection pressure one hundred years of essentially continuous cultivation has had on this group of organisms.

This generalization is at least true on mesic sites with reasonably rich soils, such as the Fermilab site. On poorer soils, or under more xeric conditions (farther west, for example), restorationists may find that the below-ground system cannot keep pace in its development with the above-ground component. This is also a commonplace problem in scrubland communities of the Great Basin, where we find essential mycorrhizal fungi are often absent or depauperate on restoration sites and must be reintroduced artificially.

Though little information exists on this point, tallgrass prairie restorationists may encounter similar problems under certain conditions. Past tillage, cropping sequence, fertilizer, and biocide usage can all affect the mycorrhizal community. Also, although mycorrhizae may be present, they may be the wrong combination of fungus and host. Symptoms of this problem include stagnation or lack of vigor of the prairie species and difficulty in establishing diversity during restoration. These symptoms would be especially prevalent during periods of ecological stress, in particular, drought and temperature extremes.

Natural successional events should be distinguishable from dysfunctional ones. Many of the plants that are successful colonists during the first year of prairie reconstruction are volunteer annuals and biennials. They are especially prevalent if no herbicides are used—as with the majority of the Fermilab reconstructions. Many of these plants are non-mycotrophic and are members of the mustard and chenopod families. They are of little consequence to the final outcome, unless for some reason they continue to dominate a site. In mesic sites, these plants usually disappear after the second year, but a more protracted phase of these nonmycorrhizal weeds can be found on xeric and highly disturbed prairie sites. Extended occupation of a site by these plants can affect the trajectory of succession by reducing the propagules of mycorrhizal fungi.

The fine crumb structure of prairie soils is a feature that makes them fertile agricultural soils. The structure deteriorates, however, as a result of the high-input management practices that are widespread in the Midwest. One of the best ways to restore these soils is to use prairie plants. Our studies of soils under restored prairie at the Fermilab site have shown that the roots and mycorrhizae of prairie plants bring about recovery of this crumb structure more rapidly than do nonprairie plants, suggesting that these prairie plants (communities) may be valuable in restoring crumb structure to soils degraded by agriculture.

This observation in turn suggests a scenario in which prairie plants might be grown in rotation with corn, soybeans, and other crops. Such rotations would be only the beginning; rather, what is needed is to mimic the prairie by using perennial polyculture. This approach would truly integrate prairie into our agricultural practices, so that native grasslands might once again cover large areas of the Midwest, with prairie plants growing in a shifting mosaic in rotation with traditional crops.

REFERENCES

Bradshaw, A.D. 1987. The Reclamation of Derelict Land and the Ecology of Ecosystems. In *Restoration Ecology: A Synthetic Approach to Ecological Research,* W.R. Jordan, M.E. Gilpin, and J.D. Aber, eds., pp. 53–74. Cambridge: Cambridge University Press.
Hetrick, B.A.D., G.W.T. Wilson, and T.C. Todd. 1992. Relationships of Mycorrhizal Symbiosis, Rooting Strategy, and Phenology among Tallgrass Prairie Forbs. *Canadian Journal of Botany* 70:1521–1528.

Hole, F.D., and G.A. Nielsen. 1970. Soil Genesis under Prairie. In *Proceedings of a Symposium on Prairie and Prairie Restoration,* September 14–15, 1968, Knox College, P. Schramm, ed., pp. 28–35.

Jackson, W. 1980. *New Roots for Agriculture.* Lincoln: University of Nebraska Press.

Miller, R.M., and J.D. Jastrow. 1992. The Application of VA Mycorrhizae to Ecosystem Restoration and Reclamation. In *Mycorrhizal functioning,* M.A. Allen, ed., pp. 438–467. New York: Chapman and Hall.

Miller, R.M., and J.D. Jastrow. 1992. The Role of Mycorrhizal Fungi in Soil Conservation. In *Mycorrhizae in Sustainable Agriculture,* G. Bethlenfalvay and R. Linderman, eds., pp. 29–44. Madison, WI: American Society of Agronomy, Crop Science Society of America, and Soil Science Society of America.

PART II

Goals and Plans

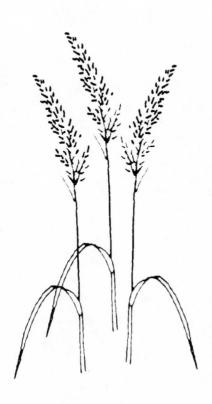

Planning a Restoration

Virginia M. Kline

This chapter discusses the factors to consider when planning your restoration. Getting started involves assessing your piece of land, making choices, and developing a plan. The plan you develop will depend on the choices you make, which in turn will depend on the characteristics of the site and also on your objectives. People involved with large-scale projects in which the objective is to restore and preserve an extensive prairie or savanna ecosystem as part of the natural heritage of the region will make different choices from those who wish to restore an example of diverse prairie or savanna in a backyard, schoolyard, city park, or industrial park, where educational, aesthetic, or economic objectives may have high priority.

You will need to choose the basic technique you will use in planting: will you plow the soil before planting, or will you use "interseeding," in which seeds are planted into the existing vegetation? Factors to consider when making this choice are discussed in this chapter. Interseeding is explained in chapter 11, while the plowing and planting approach is described in chapter 12.

Your plan should recognize the importance of continued management after the initial planting and should incorporate the techniques to be used and their timing. Techniques for burning, controlling weeds, and monitoring the changing quality of your site, as well as consideration of the issues involved in animal introductions, are explained in parts IV and V.

Some Considerations of Size

A restoration can be as small as a prairie planting in a residential yard or as large as a prairie-savanna landscape of several thousand acres. If you have a choice in the matter, make your restoration as large as possible, given the available resources.

The Importance of Large Sites

Populations of some animal species such as bison and prairie chickens can be maintained only on very large prairie or savanna sites. Insects with specialized food requirements, such as many butterflies in the larval stage, may require large populations of particular food plants, which in turn require areas of sufficient size. Large sites also can support larger and more genetically diverse populations of species that in smaller prairies might become extirpated. Extensive prairies and savannas contain soil and topographic gradients that will support a variety of savanna and prairie types, each blending naturally into the next as they did in presettlement times. Besides adding landscape interest, the presence of an array of plants adapted to different moisture levels safeguards against soil moisture changes induced by changes in climate or directly by human activities. For example, if the soil becomes drier, whether because of global warming or because of ditching of adjacent land, species adapted to the new range of moisture conditions probably would be available to shift into relocated moisture zones and keep the prairie intact.

For these and other reasons, there is growing recognition of the need for extensive prairie restorations, and a few projects involving sites of several thousand acres have been initiated. Imagine eight thousand acres, half prairie and half savanna, stretching to the Iowa horizon at the Walnut Creek National Wildlife Refuge, where the U.S. Fish and Wildlife Service is funding the transformation of the present cropland and pasture. Or the four thousand-acre Bluestem Prairie in Minnesota, part original prairie and part under restoration, which is being developed by the Nature Conservancy, a state park, and other partners. Or try to imagine twenty thousand acres of prairie and wetland with prairie groves and a stream at Midewin Prairie, a U.S. Forest Service project in Illinois, not far from Chicago. The word *midewin,* used by both Potawatomi and Ojibwa tribes, relates to healing. These projects are truly healing the land and restoring its biodiversity on a significant scale. There are many more opportunities for major restored landscape projects on appropriate federal, state, and county lands. Public understanding and support are critical to make them active projects.

Small Is Beautiful, Too

The value of small "postage stamp" prairies and savannas, however, should not be underestimated. Remnant prairies as small as one-fourth acre have been shown to harbor an amazing diversity of insects including rare species that do not occur in adjacent agricultural fields. For more than a century these isolated prairie patches have provided refuge for species that may once have been widespread. There have been a few studies of the invertebrates inhabiting planted prairies and a few attempts at introductions (see part V). Although this field of study is in its infancy, it is possible that these new prairies, like the remnants, may eventually serve as refuges not only for plants, but also for insects and other small animal life.

Prairie and savanna restorations replacing lawns in parks, schoolyards, private yards, and business grounds can include substantial numbers of prairie grasses and forbs. (My frontyard prairie patch of slightly more than one thousand square feet has sixty native prairie species.) Restoring biological diversity in this way adds beauty and interest to the neighborhood, improves environmental quality, and can foster greater understanding and appreciation of natural communities. If even one-tenth of the lawns in a community were replaced by prairie plantings, there would be a sizeable reduction in the use of water, fertilizers, and chemical pesticides and in the fuel consumption, noise, and air pollution associated with power mowers. In addition, deep prairie roots condition the soil and improve rainwater penetration, reducing runoff and recharging the water table.

The Influence of Adjacent Vegetation

The effective size of a prairie as habitat for prairie animals may be increased if surrounding land is not wooded. For example, three dry prairie remnants in southwestern Wisconsin, preserved because the bedrock was too close to the surface for plowing, have become native "islands" in a sea of corn. These patches, totaling only about thirty acres but surrounded by open, plowed fields, each year attract prairie birds, including the upland sandpiper. Similarly, scattered oaks in a cemetery, golf course, subdivision, or pasture may increase the effective habitat size of an adjacent savanna restoration.

From the prairie management standpoint, open communities such as old fields, lawns, or pastures are preferable to wooded communities as close neighbors. (Cropland would provide similar low vegetation, but there would be great risk of accidental overspray of herbicide, or of siltation if the prairie is downhill.) Trees and shrubs along the periphery, especially along south and west sides, tend to reduce sun and wind, two factors important to the prairie. Tall trees along a southern boundary will shade the adjacent prairie enough to eliminate many species, particularly the grasses. This essentially reduces the size of the prairie. In the University of Wisconsin–Madison Arboretum, a strip of pines located south of Curtis Prairie has seriously degraded a fifty-foot-wide strip of this, the oldest planted prairie in the Midwest.

Trees such as black locust and quaking aspen are of special concern in a border, since they can rapidly invade and are extremely difficult to control. Many native shrubs, including gray dogwood and smooth sumac, also advance aggressively.

Both size and shape are important to management, since these determine the edge-to-area ratio. The smaller this ratio, the easier it is to install and use fire barriers, and the less undesirable influence will be exerted by adjacent land use. In general a roughly circular site is better than a narrow corridor, and the larger the prairie, the smaller the edge-to-area ratio.

Soil Considerations

Prairies establish well on nutrient-poor soils; in fact, rich soil favors weeds over prairie species in the early years of a restoration. The addition of organic matter or fertilizer is usually not advisable. Over time the prairie will add substantial amounts of organic matter from the deep decaying roots. Prairies can be established on sites with a wide range of soil conditions, but the moisture requirements of the species planted should match the soil(s) on the site. Curtis Prairie soils vary from wet to dry, and some species were planted in soils with inappropriate moisture levels. Followup surveys showed these species disappearing from the unfavorable locations. Although in many cases they reappeared elsewhere in the prairie where conditions were more suitable, requiring plants to relocate in this way slows the restoration process, and poorly matched species may be lost from the site.

Taking advantage of even a slight moisture gradient will allow diversity in prairie composition. A four-acre addition to the Curtis Prairie planted in 1986 has a slight southeast-facing slope. Proceeding downslope, the prairie seed mixes used varied from dry-mesic to mesic to wet-mesic, and so far this very successful restoration reflects the planned diversity along the moisture gradient.

Soil texture and drainage provide the best indication of what species will be appropriate. Texture is readily determined by rubbing soil between your thumb and fingers. Sandy soils are very gritty and do not stick to your fingers; loams have a small gritty component, are slightly sticky, and have a smooth, flourlike feel because of the presence of silt. Clay soils are more sticky, but some have enough silt to give the flourlike feel. Wetness can usually be determined by simple observation: Is the area low-lying and seasonally flooded, or does it frequently have standing water for a day or two after a heavy rain? If either is true, consider planting a wet prairie mix, even if the soil is very sandy. A dry prairie mix is best for well-drained sandy soil and for shallow loamy soil on ridges or steep slopes, particularly if the slope is south or west facing. Gently sloping or level sites with loamy soil or clay soil containing some organic matter are suitable for mesic prairie mix. Heavy clay soil with little organic matter is tolerated by only a few species. It can be improved by adding organic matter or topsoil, or by growing a mix of the clay-tolerant species. (If you are concerned about your ability to interpret soil conditions, help is probably as close as your local county extension agent or soil testing service.)

Different considerations pertain to wet, mesic, and dry sites. Cultivation of wet soils for planting wet prairie may be possible only in some seasons of some years and may encourage invasion of the aggressive European strain of reed canary grass, which is highly competitive with prairie species. Establishment of trails in a wet prairie requires the extra expense of boardwalk construction; the boardwalks in turn require special protection during burns. However, a boardwalk system in a wet prairie will discourage off-trail excursions and enhance the feeling of entering a wild, hitherto inaccessible area.

Many species of mesic prairie are showy, easy to start, and provide a quick effect; here the tall grasses achieve their greatest height. However, pasture weeds can be persistent on these soils. On dry prairie sites prairie species usually outcompete weeds, but wind and water erosion may be a threat in the early stages if the site is cultivated.

Slope and Aspect

Prairies will grow well on either level or sloping land. A level site is easier to plant and is less subject to erosion and seed loss. As noted previously, a slope may provide a soil moisture gradient that will support more than one prairie type. However, planting several seed mixes, especially on a large site, is more time consuming than planting a single mix on a level site. Aesthetically, a sloping site allows better views of the prairie and may provide a vantage point from which the prairie will appear to reach the horizon.

Slope exposure also influences species selection. South slopes are the hottest and driest, followed by west slopes, which are exposed to the drying effects of the prevailing winds. East slopes experience the most moderate conditions. North slopes are the coolest, since they receive the least amount of direct sun. Soils that would favor mesic prairie on level sites may be more suitable for dry prairie on steep south or west slopes, while the reverse may be true for north slopes.

Presettlement Vegetation

If the natural communities that were found in the area before European settlement are determined, restoration can be directed to reestablishing communities known to be well adapted to the site. Information is available in the records of the original Public Land Survey; a map of the presettlement vegetation of your state may also be available. Additional sources include botanical lists made by early explorers or during military expeditions and journals of early settlers. Assembling this material can be an interesting project, especially for someone whose ancestors settled in the area.

Existing Vegetation

A critical, but frequently slighted, step in planning a restoration is a comprehensive survey of the plant species present on the site. Managers need to take time to become familiar with the existing vegetation before initiating restoration. Using a growing season to become familiar with the plants—with the help of an expert field taxonomist, if needed—is time and effort well spent.

Native Prairie or Savanna Species

It is important to determine whether a significant component of native prairie or savanna species is present so that it can be protected and encouraged during the restoration process. Some may be so suppressed by competition that they no longer flower, which means that the field expert must be able to identify nonflowering specimens. Not too long ago, a prairie enthusiast was asked to evaluate the potential of an elementary schoolyard in a small Wisconsin town for a prairie planting. On examining the site, he discovered that at least twenty species of prairie plants were already present! It was, in fact, a neglected, overgrown prairie remnant that had escaped plowing because the bedrock was too close to the surface. Knowing that prairie species were there led to development of a restoration plan that provided the protection they needed.

Troublesome Weeds

Identify the weed species present. Common exotic grasses are shown in figure 3.1. Sites selected for prairie plantings often are former pastures, hayfields, and croplands with a wide variety of weeds. The species present differ substantially between sites, and some are more difficult to control than others. The main offenders include reed canary grass, leafy spurge, spotted knapweed, Canada thistle, yellow and white sweet clover, wild parsnip, purple loosestrife, smooth brome, and quack grass. In partial shade, burdock and garlic mustard are problem species. Many of these can be controlled by active management, but it may be easier to rid the site of them prior to planting. Sites with established populations of leafy spurge, however, should be altogether avoided, since there is no effective way to eradicate that aggressive species. Alternative sites should also be considered if purple loosestrife, reed canary grass, or spotted knapweed are established; these are extremely difficult to eradicate. Species that are persistent but not usually competitive when prairies are managed by burning include Canada and Kentucky bluegrass, redtop, dandelion, and red and white clover. Compared with pastures, recently cultivated fields often have fewer of the perennial weeds that can persist in competition with prairie plants. An abandoned soybean field or cornfield can give good results, although a field recently treated with atrazine may require a waiting period prior to planting.

Two Restoration Pathways

In planning your prairie or savanna restoration, you will need to choose between two planting approaches. In the first, referred to as interseeding (see chapter 11), seeds are broadcast over existing vegetation, usually after burning the site, but without cultivation. Particularly troublesome weeds may be treated with herbicide before planting. In the second approach, prairie seeds are planted in a weed-free seedbed that has been carefully cultivated, herbicided, or both (see chapter 12). Each approach has advantages and disadvantages, and there are situations in which one will be more appropriate than the other.

A carefully cultivated, relatively weed-free seedbed will give quick results, with easily established prairie species such as black-eyed Susan, grey-headed coneflower, and wild bergamot in showy bloom the second year. This is an advantage in situations where public acceptance of a project is problematic, or where quick results are needed to sustain the interest of the participants, such as in a schoolyard prairie planted by children. Many property owners, excited about planting a prairie of their own, may also be eager to have aesthetically pleasing results quickly. Some restorationists suggest that germination and seedling survival are higher for seeds planted in a well-prepared seedbed, so that fewer seeds are required. However, not everyone agrees that this is true, and there are no published data.

Disadvantages of plowing include the time and energy required for site preparation and the potential for soil erosion. It is not a technique to

Figure 3.1. Exotic and aggressive grasses.

a. Annual foxtails (*Setaria* species): Loose cylindric head with rounded seeds. Typical annuals (very shallow root systems). Shin to waist high.

b. Meadow fescue (*Festuca pratensis*): Base of leaf blade distinctively folded in on itself. Mesic to dry soil. Thigh high.

c. Reed canary grass (*Phalaris arundinacea*): Smooth. Long papery ligule where leaf blade meets stem. Seed head dense. Low ground. Chest high.

d. Timothy (*Phleum pratense*): Tight cylindric head with flat seeds. Thigh high.

e. Orchard grass (*Dactylis glomerata*): Clumpy seed-head. Plant is pale green at flowering time. Stem flattish and keeled. Thigh high.

f. Smooth brome (*Bromus inermis*): Sod-forming. Leaf with w-shaped crimp near middle. Sheath at base of leaf blade tubular (not split except near top). Mesic to dry-mesic soil. Waist high.

g. Quack grass (*Elytrigia repens*): Sod-forming. Leaves crimped near tip. Wet-mesic to dry-mesic soil. Thigh high.

h. Redtop (*Agrostis gigantea*): Seed head at first very open and purplish-red, soon contracting and turning pale. Ligule (at leaf base) long and membranous as in reed canary grass. Wet-mesic soil. Shin to knee high.

i. Kentucky bluegrass (*Poa pratensis*): Stem round. Lower seeds held well away from stem. Leaves of both Kentucky and Canada bluegrass not long-tapering, but with a "boat-shaped" tip. Shin high.

j. Canada bluegrass (*Poa compressa*): Leaves bluish-green. Stem flattened (won't roll between fingers). Seeds near stem on lower branches. Shin high.

be used for restoration of savanna ground layer in existing oak groves, since plowing may damage oak roots. Plowing of course should also be avoided wherever there is the possibility that native prairie or savanna species may already exist on the site.

Prairies planted on cultivated sites are often not very diverse—at least not in the first few years. They tend to be predictably alike: heavily dominated by tall grass and easily established composites.

Using interseeding protects desirable species that are present, which may include some not known to be there. It can be used in prairies too wet to cultivate, and also beneath savanna trees since it causes no damage to the roots. It reduces labor and fuel costs associated with soil cultivation and protects the soil from erosion. A technique not widely used until recent years, interseeding has been remarkably successful in some situations.

Whatever the approach, the restorationist seeks to replace exotic species with a diversity of prairie or savanna species, including a good representation of "conservative" species—species that do not come in readily on disturbed sites, are found in older prairies, and are among the first to disappear when a good prairie suffers major disturbance. The success of a restoration is often measured in terms of how successful this replacement is.

Planning a Prairie Restoration

Once the site for the restoration is evaluated and selected, whether in that order or the reverse, the next move is to develop a restoration plan that takes into account the resources available, the nature of the site, and the overall goal of enhancing and preserving biodiversity. The plan should also provide for any special uses anticipated for the restoration, such as providing an educational experience for children or a scenic hiking area in a county park. Perhaps you want the prairie to serve as a model that will persuade local garden clubs to promote prairie plantings, or kindle interest in protecting remnant prairies, and therefore aesthetic considerations are important.

The cost of starting a prairie will depend on how much of the labor you or your group can provide, whether you want a more expensive mix with a substantial component of conservative species, and whether you plan to collect the seed yourselves. For a sizeable backyard prairie of 1,000 square feet, mixed forb and grass seed from a nursery will cost roughly $30 to $50 depending on the type of prairie. For one acre, the cost of seed would be roughly $1,000 to $1,500. (While that seems high, it compares favorably with the cost of putting in and maintaining a lawn.) Many groups and individuals collect their own seed. This requires a nearby prairie owned by someone willing to give permission to collect, and substantial time and labor to gather and prepare the seeds for planting.

If your site is in full sun, has uniform soil and slope, is small enough to fit your energy and funds and can be planted with a standard mix of prairie seed, go for it! Your planning needs are easily met.

Most situations, however, are more complex, and a good starting point is a map of the site showing features that should be considered in the plan, such as steep slopes, soil types, shaded areas, existing or planned paths and firelanes, and important views of the prairie or the landscape beyond. For rural sites an aerial photo or a plat map may be helpful in establishing the basic outline.

If soil and topography provide conditions for more than one prairie type, the next step is to map where each type will be planted and estimate how much area each will cover. Alternatively, the areas can be staked out and measured on the site. Areas receiving less than a half day of full sun should be mapped as separate units; a mix of savanna species having some shade tolerance will succeed better there.

The plan should include species lists for each of the units to be planted. Lists of species of prairie plants suitable for each type of prairie (wet, mesic, dry) can be found in tables 9.2–9.4, 12.1, and 12.2. Lists can also be obtained from prairie nurseries in your area (see appendix E), from books on local natural vegetation (appendix D), or from local preservation groups.

Your selection of species should include only those native to your area. Some nurseries sell mixes of seeds appropriate for wet, mesic, or dry prairie, but you may wish to make your own selections. Be sure to include early-flowering as well as late-flowering species, and conservative as well as pioneer species. The ratio of grasses and grasslike species to forb species is an important consideration. (A forb is a plant that is not woody and is not grasslike; forbs are sometimes referred to as wildflowers.)

Native prairies are dominated by grasses or grasslike plants, and grasses also form the matrix for most prairie plantings; a frequently recommended ratio is equal parts by weight of grass/sedge seed and forb seed. A higher percentage of grass seed will result in a prairie heavily dominated by grasses; a lower percentage will have a showier display of forbs but may also have more weeds. Big bluestem, Indian grass, and other tall warm-season grasses usually establish readily and spread rapidly on the silt-loam soils that are common in the midwestern Corn Belt, making them a good choice for large areas. A large stand of 10-foot big bluestem sweeping to the horizon in fall color can be spectacular. For small prairies such tall grass may be overwhelming—visually and in terms of competition with less aggressive forb species. To reduce tallgrass dominance, planting of tall grasses might be delayed until the second year. Alternatively, a shorter-grass matrix would compete less with the forbs. For loamy soils little bluestem, prairie panic grass, and prairie dropseed would be good choices, while June grass, side-oats grama, and prairie dropseed do well on sandy soils. Patches of shorter grasses add interest to large prairies as well. It would be prudent to plant the tall grasses downwind from an area where you want only the shorter grasses, to discourage seed dispersal into the short-grass area.

A detailed design of the distribution of certain species or groups of species within the planting may be part of the plan. Perhaps you want the distribution of prairie species to duplicate the pattern of the best available nearby prairie remnant. Visit the remnant and make some observations: note what forb species are in patches and what species are more evenly distributed; what species seem to occur together; whether the grass cover is uniform; what forbs grow in dense grass; and where shorter grasses occur in relation to taller grasses. A plan emphasizing aesthetic quality might show species distributed to provide a particular interplay of colors, forms, and textures, or to enhance a view or avoid blocking it. A school prairie might include an area near the beginning of a trail where as many species as possible are to be planted and labeled, and possibly an area of tall grasses and robust forbs where children could explore off the trail. As long as the species selected are among those adapted to the site conditions, such "contrived" prairie species arrangements probably match those that were present somewhere in the vast original prairies.

Timetable

A timetable is an important component of any plan. Sufficient time for becoming well acquainted with your site should be a top priority, if this has not already been accomplished. Providing adequate time for seed gathering and site preparation (see chapters 7 and 8 for techniques) is also important. For most restorations, a full year is needed for seed gathering and the initial steps of site preparation before any planting begins.

For large prairies, a common procedure is to plant an acre or a few acres each year, taking advantage of the early plantings as a seed source for those planted later. This reduces costs and can provide a useful demonstration of plots in various stages of restoration. This approach is often used in planting schoolyard prairies because it saves money and conveniently allows a sequence of classes to be involved in every stage of the prairie's development over a long time period.

Long-Term Management

Prescribed Burns

Management of the vegetation, whether savanna or prairie, will require prescribed burning. The frequency of burning required and the timing of burns will depend on the rate and extent of woody invasion, the need for control of exotics, the rate of fuel accumulation, and the type of prairie. New restorations are generally burned every year for five or more years. Mesic prairies require more frequent burning than dry prairies. Prairies severely invaded by trees and shrubs also require frequent burning, and sometimes brush cutting and treatment of the woody invaders with an herbicide as well. Keep in mind, however, that complete elimination of shrubs and trees is not necessary or even desirable. The presettlement prairies had trees and shrubs also, kept short and hidden in the tall grass by the repeated fires.

The timing of prescribed burns is currently a subject of considerable discussion. (See chapter 15 for a discussion of summer burns.) Fall burning was customary for the Native Americans in this area, while today's prairie managers have made prescribed burning a spring rite. Spring is a convenient and relatively nonhazardous time, but repeated spring burns tend to favor tall grasses at the expense of forbs and late-flowering species at the expense of early-flowering species. Perhaps the wisest course of action is to avoid repeated burns at one particular season and instead to burn at various times of the year.

It is also wise not to burn an entire prairie or savanna at once to avoid high mortality of insects and other small invertebrates in the litter. The Curtis Prairie is divided into three burn units; each year one of these is not burned, in order to provide a refuge from the fire for these small creatures. It is still possible to burn each unit two years out of three, an intensive schedule designed to control overabundant shrubs and trees.

Before you burn, inquire about local burning restrictions; get a permit if required. Some jurisdictions, especially in urban areas, prohibit fires. If burning is not allowed and your prairie is small, cut or mow the dead plant material in early spring and then rake it off. This will prevent accumulation of mulch, which is an important function of fire.

Exotic Weed Patrol

Besides maintaining ongoing procedures to control exotic species, prairie managers should exercise long-term vigilance in checking restorations for unwelcome new arrivals and take prompt action if any are found. The first discovery of a small patch of reed canary grass or a few individuals of purple loosestrife in a wet prairie, or of leafy spurge in a dry prairie, should trigger vigorous control measures for as long as it takes to eliminate the new arrival. The penalty for not reacting can be severe: failure to eradicate a small patch of leafy spurge that appeared in Curtis Prairie twenty years ago has allowed this pest species to invade over an acre of good-quality restored prairie—so far.

Species Enrichment

The diversity of a restoration in terms of the number of native species present is frequently one of the criteria for measuring the success of the restoration. The diversity of a restoration tends to increase in the early years, as the plants from species that take longer to germinate are added to those that germinate quickly. (In some prairie plantings, for reasons perhaps related to weather, it has taken as long as four or five years for significant germination to take place. This can be discouraging, but don't give up!) Eventually, however, the viable planted seeds and those in the seed bank, if any, will be used up. The manager will be able to list the native species present and determine what species should be added to the restoration.

Most of the plants to be added will be conservative species (see tables 5.1, 11.1, 11.2). The techniques for doing so have not been sufficiently tested, but some managers have had good results by interseeding after burning the prairie. You may also want to try setting out transplants of desired species in openings created by clipping or pulling.

People Management

Except for very remote and inaccessible areas, long-term management will also require people management. This is a challenge but also an opportunity to encourage visitors to enjoy and learn about these complex ecosystems and yet to protect them. Three approaches can be helpful:

1. Establish a volunteer program, preferably at the beginning of the project. Recruiting volunteers not only provides labor that can make a project possible, it also provides a core of informed and enthusiastic stewards who will spread the word. People who have

spent hours cutting buckthorn or gathering seeds tend to take a proprietary interest in the project.
2. Educate the public. Offer public tours and special tours or talks for groups. Newspaper articles and appearances on talk shows may be helpful. For some sites, posting an informative sign may be appropriate. (Consider this even for a small yard prairie!)
3. For small restorations, wet sites, or heavily used areas, provide comfortable, easily visible trails and/or boardwalks that will permit enjoyment of the site without trampling the vegetation. (Prairies and savannas are resilient enough to permit light off-trail activity on large upland sites.)

Keeping Records and Monitoring Changes

Recording all observations and management activities is important so that future managers will be able to learn from the past, avoid repeating mistakes, evaluate the effects of management, and plan future management based on the record. It may be important to take data in a systematic way in order to follow long-term changes. One of the most frequent regrets of restorationists is that they did not take sufficient data early in the restoration (see chapter 17).

It is important to share documented observations with the growing body of restorationists. This may mean sending a report on the development of a county park prairie to the journal *Restoration and Management Notes,* or presenting a paper on a landscape-scale savanna restoration at a savanna conference, or inviting people who have started prairies in their yards to get together and compare notes. Somewhere out there are restorationists who need to know what you have learned.

REFERENCES

Ahrenhoerster, Robert, and Trelen Wilson. 1981. *Prairie Restoration for the Beginner.* North Lake, WI: Prairie Seed Source.

McClain, William. 1996. *Illinois Prairie, Past and Future.* Springfield: Illinois Department of Natural Resources.

Morgan, John P., and Douglas Collicutt. 1995. *Restoring Canada's Native Prairies—A Practical Manual.* Available from Prairie Habitats, P.O. Box 1, Argyle, Manitoba R0C 0B0, Canada.

Murray, Molly Fifield. 1993. *Prairie Restoration for Wisconsin Schools.* Madison: University of Wisconsin-Madison Arboretum.

Nichols, Stanley, and Lynn Entine. 1976. *Prairie Primer.* Madison: University of Wisconsin Extension Bulletin.

Packard, Stephen. 1986. "Rediscovering the Tallgrass Prairie Savanna of Illinois," article 1.14 in *Proceedings of the Tenth North American Prairie Conference.* Dallas: Native Prairie Association of Texas.

Rock, Harold. 1974. *Prairie Propagation Handbook.* Hales Corners, WI: Boerner Botanical Gardens.

Shirley, Shirley. 1994. *Restoring the Tallgrass Prairie: An Illustrated Manual for Iowa and the Upper Midwest.* Iowa City: University of Iowa Press.

Smith, J. Robert, and Beatrice S. Smith. 1980. *The Prairie Garden.* Madison: University of Wisconsin Press.

Thompson, Janette R. 1992. *Prairies, Forests and Wetlands: The Restoration of Natural Landscape Communities in Iowa.* Iowa City: University of Iowa Press.

4
Restoration Options

Stephen Packard

"Should I cut down all these trees and restore prairie, or should I save some cherries, plant some oaks, and restore woodland?"

"Do I plow up this old meadow, or plant directly into what's already here?"

Choosing a prairie, woodland, or some other target community and selecting restoration strategies to rebuild that community require difficult choices. Yet the choices must be made before restoration can begin. This chapter will help you decide whether and how to select a target community. It includes a key that suggests specific courses of action, preceded by a section defining important terms employed in the key.

If you are not familiar with restoration decision making and if there is any natural vegetation on your site, you will find it valuable to study chapter 5 before using the key. Also, the key requires a knowledge of your region's natural communities. References describing the natural communities of the states and provinces that are the focus of this book are found in appendix D. Many regions still do not have detailed descriptions of their original natural communities—especially the savannas and open woodlands. The references listed are the best currently available to help evaluate the existing vegetation on a possible restoration site; they will in most cases also help set restoration goals by providing both species lists and an analysis of ecosystem processes.

Choosing a Target Community

Before you begin the restoration of land that may have lost its original structure, you may need to decide what specific type of community is the most appropriate target. One component of choosing a target is knowing what is possible. You need to understand the characteristics of the site and the potential impacts of restoration techniques. The presettlement vegetation (see Noss 1985), as well as soils, topography, rare plant or animal populations, and the site's current and original hydrology, should provide insights.

But the most important step is to analyze the site's existing plant communities. This analysis must be made by someone who understands the local natural ecosystems and who can identify both weed species and conservatives—plants of older, more stable communities that are among the first to disappear when an ecosystem is disrupted. Anyone planning restoration activity—as vocation, avocation, or on any other basis— needs to be able to identify the plants of the existing site and of the target communities. One alternative (much less fun) is to find and rely on some other person who knows plants. But learning to identify plants is central to the excitement of restoration, and anyone can do it. Simple field guides (for example, Peterson and McKenny 1968 or Newcomb 1977) are sufficient equipment to identify most plants.

When analyzing the current vegetation, first survey the site for rare and conservative species. Conservativeness rankings for prairie and for some savanna and woodland species can be found in appendix A and table 5.1. *If conservatives are diverse and plentiful, perhaps even with endangered species present, this fact determines your goal.* For example, if diverse woodland conservatives are plentiful, woodland is the target community or goal.

Once you have selected a target, it guides your actions. Hence, if oak woodland is the target, you would not burn so aggressively that the trees would be top-killed, since woodland conservatives will not persist in bright sun, and the "restored" site would soon be of poorer quality than when you started.

If the conservatives present are prairie species, the goal is prairie. But don't assume that an area with scattered trees and shrubs should necessarily be a savanna or woodland. In sites with remnant elements of high natural quality, the main obstacle to recognizing the most appropriate goal is likely to be invading trees. When a high-quality prairie is threatened by invading shrubs and trees, good monitoring will reveal that the community is degrading, even though the process may look "natural" to the uninformed. Once you can recognize exotic and aggressive species, especially invading trees, learn to subtract them from the scene mentally as you seek to identify a target community. For a thumbnail depiction of natural community types divided by amounts of woody canopy cover, see figure 4.1. Compare these with the degraded and subsequently restored site shown in figures 5.2 and 5.3.

Many sites, especially large ones, comprise more than one community. A valuable planning step for such sites is to map the best remnant areas of each community type. Prospect for the parts of the site with the highest frequency of conservative species. Such places are top priorities for restoration, in part because these areas will later supply the rarest and most important seed for the site.

Once the restoration is under way, monitoring changes will help you decide whether your work is succeeding. If the structure of the natural community is moving toward the one identified as your target or goal, and if natural quality is rising, then your management is probably on track. The section entitled "What Is Quality?" in chapter 5 considers the question of quality in more depth and discusses its assessment; animal and plant monitoring are described in chapters 17–21.

If, on the other hand, the quality of your site is rising, but the community is turning out to resemble a prairie or woodland, for example, rather than the savanna you expected, or if your site's quality is falling because your work is eliminating the habitat of the site's rare and conservative species, additional research and rethinking are needed. Listen to the ecosystem. Your initial goal reflected your best judgment with the information then available to you. It helped you get rolling. But as you proceed, you will learn to recognize the ecosystem's natural inclinations and healing processes; as this happens, allow nature to guide you as you work to restore the conditions under which it can follow its own course.

Some traditional conservationists may question the restorationist's practice of identifying a target community. It has been challenged as "playing God." This concern is one to take seriously. There certainly is a danger that some individual restorationists will make ecologically insensitive, destructive decisions. But there are many instances, such as when the survival of an endangered species population is at stake, when playing God is the only good option.

Consider, for example, a site that supports small numbers of an endangered prairie species that are just holding on in the spaces between invading trees. That population of rare species will survive only if the restorationist plays God to the extent of removing the trees and changing that woodland back to prairie.

Few people will question such a decision. But now consider the more difficult case of a site sufficiently degraded that it has little biodiversity to start with. In this case reseeding is necessary, but suppose you receive a recommendation not to choose a target community. Not choosing may seem to be a humble approach, but then how do you decide which types of seeds to buy or gather? Seed is costly, and wild seed is always gathered

Figure 4.1. Prairie-forest continuum.

Prairie: A grassland with few or no trees. Characteristic breeding birds: bobolink, meadowlark, Henslow's sparrow, short-eared owl.

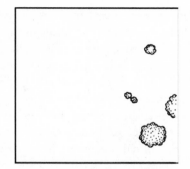

Savanna: A grassland with scattered trees. Trees are characteristically oaks, well spaced or in clusters. May have extensive areas of shrubs (especially hazelnut) and tree resprouts. Characteristic breeding birds: eastern bluebird, eastern kingbird, orchard oriole, Bell's vireo, barn owl.

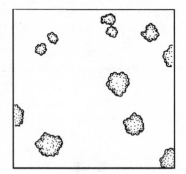

Woodland: An open forest with a vigorous turf of grasses and flowers throughout the growing season. Depends on frequent fire. Many trees have spreading lower limbs. Bright enough for oak reproduction (i.e., less than 80% canopy cover). Typically dominated by oaks but may contain hickory, walnut, elm, dogwood, plum, and many other woody species. Characteristic breeding birds: Baltimore oriole, red-headed woodpecker, whippoorwill, Cooper's hawk.

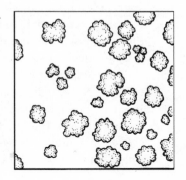

Forest: In many ways the oak forest (shown on left) is intermediate between oak woodland and maple forest. Maple forest (shown on right) is fire-intolerant. Most tree trunks have few lower limbs. Shade-tolerant species of understory trees and shrubs are present. Herbs are mostly ephemeral (dormant in summer) or scattered. Characteristic breeding birds: ovenbird, red-eyed vireo, sharp-shinned hawk.

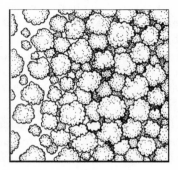

at the expense of an existing ecosystem. But woodland seed will not survive in a prairie, and vice versa. Thus, if you are planning to use seed of rare or uncommon plants, choosing a target community is a necessity.

On the other hand, there are some times when choosing a target community is not appropriate. For example, in most good and high-quality remnants, the best restoration plan is simply to attempt to restore the site's original fire regime, hydrology, and other natural processes. Assure that the degree of shade is neither so dark nor so bright that the existing plant and animal species are lost. Then let nature follow its own course.

Restorationists have developed a variety of approaches to selecting target communities. Six of these are listed below. These target options may seem to be quite distinct, but in practice they blend and overlap.

1. Restore the original vegetation of the site. Public Land Survey (PLS) records are usually the starting point for efforts to characterize a site's original vegetation. (See Noss 1985.)
2. Restore the community now best expressed by the flora and fauna of the site (particularly when a globally endangered species or community is involved).
3. Restore the rarest or the otherwise highest priority community that it is practical to restore on the site. (This is particularly appropriate for areas with little ecological integrity remaining.)
4. Restore a representative variety of communities on the site. (Two or more different habitats may be required by certain significant species.)
5. Restore as large as possible an example of a given community on the site. (See the discussion below.)
6. Restore the highest priority and most easily attainable mix of communities in the quickest and easiest way, given the best available expert judgment, which in turn is based on the best practically attainable information. (See the discussion below.)

To learn which are the rarest—and therefore often the highest priority—natural communities and species in your area, consult a Nature Conservancy office or state conservation agency. A summary of the rarest communities in the United States can be found in Grossman, Goodin, and Reuss, *Rare Plant Communities of the Conterminous United States, An Initial Survey* (see appendix D). In that publication, many of the formerly most widespread types of oak savanna and woodland communities are classified G-1—globally endangered. Many of the formerly most widespread types of prairie communities are classified G-2—globally threatened. Both are high priorities for protection and restoration.

Option 5 is often important because a large habitat of a given type may be required to support minimum viable populations of rare species. For the sake of a very significant species or group of species, for example, it may be appropriate to remove trees from a prairie even though trees of those species show up on the presettlement land survey of the site and savanna is a rarer community than prairie. Such an option would be the clear choice in this case: the survival of rare prairie birds and butterflies is threatened by some invading young oaks; no significant distinctive savanna species can be found; and ample similar land nearby is being managed for recovery of the oak savanna community.

To understand option 6, consider the following hypothetical situation. Two adjacent hundred-acre tracts are acquired by a conservation agency, which already owns all the surrounding land. One tract, originally mostly prairie, has grown up in oaks and brush and now has no herbaceous ground layer. The other tract, originally open oak woodland, has been cut, plowed, planted to pasture, and now consists of old-field vegetation. Knowing only this, the easiest plan would be to restore prairie on the pasture land (formerly wooded) and open oak woodland in the brushy oak woods (formerly prairie).

However, if the surrounding conservation area is now mostly prairie and if that prairie supports a number of animal species in populations not quite large enough for viability, and if open woodland is well represented in other nearby conservation lands, then the choice to restore both tracts to prairie might be clearly preferred. Alternatively, if no rare species are present and the adjacent land is mostly open woodland, it might be easy to decide to plant oaks in the field and restore both tracts to open woodland. Or if, in a fourth variation, the rare species present depend on the dynamic interface between prairie and woodland, then the first mentioned (and easiest) option might be recommended: restore mostly prairie in the field and mostly savanna in the brush in such a way as to maximize the acreage of transition zones. Such considerations, as reflected in the key and throughout this handbook, should be explored and weighed before making a final decision. Choosing target communities on the basis of biodiversity priority is challenging and requires complex judgments. But in many cases there is no substitute for doing that.

Important Terms

Many terms in the key have specialized connotations or definitions that are commonly used by restorationists. These are given below:

aggressive species—one that outcompetes weedy and sometimes even conservative species. Some exotic aggressives (e.g., purple loosestrife, garlic mustard, leafy spurge) can invade and degrade even high-quality natural communities.

brush—exotic or native shrubs and trees that are out of balance or out of place and thus need to be controlled. This term is used for native shrubs only when they need to be controlled because they are present in numbers greater than those believed to have been characteristic of an original natural community.

conservatives—species that thrive best in a relatively stable (successionally advanced) community with its original processes intact. Conservatives are the species with high ratings in appendix A and table 5.1. Antonym: weed. (See also *aggressive species*.)

degraded—refers to a remnant natural community that has not been destroyed but has lost some of its component species or has been invaded by aggressive species not native to the site. The main sources of degradation in the Midwest are lack of fire, exotic species invasion, hydrologic alteration, fragmentation, and overgrazing.

exotics—species native to another continent or another region but not to the region in question.

forest—as used here, a closed-canopy, wooded natural community that is not dependent on frequent fire. There are typically one or more layers of shade-tolerant trees or shrubs below the canopy trees and no grassy turf. (See *oak forest* and *woodland*.)

forest trees—canopy species, including sugar maple and basswood, and understory species, including hop hornbeam, blue beech, and other species that can complete their life cycles in considerable shade. When old oaks stand today among such species, the forest trees are usually invaders of formerly more open woodlands, and the oaks no longer reproduce.

herbaceous—nonwoody. Herb species include grasses and forbs (or wildflowers).

interseeding—planting seed directly into existing vegetation without plowing or herbiciding that vegetation.

natural communities—complex assemblages of species as they have evolved in their environments over long periods of time.

oak forest—an alternative term for oak woodland. But the dense, unburned oak community to which this term is usually applied may not be a natural community, as described in this book. It is probably in most cases an artifact of fire suppression, a new and temporary assemblage of species that is gradually being replaced, often by a few aggressive exotic or maple forest species. A forest of oak and aggressive trees can often be restored to oak woodland by fire and, if necessary, girdling and inter-seeding.

original—refers to a prairie, woodland, wetland, etc., that is essentially intact, that is, as it was for thousands of years before Euroamerican settlement. Such areas are restored by reinstating natural conditions, that is, by burning, weeding, blocking ditches, etc. (See *degraded* and *remnant*.)

prairie—a fire-maintained natural community dominated by grasses and with few or no trees. (See *savanna*.)

remnant—a site with all or part of its presettlement nature intact. (See *original*.) Such areas may be intact or may benefit from the restoration of missing species of plants and animals.

restoration—repair or reestablishment of a natural community by reinstating as many as possible of the species and processes that evolved together in response to the physical environment and to one another over thousands of years or more.

savanna—a fire-maintained natural community dominated by grasses or sedges but with scattered fire-tolerant species of trees. Hazelnut is a major shrub. (See *prairie* and *woodland*.)

savanna trees—principally oaks, especially bur (on rich soil), white (often on thinner or drier soil), black (on sand), swamp white and pin (wet), and scarlet, post, and blackjack (dry).

weed—a species that depends on unnatural or severe disturbance. Weeds are the species with low ratings in appendix A. (See *aggressive*.) Antonym: conservative.

weedy trees—species of trees that aggressively invade a site when natural processes are disrupted (e.g., hydrology altered, fires stopped, etc.).

woodland—a fire-maintained natural community with a grassy turf dominated by trees. Some woodlands have many shrub species; others have few. (See *savanna* and *forest*.)

woodland trees—principally oaks and hickories, also at times many other species including black walnut, cottonwood, elm, and black maple.

Key to Restoration Options

This key may help experienced practitioners organize their decision-making process and review options. It should help less experienced people learn the components of the restoration decision-making process. In the case of difficult decisions it may be wise to consult with expert ecologists and restoration practitioners.

The key covers the fire-dependent communities of the Midwest—the prairies and associated savannas and woodlands. Some associated wetlands are covered as wet prairie, wet savanna, and wet woodland. Because the key (like the rest of this book) includes only communities that depend on frequent fire, it does not cover deep-water aquatic communities or others (e.g., beech-maple forest) that were not subject to frequent fire in the past.

This key works much like the keys that help taxonomists identify specific plants or animals: The reader is led through a set of decisions and at each step chooses one of two possible routes to follow. Each route leads to an ever-narrower range of options, until the concluding choice is made. To use the key, start at the top, decide whether a statement is correct or not, and proceed to the number indicated. Repeat the process. When your choice leads to a "restoration option," you have finished the key. (The restoration options follow the key.) If along the way you reach a step where both options are partially true, follow first one lead and then the other; then choose between the two suggested approaches. Consider your chosen option as a basis for your restoration plan. In cases where more than one option appears under the same letter, a judgment decision by the land manager is called for. Read all options. If the option you reach seems inappropriate, begin the key again and reconsider your decisions at each step; you may be led to a more appropriate option.

1. If the land is wooded, go to 2. (If not, go to 14.)
2. If trees include mature oaks, go to 3. (If not, go to 9.)
3. If the ground has continuous grass or oak leaf cover so that brush can be controlled gradually through fire alone, go to 4. (If not, go to 6.) *Note: This condition most often applies to relatively healthy savannas or to woodlands with a thick carpet of oak leaves.*
4. If the ground layer consists largely of native grasses and forbs, consider restoration option A1 or A2. (If not, go to 5.)

5. If the ground layer consists largely of weeds, dry leaves, or bare ground, consider restoration option B1 or B2.

6. Insufficient fuel accumulates to sustain burns adequate to control brush. If the restoration goal is woodland, consider restoration option C1, C2, or C3. (If not, go to 7.) *Note: This condition most often applies to savannas in which shrubs have shaded out most of the grasses, or woodlands in which invader species have replaced many of the oaks.*

7. If the restoration goal is savanna, consider restoration option D1 or D2. (If not, go to 8.)

8. If the restoration goal is prairie, clear all trees and exotic or aggressive brush. Go to 14.

9. If many of the small trees are oaks, go to 10. (If not, go to 11.)

10. If your goal is savanna or woodland, consider restoration options C and D. (If the restoration goal is prairie, clear all trees and exotic or aggressive brush. Go to 14.)

11. If few or none of the trees are oaks and the goal is oak wood-land, consider restoration option E1. (If your goal is savanna or prairie, go to 12).

12. If your goal is savanna, consider restoration option E2. (If not, go to 13.)

13. If your goal is prairie, clear all trees and consider restoration option J.

14. If the land is not wooded and the vegetation (other than brush) consists principally of native grasses and forbs, go to 15. (If not, go to 17.)

15. If diversity is good and conservative species are present, consider restoration option F. (If not, go to 16.)

16. If diversity is poor or conservative species are absent, consider restoration options G1 and G2.

17. If the vegetation is a diverse stand of perennial herbs (i.e., the site is an "old field"), consider restoration option H1 or H2. (If not, go to 18.)

18. If the vegetation is predominantly annual weeds (perhaps because it is a recently cultivated field) or a dense stand of one or a few rank species (e.g., smooth brome, reed canary grass), consider restoration options H2, I1, or I2. (If not, go to 19.)

19. If soil is bare and the weed threat slight because dense brush was recently removed, consider restoration option J.

Restoration Options

A1. Woodland and Savannah Management: In early years, burn one-third to two-thirds of the site every spring or fall on a revolving schedule. Remove problem weeds. This option requires minimal work if all goes well, and there is no need to fear (as some managers do with option A2) that some inappropriately planted species will outcompete those native species existing on the site. (Note: If the trees are widely spaced, the site is a savanna. On sand or other dry, poor soil and rarely elsewhere, savannas may still be found with sufficient native grass fuel to sustain fire. Such areas should be managed as in A1 or A2.)

A2. Woodland and Savannah Restoration with Interseeding: Manage as in A1 with the following additions: Remove most weed trees (see "Savannas" and "Woodlands" in chapter 11). Remove excessive stocking of even such native trees as oaks, hickories, and black walnut in areas where artificially dense tree or shrub reproduction prevents restoration of ground-layer vegetation or tree reproduction. Collect appropriate seed and sow in areas opened up as brush is removed mechanically or by fire. (This option has the advantages that: a. there is less chance that weeds will take over in areas where brush had killed off the herb layer; and b. it provides a strategic opportunity to restore some of the natural diversity of the many herbaceous species that disruption may have reduced or eliminated from the site.)

B1. Degraded Woodland Management (1): Follow option A1 in some test plots for two or more years to determine whether natural vegetation will return and gain control of the ground. A hypothesized "soil seed-bank" often fails to materialize, but plants sometimes emerge from shade-suppressed root stocks. Caution: Weed problems that develop in the absence of seeding may be severe for a decade or longer. If native vegetation does not regain control of the ground, then manage as in A2 (but weeds may get quite a head start in the meantime).

B2. Degraded Woodland Management (2): Manage as in A2. Plant appropriate seed immediately (see tables 11.1 and 11.2). Control weeds. This option has a strong advantage on moist, fertile soil. It gives restored native species the jump on weeds. Be careful to clear brush (by cutting and burning) from *only* as much ground as you have seed to plant. Experiment for a year or two to determine how much area you can handle. How much seed can you gather? How dense do you need to plant it?

(The thinner the seed is planted, the larger the acreage you can plant—and the worse the weed problems will be. If you try to restore too large an area and cannot handle the weeds, then you may have a persistent weed community for a considerable period of time and the conservative seed planted may have been wasted. Weedy or aggressive species can prevent conservatives from becoming established. In the long run, however, most weeds can't compete once a dense and diverse turf of conservatives has begun to form.)

C1. Oak Rescue: Control weed tree species in order to encourage oaks; as adequate fuel accumulates, begin restoration as in A1, A2, B1, or B2 as appropriate. (This method is simple and straightforward, particularly if large numbers of young oaks are already present. A disadvantage is that the restoration time scale may be so long—many decades—that the restoration will not help conserve the gene pools of locally threatened populations of many species. For that reason, this option may be most valuable as a "holding action" while resources are being invested in restoration of the same community type on other sites nearby.)

C2. Gradual Woodland Restoration: Control weed tree species except to leave sufficient shade to provide good growing conditions for herbs of dense woodlands. (Otherwise, invasion by aggressive weeds may be severe.) Plant seed of the common herbs of dense woodlands if necessary. Plant herbs of more open woodlands as appropriate habitat develops.

C3. Savanna Restoration for Succession to Woodland: Remove all weed trees. Plant open savanna or prairie seed in areas too bright to sustain woodland species. Maintain site with low-intensity fire as oak dominance increases. Sow woodland herbs as necessary when the restored canopy permits.

D1. Gradual Savanna Restoration: Remove nonsavanna trees from limited parts of the areas to be most open. Restore prairie. In the areas with the most oak leaves, restore woodland herbs. Burn both restored communities biennially. Expand the edges of the fire community by burning, cutting brush, and planting prairie, savanna, or woodland vegetation until the unburnable areas are gone or mostly gone.

D2. Rapid Savanna Restoration: Cut all or most areas of unburnable brush. Seed with prairie, savanna, and woodland mixes (see tables 11.1–2). Burn. Pay particular attention to the open savanna areas, which may be the slowest to develop enough fuel to ward off reinvasion by brush.

E1. Planting a Woodland: Clear enough brush to reestablish woodland tree species at a density greater than ultimately needed. Plant woodland trees, particularly oaks. Occasionally trim back weed trees that threaten to shade the slow-growing oaks. There will be little else to do on this site for a few decades. Proceed with herb-layer restoration when there are a sufficient number of trees big enough to withstand moderate fire and provide sufficient fuel to control brush.

E2. Planting a Savanna: Remove exotic and weedy trees. Plant prairie mix and savanna tree species. While they're young, protect trees from fire. Remove or wet down dry vegetation surrounding the trees prior to burning. (Or leave the site unburned for several to many years after the prairie vegetation is well established; considerable mechanical or herbicide brush control may be needed during this time. Begin to burn when a sufficient number of trees are large enough to withstand burning.) Plant the distinctive savanna grasses and forbs that require partial shade only after the trees have grown large enough to provide sufficient shade.

F. Prairie Management: Burn. Clear exotic or aggressive brush if necessary. If some conservative species are missing or present only in low numbers, and especially if high-quality remnants nearby are being lost, it may be desirable to restore missing conservatives by interseeding with seeds collected from those remnants.

G1. Prairie Restoration through Interseeding: Burn and sow seed of conservative (and other missing) species. Soil biota may be restored with sods from areas being destroyed (especially from unprotectable remnants that are similar to and of higher quality than the restoration site). Cut and remove dominant vegetation when it's in bloom or even twice during a growing season if necessary to prevent heavy shading of the new seedlings.

G2. Prairie Maintenance: Burn only. The advantage of this minimal level of restoration is that it allows study of how much recovery will result from the seed bank, suppressed root stocks, and chance processes. Certainly this experiment should be done in a few cases. The disadvantages are that a degraded system will probably be maintained in that poor state, and the site will not contribute to the conservation and continuing evolution of the extirpated rarer species (and associated processes) of high-quality ecosystems.

H1. Restoring Prairie Conservatives in an Old Field: Restore seed of conservative species using techniques described in chapter 11. This is the preferred alternative, if practical, but see H2. Burn every year or two at first. Add any missing aggressive prairie species in later years—after the conservative species control most of the ground.

H2. Restoring Prairie in an Old Field: H1 may not be practical because insufficient conservative seed is available or because of the threat of overgrowth by brush or briars (which can actually be stimulated when an old field is first burned). In these cases sow the best areas with conservative seed and sow the balance, especially those areas most threatened by brush or aggressive weeds, with aggressive species such as the bluestems and Indian grass. Burn annually or biennially until the prairie turf controls the ground. Strategic mowing or grazing may help.

I1. Restoring Prairie on Bare Soil: Herbicide or plow, then plant, as described in chapter 12. This approach is tried and true, well understood, and predictable. But consider I2.

I2. Restoring Prairie Conservatives on Bare Soil: Restore as in H1 or H2. Be careful not to bury the smaller seeds under more than twice their thickness of soil. Mow once or a few times each year, whenever rank vegetation begins to cast such dense shade at the ground level that seedlings may die. Under some conditions this method will produce a high-quality prairie while minimizing erosion and the need for herbicides.

J. Restoring Prairie on Stable Soil: Herbicide stumps carefully (or else, in a few years, the site is likely to consist of dense brush). If necessary, control seedling or resprouting brush mechanically or with herbicide until fire is a sufficient control. Do not plow. Broadcast prairie mix as in H1 or H2. Since agricultural weeds should be in short supply (because of the lack of recent cultivation or other disturbance), you should be able to plant in fall or early spring. Carefully control any aggressive weeds that appear during the first year or two. If you are confident that brush control is thorough, try a conservative mix. Most often, however, the brush-regrowth threat will be severe; in that case, plant an aggressive prairie mix (strong on tall grasses) to provide adequate fuel so that fire will quickly be able to control brush.

REFERENCES

Newcomb, Lawrence. 1977. *Newcomb's Wildflower Guide.* Boston: Little, Brown and Co.

Noss, Reed F. 1985. "On Characterizing Presettlement Vegetation: How and Why." *Natural Areas Journal* 5:1.

Peterson, Roger Tory, and Margaret McKenny. 1968. *A Field Guide to Wildflowers.* Boston: Houghton Mifflin Co.

5
Restoring Remnants

Stephen Packard and Laurel M. Ross

We in the turn-of-the-century Midwest are honored and challenged to be among the first on earth to recognize that we have with us the tattered remnants of a nearly lost ancient ecosystem. Just tattered remnants. Nowhere do whole communities of our plants and animals thrive as they once did. The protection and stewardship of the tiny remaining pristine natural areas is a high conservation priority, but these areas are often too small for long-term viability of many of their original species. Ecologist Dan Janzen wrote in 1988 of a comparable situation:

> The increasingly vigorous efforts to protect some of the relatively intact portions of tropical nature come too late and too slow for well over half of the tropics—especially the half best suited to agriculture and animal husbandry. Its remaining wildlands are hardly more than scattered biotic debris. The only feasible next step is conservation of biodiversity by using the living biotic debris and inocula from nearby intact areas to restore habitats. If this step is not taken quickly, natural and anthropogenic perturbations will extinguish more of the habitat remnants, small fragments, and the living dead—the organisms that are living out their physiological life spans, but are no longer members of persistent populations.

This chapter discusses restoration for the purpose of conserving biodiversity. Remnant restoration is the process of nursing the full biota back to good health as much as possible, restocking species as necessary, and reestablishing natural processes. The building blocks of this work are burning, brush and weed control (including strategic herbiciding but not broadcast herbiciding), mowing, interseeding, and the interplanting of sods. Many of these techniques are addressed in detail in later chapters of this book. In this chapter we introduce them and discuss how managers can decide what combination and sequence of these techniques will be most effective and most appropriate to meet their management objectives. The key in chapter 4 provides initial guidelines for reading the landscape and selecting options.

The term *remnant,* as used in this book, refers to communities that have some components of their natural character surviving, although often in highly degraded form. According to this definition, it may not be principally the survival of diverse native vegetation that qualifies a site as a remnant. It may instead be intact soils, for example, or hydrology, or old oaks, or breeding birds that make a remnant ecologically significant. The level at which the original biota survives in remnants varies from 99 percent to 1 percent.

To some, restoration means "plow the ground and plant the seed." The purpose of plowing, of course, is to kill existing vegetation. The vegetation-dependent animals, of course, are lost too. In remnant restoration, techniques may be more subtle or more complex. The patient—the ecosystem—is still alive. The prescription may include any measure that may foster recovery of the original biota.

The philosophy and techniques described here are most directly applicable to conservation lands such as those owned by public agencies and conservation organizations, although homeowners, landscapers, and others can adapt much of this thinking to their own purposes. Indeed, public participation, in the form of backyard gardeners as well as restoration volunteers on public lands, is critical to the success of conservation efforts generally.

When restoring a weedy quarter-acre on a home lot, it might be considered a matter of personal taste whether grassland or woodland is chosen as the goal. But even on small sites, choosing the most appropriate option can make a big difference in the amount of work necessary and in the quality of the result.

On the other hand, when restoring hundreds of acres of county conservation land, the life and death of millions of individuals and populations of hundreds of species hang in the balance. It is sometimes tempting to say, "These decisions require research that we can't afford. We'll have to wait." But to wait and do nothing is a powerful and potentially destructive alternative. Thus, more and more people must develop the ability and confidence to make restoration decisions and act on them. The clear imperative in most situations is to make restoration progress in a timely way, using the best thinking and resources available.

What Is Quality?

Restoration is the work of enhancing ecological quality. High-quality prairies and woodlands are, by definition, rich in conservative species and have most natural processes intact. Disrupted or degraded systems (those that have been plowed, drained, overgrazed, protected from fire, etc.) lose their conservatives. Species that are most conservative, also by definition, are the first ones to be lost to disruption and the least likely to return if the disruption ceases. The principal challenge in remnant restoration is to release or speed up the processes that allow conservative species of plants and animals to regain their important roles in the system. Biodiversity rises from and at the same time actively influences a site's physical characteristics (minerals, water, and air) as well as its natural processes (erosion, fire, evolution, etc.).

The presence of high-quality *plant* communities does not necessarily imply similarly high-quality *animal* communities. Consider the case of the grade A ("very high quality") black-soil prairies identified as conservation priorities by the vegetation-based Illinois Natural Areas Inventory in 1979. They are all very small—mostly in the one- to five-acre range. None was large enough to support even a single pair of breeding prairie birds. Although no similar animal-based inventory was conducted, it would have been possible to select other sites with relatively "high-quality" assemblages of prairie birds, mammals, reptiles, and amphibians. These sites are generally much larger but very often with only poor or fair plant diversity present. (A site that merited an *overall* high-quality rating, of course, would have a relatively complete assemblage of its original biota, both plants and animals.)

There are many complex interdependent relationships among species of plants and invertebrate animals (insects, etc.). Many plants depend on certain insect species for pollination and other services. Many insect species depend on certain species or small groups of plants for food and other less obvious requirements. Those species that seem to require a fair- to high-quality prairie or woodland for survival have been called "remnant dependent" by Ron Panzer (1995; see chapter 18). Such insects have also been called "conservative" in that they are associated with the relatively stable remnants of ancient plant communities. They are rightly becoming a principal focus of conservation efforts.

Monitoring the progress of ecosystem recovery requires a system for assessing community quality. Assessing quality requires standards. One of the first systems for setting biodiversity standards was developed for the

Illinois Natural Areas Inventory in the mid-seventies. Such systems have subsequently been developed by most state conservation agencies. The basic goal of the Illinois system was to identify sites that had not been degraded by what was then called disturbance. (In this chapter, sources of degradation are referred to as disruption, since the term "disturbance" has come to be used to refer to natural processes such as fire, many of which are actually required for healthy systems.) The botanists who evaluated sites for the inventory developed three lists of plant species characteristic of "very high quality," "high quality," and "good" sites to help them distinguish grades A, B, and C prairie remnants. Lack of disturbance and its indicator species (the conservatives) became the basis of the professional judgments that determined whether a site was selected as a priority for "preservation." Subsequently, these community inventories, based on the judgment of individuals, and supplemented by more hard-data-reliant inventories of rare species, have been combined in state Heritage Programs to help prioritize land for conservation. However, these systems for judging ecosystem health that depend largely on expert judgment, though widely respected for setting land acquisition priorities, are not easily adapted for use in assessing and comparing the results of restoration efforts or evaluating degraded land for restoration potential.

Other tools for evaluating ecosystem quality, based on species conservatism, have been developed by Gerould Wilhelm, Doug Ladd, and others (see chapter 17). These systems expanded on the lists of indicators for "undisturbed" prairie by assigning conservatism rankings to each species of the flora of a region. Once expert judgment has assigned conservativeness values to species, the system can then be used by any botanist to evaluate and compare sites or plots objectively. This system, called the floristic quality assessment, has in recent years been increasingly used by local, state, and national public and private conservation agencies in the Midwest. It is described in detail in chapter 17 and applied to restoration decision making under "Restoration Triage" below.

With experience an observer can readily distinguish between areas of differing quality. A good way to get a feel for quality comparisons is to do the work of sampling plots at a variety of sites, compute floristic quality indices for each sample, and gradually begin to recognize different levels of quality. (See figure 5.1.)

High-quality prairies are readily identified by their richness in conservative prairie flora and the relatively limited proportion of exotics. Prairies that have been somewhat degraded by overgrowth of brush and trees are recognizable in the same way. If the conservative flora mostly survives, restoration to high quality can be relatively easy.

Important savanna and woodland remnants are harder to recognize for two reasons. One problem is few high-quality remnants have been found, managed, and studied. Thus there is relatively little literature that provides a search image, and there are few pristine examples to visit and few experts to consult. The other problem is that virtually all savanna and open oak woodland remnants that haven't suffered from overgrazing have by now been heavily overgrown by brush and trees. Their appearance has been altered, but to a greater or lesser degree the ground-layer flora and associated small animals may for a time survive.

Conservativeness rankings for some representative and distinctive savanna and woodland plants are given in table 5.1. This table was prepared by Gerould Wilhelm, who also contributed much of the language in this and the preceding paragraph. He selected species that are for the most part restricted to contemporary savanna and open woodland remnants across the central and eastern parts of the tallgrass region. Many of these plants are commonly thought of as forest species since today they are often found in more closed woodlands. But these "forests" may in fact be overgrown savannas. While the species in question can persist in heavy shade for a time, shady woodlands are not their preferred habitat. Each of these species tends to increase in vigor and number when woodlands are burned and most pole-sized undergrowth is removed, allowing more light to reach the ground.

The selective list in table 5.1 includes only the relatively small number of savanna and open woodland species that are 1) conservative, 2) geographically widespread, and 3) relatively restricted to intermediate canopy conditions. A comprehensive list of the species of savannas and woodlands would also include most species that have been thought to be more characteristic of prairies and forests. Thus the selective list in this table has been designed as a tool to be used for two purposes: it can help you distinguish an open oak community of understory species from prairie or forest communities, and it can help distinguish between high-quality and low-quality remnants.

Animals are as important to an ecosystem as plants. Zoological quality assessment, however, is considerably more challenging than botanical is. A botanist can often adequately assess the vegetation of most of a five hundred-acre site in a day or two. But to assess in a comparable way the site's birds, mammals, reptiles, amphibians, fish, and invertebrates would take many people and many, many days. No system comparable to

Figure 5.1. Prairie quality: Three examples.

Original prairie. Very high quality. Highly diverse (about twenty native species per ¼m²). Conservative species comprise a substantial component of the biomass. Shown here are thirteen dry-mesic species including such conservatives as white prairie clover, prairie dropseed, and prairie gentian. FQI for a very high quality prairie per ¼m² is typically 20 or higher.

Degraded remnant. Grazing-tolerant natives mix with exotics. Diversity often low (five to fifteen native species per ¼m²). Conservatives absent or rare. Shown here are native Indian grass and ironweed with exotic timothy and white sweet clover (exotics drawn with hatched lines). FQI for degraded remnants per ¼m² is typically between 5 and 10.

Low-quality restoration. One or a few native grass species dominate overwhelmingly (often five or fewer native species per ¼m²). Shown here are big bluestem, Indian grass, bush clover, and compass plant. FQI per ¼m² is typically between 2 and 5.

Table 5.1.

Conservative Savanna and Woodland Plants

Coefficients of conservatism, listed for areas for which they have been developed: Illinois (IL), Michigan (MI), Missouri (MO), northern Ohio (OH), southern Ontario (ON), and the Chicago region (CR), are explained in chapter 17. Numbers indicate, on a scale of 0 to 10, the degree to which the species is faithful to high-quality habitats.

Scientific Name	Common Name	IL	MI	MO	OH	ON	CR
Agastache scrophulariifolia	purple giant hyssop	5	5	9	4	10	5
Agrimonia pubescens	soft agrimony	4	5	3	5	7	5
Amphicarpaea bracteata	hog peanut	4	5	4	5	4	4
Anemone quinquefolia	wood anemone	8	5	10	5	7	7
Anemone virginiana	tall anemone	4	3	4	3	4	5
Apocynum androsaemifolium	spreading dogbane	6	3	5	6	3	5
Aquilegia canadensis	columbine	6	5	6	5	5	6
Arabis laevigata	smooth bank cress	4	5	5	4	5	5
Aralia nudicaulis	wild sarsaparilla	8	5	10	5	4	8
Arisaema dracontium	green dragon	5	10	6	5	9	7
Arisaema triphyllum	Jack-in-the-pulpit	5	5	6	4	5	4
Asclepias exaltata	poke milkweed	10	6		8	8	9
Asclepias purpurascens	purple milkweed	7	10	6	8	10	8
†*Aster cordifolius sagittifolius*	arrow-leaved aster	6	7	6	7	6	7
Aster ontarionis	Ontario aster	4	6	5		6	4
Aster shortii	Short's aster	6	5		4	7	8
Athyrium filix-femina	lady fern	6	4	8	5	4	8
Blephilia hirsuta	wood mint	5	8	7	4	10	8
Botrychium dissectum	cut-leaved grape fern	5	5	6	5	6	6
Botrychium virginianum	rattlesnake fern	4	5	4	5	5	6
Brachyelytrum erectum	long-awned wood grass	7	7	6	6	7	10
Bromus latiglumis	ear-leaved brome	5	6	10	7	7	5
†*Bromus pubescens*	woodland brome	7	5	5	4	7	5
Camassia scilloides	wild hyacinth	7	9	6	5	10	6
†*Campanulastrum americanum*	tall bellflower	3	8	4	4	8	3
Carex albicans	blunt-scaled oak sedge	5	3	8	3	9	8
Carex davisii	Davis's sedge	3	8	4	6	10	7
†*Carex hirsutella*	hairy green sedge	5	3	4	2	8	4
Carex hirtifolia	hairy wood sedge	6	5	7	3	5	5
Carex hitchcockiana	hairy gray sedge	10	5	9	7	6	10
Carex jamesii	grass sedge	4	8	5	7	8	5
Carex oligocarpa	few-fruited gray sedge	6	8	6	8	9	9
Carex pensylvanica	Pennsylvania sedge	5	4	6	3	6	5
Carex rosea	curly-styled wood sedge	5	2	7	5	5	4
Carex sprengelii	long-beaked sedge	8	5		10	6	9

†Precedes scientific name cross-referenced in appendix C.

continues

Table 5.1. (*Continued*)

Scientific Name	Common Name	IL	MI	MO	OH	ON	CR
†*Caulophyllum giganteum*	blue cohosh	7	5	8	6	6	8
Chenopodium standleyanum	woodland goosefoot	3	5	3	6	8	4
Cirsium altissimum	tall thistle	3	5	4	5		6
†*Calystegia spithamaea*	low bindweed	10	8	9	6	7	10
Corylus americana	hazelnut	4	5	2	5	5	5
Cystopteris protrusa	fragile fern	5	5	5	5	9	6
Desmodium cuspidatum	hairy-bracted tick trefoil	6	5	4	4	10	6
Desmodium glutinosum	pointed tick trefoil	4	5	3	5	6	5
Desmodium nudiflorum	bare-stemmed tick trefoil	5	7	4	5	7	9
Desmodium paniculatum★	tall tick clover	5	4	3	4	8	6
Diarrhena americana	beak grass	7	9	6	8	10	10
Dioscorea villosa	wild yam	4	4	5	4	7	7
Echinacea purpurea	purple coneflower	6	10	5	8	10	3
Erigeron pulchellus	Robin's plantain	5	5	5	6	7	10
†*Festuca subverticillata*	Nodding fescue	5	5	4	5	6	5
Galium circaezans	hairy wild licorice	4	4	4	5	7	7
Galium concinnum	shining bedstraw	4	5	4	4	9	5
Galium triflorum	sweet-scented bedstraw	4	4	4	5	4	5
†*Gentiana alba*	yellowish gentian	9	10	8	10	10	9
Geranium maculatum	wild geranium	4	4	5	4	6	4
Helianthus divaricatus	woodland sunflower	5	5	6	5	7	5
Helianthus strumosus	pale-leaved sunflower	4	4	4	5	7	5
†*Hepatica nobilis acuta*	sharp-lobed hepatica	7	8	7	5	6	6
Hieracium scabrum	rough hawkweed	5	3	6	5	7	8
Hydrophyllum virginianum	Virginia waterleaf	5	4	4	5	6	5
Hypericum punctatum	spotted St. John's wort	3	4	3	3	5	4
Krigia biflora	false dandelion	5	5	5	7	10	7
Lactuca floridana	blue lettuce	4	4	3	4	6	5
Lathyrus ochroleucus	pale vetchling	10	8		9	8	10
Lathyrus venosus	veiny pea	9	8	8	8	8	9
Leersia virginica	white grass	4	5	4	3	6	7
Lespedeza violacea	violet bush clover	5	5	4	4	10	7
Lespedeza virginica	slender bush clover	5	7	5	2	10	4
Lithospermum latifolium	broad-leaved puccoon	9	10	9	7	9	9
†*Lonicera reticulata*	yellow honeysuckle	5		6	7		7
†*Maianthemum racemosum*	false Solomon's seal	4	5	4	5	4	3
Menispermum canadense	moonseed	4	5	4	5	7	6
†*Moehringia lateriflora*	wood sandwort	7	5	10	8	7	8
Muhlenbergia sobolifera	rock satin grass	5		4	8	10	10
Muhlenbergia sylvatica	woodland satin grass	7	8	5	6	9	10
Muhlenbergia tenuiflora	slender satin grass	6	8	5	8	9	10

Table 5.1. (*Continued*)

Scientific Name	Common Name	IL	MI	MO	OH	ON	CR
Paronychia canadensis	tall forked chickweed	5	8	4	4	10	6
Pedicularis canadensis	lousewort	7	10	5	6	7	9
Perideridia americana	thicket parsley	7		8	10		8
Phlox divaricata	woodland phlox	5	5	4	6	7	5
Phryma leptostachya	lopseed	4	4	2	5	6	4
Poa sylvestris	woodland bluegrass	5	8	5	6	10	10
Podophyllum peltatum	Mayapple	4	3	4	5	5	4
Polemonium reptans	Jacob's ladder	5	10	4	6		5
Polygala senega	Seneca snakeroot	7	8	6	7	7	8
Polygala verticillata	whorled milkwort	5	5	4	4	7	7
Prenanthes alba	white lettuce	5	5	9	5	6	5
Ranunculus fascicularis	early buttercup	5	10	5	8	9	6
Rosa setigera	prairie rose	5	5	4	6	5	7
Sanguinaria canadensis	bloodroot	5	5	5	5	5	6
Sanicula canadensis	Canadian black snakeroot	4	8	3	4	7	7
Scrophularia marilandica	late figwort	4	5	3	5	7	4
Scutellaria ovata	heart-leaved skullcap	5	10	5	7		10
Silene stellata	starry campion	6	10	5	6		6
Silene virginica	fire pink	9	10	7	7	10	10
Smilax ecirrata	upright carrion flower	5	6	5	6	6	5
Smilax tamnoides	bristly cat brier	3	5	3	5	6	5
Solidago flexicaulis	broad-leaved goldenrod	6	6	6	6	6	7
Solidago ulmifolia	elm-leaved goldenrod	5	5	4	6	9	5
Taenidia integerrima	yellow pimpernel	7	8	6	6	9	9
Thalictrum dioicum	early meadow rue	5	6	7	6	5	7
†*Thalictrum thalictroides*	rue anemone	5	8	5	6	8	7
Thaspium trifoliatum	meadow parsnip	6	8	6	3	9	7
Trillium flexipes	declined trillium	7	7	8	7	10	6
Trillium recurvatum	red trillium	5	8	6			5
Trillium sessile	toad trillium	8	9	5	7		10
Triosteum aurantiacum	early horse gentian	5	5	6	5	7	5
Triosteum perfoliatum	late horse gentian	5	5	4	5	9	5
Uvularia grandiflora	bellwort	7	5	6	5	6	7
Veronicastrum virginicum	Culver's root	6	8	7	9	10	7
Viburnum prunifolium	black haw	4	7	4	5		5
Viburnum rafinesquianum	arrow wood	6	5	7	8	7	5
Vicia caroliniana	wood vetch	9	8	6	7	10	10
Viola pubescens	yellow violet	7	5	5	5	5	5

Note: This table was compiled by Gerould S. Wilhelm.

★Indicates nomenclature differs from Kartesz.

†Precedes scientific name cross-referenced in appendix C.

floristic quality assessment has been developed for terrestrial animals, but steps in that direction are being taken. One system was proposed in 1995 by Dan Ludwig. In Missouri, Ballard and Greenlee (1995) have assigned coefficients of conservatism to the orthopterans, a prominent invertebrate group.

A zoologically based method for assessing the quality of streams and rivers has been developed by Karr and others (1986). This Index of Biological Integrity applies to fish species numerical values that reflect a given species' tolerance or intolerance of pollution as well as other factors. The quality rating of a stream is proportional to the numbers and pollution intolerance of the fish species in the stream and inversely proportional to the numbers of stunted and diseased individuals.

What Is a Weed?

The role of weeds in restoration may be a source of confusion at first because the word *weed* has been used to refer to two groups of species—classic weeds and invasive species. Once the difference is understood, it is only necessary for remnant restorationists to worry about one group—the invasives. Here is why.

Classic weeds are the bane of gardeners. These are the species that thrive in disrupted habitats: in other words, they are nonconservatives. Such species, whether native or exotic, are not found in mature prairie except at the site of disturbances such as badger holes, ant mounds, and bison wallows. A good way to understand the difference between these weed species and conservative species is to realize that if you throw classic weed seeds into a mature, healthy prairie, they will have no impact. Conservatives utterly outcompete the weeds, and none will appear, unless that badger rips up the conservatives and makes an ecologically appropriate, temporary place for weeds. We don't have to think too much about these plants. Exotics like dandelion and Queen Anne's lace don't have a chance against conservatives and will appear only if some disruption occurs and will recede docilely as the disturbance naturally heals. Nor do remnant restorationists normally pay much attention to "weedy" native species like common ragweed, daisy fleabane, or common cinquefoil—not because they don't belong or because they lack value to the system, but because these species in most cases have a genius for thriving without our help. Seeds of conservatives thrown into a weed patch—given natural conditions and enough time—will entirely outcompete and replace most weeds. Encouraging and speeding up this process is the central idea in the restoration of degraded remnants. For this reason such work has been called successional restoration or successional encouragement.

The above scenarios, however, do not hold for the other class of species that is also referred to as weeds. This second group—perhaps better called *aggressive* or *invasive* species—is not restricted to disturbed situations: These species may thrive among or replace conservatives even under apparently unstressed conditions. This group includes, among others, leafy spurge, purple loosestrife, and garlic mustard. Such species can seriously degrade or even destroy high-quality natural communities and are particularly dangerous in disrupted or recovering systems. These out-of-balance species often came to this continent from other parts of the world, where they were functioning parts of some natural system. But they arrived here without the insect pests or disease organisms that kept their numbers in balance. In these new environments they can sometimes reproduce cancerously until they have eliminated or seriously depleted the diverse species of ancient natural communities. They are powerful reminders of the complexity of relationships on which healthy natural systems depend.

One of the simplest and most effective acts of restoration is removal of the first few individuals of such species from high-quality communities before the invaders have had a chance to spread and become a serious problem. An important function of stewards of natural areas is to notice and remove these invaders as they appear, and a valuable benefit of increased attention to natural areas in recent years has been the increased probability that someone will be present to do that. Protecting high-quality areas in this way protects the raw materials for restoration.

First, Do No Harm . . .

How does one decide when, and how aggressively, to act?

Particularly in the case of high-quality remnants, managers need to heed a central principle of the healing arts, "First, do no harm." Only a few tiny shreds of our prairies and savannas have their plant communities essentially intact. In the Corn Belt states inventories have consistently found that high-quality prairies and savannas survive on less than 1/100 of 1 percent of the land. These precious lands should be protected, weeded, burned, cherished, and left alone.

Some larger fragments of our natural landscape have been only moderately overgrazed and have lost only the most conservative plant species. These lands have largely been ignored by inventories, yet their plant diversity can often be restored by collecting the seeds of their lost species from nearby surviving remnants, such as those on railroad rights-of-way or in old pioneer cemeteries, and scattering those seeds among the existing flora of the restoration site. Other elements of a plan to restore a fair- or good-quality remnant may include brush and weed control, prescribed burning, the stewardship of animal populations, and monitoring. The restoration or stewardship of good-quality natural communities should be coordinated with the local academic or conservation institutions that specialize in such work.

In much of the range of the tallgrass prairie, however, there are few good-quality remnants. Most of the original landscape is seriously degraded, typically by severe overgrazing and decades of fire suppression (see figures 5.2 and 5.3). Learning to restore these languishing remnants—ranging in size from a backyard to thousands of acres—is a challenging and urgent task. It requires all the techniques described for high-quality sites as well as one additional technique: interseeding. But how do we decide exactly which techniques to prescribe for which damaged lands and when to intervene?

What may not be immediately obvious and needs to be underscored is that the decision to withhold restoration "until we have better information," perhaps for decades, although it seems "conservative," is in fact a dangerous decision that *will very likely do harm.* Many of these patients are dying and desperately need treatment. "First, do no harm" does not mean "do nothing until the patient dies."

For any person who would be a physician to ecosystems, three types of knowledge are crucial. First, learn to recognize signs of health in an ecosystem. Second, learn to recognize signs and causes of disruption and degradation. Third, learn to recognize the natural processes and restoration measures that nurture an ecosystem back to good health. These skills and their ecological underpinnings are introduced below.

Restoration Triage

How do you decide whether a given site is, at one extreme, highly sensitive and in need of very careful restoration, if any—or, at the other extreme, so degraded that virtually any well-intentioned restoration would make it better? Described below is a system of triage based on the floristic quality of the site and coefficients of conservatism (C) using the floristic quality index (FQI) as described in chapter 17. Coefficients of conservatism have been included in appendix A (for prairie plants) and table 5.1 (for selected savanna and woodland plants), for those areas for which they are being developed.

Figure 5.2. Savanna succession without fire.

Original savanna. These drawings show one fate for a "preserved" savanna that receives no burning or other restoration. In 1800 the savanna looked as it may have looked five thousand years ago. Most likely, in that period, this site had spent some time as both prairie and forest.

1890 pasture. This hypothetical site had been used for half a century as pasture. Despite the cessation of fire, the overall savanna physiognomy and much of its biota persisted because grazing kept the brush down, although many savanna herbs, butterflies, etc., survived only on an adjacent railroad right-of-way, which remained ungrazed and burned regularly because of sparks from passing trains.

1980 "preserve." The site was acquired in 1960 by a conservation agency, but at that time there was little appreciation of the savanna's need for fire. At first the native fauna and flora began to recover from 140 years of grazing, but at the same time brush began to invade.

2010 "preserve." The understory herbs have been almost entirely shaded out, and most original plant and animal species are gone. Unlike an original forest, this new forest has little biological diversity. Most of the original (and now rare) species of this site have been lost—replaced by a relatively common aggressive species.

Figure 5.3. Savanna restoration.

1981 *Restoration begins.* In these drawings, the site shown in figure 5.2 is restored, beginning with its condition as shown in 1980. That fall it was burned, and the girdling of invasive tree species was begun in May 1981.

1983 *Intensive restoration.* For the first few years, aggressive weeds and brush were carefully controlled. Seeds gathered from nearby threatened remnants were broadcast throughout the site.

1990 *Restoration "completed."* Aside from regular prescribed burning, this site may now need little additional work.

2010 *Nature proceeds.* In centuries to come, such sites may be the only places at which hundreds of savanna species survive. The restored savanna is different from the 1800 savanna, but it is a natural descendant from it and contains most of its original species.

We'll start with the easiest case. If the site is high quality (mean C greater than 4; mean FQI per .25m^2 greater than 15; site FQI greater than 50), then your restoration goal in nearly all cases will be to restore the conditions in which the three indices cited above will remain stable or increase. Such sites are high priority for protection and for restoration when needed. All restoration for high-quality sites should have the benefit of counsel from the best experts you can attract. With the most knowledgeable ecologists and most experienced restorationists, you can find, identify, and protect whatever the conservative biota of the site depends on (e.g., prairie, shrubs, oaks, transition zones, maples, dry-mesic soil, mineral water seepage, etc.). In most cases, begin control of any invasive species immediately and, if prairie or oaks are crucial, burn.

If, at the other extreme, the floristic quality of the site is low (mean C of 0–2; mean FQI per .25m^2 of 0–8; site FQI of 0–20), and if no rare species or communities are involved, then freely set your goal according to other considerations (habitat expansion needs of adjacent rare species or communities, flood control, economy, aesthetics, or whatever).

The most difficult decisions are in the intermediate range (mean C of 2–4; mean FQI per .25m^2 of 8–15; site FQI of 20–50). To make the best decisions in these cases, read chapter 4 carefully, use its key to determine the most appropriate options, and, if possible, become familiar with the decision-making processes of experienced restorationists at similar sites nearby. A good way to learn is to do a bit of apprentice volunteer work in exchange for your education.

If the site is not in one of the states where coefficients of conservatism are available (see appendix A), you can perform a less authoritative but still valuable assessment by using coefficients from nearby states or developing the coefficients yourself, according to the directions provided in chapter 17.

If a site is a prairie, a prairie floristic quality index can be calculated using the coefficents in appendix A. But, as described under "What is Quality?," a site that appears to be a brushy prairie may in fact be a degraded savanna or woodland. For these latter communities, the distinctive species of which are not found in appendix A, a rough assessment can be made by looking for species listed in table 5.1. A site with oaks is likely to have a degree of recovery potential proportional to the numbers of such species that survive in it. In other words, high numbers of such species suggest high potential for recovery. Since the areas covered by this table (those for which coefficients of conservativism were available) are all in the central or eastern parts of the tallgrass region, sites elsewhere will require alternative analysis.

The above discussion summarizes an approach to restoration goal setting and decision making based on floristic quality. Expert judgment is another approach. Traditionally, when a decision-making process was under way, a manager would bring together individuals who were knowledgeable and experienced in conservation biology, who would hike the site, consider the options, and deliver an opinion. In a given hypothetical case, the advisory team might include two botanists and a herpetologist. If the individuals involved were up-to-date, creative conservation biologists, the product of their efforts would often be excellent. There are often more sites needing work than experts to visit them, however, and biologists consulted for these purposes, though accomplished in their own fields, are often not expert in either restoration or conservation priority setting.

Whatever the decision-making process, if the decision is difficult, start slowly with any of the more aggressive restoration options (cutting conservative shrubs, interseeding, hydrologic restoration, burning in areas with large maples, etc.). As your work proceeds, monitor the site; your data will help guide future efforts, as will your growing intuitive understanding of the site. With continued counsel of the most expert available colleagues, you will be able to make difficult decisions with increased confidence and improved results.

To Burn or Not to Burn

This is an easy decision. Burn! Prairies and their associated wetlands and woodlands are fire-dependent communities. If for some reason it is not possible to burn a fire-dependent community, then it is probably not possible to restore and maintain that community.

Three exceptions test this rule.

1. A small prairie might be maintained amid lawns and gardens without burning. Each fall or spring the dead above-ground thatch can be mowed and raked off (perhaps even mulched and reapplied). The brush and exotic herbs that invade are then weeded by hand. A small prairie can thus be maintained as a garden.
2. Many high-quality prairies have hay cut and removed every year. This is an economical way to maintain prairie habitat in some areas. Over the years, however, some plant and animal species (with life cycles that make them relatively vulnerable at haying time) may eventually be lost. In seeking to maintain prairie by

mowing, it is important not to let thick thatch lie too long, since it can smother and kill some species. Mowed prairies can benefit from being left unmowed periodically and from being burned occasionally.

3. A prairie that has lost many species to overgrazing is likely to have invading brush and a significant component of exotic weeds and aggressive natives. It is *not* a good idea to burn such an "old field" until resources are available to control brush and, if possible, to interseed conservative natives. Burning will kill off many weeds, but many other exotic and more or less aggressive native species (e.g., white sweet clover, tall goldenrod, briars, and shrubs) will quickly take their places. In this scenario resprouting shrubs often gradually outcompete the grassy fuel species and thus make the site unburnable, eliminating the potential for restoring the essential dynamic that allows for prairie recovery. At the same time, an important window for the restoration of missing conservative species will have been missed (see chapter 11, "Interseeding"). The relatively stable, weedy old field may thus be best left unburned for a time—perhaps managed by selectively cutting shrubs and weeding or herbiciding aggressive exotics—until there is sufficient seed and other resources to begin full restoration.

To Plow or Not to Plow

All high-quality natural communities in the tallgrass region are too small for the long-term survival of many of their species of plants and animals. Many, however, have adjacent land that could be restored, expanding their size and thereby increasing the long-term viability of the populations of the many species that may survive in these fragments in perilously low numbers. For this reason restoration of land adjacent to high-quality communities deserves to be undertaken as expeditiously as is practical. When should such land be plowed, and when should it be interseeded?

The quickest way to restore prairie vegetation to an old field is to plow and plant. But that may not be the quickest way to restore the conservative species and diverse structures that are essential to the habitats of most species that need conservation. The discussion below should help managers answer the question of whether plowing, interseeding, or only burning is the best choice for a given area. (See also the key in chapter 4.) Which route to follow is often a difficult decision. Let's start where the choice is clear:

Do not plow if the site already has many prairie plants, especially if they include rare species or the difficult-to-restore, spring-blooming species. Plowing will do more harm than good, destroying existing native vegetation.

Do not plow if the site has a diverse, open turf. Such a site is a prime candidate for interseeding conservatives.

Do not plow among the trees in a woodland. Plowing damages tree roots and soil biota.

Do not plow steep slopes. Erosion can be severe.

Do plow (or disk or herbicide or plant a "smother crop" on) agricultural fields thick with annual weeds. (See chapter 12.)

Do plow (or herbicide) dense concentrations of the worst perennial weeds.

Now for the harder cases. Suppose you hope to restore one acre currently thick with white sweet clover and smooth brome; this acre adjoins a high-quality remnant prairie. Or suppose you manage land for a county conservation district and have one hundred acres of former cornfield that has been fallow for ten years. In these and many other cases, you might go either way on the question of plowing, but you would want to consider these tradeoffs:

Difficulty. For small areas, the easiest approach is to mow (or scythe) and interseed. But above a few acres the easiest approach is to plow and plant relatively dense tall grasses that will subsequently control weeds and brush.

Quality. Generally speaking, plowing is an easy, quick way to restore a low-diversity prairie dominated by aggressive native grasses. Interseeding is an effective way to restore the diverse rare conservative species of high-quality prairie. However, both plowing and interseeding, depending on the seed mixes used, can produce either high-quality diverse prairie or fair-quality prairie dense with tall native grasses.

Economy. Interseeding saves the expense of plowing, but the conservative seed often used with this technique is much more expensive than the tallgrass seed typically emphasized in plowed-ground restoration. If you were to compare two plantings using a seed mix emphasizing common aggressive prairie species, plowing would probably require less seed than interseeding to achieve the same result. Mowing a plowed-ground restoration for the first few years may allow conservatives to survive well. But the expensive seed of some rare conservatives may reproduce best interseeded in turf.

Speed. Plowing produces noticeable results faster than interseeding. Most planted species of flowers and grasses will begin to bloom in two to three years following plowing compared to four to five years with inter-seeding—even longer for many of the highly conservative species.

Aesthetics. Plowed-ground restorations often have impressive stands of tall grasses and colorful masses of tall prairie flowers. Interseeded prairies often have less dense and shorter grass but more complexity and more color close up.

Reliability. Both methods will likely fail during severe droughts. Plowed-ground restoration is a more fully developed practice and therefore may on average be more reliable.

Conservation. Plowing, especially on slopes, exposes the soil to erosion. Interseeding is particularly valuable on a site with remnant populations of prairie plants, animals, and soil biota since these will remain as original parts of the restored ecosystem. Many prairie animals require the presence of conservative plant species or a complex vegetation structure, both of which are more characteristic of interseeded than plowed-ground restorations.

To Seed or Not to Seed

In many cases, the principal management question will be, should this site be interseeded or not? To answer, begin by categorizing a remnant as lightly, moderately, or heavily degraded. Some managers argue compellingly that species should not be added to lightly degraded remnants. "This land has been meddled with enough! Leave it alone, and let nature take its course!" Other managers argue that our respect for the sanctity of nature requires us to restore, as best we know how, the full complement of original species and processes—at least at some sites. How do we decide? For lightly degraded sites, *both* of these approaches, and others as well, should be pursued. Particularly in this early stage of the development of our knowledge, we should operate on the principle that there is no single answer for many questions. In fact, choosing a variety of management approaches is in itself valuable, because that gives us the benefit of learning from many different experiments while the young discipline of ecological management is in its formative decades.

Degraded prairie sites of fair or good quality may indeed recover through burning alone, and that approach deserves special consideration. If a large site supports conservative prairie species in a matrix of weeds—perhaps, for example, the only source of degradation has been moderate grazing—then one approach is to start by burning the site for two years. However, if you're skeptical about the recovery potential of a degraded site, then you would be wise to test the site's recovery potential by burning only a part (see "Prepare the Ground" in chapter 11.) Afterward, carefully study the resulting vegetation throughout the growing season, looking for examples of returning species, which at first would probably be only small nonflowering individuals. After two to five years of burning, make a decision on interseeding. If many conservative species are absent (and especially if they are present in high-quality sites nearby), a strong case can be made for restoring them. If, on the other hand, most original species seem to be recovering on their own, then don't interseed except for those missing or endangered species, which often thrive only in high-quality original or restored communities. Consider chapter 6, "Restoring Populations of Rare Plants": Most of the approaches Jim Reinartz describes there apply to prairie conservatives generally.

In many cases, burning alone will not restore most species to seriously degraded areas. Once a site has been weeded, brushed out, and burned, the quality will generally rise somewhat, but an area that starts out in very poor condition will most often improve only modestly without reseeding. If a manager is concerned about the impact of interseeding on the existing vegetation, a good rule of thumb is to interseed with species of higher conservatism than the average of those present. This way, there is no danger that restored or introduced conservatives will outcompete existing species that are native to the site. Conservatives are the least aggressive of species and are also those most adapted to highly diverse and relatively stable communities. On the original natural landscape, most land was carpeted by diverse plant assemblages with many, many conservatives. Those species that cannot compete with conservatives survived on disturbed ground, as they do today.

In contrast, restorationists should be cautious about introducing weedy natives (identified by very low coefficients of conservatism) into recovering communities with surviving conservatives. When massive amounts of brush are cut and the first burning in decades is conducted, the system enters a highly fragile "intensive care" phase. Although a step on the road to recovery, this phase is potentially dangerous. Aggressive species, including natives, can become so dense as to shade out the conservatives we want to protect. It may be best to withhold seed of potentially rank and aggressive natives in the early stages of restoration of sites with surviving rare or conservative species. Such aggressive natives include white snakeroot, tall goldenrod, and briars. Once the community has restabilized, then all species native to the site can be restored without concern. Weedy natives will play only a modest role once a diverse turf is reestablished.

In the case of heavily disturbed remnants, interseeding is generally necessary for timely restoration. The basics of seed gathering and processing as described in chapters 7–10 apply here. But some additional practical, ethical, and genetic questions are of particular concern in remnant restoration. There are no simple answers to any of these questions. But being aware of the following issues will help in formulating policies at the project level and in answering day-to-day questions:

1. To what extent is it acceptable to put stress on spontaneous populations of plants and animals by removing seed? What are the tradeoffs?

2. How close and similar (in geology, soils, aspect, hydrology, etc.) to the recipient site does the seed donor site need to be? What are the tradeoffs?

3. How important is it to protect local gene pools from being overwhelmed by distant ones?

4. When is it important to restore diversity to depauperate local gene pools?

5. How does the conservation community arrive at and enforce seed gathering and species introduction standards, and how much uniformity should our standards encourage among projects?

Many of these questions have been well addressed by Jim Reinartz in chapter 6. The conservative biology of seeds is a subject, like many in this field, that urgently needs and deserves a more fully developed science on which to base our ongoing decisions. As that science is being assembled, however, conservation action should proceed vigorously using a diversity of complementary strategies. These include:

1. Maintenance and monitoring of some high-quality preserves without any introduction of seed.

2. Maintenance and monitoring of a small number of degraded preserves without any introduction of seed.

3. Restoration of as full as possible a complement of natural genetic diversity to most degraded conservation lands, emphasizing seed of threatened populations from as nearby as practical, typically a few miles or tens of miles for most species, with careful monitoring of results wherever possible.

4. Designation of a few large, diverse "assembly preserves" with extensive introduction of seed. Formerly common (that is, not rare) conservative species should be the main focus of this effort, although all local native species have a place. Restoration should use seed from many populations from as far away as fifty miles (north or south) or one hundred miles (east or west). The seed-gathering areas of such preserves should overlap. In the long run (particularly in light of such long-term phenomena as global warming), seeds or pollen from plants and small numbers of animals should be interchanged between the assembly preserves that are nearest to each other. In choosing assembly preserves, it would be wise to look for high-quality core sites surrounded by the most restorable land. It may also be a good investment—if unprotectable, small, high-quality sites within the seed-gathering range are being lost—to import tree-spade plugs from these areas, since these plugs may bring in invertebrates, fungi, bacteria, etc. Many of these obscure taxa may be important to the community, and they are not otherwise readily restored.

In many of the regions in which natural communities most need restoration, there are pitifully few populations from which to harvest seed. Already beleaguered by brush, weeds, road maintenance crews, agricultural herbicide drift, land development, fragmentation, and such stresses, these remnant populations are now also threatened by overcollection of seed. Before such threats become severe in any region, seed ethics policies need to be developed. Once they are widely understood, they need to be enforced legally and/or morally as appropriate.

However, the restoration of protected conservation lands should not be put off because of a lack of seed. Protecting the biota is no less important than acquiring the real estate. The necessary levels of resources should be found for restoration and stewardship of the biota just as we find funds to buy land.

Therefore, in addition to the recommendations in chapter 7, there are a variety of options worth considering by anyone seeking large amounts of rare conservative seed. For Walnut Creek National Wildlife Refuge, Pauline Drobney searched out the best remnant prairies in south-central Iowa and contracted with the owners to harvest a portion of their seed each year. At the McHenry County (Illinois) Conservation District, Ed Collins developed efficient methods of growing such seed in nursery beds, which produce seed valued at over $50,000 annually. The Forest Preserve District of Cook County (Illinois), in addition to judicious collection from high-quality remnants and increasing harvests from nursery beds, has volunteer projects in which more than four hundred backyard gardeners, led by volunteer Lindsay McGee, produce large amounts of the seed of some very finicky species. The individuals who grow this rare seed are creative, ethical, and energetic; they do such good work because their daily attention to these gardens gives them a powerful connection to wild nature and a role in its gradually reviving good health. In addition to increasing their restoration expertise, such people often develop insight and motivation as constituency for local and global biodiversity conservation, and for global health and justice generally.

A Complex Vision

Often a given tract of land is not ecologically homogeneous, comprising brushy woods, wooded pasture, cornfield, marsh, etc. The best management in these cases involves combining a number of approaches—for philosophical, practical, political, and other reasons. This section concludes with the story of a plan for one such site, told here in hopes of conveying how restoration can bring diverse human and natural elements together for conservation. The players in this tale are, in order of appearance: original nature, a county board president, heavy machinery, volunteers, and a large predator. Biodiversity in this case depends on all of these.

Shoe Factory Road Prairie sits atop a glacial kame fifteen miles west of Chicago in a forest preserve. Although this nine-acre site, dedicated as an Illinois Nature Preserve, contains two plant species on the federal endangered list, as well as the region's highest-quality dry prairie, the preserve was degrading rapidly. Aggressive black locust brush covered one-third of the prairie. The bur oak savanna on the east slope of the kame was so densely choked with brush that little summer or fall flora survived. Although the adjoining four thousand acres of forest preserves should have had high priority for restoration, the county board and local mayors were instead developing a plan to use five hundred acres of it for a garbage dump.

In 1983, Audubon Society volunteers and Nature Conservancy staff began a campaign to reverse the tide. After a contentious hearing, the county board voted not to permit garbage dumps on this or any preserve site. Cook County Board President George Dunne, speaking to a small crowd at the site, promised a new era. The board approved a restoration plan for six hundred acres. The plan included dedication of significant Forest Preserve District resources (ranging from scientists to trucks). The Conservancy hired interns to chainsaw twenty acres of brush from the savanna and a farmer to plow 8.4 miles of 20-foot-wide contour strips through two hundred acres of Eurasian meadow. A new group, the Poplar Creek Prairie Stewards, pulled weeds, gathered seeds, planted the plowed strips, and interseeded the old fields and savanna. When a nearby railroad prairie was to be destroyed by road widening, the stewards arranged for a tree-spade to rescue 6x5-foot plugs and moved them to some of the old-field restoration areas.

Coyotes, which have moved back into the forest preserves of the region after having been absent for decades, now have a den on the site. In 1992 the international headquarters of the Sears Corporation moved to adjacent land. Sears landscaped the campus with prairie and savanna and restored a prairie and wetland corridor through the center of the site. The corridor now links the four thousand-acre Poplar Creek Preserve with the three thousand-acre Spring Creek Preserve. The stewardship group sponsors tours, festivals, lectures, and social events. Many members grow rare plants in their gardens to supply seed for restoration. In response to the initiative shown by this group and others, Forest Preserve Superintendent Joseph Nevius in 1994 announced a plan to restore fifty-four thousand acres within the sixty-seven thousand-acre preserve system.

Efforts like this are inspiring to the human participants and mean the difference between life and death for some natural areas. They are a great beginning. But in the Midwest as a whole today, even on most of our protected conservation land, there is probably more biodiversity being lost than is being securely protected or restored by good stewardship. Does this sound pessimistic? It isn't. The need for restoration has only recently been recognized. Unlike much of the rest of the "developed" world, the Midwest still supports most of the elements of biodiversity that have thrived here for thousands of years. We have the historic opportunity to rescue

Janzen's "living dead" from the edge of oblivion and restore these tattered remnants as a permanent part of our cultural landscape.

REFERENCES

Ballard, H. Jr., and E.S. Greenlee. 1995. *Preliminary Checklist of Missouri Orthopterans with Coefficients of Conservatism.* St. Louis, MO: Nature Conservancy.

Falk, Donald A., and Kent E. Holsinger, eds. 1991. *Restoring Diversity: Strategies for Endangered Plants.* New York: Oxford University Press.

Janzen, Daniel H. 1988. Tropical Ecology and Biocultural Restoration. *Science* 239:243–244.

Jordan, William R. III, Michael G. Gilpin, and John D. Aber. 1987. *Restoration Ecology: A Synthetic Approach to Ecological Research.* Cambridge University Press.

Karr, J.R., K.D. Fausch, P.L. Angermeir, P.R. Yant, and I.J. Schlosser. 1986. "Assessing Biological Integrity." *Running Waters: A Method and Its Rationale.* Illinois Natural History Survey Special Publication 5. Champaign: Illinois Natural History Survey.

Kusler, Jon A., and Mary E. Kentula, eds. 1990. *Wetland Creation and Restoration: The Status of the Science.* Washington, DC: Island Press.

Ladd, Douglas. 1991. Reexamination of the Role of Fire in Missouri Oak Woodlands. In *Proceedings of the Oak Woods Management Workshop*, George V. Burger, John B. Ebinger, and Gerould S. Wilhelm, eds. Charleston, IL: Eastern Illinois University.

Leach, Mark K., and Laurel Ross, eds. *Midwest Oak Ecosystems Recovery Plan: A Call to Action.* Nature Conservancy, Illinois Field Office, and Environmental Protection Agency, Great Lakes National Program Office (available from EPA at 77 W. Jackson Blvd., Chicago, IL 60604–3590).

Ludwig, Daniel. 1995. "Assessment and Management of Wildlife Diversity in an Urban Setting." *Natural Areas Journal* 15, no. 4.

Noss, Reed F. 1985. On Characterizing Presettlement Vegetation: How and Why. *Natural Areas Journal* 5:1.

Noss, Reed F., and A.Y. Cooperrider. 1994. *Saving Nature's Legacy: Protecting and Restoring Biodiversity.* Washington, DC: Island Press.

Panzer, Ronald. 1995. "Prevalence of Remnant Dependence among the Prairie-Savanna–Inhabiting Insects of the Chicago Region." *Natural Areas Journal* 15:4.

Samson, Fred B., and Fritz L. Knopf. 1996. *Prairie Conservation: Preserving North America's Most Endangered Ecosystem.* Washington, DC: Island Press.

White, John. 1978. *Illinois Natural Areas Inventory Technical Report.* Urbana: Illinois Natural Areas Inventory.

Wilson, E.O. 1992. *The Diversity of Life.* New York: W.W. Norton.

Some of the best places to keep up with the latest developments in this field include the journals *Conservation Biology*, *Natural Areas Journal*, *Restoration and Management Notes*, and *Restoration Ecology*, as well as the biennial North American Prairie Conference and Midwest Oak Ecosystems Conference. When they are held in the tallgrass region, the annual conferences of the Society for Ecological Restoration and the Natural Areas Association are important sources of information as well. Information about these conferences can be found in the above journals.

6
Restoring Populations of Rare Plants

James A. Reinartz

In a broad sense, any plant that is uncommon or infrequently occurring is rare. The federal and state governments have more narrowly defined what are considered to be the rarest of the rare species and categorized them as endangered or threatened. A species that is in danger of extinction at the national or state level is called federally or state endangered, respectively. A threatened species is one that is likely to become endangered within the foreseeable future unless the decline in its population can be stopped and even reversed. Most states recognize a third category of rare plants, listed as special concern species, which are thought to be likely to become threatened within the foreseeable future. In this chapter I discuss mostly endangered and threatened (ET) plants, although most of the special considerations I recommend for restoring populations of rare plants are appropriate for any native species. ET plants are given a special protected legal status. It is illegal to possess or plant a federally ET species; in most states, state ET species may be planted in restorations only with a permit from the state. Because a species is rare, the likelihood that it previously occurred precisely at the site of a community restoration is small. Hence, I refer to the creation of a population of a rare plant rather than restoration of that species.

Many plants listed as ET in a midwestern state are at or near the margin of their range in that state and are more common elsewhere. These species are, nonetheless, worthy of preservation at the state level for the maintenance of biodiversity and aesthetics within the state and because these marginal populations may harbor a disproportionate amount of unique genetic diversity within the species. There are many types and causes of rarity: *Sparse species,* those that typically occur at low local density, may have a wide geographical range but tend to grow only in very small populations. *Geographically restricted species* have very small geographical ranges and often only a small number of populations.

Habitat specialists require specific habitat conditions that are uncommon. These habitat specialists can be divided into two groups: 1) Natural—species requiring a naturally rare habitat, e.g., a specific, unusual soil type or climatic condition. 2) Manmade—species that have been made rare by postsettlement destruction of their previously widespread habitat.

Rarity is the natural state of many plant species; however, I doubt we could find any examples of rare plants in the Midwest that have not been made more rare by habitat destruction. On the other hand, midwestern prairies offer some of the best examples of "habitat specialists" that were once much more common and have been made rare by destruction of the prairie habitat. Ladd (appendix A) shows that over half of the 990 plant species he lists as occurring in midwestern tallgrass prairies are designated as rare or protected by one or more states in the region. These plants are specialists to the prairie habitat, which has been made exceedingly rare relative to its former distribution. For many of these species, rarity is a very recent condition.

The Consequences of Rarity

Plants that have been rare (existed in small, isolated populations) for a long time have rarity as a natural feature of their population biology. Because there has been no flow of genes (pollen or seeds) among populations, these rare plants tend to have populations that have differentiated genetically over time. Each population has developed a unique set of genetic characteristics that may or may not be particularly adaptive to the local environment, but that differentiates it from other populations of the species. Since populations are isolated and often small, these rare plants have evolved under conditions that include breeding with close relatives, and they tend not to suffer severe deleterious effects from inbreeding. In short, the entire population's genetic structure has been formed to a large extent by rarity.

Many prairie plants that have been made very rare as the result of recent habitat destruction have evolved in larger, better connected populations. These plants are not accustomed to the same level of inbreeding as naturally rare plants, and offspring produced by breeding with close relatives may suffer more adverse consequences. Plants that until recently have been more common are also less likely to have highly differentiated populations than naturally rare plants. More common plants tend to have a much higher proportion of their genetic variability contained within individual populations. Naturally rare plants often have populations that differ genetically from one another but have relatively less genetic variability within single breeding populations.

Making an always-rare species more common would be creation of a novel condition. We cannot "restore" what never was. On the other hand, increasing the abundance of a formerly more common species constitutes restoration of a more natural condition.

Risks and Benefits of Creating Populations of Rare Plants

In a previous paper (Reinartz 1995), I discussed in detail both the risks and the benefits of planting rare species, and some ways in which risks can be minimized and advantages maximized. The potential risks and benefits associated with a rare species planting program depend to a great extent on the species, and on methods used for selection or production of genetic stock to be planted, selection of planting location, and planting methods.

Potential benefits derived from creating new populations of a rare plant include: 1) increased security from extinction gained from having more successful breeding populations; 2) the potential to restore opportunity for gene flow among populations that more nearly emulates that available before habitat destruction; 3) educational opportunities afforded by enabling the public to have more contact with some of our rarer flora, and the public support for rare plant programs that can be derived from having successful intervention programs; and 4) increased opportunities to learn more about the ecology, population biology, and horticulture of the species. Although there may be few ET species that currently require creation of new populations to avoid total extinction, this sort of intervention can become necessary for a species within a very short time and may frequently be required to mitigate the potential for local extinction. We really know very little about the habitat preference, environmental tolerance, and horticulture of most ET species, and planting attempts can be one excellent way to learn.

The major risks associated with creation of new populations of state ET species include: 1) the potential for overcollecting of propagules from, and damage to, remnant natural populations of an ET species if nursery-grown stock of local genotypes is unavailable; 2) the possibility that remnant natural populations and restored populations will be confused in the future, thus jeopardizing our ability to provide protected status for relict populations, and compromising opportunities to study naturally evolved populations; 3) the possibility of creating inappropriate gene flow between restored and remnant populations, causing the unique genetic structure of relict populations to be swamped by the foreign genotypes of planted stock.

It is apparent from these lists that the creation of both new populations and new opportunities for gene flow among populations can either benefit or damage efforts to preserve the ET species within the state. The success of these efforts depends on the care taken to ensure an appropriate planting program.

Maximizing Benefits, Minimizing Risks

Creation of new populations of our state ET species appropriately requires a permit from the state, which allows the state rare plant biologists to review planting plans on a case-by-case basis. The requirement for a permit should not be interpreted as an absolute ban on the use of any listed species in restorations. Following several general rules will help ensure that the creation of new populations has the highest likelihood of being beneficial for preservation of the species in the state. Most of these rules apply to any native species and should form some of our goals in any restoration effort regardless of whether ET species are planted.

1. Species that have been made rare by habitat destruction (e.g., many prairie species) are much better candidates for creation of new populations than are species that have always been rare. Creation of new opportunities for flow of pollen and seeds among populations is more likely to restore a natural level of gene flow for species that were once more common. Intervention to preserve species that have always been extremely rare is best undertaken only after careful study and as part of a well-planned recovery effort.

2. Only local genotypes should be used for restoration. Importation of foreign genotypes (e.g., from other states or ecoregions) can bastardize local flora by allowing foreign genes to swamp and destroy what is genetically unique about local types. Long-distance, unnatural migration may be particularly corrupting to rare plants, which are likely to be at the margins of their ranges, because these plants may lack the population size and genetic resilience to resist swamping by foreign genotypes. As a practical matter, genotypes from areas that differ substantially in climate or habitat may also be poorly adapted to local conditions and have a

lower likelihood, therefore, of establishing successful breeding populations.

3. Nursery production of stock is much preferable to collection of propagules from remnant populations, since such production minimizes the risk of damage to those populations we value most. Nursery practices should make a conscious effort to avoid selecting for nursery genotypes by, among other things, using only wild-collected propagules to establish plants in the nursery. A large number of populations can be created from the stock in a single nursery that has been formed by a single collection of wild propagules. If we lack sufficient horticultural knowledge of an ET species to produce stock in a nursery, then the chances of successfully establishing naturalized populations is probably low. Nursery experimentation is a more appropriate and profitable place to start than in the field.

4. I believe it is preferable to use multiple-source populations for collection of the genetic stock for nursery establishment rather than collecting propagules from only one population, but this opinion is in many ways a personal philosophy. A nursery established from a single-source population may more or less faithfully reproduce the general genetic type, if not the population genetic structure, of an existing remnant population. The single-source stock will be lower in genetic variation than stock produced by combining multiple-source populations and may be well adapted to a more limited range of microhabitats. Although using a single genetic source more closely approaches the re-creation of an existing remnant population, I would, in most cases, prefer creation of an entirely new genetic population. The new genetic population created by combining genotypes of several relict populations will form novel genetic combinations, having the potential to evolve entirely new genotypes in a novel habitat. The multiple sources used for establishing the nursery must all be found in the same local area (at least state or region) as the site where the new population will be created.

5. All newly created populations should be separated by at least half a mile from any existing remnant populations. Augmentation of existing, natural populations should be carried out only as part of well-researched recovery efforts. Spatial separation of restored

and remnant populations will minimize the risks of swamping a unique local ecotype with artificially introduced genes and will instead restore the low level of gene flow typical of that found when the species was more common. Care should also be taken to ensure that introduction of the species to the transplant site will not damage existing vegetation of high natural integrity.

6. Careful records should be made of the precise location and size of the restored population. Ideally, these records would also include detailed notes pertaining to the restoration methods used, especially those that apply to the treatment of the rare species. These records should be provided to the rare plant biologists within the state government responsible for granting permits to plant ET species. Adequate records will ensure that remnant and planted populations are not confused and may help to establish successful restoration methods for the ET species.

7. The newly restored population should be monitored. Only by maintaining records allowing evaluation of the success or failure of our restoration efforts will we improve our methodology and understanding for the time when intervention becomes more necessary.

Restoration of Rare Plant Populations in Practice

Creation of new populations to aid in the recovery of our ET flora can be of great value and will likely become necessary for some species. I hope that the special considerations listed above will not dampen the enthusiasm of those who are serious about incorporating rare plants into their restorations. I encourage those engaged in restoration to explore the possibility of working with some rare plants. It is vital, however, that any such project be viewed as a cooperative effort with biologists employed by the state agency regulating ET plants.

As a practical matter, the first step when considering planting a rare plant in a restoration should be to discuss the project with a state rare plant biologist. Those working in rare plant programs will often have ongoing projects, or species with which they would value help. The restorationist may find an enthusiastic partner in someone who is already searching for suitable outplanting sites for one or more species. Becoming involved in an existing or planned rare plant project will increase the value of your restoration efforts to the recovery of rare species statewide. Contacting the state rare plant biologists with an eagerness to work with rare plants, and a willingness to incorporate the special efforts outlined above, should get you solidly involved in rare plant recovery, even if there are no current projects.

REFERENCES

Allendorf, F. W. 1983. "Isolation, Gene Flow, and Genetic Differentiation among Populations." In C. M. Schoenwald-Cox, S. M. Chambers, B. MacBryde, and W. L. Thomas (eds.), *Genetics and Conservation,* pp. 51–65. Benjamin/Cummings, Menlo Park, California.

Brown, A. H. D., and J. D. Briggs. 1991. "Sampling Strategies for Genetic Variation in *ex sita* Collection of Endangered Plant Species." In D. A. Falk and K. E. Holsinger (eds.), *Genetics and Conservation of Rare Plants,* pp. 99–119. Oxford University Press, New York.

Center for Plant Conservation. 1991. "Genetic Sampling Guidelines for Conservation Collections of Endangered Plants." In D. A. Falk and K. E. Holsinger (eds.), *Genetics and Conservation of Rare Plants,* pp. 225–238. Oxford University Press, New York.

Frankel, O. H. 1983. "The Place of Management in Conservation." In C. M. Schoenwald–Cox, S. M. Chambers, B. MacBryde, and W. L. Thomas (eds.), *Genetics and Conservation,* pp. 1–14. Benjamin/Cummings, Menlo Park, California.

Geurrant, E. O., Jr. 1992. "Genetic and Demographic Considerations in the Sampling and Reintroduction of Rare Plants." In P. L. Fiedler and S. K. Jain (eds.), *Conservation Biology: The Theory and Practice of Nature Conservation, Preservation, and Management,* pp. 321-344. Chapman and Hall, New York.

Rabinowitz, D. 1981. "Seven Forms of Rarity." In H. Synge (ed.), *The Biological Aspects of Rare Plant Conservation,* pp. 205-217. John Wiley, New York.

Reinartz, J. A. 1995. "Planting State-Listed Endangered and Threatened Plants." *Conservation Biology* 9: 771–781.

PART III

Seeds and Planting

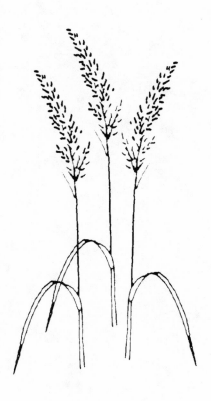

7
Obtaining and Processing Seeds

Steven I. Apfelbaum, Brian J. Bader,
Fred Faessler, and David Mahler

Before agricultural practices prompted the formation of complex human societies, nomadic hunter–gatherer cultures developed practical techniques for seed collecting and processing. Today's harvesters of prairie seed, although they may use machine technology, follow many of those old ways— traveling lightly over the landscape, collecting and processing seeds from various plants as they mature throughout the season.

Every year, restorationists and seed purveyors harvest and clean thousands of pounds of seed for prairie, wetland, and savanna restorations. In this chapter, we describe the various techniques and equipment needed to collect and process seeds and formulate seed mixes for such restorations.

Obtaining Seed

Restorationists can either buy or collect seed. Purchasing seed from a reputable supplier of locally collected seed has several advantages. First, producers who can efficiently grow and machine-harvest large quantities of certain species can offer those species at prices below the cost of hand collecting. Second, purchased seed often has fewer unwanted species, less chaff, and reduced overall bulk. This results in a product that works better in commercial seed drills and has lower shipping and storage costs. Finally, dealers usually provide information on the quality of the seeds they sell—including information about pure live seed (PLS) and the number of seeds per unit weight. This information can help you decide how much seed you will need for your projects.

As when buying any product, check with colleagues regarding the reputation of the suppliers you are considering doing business with. Ask the suppliers about their seeds and plants, as well. For example, are they nursery-grown or wild-collected? Are they of a local ecotype cultivars, or out-of-the-region native species? (See appendix E.)

Collecting seed has advantages, too. First, restorationists can often collect species that are not available commercially. Second, some commercially available seed may not be genetically appropriate for the restoration site. Most restorationists agree that seed (including commercially grown seed) should be locally derived. How "local" remains open to debate (see "Ethics of Seed Collecting" below). However, mixes designed to maintain strictly local gene pools often require such careful and labor-intensive efforts that paid labor makes the seed far too expensive, and dedicated volunteers are the only practical option. Third, seed collecting is fun and provides an effective means of bonding and educating the wide variety of people who are happy to assist in this engaging and rewarding pursuit.

Finding Sources of Seed

Seed collectors are always on a treasure hunt. They constantly scan hillsides and road rights-of-way for the hints of color and texture that suggest plant species associated with prairie and savanna remnants. Once they have found a site, they may use a local county map or plat map to identify the owner of the property. Collectors should always seek permission from landowners before collecting. This is a common courtesy that also gives collectors an opportunity to educate landowners about the special qualities of native plant remnants. While some landowners can be confrontational, many are surprised and, later, pleased to learn that they own something unusual. Some may be willing to learn more about native plants and how to manage them.

Land that has been disturbed but not overrun by undesirable species often provides large quantities of seed from early-successional native species. Native habitats that have not been overgrazed or invaded by exotic species often provide large quantities of more conservative species.

Seed collectors should map their discoveries for future reference and use common sense about whether it would be ethical, wise, and profitable to conduct a harvest. Small populations or thin stands of rare and much-needed species may be reason enough to make an ethical deal with nature and the landowner. Through informal agreement, or a lease, you might be able to manage the site for several seasons until the desired population is healthy enough to harvest.

Harvest Readiness

To learn when seeds are ready for harvesting, you will need to develop an intimate familiarity with the plant species, its phenology, and the difference between good and poor seed. Developing seed should be examined regularly and harvested only when significant amounts of ripe seed are present. (Figure 7.1 shows the differences between two types of seeds and other parts of their seed heads.) Many species produce only small quantities of viable seed. For example, prairie clovers and prairie cord grass seed may be less than 5 percent viable in the wild.

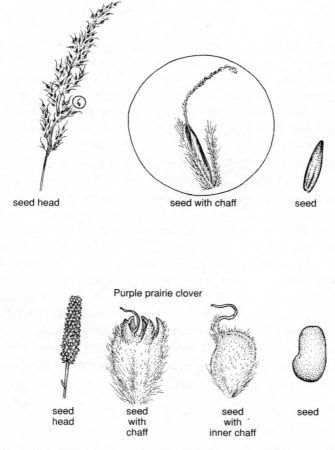

Figure 7.1. Seed heads and seeds.

Here are four common indicators of harvest readiness:

- Seeds are full-sized.
- Seed coats are changing color—usually from green to a darker hue.
- Stems are dry and no longer nourished by the roots and leaves.
- Earliest formed seed is dropping.

There are two stages of seed formation: the "soft-dough" stage, followed by the "hard-dough" stage. A seed in the soft-dough stage will reveal a doughy substance when you squeeze it between the fingernails of your forefinger and thumb. Seeds collected at this time are generally not viable. As the seed matures, it enters the hard-dough stage, which can be detected by biting the seed. If the seed is mature, it is usually too hard to bite, signaling that seed collection should begin. Some collectors look at seeds under microscopes to determine whether they have filled out and, therefore, are ready to harvest.

Species that have capsules or fruits that burst at maturity can present a timing problem. Collectors of species such as New Jersey tea, lupines, violet wood sorrel, phloxes, and violets often harvest them prior to seed ripening or place nylon or mesh bags over the plant to catch the seed as the seed capsules shatter. Spiderworts can also be difficult because they ripen over a period of three to four weeks. They should be collected by plucking the entire seed head cluster from plants with only one remaining flower bud. Some species have flower heads that bloom gradually from top to bottom, or vice versa—and the seed at the lower or upper end of the stalk ripens first. With these species, such as the blazing stars and Culver's root, collectors should harvest after the first seeds have fallen. This allows for some initial seed release while providing mature seed for harvest.

Each species within a given region produces ripe seed during a particular period. Some are consistent, while others are more opportunistic and produce seed over considerable intervals of time depending on available moisture, pollinator efficiency, and life-history strategy. It is helpful to develop a plant species list, arranged in the order in which the various species mature (see table 7.1). Correlate the lists with a calendar to check the progress of the seed. Although the exact date that the plants mature may vary annually, they will generally follow the same order from year to year.

Ethics of Seed Collecting

Like hunter-gatherer cultures, seed collectors must work within a code of ethics to ensure continued growth of the wild plant populations from

Table 7.1.

Seed Collection Dates

The following seed collection dates were derived from several sources in northeastern Illinois. In latitudes other than northeastern Illinois seed ripening may occur earlier or later. Dates also will vary from year to year, depending on the weather. Because the data for some species were limited, some collection periods may be shown in the table as shorter than they actually are, although other short collection intervals may be accurate, especially for species that eject seed. Also, some species with short seed collection periods in the wild may produce seed over extended periods in cultivation.

Species	Common Name	MAY	JUNE	JULY	AUG	SEPT	OCT	NOV
Acorus calamus	sweet flag							
Actaea pachypoda	white baneberry				—			
Actaea rubra	red baneberry		——					
†*Agalinis purpurea*	purple false-foxglove					——		
†*Agalinis tenuifolia*	slender false-foxglove						—	
Agastache nepetoides	yellow giant hyssop				—			
Agastache scrophulariifolia	purple giant hyssop					——		
Agrostis perennans	upland bent grass					—		
†*Allium burdickii*					—			
Allium canadense	wild garlic			——				
Allium cernuum	nodding wild onion					—		
Allium tricoccum	wild leek					—		
Amorpha canescens	lead plant					——		
Amphicarpaea bracteata	hog peanut						—	
Andropogon gerardii	big bluestem					——		

continues

---

†Precedes those scientific names cross-referenced in appendix C.

Table 7.1. (Continued)

Species	Common Name	MAY	JUNE	JULY	AUG	SEPT	OCT	NOV
Anemone cylindrica	thimbleweed				—	—		
Anemone quinquefolia	wood anemone	—						
Anemone virginiana	tall anemone		—	—	—	—		
Antennaria plantaginifolia	pussy toes	—						
Apocynum androsaemifolium	spreading dogbane		—	—	—			
Aquilegia canadensis	columbine							
Arabis glabra	tower mustard			—	—			
Arabis laevigata	smooth bank cress		—	—				
Aralia nudicaulis	wild sarsaparilla		—					
†*Arisaema triphyllum*	Jack-in-the-pulpit			—	—	—		
†*Arnoglossum atriplicifolium*	pale Indian plantain			—	—	—		
Asclepias amplexicaulis	sand milkweed				—			
Asclepias exaltata	poke milkweed		—	—	—	—		
Asclepias incarnata	swamp milkweed			—	—	—	—	
Asclepias purpurascens	purple milkweed			—	—	—		
Asclepias tuberosa	butterfly weed			—	—	—		
Aster cordifolius	heart-leaved aster					—	—	
†*Aster cordifolius sagittifolius*	arrow-leaved aster				—	—	—	
Aster ericoides	heath aster						—	—
Aster furcatus	forked aster				—	—	—	—
Aster laevis	smooth blue aster					—	—	—
Aster lateriflorus	side-flowering aster					—	—	
Aster macrophyllus	big-leaved aster					—	—	

continues

Scientific name	Common name
Aster novae-angliae	New England aster
†*Aster oolentangiensis*	azure aster
Aster sericeus	silky aster
Aster shortii	Short's aster
†*Aureolaria grandiflora*	yellow false-foxglove
†*Baptisia alba macrophylla*	white wild indigo
†*Baptisia bracteata leucophaea*	cream wild indigo
Blephilia ciliata	Ohio horse mint
†*Boltonia asteroides*	false aster
Bouteloua curtipendula	side-oats grama
Brachyelytrum erectum	long-awned wood grass
†*Brickellia eupatorioides*	false boneset
Bromus kalmii	prairie brome
Bromus latiglumis	ear-leaved brome
†*Bromus pubescens*	woodland brome
Calamagrostis canadensis	blue joint grass
Callirhoe triangulata	clustered poppy mallow
†*Calystegia spithamaea*	low bindweed
Camassia scilloides	wild hyacinth
Campanula aparinoides	marsh bellflower
†*Campanulastrum americanum*	tall bellflower
Cardamine bulbosa	bulbous cress
†*Cardamine concatenata*	toothwort
Cardamine douglassii	purple spring cress

†Precedes those scientific names cross-referenced in appendix C.

Table 7.1. (*Continued*)

Species	Common Name	MAY	JUNE	JULY	AUG	SEPT	OCT	NOV
Carex albursina	blunt-scaled sedge		—					
Carex bromoides	brome hummock sedge		—					
Carex cephalophora	woodbank sedge							
Carex crus-corvi	raven's foot sedge							
Carex davisii	Davis's sedge							
Carex gracilescens	slender wood sedge							
Carex gracillima	graceful sedge							
Carex grayi	bur sedge							
†*Carex hirsutella*	hairy green sedge							
Carex hirtifolia	hairy wood sedge							
Carex hystericina	porcupine sedge							
Carex lacustris	lake bank sedge							
Carex lupuliformis	knobbed hop sedge							
Carex lupulina	hop sedge							
Carex muskingumensis	swamp oval sedge							
†*Carex pellita*★	wooly sedge							
Carex pensylvanica	Pennsylvania sedge							
Carex radiata	straight-styled wood sedge							
Carex sartwellii	running marsh sedge							
Carex shortiana	Short's sedge							
Carex squarrosa	squarrose sedge							
Carex stipata	sawbeak sedge							

Scientific name	Common name
Carex stricta	tussock sedge
Carex swanii	downy green sedge
Carex tenera	slender sedge
Carex tuckermanii	bent-seeded hop sedge
Carex utriculata	beaked sedge
Carex vesicaria	inflated sedge
Carex vulpinoidea	fox sedge
†*Caulophyllum giganteum*	blue cohosh
Ceanothus americanus	New Jersey tea
Cephalanthus occidentalis	buttonbush
Chelone glabra	turtlehead
Cicuta maculata	water hemlock
Cinna arundinacea	wood reed
Cirsium altissimum	tall thistle
Claytonia virginica	spring beauty
†*Comandra umbellata*	false toadflax
Coreopsis palmata	prairie coreopsis
Coreopsis tripteris	tall coreopsis
Corylus americana	hazelnut
†*Dalea candida*	white prairie clover
†*Dalea purpurea*	purple prairie clover
Danthonia spicata	poverty oat grass
Desmodium canadense	showy tick trefoil
Desmodium cuspidatum	hairy-bracted tick trefoil

---

*Indicates nomenclature differs from Kartesz.

†Precedes those scientific names cross-referenced in appendix C.

continues

Table 7.1. (*Continued*)

Species	Common Name	MAY	JUNE	JULY	AUG	SEPT	OCT	NOV
Desmodium glutinosum	pointed tick trefoil					—		
Desmodium illinoense	Illinois tick trefoil					—		
Desmodium paniculatum★	tall tick clover					—		
Diarrhena americana	beak grass					—		
Diervilla lonicera	dwarf honeysuckle				—			
Dodecatheon meadia	shooting star				—			
Echinacea pallida	pale purple coneflower							
Elymus canadensis	Canada wild rye					—		
†*Elymus hystrix*	bottlebrush grass				—			
†*Elymus trachycaulus*	slender wheat grass			—				
Elymus villosus	silky wild rye				—			
Elymus virginicus	Virginia wild rye						—	
†*Enemion biternatum*	false rue anemone		—					
Eragrostis spectabilis	purple love grass		—					
Erigeron pulchellus	Robin's plantain							
Eryngium yuccifolium	rattlesnake master							
Erythronium albidum	white trout lily	—						
Eupatorium maculatum	spotted Joe-Pye weed					—		
Eupatorium perfoliatum	common boneset						—	
Eupatorium purpureum	purple Joe-Pye weed							
Euphorbia corollata	flowering spurge							
†*Euthamia graminifolia*	grass-leaved goldenrod						—	
†*Festuca subverticillata*	nodding fescue			—				

Scientific name	Common name
Galium boreale	northern bedstraw
Galium circaezans	hairy wild licorice
†*Gentiana alba*	yellowish gentian
Gentiana andrewsii	closed gentian
†*Gentianella quinquefolia*	stiff gentian
†*Gentianopsis crinita*	fringed gentian
Geranium bicknellii	northern cranesbill
Glyceria septentrionalis	floating manna grass
Glyceria striata	fowl manna grass
Helenium autumnale	sneezeweed
Helianthemum bicknellii	rockrose
Helianthus divaricatus	woodland sunflower
†*Helianthus pauciflorus*	showy sunflower
Heliopsis helianthoides	false sunflower
Heracleum maximum	cow parsnip
Heuchera richardsonii	prairie alum root
Hieracium longipilum	long-bearded hawkweed
Hydrastis canadensis	golden seal
Hydrophyllum virginianum	Virginia waterleaf
Hypoxis hirsuta	yellow star grass
Iris virginica shrevei	blue flag iris
Juncus nodosus	joint rush
Juncus torreyi	Torrey's rush
Krigia biflora	false dandelion
Lactuca biennis	tall blue lettuce

*Indicates nomenclature differs from Kartesz.

†Precedes those scientific names cross-referenced in appendix C.

continues

Table 7.1. (Continued)

Species	Common Name	MAY	JUNE	JULY	AUG	SEPT	OCT	NOV
Lactuca floridana	blue lettuce					—		
Lathyrus palustris	marsh vetchling				—			
Lathyrus venosus	veiny pea			—				
Leersia virginica	white grass					—		
Lespedeza capitata	round-headed bush clover							—
Lespedeza violacea	violet bush clover					—		
Liatris aspera	rough blazing star					—	—	
Liatris pycnostachya	prairie blazing star					—		
Liatris spicata	marsh blazing star						—	
Lilium michiganense	Michigan lily					—		
Lithospermum canescens	hoary puccoon		—					
Lithospermum latifolium	broad-leaved puccoon					—		
Lobelia cardinalis	cardinal flower					—		
Lobelia inflata	Indian tobacco				—	—		
Lobelia siphilitica	great blue lobelia				—	—		
Lobelia spicata	pale spiked lobelia				—			
†*Lonicera reticulata*	yellow honeysuckle			—				
Ludwigia polycarpa	false loosestrife					—		
Lycopus americanus	common water horehound						—	
Lycopus uniflorus	northern bugle weed					—		
Lysimachia ciliata	fringed loosestrife					—		
Lysimachia quadriflora	narrow-leaved loosestrife					—	—	

Scientific name	Common name
Lythrum alatum	winged loosestrife
†*Maianthemum racemosum*	false Solomon's seal
†*Maianthemum stellatum*	starry false Solomon's seal
Mimulus ringens	monkey flower
†*Moehringia lateriflora*	wood sandwort
Monarda fistulosa	wild bergamot
Muhlenbergia mexicana	leafy satin grass
Muhlenbergia tenuiflora	slender satin grass
Oenothera perennis	small sundrops
Orobanche uniflora	one-flowered broom rape
Oryzopsis racemosa	black-seeded rice grass
Osmorhiza longistylis	smooth sweet cicely
Oxalis violacea	violet wood sorrel
Oxypolis rigidior	cowbane
†*Panicum languinosum implicatum*★	slender-stemmed panic grass
Panicum latifolium★	wide-leaved panic grass
Panicum leibergii★	prairie panic grass
Panicum virgatum	switch grass
Parthenium integrifolium	wild quinine
Pedicularis canadensis	lousewort
Pedicularis lanceolata	swamp lousewort
Penstemon calycosus	smooth beard tongue
Penstemon digitalis	foxglove beard tongue

★Indicates nomenclature differs from Kartesz.

†Precedes those scientific names cross-referenced in appendix C.

continues

Table 7.1. (*Continued*)

Species	Common Name	MAY	JUNE	JULY	AUG	SEPT	OCT	NOV
Penthorum sedoides	ditch stonecrop						—	
Perideridia americana	thicket parsley			—				
Phlox divaricata	woodland phlox		—					
Phlox glaberrima	marsh phlox			—				
Phlox pilosa	sand prairie phlox		—					
Phryna leptostachya	lopseed				—			
Physostegia virginiana	obedient plant					—		
Poa palustris	marsh blue grass				—			
Polemonium reptans	Jacob's ladder		—					
Polygala senega	Seneca snakeroot		—					
†*Polygonatum biflorum commutatum*	smooth Solomon's seal							
Potentilla arguta	prairie cinquefoil					—		
Prenanthes alba	white lettuce					—		
Prenanthes racemosa	glaucous white lettuce					—		
Pycnanthemum tenuifolium	slender mountain mint					—		
Pycnanthemum virginianum	common mountain mint					—		
Ranunculus fascicularis	early buttercup	—						
Ratibida pinnata	grey-headed coneflower					—		
Rosa spp.	roses					—		
Rudbeckia hirta	black-eyed Susan						—	
Rudbeckia subtomentosa	sweet black-eyed Susan					—		
Rudbeckia triloba	brown-eyed Susan					—		

†*Samolus valerandi*
  ssp. *parviflorus* — water pimpernel
Sanguinaria canadensis — bloodroot
Sanicula marilandica — black snakeroot
Saxifraga pensylvanica — swamp saxifrage
†*Schizachyrium scoparium* — little bluestem
Scrophularia lanceolata — early figwort
Scrophularia marilandica — late figwort
Scutellaria lateriflora — mad-dog skullcap
Scutellaria parvula — small skullcap
Senecio aureus — golden ragwort
Silene antirrhina — sleepy catchfly
Silene stellata — starry campion
Silene virginica — fire pink
Silphium integrifolium — rosinweed
Silphium laciniatum — compass plant
Silphium terebinthinaceum — prairie dock
Sisyrinchium albidum — common blue-eyed grass
Sisyrinchium angustifolium — pointed blue-eyed grass
Smilax ecirrhata — upright carrion flower
Solidago caesia — blue-stemmed goldenrod
Solidago flexicaulis — broad-leaved goldenrod
Solidago patula — swamp goldenrod
Solidago riddellii — Riddell's goldenrod
Solidago speciosa — showy goldenrod

†Precedes those scientific names cross-referenced in appendix C.

continues

Table 7.1. (*Continued*)

Species	Common Name	MAY	JUNE	JULY	AUG	SEPT	OCT	NOV
Solidago ulmifolia	elm-leaved goldenrod						—	
Sorghastrum nutans	Indian grass						—	
Spartina pectinata	prairie cord grass					—		
Sphenopholis intermedia	slender wedge grass	—						
Spiranthes cernua	nodding ladies' tresses						—	
Sporobolus heterolepis	prairie dropseed					—		
Stachys tenuifolia	rough hedge nettle			—				
Taenidia integerrima	yellow pimpernel					—		
Thalictrum dasycarpum	purple meadow rue				—			
Thalictrum dioicum	early meadow rue		—					
†*Thalictrum thalictroides*	rue anemone	—						
Tradescantia ohiensis	common spiderwort					—		
Trillium flexipes	declined trillium				—			
Trillium grandiflorum	large-flowered trillium					—		
Trillium recurvatum	red trillium				—			
Triosteum aurantiacum	early horse gentian			—				
Uvularia grandiflora	bellwort			—				
Verbena urticifolia	hairy white vervain					—		
Veronica scutellata	marsh speedwell				—			
Veronicastrum virginicum	Culver's root		—					
Vernonia fasciculata	common ironweed				—			
Vicia americana	American vetch			—				
Zizia aptera	heart-leaved meadow parsnip				—			
Zizia aurea	golden Alexanders				—			

Note: This table was compiled by James F. Steffen.

*Indicates nomenclature differs from Kartesz.

†Precedes those scientific names cross-referenced in appendix C.

which they collect. Collectors who work in areas of intensive wild seed harvest follow (and do their best to enforce) rules like the following:

- From a given population take no more than 50 percent of the seed of a strong perennial or 10 percent of the seed of an annual species.
- Especially with rare and conservative species, take wild seed only when you are prepared to plant it in a properly prepared protected area and propagate it with appropriate conditions of soil, moisture, and exposure. Do not collect from state- or federally listed species without a permit.
- Be aware that taking seed may disrupt relationships between plants and animals. Many species depend on seed for food.
- Trampling can damage plants. Walk lightly during the growing season.
- Get to know other local seed collectors and propagators. Exchange information with them about the species and the areas in which you are all collecting to avoid duplication. Remember, even though everyone is following the collecting code, plants may become over-harvested if more than one person has collected at a site.
- If you are considering collecting from gardens or other landscaped areas, check the source of the plant material. Seeds from horticultural cultivars should not be used in restorations.
- Collecting from small, high-quality remnants should be done only in very small quantities unless the site is immanently threatened by destruction.
- Some experts suggest that, to maintain local gene pools, seed should be collected within 100 miles north or south and 200 miles east or west of the restoration site. Others recommend much narrower limits, perhaps as local as 25 miles or less. As a general rule, seeds should be collected as close to the restoration site as is practical. They should also be collected from a site as similar as possible to the restoration site in terms of soil type and topography.

Harvesting: Single Species or Mixes?

There are two general approaches to seed harvesting—collecting one species at a time and collecting mixes. Seed purveyors usually harvest seeds of single species and then mix them as necessary to meet their orders. Restorationists who plan to do the whole task—design their own planting plan, collect, and plant seed—need not follow the same strategy. In the latter situation, the most effective way to harvest may be to collect all ripe species of a given habitat simultaneously and place them in the same bag. This is true whether seed is harvested by hand or with equipment (see "Seed Harvesting with Machines" below).

Collecting Methods

When considering whether to collect seed by hand or with a machine, keep in mind that the techniques that use the least expensive equipment are usually the least efficient, though the most selective. Conversely, methods that use more expensive equipment tend to be more efficient but less selective. For many species, in many situations, there is no more efficient collecting equipment than a paper bag and two hands. When bags are full, they should be labeled with at least the species name, date, and site.

COLLECTING SEED BY HAND   Hand harvesting is a basic, ancient, accurate, and enjoyable method. To collect large quantities, it is best done with a seed bag or other receptacle attached to the body. This leaves both hands free to collect seed. Some collectors construct a seed bag by folding over and creasing the top inch of a paper grocery bag, tucking a firm wire into the crease to hold the bag fully open, and clamping a cord (with a spring clamp at each end) onto the bag for hanging around the collector's neck. In mixed stands, some people use a shoe box divided into several compartments. Others attach several gallon-sized plastic containers to their waist belts.

Methods of hand collecting vary from person to person and species to species (see chapter 8, "Tips for Gathering Individual Species"). The seed of some species such as Indian grass and prairie clover can be removed easily by grasping just below the flower head and then moving with a slightly open hand upward across the seed head. Others such as alum root, columbine, shooting star, and the wild indigos form their seeds in capsules that must be emptied. Collectors often use pruning shears to cut off the entire seed head of species such as nodding wild onion, purple coneflower, rattlesnake master, wild bergamot, and the goldenrods. Some collectors feel gloves are necessary, although bare hands give a more precise feel. Veteran collectors will tape their fingers to avoid cuts and callouses brought on by harvesting some species.

For transporting and storing bulk seed, it's hard to beat the seed bags that farmers discard after sowing the seed corn or soybeans that came in them. Those bags are very strong (and aren't easily torn by briars and twigs), and they allow the gathered seed to "breathe," thus discouraging rot and mold.

Some collectors are using small, low-tech devices. Applied Ecological Services, for example, is experimenting with a device modeled after hand-held blueberry and cranberry strippers. One design uses a disposable, two-gallon plastic jug with the top cut off. A handle is attached to the broad side and held horizontally. A row of pointed teeth, each 1 inch wide and 2 inches long, is cut along the bottom edge of the opening. This device has worked well with little bluestem, side-oats grama, and several other species. Others have used a similar comb-shaped device, made of wood and sheet metal, for stripping seed from plants into a collecting bin. Ron Bowen, of Prairie Restorations, uses a hand-held vacuum for collecting fine seeds. Whatever the technique, collecting by hand remains the only option in situations where plants are widely dispersed and in areas that are inaccessible to machinery or where machinery might inflict substantial damage to plants or soil.

SEED HARVESTING WITH MACHINES   Harvesting machines can be grouped into four categories: 1) portable seed strippers, 2) pull-type seed strippers, 3) combines, and 4) modified seed strippers and other mechanical harvesters. Small machines can be used effectively to harvest individual species which are growing in discrete patches in rough, wild terrain. These machines can also harvest seeds from rows of nursery-grown plants. Large machines are less portable, but they can supply the increased volumes of seed required for large-scale restorations. Sources of harvest machinery are listed in appendix E.

Portable Seed Strippers. These are simple, efficient, relatively inexpensive, and readily available. A by-product of the ubiquitous "weed whacker," these gasoline-powered machines consist of a high-speed rotating reel that combs seed off plants, throwing it into a screened hopper. The seed falls into a bag that is easily emptied. Working into the wind is the most efficient means of harvesting with a portable seed stripper.

David Mahler developed one of the earliest portable seed strippers, which he dubbed the Grin Reaper (Mahler 1988). The device weighs about eighteen pounds, provides a great deal of selectivity, and is highly maneuverable even in steep, brushy terrain. Most operators must stop every ten to thirty minutes to empty the one-bushel collection bag. Although the Grin Reaper does not strip the seeds out of seed heads, Mahler says extra processing is not needed when collecting multiple species.

Doug Collicutt developed another portable seed stripper, which uses a high-speed rotating brush that spins parallel to the ground (Morgan and Collicutt 1994). The machine weighs fifteen pounds and is carried on a shoulder harness. It can be used to harvest individual plants or sweep through a prairie taking a mix of species in an 18-inch-wide swath. In the hands of an experienced operator, it takes the seed in clean so that little processing is required to remove straw and chaff. The machine captures 50 to 85 percent of the ripe seed in one pass and will harvest plants ranging in height from 2 inches to more than 6.5 feet. Collicutt and his colleagues report that by using this machine, they can collect bulk seed in wild stands at the following rates per hour: big bluestem, 8.8 pounds; little bluestem, 2.2 pounds; prairie dropseed, 4.4 pounds; switch grass, 4.4 pounds; indigo bush, 5.1 pounds; Maximilian sunflower, 5.1 pounds; purple prairie clover, 12 pounds; and long-headed coneflower, 4.4 pounds. Harvesting in single-species stands like those in nurseries produces even higher collection rates.

Portable seed strippers are designed for harvesting areas that are difficult to reach or too sensitive in which to use other machinery. Other than the impact of the operator walking through them, there are no detrimental effects on the prairies being harvested. This allows collectors using this device to harvest the same area several times during the year.

Pull-Type Seed Strippers. Commercial pull-type seed strippers were common harvesting tools during the early part of this century. Now they exist mostly in farm machinery junkyards, a reminder of another era. Working from the basic plan used for these older machines, Don Pomeroy and John Morgan (Morgan and Collicutt 1994) developed a modern version that can be pulled behind a small tractor or all-terrain vehicle. It consists of a nylon bristle brush, which is powered by a five-horsepower gasoline engine, mounted on a chassis with two low-ground pressure tires. The adjustable machine height along with variable brush speed and angle enables harvesting of various prairie types and species. The nylon brush is gentle on the plants, harvesting the ripe, clean seed and leaving stalks intact for nesting cover and managed burns. Prairies can be harvested several times a season. The usual procedure for harvesting is to select a patch and then make rounds with the stripper. Morgan reports that seed harvesting of light, fluffy species is most efficient when done into the wind.

Hourly harvest rates in wild stands include big bluestem, 66 pounds of bulk seed; blue grama, 10 pounds; Canada wild rye, 40 pounds; Indian grass, 38 pounds; little bluestem, 15 pounds; tufted hair grass, 13 pounds; cinquefoils, 18 pounds; and purple prairie clover, 30 pounds. One machine can harvest from ten to fifteen acres per day. Two or three strippers can be hitched together to double or triple the daily area harvested on large prairies. Strippers can be transported by pickup truck or on a small trailer. They are ideal for roadside rights-of-way and harvesting in rocky or uneven terrain.

When pulled in an offset manner behind a small tractor or all-terrain vehicle, the resulting imprint is that of six to eight people walking single file through a prairie. These machine tracks usually disappear within a few weeks. Morgan and his colleagues have monitored the vegetation harvested with this machine and have found no negative effects on the harvested prairie when compared to unharvested controls.

Pull-type seed strippers should not be used when soil is wet and a chance of soil rutting exists.

Combines. Harvesting large areas is most efficient with large machines such as agricultural combines. However, their benefits must be weighed against the considerable costs of purchasing, modifying, and transporting these machines. For example, their purchase price alone deters many would-be users—a new combine can cost more than $120,000, and used combines range from $500 to $10,000.

Most combines are designed to harvest heavy-seeded grain crops. They use a cutting sickle and reel to cut and ingest large quantities of plant material. A system of screens, augers, and fans separates the large and small seeds, chaff and stem material, and other debris gathered by the combine. It is essential to modify a combine in order to harvest the chaffy, low-density seeds of most native wildflowers and grasses. Otherwise, a combine's high-volume fans tend to shoot light seeds past their collection box, while fluffy seeds do not easily flow through the elevators and augers.

Combines have been successfully modified by reducing the amount of intake air, which allows lightweight seeds to stay in the machine. This can be done either by removing some fans or by covering them with pieces of metal or cardboard. Sealing gaps and spaces, where small seeds collect, prevents combines from jamming. Some practitioners remove all moving parts and augers in the grain bin and build a special hood and bagging unit that allows the elevator to feed seeds directly into attached feed bags.

Modified Seed Strippers and Other Mechanical Harvesters. Machine designers and developers have made several modifications to the seed harvesters mentioned above. For example, instead of pulling a seed stripper, some machines have the brush and collection box mounted on the front of a tractor or other mobile unit. One such machine is marketed as a flail vac seed stripper. It costs about $10,000 new and will harvest large quantities of prairie grasses. A large, hydraulically powered brush assembly is mounted on a front-end loader (bucket removed) of a tractor. The spinning brush creates a vacuum that pulls the seed head into the brush, which removes the seed and deposits it into a hopper.

Applied Ecological Services, Inc., developed a smaller version of this machine, which uses an all-terrain vehicle mounted on half-tracks. They report that it is useful in both wetlands and prairies, although it will collect unwanted plant parts if those parts dislodge more easily than the seed heads (Apfelbaum and Faessler 1988).

Others have designed and made what might be described as mini-harvesters. Environmental Survey Consulting, for instance, developed a machine that it uses extensively for harvesting in large, mixed stands of prairie species (Mahler 1989). It is much easier to operate on rough land and more maneuverable than a combine, and unlike the combine, this reaper takes and saves everything. The unit consists of a box about 7.5 feet wide, 2.5 feet high, and 5 feet deep mounted on the loader arms of a tractor (bucket removed). A cutting bar from a sickle bar mower is attached near the bottom of the box, and a set of four rotating paddles is mounted near the top of the box. The operator can control the speed of the hydraulically powered cutting bar and paddles through separate control valves. When the box is full, the operator unloads it by tilting it back and releasing the collected material through a trap door at its rear. The cut material, which resembles seed hay, does not suffer the loss of seed inherent in cutting, raking, and baling hay.

Bill Whitney of Prairie/Plains Resource Institute in Aurora, Nebraska, has designed and built a harvester that attaches to the side of a pickup truck (Whitney 1992). This small harvester incorporates a reaper, a vacuum fan-processor, and a collection box. In one season, Whitney harvested approximately four hundred pounds of tall dropseed, switch grass, prairie cord grass, big and little bluestem, Indian grass, asters, goldenrods, bundleflowers, and sunflowers. He claims especially good success harvesting plants growing in the ditches of country roads.

Processing Seed

The seed of most species, as gathered, is not ready to be planted. Large numbers of seeds joined in seed heads need to be separated. Some seeds need to have their surfaces scratched, need wet or cold treatment, or need other treatments that apparently replace natural process to germinate well (see chapter 10 for details of propagation methods that are not described below). Many people who restore small areas (up to an acre or two) process harvested seed by hand. It's good winter work that gives the worker a greater knowledge of seeds and other plant parts. Learning to detect the seed buried in the spiny head of pale purple coneflower, for example, can be a small triumph. Most seed cleaners use a small knife to separate plant parts, cut open tough seed heads, and scarify legume seeds. They use various techniques to separate the chaff from the seed. A kitchen table covered with newspapers can provide a ready-made cleaning surface.

For those working with large amounts of seed, initial seed processing involves five basic steps: drying, threshing, scalping, cleaning, and storing. However, the nature of this processing can take a variety of forms depending on the characteristics of the seed, the amount of inert material and weed seed collected in the harvest, and the desired purity of the final product. Consider your situation: Did you harvest mixes or single species? Do you need to reduce the bulk for storage, stratification, or transportation? Will it be sown by hand or with equipment? Processing seed is expensive, but it may cut other costs or meet other requirements.

Seeds with fleshy fruits, typical of many savanna species, often require special handling before drying. Germination of these species improves when the pulp, which contains germination inhibitors, is removed immediately after collection. Dirr and Heuser (1987) describe a simple method that uses a food processor to remove the pulp from small quantities of seed. They recommend thickly wrapping the blades with electrical tape or covering them with tygon tubing or some type of plastic. Then, fill the container one-third full with water and add an equivalent amount of seed. Set the machine to a low speed and operate it at short bursts. The seeds, if solid, will sink, while the pulp floats to the top. Decant the seeds onto a properly sized screen, wash to remove debris, and let air dry for twenty-four to forty-eight hours before storing.

Drying Seed

Seeds should be dried shortly after harvesting to make them easier to clean and to prevent loss during storage. Properly dried prairie seeds should have a 5–14 percent moisture content (Harrington 1972, 1973). If seeds are dried below 5 percent moisture content, their cell walls break down and their enzymes become inactive. Meanwhile, seeds with a moisture content from 14 to 30 percent are often lost to microorganisms and fungi. Seed moisture content above 30 percent will induce germination in nondormant seeds.

Drying seeds depends on the temperature, relative humidity in the drying area, and moisture content of the seed. The key to drying seeds is to create a situation in which the seeds release their moisture to the air.

This can be accomplished in two ways: either spread the seeds on wire-mesh trays and circulate air around all sides of the seeds, or place the trays in a warm greenhouse, or place the seeds in paper bags in a drying room where the relative humidity is controlled, usually by a dehumidifier. Care should be taken, however, not to raise the temperature in a drying room too rapidly or too high (95° F maximum), as either action may damage the viability of the seeds.

Threshing

Threshing separates the seed from the seed head and can be done either by hand or by machine. There are several methods of hand threshing. The plant material can be rubbed against a coarse screen (⅛- to ½-inch hardware screen: ⅛ to ¼ inch for most species, ½ inch for *Silphiums*) with a gloved hand or with a rubber-covered paddle. It can also be rubbed between two paddles or with a rolling pin in a wooden tray. These methods are time-consuming, however, and inefficient for large quantities of seed.

If used properly, a mechanical hammermill can effectively thresh large quantities of seed. The device, which costs about $2,000 new for a small version, uses many fingerlike hammers to separate the seed from the chaff. The operator of a hammermill controls the speed of the hammers, the size of the bottom grate, and the rate of feed. For most species, the hammer speed should be from 1,200 to 1,400 revolutions per minute. High speeds (2,400 rpm) are used primarily to remove pappus from species of blazing star. The grate hole size is selected according to the size and condition of the seed—the smaller the seed, the smaller the hole size; the cleaner the plant material, the smaller the hole size. Material should be fed into the hammermill so it is nearly full always; otherwise, seeds may be damaged (Young and Young 1986).

Scalping

Scalping can be thought of as rough cleaning. The object is to remove bulky material such as stems and leaves. A scalping screen is selected by determining if it will allow the seed to drop through while keeping the other plant parts on top. The scalper screen is then placed over a screen with a smooth surface and the material is worked much as in hand threshing. The seeds fall onto the lower screen, which holds the seeds but passes through smaller chaff. Mechanical scalpers, which are essentially fanning mills without fans, are also available.

Cleaning

Seed cleaning can be done by hand or mechanically. Hand cleaning involves the repeated use of increasingly smaller cleaning screens (see sketches of these screens in chapter 8). Cleaning screens can be made by securing a piece of screening or hardware cloth to the bottom of a four-sided wooden frame. They can be made with varying mesh sizes of cloth from 1/32 inch to 1/2 inch or more. Cleaning screens of various sizes and premade frames are available at supply houses (see appendix E).

Seed impurities can also be separated by various machines that sort by density, size, specific gravity, minimum and maximum lengths and widths, and seed coat texture. A typical refining operation often involves more than one piece of equipment, several kinds of which are discussed below.

A fanning mill or air-screen cleaner is a common piece of equipment in the seed-cleaning shops of many prairie nurseries and restoration-related management agencies. New fanning mills cost from $500 to $20,000. However, an ad placed in a farm journal or rural weekly newspaper may bring offers of used fanning mills for $50 to $1,000. Sellers may include sets of different-sized screens, which are essential for a fully operating unit and usually cost from $50 to $100 or more at supply houses. Fanning mills range in size and power supply from small, hand-powered benchtop units to large, electrically powered floor models. A typical mill uses vibration, pressure, and air to separate seed from chaff. Some people hand screen their seed and then use the fanning mill as the final stage of their cleaning process. However, Wayne Pauly of the Dane County Parks Department in Madison, Wisconsin, reports that he cleans about 75 percent of the department's seed in a fanning mill without prior hand screening.

Other Cleaning Methods

Mel Hoff of the volunteer stewardship group at the West Chicago (Illinois) Prairie uses a commercially available shredder-mulcher to clean seed. It shatters the tough seed heads and stems of species such as rattlesnake master, pale purple coneflower, shooting star, and big bluestem. The result is a mulch that contains the seed, stems, and other parts. This material is suitable for hand broadcasting and raking-in. Hoff notes that if the bags provided with the machine will not contain the mulch, you can make your own bags from fine-mesh nylon screening. For very fine seeds, he recommends buying polyester tulle from a fabric shop and making bags with a sewing machine. He reports that these homemade bags will last several seasons.

Environmental Survey Consulting uses a tractor-powered shredder to shred collected bulk plant material. This single-step process releases the seed and creates a mixture of manageable particle sizes for later seeding. Scarifying machines used in agriculture will also work on prairie legumes, although they are expensive and, therefore, practical only for very high-volume operations.

Seed Storage

Storing seeds correctly assures restorationists that the effort of collecting and cleaning seed will not be lost to climatic extremes, microorganisms, fungi, insects, or small mammals. Seed moisture content, storage temperature, and relative humidity are the three most important factors that affect the viability and longevity of stored seeds. Harrington (1972, 1973) developed three rules of thumb that express the relationships between these factors: 1) Each 1 percent reduction in seed moisture doubles the life of the seed, with an optimum range from 5 to 14 percent for most nonaquatic, herbaceous seeds; 2) each reduction of 9° F in seed temperature doubles the life of the seed; and 3) the sum of the relative humidity (%) and temperature (° F) should not exceed 100.

There are three general ways to store seed. Unsealed containers of seed can be placed in a specially constructed room where the temperature and relative humidity can be controlled. Seeds can also be stored in gasketed containers with a silica gel desiccant, which are then placed in a refrigerator that is kept at 35–40° F. Plastic buckets with sealable lids also work well, especially when the seeds are first placed in sealed plastic bags. The desiccant, which turns from blue to pink when exposed to moisture, will keep the seeds at equilibrium with 45 percent relative humidity. (Silica gel desiccants are available at lab supply stores.) Finally, seed can be stored in paper bags or burlap bags in an unheated building such as a shed or barn. Hang the bags out of reach of rodents and above damp floors. For long-term storage, seeds can be frozen if the moisture content is below 14 percent, the point at which ice crystals will form. Seeds that are frozen should be placed in a sealed container.

Testing Seed

Testing seeds for their purity and viability provides the most accurate measure of their germination potential. The results of these tests can be translated into what is known as pure live seed (PLS), which is obtained by multiplying the bulk seed weight by the purity and germination percentages. Knowing how much PLS there is in a given quantity of seed can help determine how much seed to plant and improve a collectors' assessments of their harvesting methods. However, the effort and expense required to quantify and test seed should be kept in line with the scope of the project and the project goals. Testing seed for diverse plantings, for example, is more expensive and time-consuming than testing for simple plantings. Yet it may be less important to know the exact viability of all the species in a diverse planting because there are more species to fill in the niches created during site preparation. You simply plant it all and expect that at least some will "take."

Techniques for Testing Seed Purity and Germination Potential

Seed testing is a laboratory procedure that evaluates at least four subsamples of one hundred seeds for their purity and germination potential. Measuring purity involves removal, identification, and recording of all seed and all impurities. Seed technicians use established standards to separate samples into weed fractions, inert fractions, and desirable seed fractions. This is accomplished by running material through sophisticated, small-scale fanning mills and other desktop apparatus such as pneumatic seed shuckers (Miller 1994) to refine the samples. The percent by weight of each fraction is then calculated to derive a purity index.

The simple but time-consuming process of actually growing plants provides the standard against which seed scientists measure all other viability testing techniques. In the standard process, technicians place specified numbers of seeds on moistened blotter paper inside growth chambers where they can control the photoperiod, temperature, and humidity. These tests often take from three to eight weeks but produce accurate results. They also produce an estimate of the "hard-seed component," or seeds that are viable but have longer dormancy requirements.

A simpler but less accurate method involves slicing open the seed and examining the embryo under a hand lens or microscope. This may show whether an embryo formed, but it does not indicate if a seed has been damaged or is no longer viable.

Enzyme-sensitive chemicals are also used to test seed viability. These chemicals can provide quick results, typically within six to thirty hours. Tetrazolium chloride, a commonly used chemical for this purpose, stains a healthy seed embryo red, thus showing that the seed is viable (Moore 1973).

Many labs will test prairie seeds (see appendix E). Standardized tests have been developed for the common species, especially grasses, but there are no existing standards for most forb species. It is a good idea to write or phone a lab to explain your situation before sending seeds for testing.

REFERENCES

Apfelbaum, S., and F. Faessler. 1988. "Large-Scale Harvesting of Prairie Seed." *Restoration and Management Notes* 6, no. 2:79–80.

Bader, B.J. 1993. *Seed Handling: Basic Concepts.* Madison: University of Wisconsin Arboretum. Unpublished.

Dirr, M.A., and C.W. Heuser. 1987. *Reference Manual of Woody Plant Propagation: From Seed to Tissue Culture.* Athens, GA: Varsity Press.

Harmond, E., N.R. Brandenburg, and L.M. Klein. 1968. *Mechanical Seed Cleaning and Handling.* USDA Agricultural Handbook No. 354. Washington, DC: U.S. Department of Agriculture.

Harrington, J.F. 1972. "Seed Storage and Longevity." In *Seed Biology,* vol. 3, T.T. Kozlowski, ed. New York: Academic Press.

———. 1973. "Problems of Seed Storage." In *Seed Ecology,* W. Heydecker, ed. University Park: Pennsylvania State University Press.

Mahler, D. 1988. "New Device Speeds Seed Harvest." *Restoration and Management Notes* 6, no. 1:23, 25.

———. 1989. "Development of Front-End Tractor Reaper (Texas)." *Restoration and Management Notes* 7, no. 2:103.

Miller, W. 1994. Pneumatic seed shucker product brochure. Weatherford, OK: Ag-Renewal, Inc.

Moore, R.P. 1973. "Tetrazolium Staining for Assessing Seed Quality." In *Seed Ecology,* W. Heydecker, ed. University Park: Pennsylvania State University Press.

Morgan, J.P., and D.R. Collicutt. 1994. "Seed Strip Harvesters: Efficient Tools for Prairie Restoration." *Restoration and Management Notes* 12, no. 1:51–54.

Murrell, D., P. Curry, G. Kruger, and G. Pearse. 1995. *Production and Marketing of Native Grass Seed.* Regina, SK, Canada: Saskatchewan Agriculture and Food.

Nernberg, D. 1995. *Native Species Mixtures for Restoration in the Prairie and Parkland Regions of Saskatchewan.* Simpson, SK, Canada: Canada Wildlife Service.

Rock, H.R. 1977. *Prairie Propagation Handbook.* Franklin, WI: Wehr Nature Center, Milwaukee Department of Parks, Recreation, and Culture.

Whitney, B. 1992. "Large-Scale Prairie Restoration Underway; Harvester Devised (Nebraska)." *Restoration and Management Notes* 10, no. 1:62–63.

Young, J.A., and C.G. Young. 1986. *Collecting, Processing and Germinating Seeds of Wildland Plants.* Portland, OR: Timber Press.

8

Tips for Gathering Individual Species

Richard R. Clinebell II

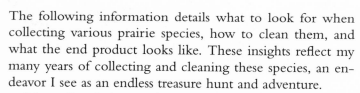

The following information details what to look for when collecting various prairie species, how to clean them, and what the end product looks like. These insights reflect my many years of collecting and cleaning these species, an endeavor I see as an endless treasure hunt and adventure.

I have found that expensive seed-cleaning equipment is not necessary to provide seed that will blend well and work in a seed drill. I use a set of wooden frames to clean prairie seed. Each one has a different size of screening: $1/16$-inch mesh, $1/8$-inch mesh, and $1/4$-inch mesh. These frames, which are easy to make, are 2 feet wide by 4 feet long by 4 inches tall (see figure 8.1). I use them two different ways. First, with the mesh side up, I rub seed through the screen. This more conventional technique works with some composites, legumes, and grasses. Second, I perform the "coneflower stomp," in which I set the frame on the floor with the mesh side down, put the seed heads in the frame, and then run in place over the seed heads. In both cases the seed falls through the screen onto newspaper.

Most seed should be dried before cleaning, although some species are easier to clean while their pods are slightly wet. Collected seed should be stored in paper bags because moist seed stored in plastic bags often molds. I usually store seed in paper bags in the basement, although seed can be stored in a refrigerator if it is kept in sealed bags or other airtight containers.

Seed that has been screened will contain various other parts of the plant. These can often be removed by vigorously shaking the storage bag or by using an air gun to winnow out these unwanted parts.

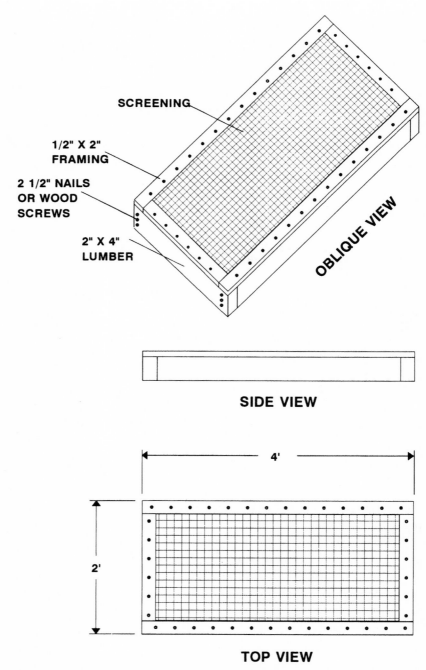

SCREENING

1/2" X 2" FRAMING

2 1/2" NAILS OR WOOD SCREWS

2" X 4" LUMBER

OBLIQUE VIEW

SIDE VIEW

4'

2'

TOP VIEW

Figure 8.1. Seed–cleaning screen. Mesh size varies from to ⅟₁₆ to ¼ inch. Some people build an additional tray that fits under the screen to catch the seeds.

The Sunflower Family

Asters

Collect New England aster when most of the plant's leaves have dropped and just before the inflorescences have fluffed out. By that time, the seed is brownish and hard (unripe seed is white and squishy). I cut off the top 12 inches of the plant with pruning shears and then stuff the top upside down into a paper bag. If you find a big patch, you can collect in large plastic bags. However, once you return from the field, the inflorescences should be laid out on newspaper to dry. To clean this species, I pour about four or five well-stuffed, grocery-sized paper bags of inflorescences onto a ¼-inch cleaning screen and rub the inflorescences across the mesh. This will usually produce about a grocery bag of seed that weighs several pounds. I remove unwanted plant parts ("sticks") by hand.

I use the same techniques to collect and process smooth blue aster, which has bright, flaming purple-red seeds when ripe, flax-leaved aster, azure aster, and stiff aster. I cut off the top 6–8 inches of the plant with pruning shears, lay the inflorescences on their sides in a paper bag, then take them home and clean them like New England aster.

Heath aster is densely covered with leaves, which makes it difficult to clean if you do not have a fanning mill. While I find that the little leaves and seed are hard to separate by screening, it's probably not necessary. Leaving in the leaves as "mulch" seems to work fine.

Silphiums

I collect the silphiums while the seed heads are green. I check the seed by cracking open the seed head to see if the seed is plump and darkly colored (wine-red in compass plant, for example). The seed heads of compass plant can be clipped off individually with pruning shears, while prairie dock seed heads can be taken in small clusters. I like to hold the stalk of the plant still when cutting off a seed head because that minimizes the amount of seed likely to be dislodged from the other seed heads before I harvest them. (I protect my skin from the coarse stalks by wrapping my fingers with band-aids.) The harvested seed heads should be laid out to dry or, if kept inside the collecting bag, turned every day during the collecting season. Seed can also be left to dry on the plant and then collected during the autumn, usually in October.

The disk flowers of silphiums are sterile and form dozens of ½-inch pieces of "straw." This material can be removed with the ⅛-inch cleaning frame. I roll and shake the uncleaned seed heads against the screen, which forces the "straw" through the screen, leaving the seeds and some galls and seed bracts on top. I pick out all the galls and the largest bracts. This usually provides a 50:50 mixture of seed and bracts. A grocery bag full of this mixture typically weighs five pounds.

Coneflowers

To collect pale purple coneflower, purple coneflower, and narrow-leaved coneflower, I use pruning shears to snip off the individual heads just below the inflorescence. I clean all these species by doing the aforementioned coneflower stomp. I first spread some newspaper on the floor. Then I place either a ¼-inch or a ⅛-inch cleaning screen with the mesh side down over the newspaper. Next, I fill the cleaning screen with seed heads and then run in place across the seed heads for one hundred steps. After carefully turning over the crushed seed heads, I run in place for another one hundred steps. Last, I lift the screen and shake it over the newspaper about twenty-five times and then lay it atop an adjacent arrangement of clean newspaper. What falls through the screen is about half bracts and half seed. The bracts are dark brown and awl shaped, while the seed is whitish with a little brown stripe on top. The seed can be separated from the bracts by winnowing.

The rest of the coneflowers—grey-headed coneflower, black-eyed Susan, golden glow, Missouri black-eyed Susan, and sweet black-eyed Susan—are easily snipped off with pruning shears. I lay the inflorescences sideways in a paper bag and then smash them down with my foot. I then pour the inflorescences into a ⅛-inch cleaning screen and perform the stomp. The first stomp yields pure seed—about half a pound for every grocery bag of inflorescences. The second and succeeding stomps are increasingly filled with other plant material. This is best removed by running the mixture several times through a ¼-inch cleaning screen with the mesh side up. This may sound compulsive, but it is much easier than picking individual plant parts out of the coneflower seed.

Blazing Stars

I find that it is best to pick this species while the bracts still have a little green color because the plants become very abrasive when totally dry. While slightly green, all *Liatris* species can be harvested by running a cupped hand up the stem to catch the seed. The seed can then be dried either by turning it inside a paper bag or by laying it out to dry on newspaper. Seed heads of rough blazing star and prairie blazing star tend to cling together, so I roll them over the ¼-inch cleaning screen. Cylindrical blazing star has very leafy inflorescences that require the use of ½-inch mesh to clean properly.

Goldenrods

I like to collect goldenrods when they are still a little green because it is easier to rub the inflorescences through a cleaning screen. Otherwise, I clean them just like the asters—through a cleaning screen with the mesh side up.

Coreopsis

All species of coreopsis should be picked when their seed heads turn brown. I clean them all with the coneflower stomp. The seeds are dark brown, rectangular, and strap-shaped.

Wild Quinine

The insects may beat you to the wild quinine if you don't pick it early. If there is a lot of dust, insect droppings, and irregularly shaped fragments, you are most likely too late. If you get there before the insects, you will find that separating the seed from the twiglets is very difficult. I recommend using a fanning mill to clean this species.

Wetland Composites

Wetland composites such as sneezeweed, tall swamp marigold, and false aster can all be treated like the coneflowers.

The Legume Family

Legumes are harder to process than composites but just as important. I clip the inflorescences of wild indigos with pruning shears and store them in paper bags. To clean them, I use the coneflower stomp. This results in a mixture of hard yellow or brown seeds and fragments of the legume pod left on the newspaper. Most of the stems and other plant material remain on the screen. I remove the fragments that remain with the seed by placing the mixture in a paper bag and shaking it vertically. The seed is so much heavier that it naturally falls to the bottom. Any sort of air gun will accomplish the same end. I use the same technique to clean Maryland senna and partridge pea.

White prairie clover and purple prairie clover are easy to collect by simply stripping the seed from the vertical seed head. Seeds that do not strip off easily are not ready to pick. After rubbing away the withered flowers, you will find tiny, olive-green seeds.

The seed pods of tick trefoils stick together and must be rubbed through a ¼-inch cleaning screen to separate the seeds. I collect and process lead plant and round-headed bush clover just like the asters. The bush clover seeds are light brown and oval shaped with a pointed end.

The Parsley Family

I clip off the seed heads of rattlesnake master with pruning shears and place them in a paper bag. The structure of the inflorescence allows air to pass around the seed heads, so they tend to dry themselves. I like to collect rattlesnake master before the insects get to it. To make sure that I am not collecting too early, I use the "cotyledon test." With sharp pruning shears, I bisect a green but ripening seed head and look for indication that the seed, though barely formed, will mature adequately on the head after harvest. Look for hard, white ovals that are about as large as the inside part of a mature seed. They may actually be slightly larger, since seeds dry and shrink as they mature. The starchy white ovals will be surrounded by reddish or purplish seed coat material. (I also use this test with silphiums, coneflowers, and other composites that tend to suffer severe insect damage before they're fully ripe.)

I clean dry rattlesnake master using the coneflower stomp. The product is a gorgeous, aromatic mixture of 50 percent seed and 50 percent bracts. The bracts are awl shaped, while the seeds have an ornamentation reminiscent of trilobites. I remove any larger, unwanted plant parts. I find that this method works best when there is just a little moisture remaining in the plant.

Heart-leaved meadow parsnip and golden Alexanders should be collected by clipping the umbels and drying them in paper bags. The best time to pick them is when half the seed is green and the other half is turning brown. They can be cleaned just like asters. The ripe seeds are dark and hard.

The Milkweed Family

I treat all species of milkweeds the same. First, I cut off the pods while they are still green to ensure that the comas ("fluff") will mat together during the cleaning process. This means that some of the seed will be immature (white), but as long as the majority is brown, you are not too early. I then rub the seed through a ¼-inch cleaning screen. The seed may still be moist after screening, so it is necessary to turn it inside the storage bag until it dries out. Once dry, I fill a small paper bag half full of seed, take it outside, and shake it gently for a few minutes. When I open the bag, the unwanted plant parts and dust billow forth, leaving only the milkweed seed inside.

The Figwort Family

This family contains a genus, the beard tongues, and a species, Culver's root, that I have collected for restorations. I clean the beard tongues using the coneflower stomp. This produces small seeds and larger capsule fragments. Because of their different sizes, they can be easily separated by sieving through a ¼-inch cleaning screen. Culver's root has spikes of capsules, but these are not the seed. The seed, which is contained in the capsules, is very small and powdery. To check a Culver's root plant for seed, you should shake a couple of the spikes onto the palm of your hand. If your hand is coated with fine, reddish-brown, dustlike seed, you are in luck. If not, the seed has already fallen.

The Borage, Phlox, Milkwort, and Lobelia Families

Plants within these four families eject their seed, so collectors must treat them somewhat differently. Still, it is easy to collect seed from species such as the puccoons, the phloxes, Seneca snakeroot, and cardinal flower by covering the plants with old nylon stockings after the corollas have withered. A few holes or runs are okay. Simply cut each leg of the stocking into thirds; close one end of each piece with a twist tie and place the open end over the plant. Then, using another twist tie, gently fasten the open bottom of the nylon to the plant stem below the inflorescence. This allows the mature seed to drop into the nylon bag.

The Grass Family

Except for a few grasses, I treat members of this family the same way as the asters—clipping inflorescences with pruning shears and rubbing the seed heads through a ¼-inch cleaning screen. The exceptions are big bluestem, Canada wild rye, and Indian grass, which I usually strip from the plants by hand before screen cleaning. (All three are abrasive, so I like to tape up my hands.) It is important to check for mature seed, especially when collecting Indian grass and cord grass. Excepting prairie cord grass, which is very abrasive, I often rub grass seed head between my moistened palms to help break down the glumes until I find tiny "ricelike" seeds. The seed of some grasses such as June grass is very small and can be seen only with a hand lens.

The Sedge Family

I snip the following sedges and roll them through a ¼-inch or ½-inch cleaning screen (depending on their seed size): *Carex annectens, C. bicknelli, C. crestatella, C. normalis,* and similar sedges with lenticular seeds and flat perigynia. (Note: These species will slice your skin if carelessly stripped by hand!) I do hand collect the "corncob" sedges such as *C. hyalinolepis, C. hystericina, C. lupulina,* and *C. lurida* when they are still a little green. The tassels at the end of the stalk are the male inflorescences, and the "corncobs" below them are the seed-bearing females. Other sedges that can be hand collected include *C. crus-corvii* and species with three-sided seeds and roundish perigynia such as *C. bushii* and *C. shortiana.* They all can be cleaned with screens. I treat the unusual *C. frankii* like the asters—clipping the florescences and rolling through a ¼-inch cleaning screen.

Bulrushes are also easy to collect and process with cleaning screens. These include *Scirpus atrovirens, S. validus,* and *S. lineatus.*

9
Designing Seed Mixes

Neil Diboll

A properly designed seed mix plays a pivotal role in establishing a high-diversity, low-maintenance prairie or savanna restoration. To design a reliable seed mix, a restorationist must take into account several different factors, including:

- site conditions (soil moisture and texture, slope aspect, amount of sun or shade, existing vegetation)
- goal(s) of the restoration (tallgrass prairie, savanna, wildlife habitat, etc.)
- grass-to-forb ratio
- seed quality
- seeding rates and seed size
- germination rates and reliability of each species
- each species' ecological behavior
- efficiency of seeding technique (hand-broadcast, drilled)
- season of planting
- budget

This chapter presents seed mixes for plowed-ground prairies (see also tables 12.1 and 12.2). Mixes for interseeding prairies and woodlands are included in tables 11.1 and 11.2.

Site Conditions and Goals of the Restoration

Although other contributors to this book cover these two topics, I want to emphasize that proper site analysis and recognition of project goals are essential when developing a balanced seed mix. They are the foundation upon which the restoration project, in general, and the design of the seed mix, in particular, rest. If you fail to take the time to properly analyze your site and your own goals, you may be disappointed with the results.

Grass-to-Forb Ratio

Prairie restorationists should have some rough estimate of the amount of grasses and forbs they want in their plantings. Although most wish to achieve a diverse prairie community with areas of both forbs and grasses, others may want more or less grass coverage to meet their goals. Mixes with lower percentages of forbs (20–40 percent by weight) and higher percentages of grasses (60–80 percent by weight) tend to result in grass-dominated prairies in a very short time. This is especially true in restorations planted heavily with big bluestem and/or switch grass. On the other hand, mixes with larger percentages of forbs (50–60 percent by weight) usually produce a more diverse prairie community with a good cover of both grasses and forbs. I caution restorationists against using mixes with more than 70 percent forbs because plantings of mainly forbs do not burn very well, and the increased number of forbs will significantly raise the cost of the planting.

Seed Quality

Knowing the quality of the seed you plan to use is critical when designing a predictable seed mix. The level of quality for each species is known as its pure live seed (PLS) value. This numerical value is obtained by testing seed of each species for its purity and germination potential. The percent purity is then multiplied by the percent germination to obtain the percentage of pure live seed. This percentage can then be multiplied by the number of seeds in a given weight to determine the PLS for that weight. This gives an accurate estimate of the number of viable seeds per unit weight. This, in turn, helps determine how much seed you will need. Since seed quality varies from year to year, it is important to get PLS values for each annual harvest.

Restorationists should also be aware that seed quality varies because nurseries and seed collectors do not necessarily clean, prepare, and store their seeds in a uniform manner. Restorationists interested in quality seed mixes should make the effort to familiarize themselves with suppliers from whom they are purchasing seed. It is a good idea to compare different suppliers by purchasing small sample amounts of seed before placing a large order. Remember, a lower price may mask an inferior product that contains only a small percentage of viable seed.

Those restorationists working with seeds they have collected themselves should make every effort to clean and store their seeds properly. Testing for seed viability is very important. If you cannot match commercial standards for seed cleaning and storage, then you must be prepared to plant the site at a higher seeding rate to compensate for lower-quality, wild-collected seed.

Seeding Rates and Seed Size

Knowing the number of viable seeds per ounce for each species is very important. That is why prairie seed suppliers who produce a consistent, high-quality product will list the number of seeds per ounce for the species they sell. With this information, the restorationist can begin to calculate how much seed of a given species to include in a mix. Designers of seed mixes must also account for the differences in seed size, which translate into differences in the number of seeds per unit weight. The contrast between small and large seed is quite dramatic. For example, the large-seeded silphiums average 800 seeds per ounce, while alum root and Culver's root produce nearly 800,000 seeds per ounce. Although the number of seeds per ounce for many species is roughly similar, the designer of machine-planted seed mixes must correct for seed size. This is necessary because smaller seeds do not always get planted at the correct depth when planted with a seed drill. To compensate for this lower rate of germination, I generally increase the amount of any smaller-seeded species in a mix. Another option is to plant these species by hand either at the time of planting or in fall after the prairie has become established (see, for example, species indicated in table 9.4).

Germination Rates and Reliability of Species

Designers of seed mixes must also consider the germination potential of each species when calculating seeding rates. Some prairie plants germinate quickly and easily reseed themselves under good conditions. This includes the warm-season grasses and certain highly adaptable forbs such as wild bergamot, grey-headed coneflower, black-eyed Susan, purple coneflower, and some legumes. Many species will overwinter in the soil and germinate the second year, while still others may not germinate until environmental conditions are just right—sometimes not for three or four years. Some of these less adaptable, "conservative" species may never show up in the planting because conditions for their germination and survival did not present themselves before the seed either lost its vitality or was consumed by soil organisms. This is especially true of the finer-seeded, slow-growing forbs such as shooting star, Culver's root, alum root, gentians, and lilies. These species should be hand scattered during the fall of the second, third, or fourth year after the initial planting. For more information about interseeding conservative species, see chapter 11.

Species' Ecological Behavior

It is also important to understand the growth patterns of each species when developing a prairie seed mix. For example, if a mix contains only short-lived species such as black-eyed Susan, Canada wild rye, purple coneflower, and blue vervain, the planting will have no staying power and will not develop into a sustainable grassland ecosystem. On the other hand, a mix that contains only slow-to-establish, long-lived species such as lead plant, prairie dropseed, gentians, New Jersey tea, and compass plant requires waiting several years before anything even remotely resembling a prairie begins to emerge.

Several aggressive prairie plants can overwhelm an otherwise good prairie mix. This is particularly true of aggressive, clonal, or rhizomatous forb species such as grass-leaved goldenrod, Missouri goldenrod, Canada goldenrod, showy sunflower, false sunflower, and coreopsis. If planted too heavily, some early-successional species such as wild bergamot, common and whorled milkweed, and black-eyed Susan can also stunt the emergence of slower-germinating species. Tall, long-lived prairie grasses such as big bluestem and switch grass can also be a problem. Their dense, tightly knit root systems can exclude all but the most competitive forbs and grasses. I recommend including these aggressive species at low seeding rates or planting them in designated areas where they can form natural clones.

Some species occur in natural prairies as occasional individuals, while other species occur more commonly. Visiting local prairie remnants and taking field notes will give you a good idea of the occasional and common species in your area.

Efficiency of Seeding Technique

There are two basic ways to plant a prairie: hand seeding and machine seeding. If all variables are equal, machine seeding is more effective than hand seeding because the seed drill does a better job of placing the seed at the correct seeding depth, thus ensuring more uniform germination. I recommend increasing the seeding rate by 25 percent when hand planting a prairie. This rate can be less if you follow explicitly the instructions for hand seeding and have a well-prepared seedbed. Anyone using hand-collected seeds probably should increase this amount to compensate for nonviable seed.

Season of Planting

Most spring-blooming species germinate best when planted shortly after collection (fresh). Other species do better when planted in early spring, late spring, or early summer, and still others, especially forbs, are favored by fall plantings (see table 9.1). Restorationists should recognize these natural tendencies and should utilize them to increase germination potential by adjusting the amount of seed in their mixes accordingly. Most warm-season grasses, legumes, and many composites do well in late spring plantings.

Budget

Planting prairies or savannas takes a certain amount of energy, which often translates into dollars. Restorationists can develop seed mixes that fit a range of budgets from the "budget prairie mix" to what I call the "dream prairie mix." In most cases, restorationists develop a mix that finds the middle ground between these two extremes, depending on the goals of the project. This generally means developing a mix that includes a good variety of reliable species that could be interplanted with other species once the prairie becomes established. There are a few other ways to help keep costs down, although they must be balanced against a loss in quality. First, plant in the fall, because those plantings require smaller amounts of forb seed due to the better rates of forb germination. Second, use larger amounts of inexpensive seed such as black-eyed Susan, blue vervain, grey-headed coneflower, and many of the grasses. Third, if absolutely necessary, judiciously reduce the overall seeding rate.

The General Process

When all is said and done, each restorationist designs a seed mix after analyzing these factors and including personal biases—be they scientific, artistic, or some hybrid of both. From a general perspective, however, I recommend working toward developing a good balance of species. A good seed mix should include many different species, especially those of the major plant families found on tallgrass prairies—grasses, composites, and legumes. Of course, restorationists should not overlook significant species from the other plant families.

When planting a diverse mix of forbs and grasses, most restorationists use a seeding rate of ten pounds per acre with pure, clean seed and as high as thirty to forty pounds per acre with rough-cleaned, wild-collected seed. A highly diverse mix on good soils typically produces a prairie with as many as forty or fifty species. Similar plantings on heavy clays with poor soil structure are usually not as diverse—only fifteen to twenty-five species. Restorationists can increase the diversity in both these situations by waiting a few years after the initial seeding and then interseeding with certain prairie species that do not grow well on an open seedbed.

Table 9.1.

Seasonal Planting Mixes
Seeds of the following species are best planted when indicated:

Scientific Name	Common Name

Immediately

Carex spp.	sedges
Geum triflorum	prairie smoke
Oxalis violacea	violet wood sorrel
Pulsatilla patens	pasque flower
Ranunculus fascicularis	early buttercup
Ranunculus rhomboideus	prairie buttercup
Stipa spartea	porcupine grass
Tradescantia ohiensis	common spiderwort

Spring (cool soil temperatures)

Aristida spp.	three-awn grass
Bromus kalmii	prairie brome
Calamagrostis canadensis	blue joint grass
†*Koeleria macrantha*	June grass
Lupinus spp.	lupines
Penstemon digitalis	foxglove beard tongue
Silphium spp.	silphiums
Sporobolus heterolepis	prairie dropseed

Late Spring or Early Summer (warm soil temperatures)

Amorpha canescens	lead plant
Andropogon gerardii	big bluestem
Anemone cylindrica	thimbleweed
Asclepias incarnata	swamp milkweed
Asclepias tuberosa	butterfly weed
Astragalus canadensis	Canadian milk vetch
Bouteloua curtipendula	side-oats grama
†*Dalea candida*	white prairie clover
†*Dalea purpurea*	purple prairie clover
Lespedeza capitata	round-headed bush clover
Panicum virgatum	switch grass
†*Schizachyrium scoparium*	little bluestem
Sorghastrum nutans	Indian grass
Verbena hastata	blue vervain
Verbena stricta	hoary vervain

Table 9.1. (*Continued*)

Scientific Name	Common Name
Fall (dormant)	
Allium cernuum	nodding wild onion
Aster spp.	asters
Baptisia spp.	wild indigos
Dodecatheon meadia	shooting star
Echinacea pallida	pale purple coneflower
Eryngium yuccifolium	rattlesnake master
Eupatorium maculatum	spotted Joe-Pye weed
Euphorbia corollata	flowering spurge
Gentiana spp.	gentians
Helianthus spp.	sunflowers
Iris virginica shrevei	blue flag iris
Liatris spp.	blazing stars
Lobelia cardinalis	cardinal flower
Lupinus spp.	lupines
Parthenium integrifolium	wild quinine
Penstemon spp.	beard tongues
Silphium spp.	silphiums
Vernonia fasciculata	common ironweed
Veronicastrum virginicum	Culver's root
Zizia spp.	golden Alexanders
Anytime, Spring Through Fall	
Desmodium canadense	showy tick trefoil
Echinacea purpurea	purple coneflower
Elymus canadensis	Canada wild rye
Heliopsis helianthoides	false sunflower
Lilium spp.	lilies
Monarda fistulosa	wild bergamot
Ratibida pinnata	grey-headed coneflower
Rudbeckia hirta	black-eyed Susan
Solidago rigida	stiff goldenrod

Note: This table was compiled by Neil Diboll and Dave Egan.
†Precedes scientific names cross-referenced in appendix C.

Calculating Seeding Rates

Prairie restorationists have had good results with seeding rates from forty to sixty seeds per square foot. Depending on the species within the mix, prairies planted at a rate of thirty seeds per square foot can be successfully established on well-prepared sites with good soil structure. With excellent soil preparation, restorationists can obtain good results with plantings of the major warm-season prairie grasses at rates as low as twenty seeds per square foot. This seeding rate translates to roughly seven pounds per acre, if the seed is 95 percent pure.

To get an idea of what this means, let's look at big bluestem planted at a rate of 40 seeds per square foot. Since there are 43,560 square feet in an acre, this mix requires 1,742,400 total seeds (40 times 43,560) to plant one acre. It is easy to calculate a seeding rate for a solid stand of any species. For example, to plant just big bluestem, which has approximately 8,000 seeds per ounce, at 40 seeds per square foot would require a planting rate of 13.6 pounds per acre (1,742,400 seeds/acre divided by 8,000 seeds/oz equals 218 oz/acre divided by 16 oz/lb equals 13.6 lbs/acre).

This calculation becomes necessarily more complex when you develop a seed mix with more than one species. I follow this process: 1) decide on the seeding rate (seeds per square foot); 2) decide on the forb-to-grass ratio; 3) choose a list of species appropriate to the site conditions and project goals; and 4) decide what percentage of the mix each species will occupy, taking into consideration all the factors mentioned above, especially seed size, ecological behavior of species, personal preferences, and budget constraints. A review of the seed mix chart for a short prairie planting of 10,000 square feet offers an opportunity to explain the process more fully (see table 9.2).

In that case, I decided to plant at a rate of 50 seeds per square foot, which on a 10,000-square-foot area requires 500,000 total seeds. Since the particular project goal called for a "diverse, forb-rich" prairie, I chose a grass-to-forb ratio of 40:60. This means that 300,000 seeds will be forbs and 200,000 will be grasses. I then selected twenty-nine forbs and four grasses and began to assign them different percentages of the mix. Working back from the total number of seeds meant that any species that represents 2 percent of the mix will have a seeding rate of one seed per square foot (500,000 total seeds times 0.02 equals 10,000 or one seed per square foot). Species with percentages more than 2 percent would have a higher seeding rate, and those with percentages less than 2 percent would have a lower seeding rate. For example, the number of seeds needed for spiderwort is calculated by multiplying the total number of seeds by the percentage of the mix for spiderwort (500,000 total seeds times 0.03 equals 15,000 seeds needed). This number divided by the number of seeds per unit of weight (in this case grams but often done in ounces) provides the weight of seed needed (15,000 seeds divided by 280 seeds/gram equals 53.57 grams). I calculated each of the forb species in the same manner, adjusting them as necessary to meet the seeding rate and weight requirements. The grass portion of the mix is then calculated using the same procedure. Tables 9.3 and 9.4 offer two more examples of mixes for different types of prairie plantings. I used the same procedure to develop them.

These are hypothetical lists for hypothetical sites. In virtually every case, there are special considerations. For example, in the mesic list I included Canadian milk vetch, purple coneflower, and sweet black-eyed Susan despite my expectation that none of those will remain in that prairie over the long haul. But they will supply early color and variety that will help the new planting gain quick acceptance while some of the prairie slowpokes are sinking the deep roots that will help them flower for decades.

Although every seed mix for every real site will be a little different, there are standard lists of potential components for various types of seed mixes. Examples of these are given in tables 11.1–2 and 12.1–2.

Designing reliable seed mixes is not difficult if you know what you want to achieve, have experience with the species you are considering, and consider all the factors outlined in this chapter. Finally, remember that your attention to detail in designing your seed mix will help determine the success of your prairie restoration for years to come.

Table 9.2.

Seed Mix for Short-Prairie Planting (10,000 square feet of dry sandy soil)

Forbs	Common Name	% of Mix	# Seeds Needed	Seeds/Gram	# Grams	Seeds/Sq Ft
Amorpha canescens	lead plant	1	5,000	600	8.33	0.50
Anemone cylindrica	thimbleweed	1	5,000	530	9.43	0.50
Asclepias tuberosa	butterfly weed	1	5,000	110	45.45	0.50
Asclepias verticillata	whorled milkweed	1	5,000	350	14.29	0.50
Aster ericoides	heath aster	1	5,000	4,900	1.02	0.50
Aster laevis	smooth blue aster	2	10,000	1,600	6.25	1.00
†*Aster oolentangiensis*	azure aster	3	15,000	2,800	5.36	1.50
Astragalus canadensis	Canadian milk vetch	2	10,000	600	16.67	1.00
Campanula rotundifolia	harebell	2	10,000	28,200	0.35	1.00
†*Dalea candida*	white prairie clover	2	10,000	15,900	0.63	1.00
†*Dalea purpurea*	purple prairie clover	3	15,000	700	21.43	1.50
Echinacea pallida	pale purple coneflower	2	10,000	180	55.56	1.00
Euphorbia corollata	flowering spurge	2	10,000	10,000	1.00	1.00
Helianthus occidentalis	western sunflower	1	5,000	450	11.11	0.50
†*H. paucifloris*	showy sunflower	1	5,000	160	31.25	0.50
Lespedeza capitata	round-headed bush clover	2	10,000	350	28.57	1.00
Liatris aspera	rough blazing star	3	15,000	480	31.25	1.50
Lupinus perennis occidentalis★	lupine	1	5,000	40	125.00	0.50
Monarda punctata	spotted bee balm	3	15,000	3,300	4.55	1.50
Penstemon grandiflorus	large-flowered beard tongue	3	15,000	388	38.66	1.50
Ranunculus rhomboideus	prairie buttercup	2	10,000	990	10.10	1.00
Rudbeckia hirta	black-eyed Susan	4	20,000	3,530	5.67	2.00

	Common Name	% of Mix	# Seeds Needed	Seeds/Gram	# Grams	Seeds/Sq Ft
Ruellia humilis	hairy ruellia	1	5,000	150	33.33	0.50
Solidago nemoralis	old-field goldenrod	1	5,000	8,500	0.59	0.50
†*Solidago ptarmicoides*	white upland aster	2	10,000	2,400	4.17	1.00
Solidago rigida	stiff goldenrod	3	15,000	1,600	9.38	1.50
Solidago speciosa	showy goldenrod	4	20,000	3,700	5.41	2.00
Tradescantia ohiensis	common spiderwort	3	15,000	280	53.57	1.50
Verbena stricta	hoary vervain	3	15,000	1,130	13.27	1.50
29 Total Forbs		60	300,000		591.64	30.00

Grasses	Common Name	% of Mix	# Seeds Needed	Seeds/Gram	# Grams	Seeds/Sq Ft
Bouteloua curtipendula	side-oats grama	10	50,000	280	178.57	5.00
†*Koeleria macrantha*	June grass	5	25,000	1000	25.00	2.50
†*Schizachyrium scoparium*	little bluestem	15	75,000	310	241.62	7.50
Sporobolus heterolepis	prairie dropseed	10	50,000	500	100.00	5.00
4 Total Grasses		40	200,000		545.19	20.00
33 Total Forbs and Grasses		100	500,000		1,136.83	50.00

†Precedes scientific names cross-references in Appendix C.

*Indicates nomenclature differs from Kartesz.

Table 9.3.

Seed Mix for Tall-Prairie Planting (10,000 square feet of mesic soil)

Forbs	Common Name	% of Mix	# Seeds Needed	Seeds/Gram	# Grams	Seeds/Sq Ft
Allium cernuum	nodding wild onion	2	10,000	270	37.04	1.00
Amorpha canescens	lead plant	1	5,000	600	8.34	0.50
Aster laevis	smooth blue aster	3	15,000	1,700	8.82	1.50
Aster novae-angliae	New England aster	3	15,000	2,400	6.25	1.50
†*Aster oolentangiensis*	azure aster	3	15,000	2,900	5.17	1.50
Astragalus canadensis	Canadian milk vetch	3	15,000	560	26.79	1.50
†*Baptisia alba macrophylla*	white wild indigo	0.5	2,500	60	41.67	0.25
†*Baptisia bracteata leucophaea*	cream wild indigo	0.5	2,500	60	41.69	0.25
†*Dalea purpurea*	purple prairie clover	3	15,000	700	21.43	1.50
Desmodium canadense	showy tick trefoil	0.5	2,500	160	15.63	0.25
Echinacea pallida	pale purple coneflower	3	15,000	180	83.33	1.50
Echinacea purpurea	purple coneflower	2	10,000	230	43.48	1.00
Eryngium yuccifolium	rattlesnake master	2	10,000	280	35.71	1.00
†*Helianthus pauciflorus*	showy sunflower	0.5	2,500	160	15.63	0.25
Heliopsis helianthoides	false sunflower	2	10,000	230	43.48	1.00
Lespedeza capitata	round-headed bush clover	2	10,000	350	28.57	1.00
Liatris pycnostachya	prairie blazing star	4	20,000	420	47.62	2.00
Monarda fistulosa	wild bergamot	3	15,000	2,750	5.45	1.50
Parthenium integrifolium	wild quinine	1	5,000	240	20.85	0.50
Penstemon digitalis	foxglove beard tongue	4	20,000	3,530	5.67	2.00
Ratibida pinnata	grey-headed coneflower	4	20,000	950	21.05	2.00
Rudbeckia hirta	black-eyed Susan	4	20,000	3,530	5.67	2.00

	Common Name	% of Mix	# Seeds Needed	Seeds/Gram	# Grams	Seeds/Sq Ft
Rudbeckia subtomentosa	sweet black–eyed Susan	1	5,000	1,620	3.09	0.50
Silphium integrifolium	rosinweed	0.5	2,500	140	17.86	0.25
Silphium laciniatum	compass plant	0.5	2,500	25	100.00	0.25
Solidago rigida	stiff goldenrod	2	10,000	1,620	6.17	1.00
Solidago speciosa	showy goldenrod	3	15,000	3,700	4.05	1.50
Zizia aptera	heart-leaved meadow parsnip	2	10,000	320	31.25	1.00
28 Total Forbs		60	300,000		731.74	30.00
Grasses	Common Name	% of Mix	# Seeds Needed	Seeds/Gram	# Grams	Seeds/Sq Ft
Andropogon gerardii	big bluestem	4	20000	290	68.97	2.00
Elymus canadensis	Canada wild rye	7	35000	150	233.33	3.50
†*Schizachyrium scoparium*	little bluestem	12	60000	310	193.55	6.00
Sorghastrum nutans	Indian grass	10	50000	300	166.67	5.00
Sporobolus heterolepis	prairie dropseed	7	35000	490	71.43	3.50
5 Total Grasses		40	200,000		733.94	20.00
33 Total Forbs and Grasses		100	500,000		1465.69	50.00

†Precedes scientific names cross–referenced in appendix C.

Table 9.4.

Seed Mix for Wet-Prairie Planting (10,000 square feet)

Forbs	Common Name	% of Mix	# Seeds Needed	Seeds/Gram	# Grams	Seeds/Sq Ft
Angelica atropurpurea	great angelica	2.00	10,000	230	43.5	1.00
†Arnoglossum atriplicifolia	pale Indian plantain	2.00	10,000	225	44.4	1.00
Asclepias incarnata	swamp milkweed	2.00	10,000	155	64.5	1.00
Aster novae-angliae	New England aster	3.00	15,000	2,400	6.3	1.50
Aster puniceus	bristly aster	3.00	15,000	2,800	5.4	1.50
†Cassia hebecarpa	wild senna	0.50	2,500	50	50.0	0.25
Coreopsis tripteris	tall coreopsis	0.25	1,250	400	3.1	0.13
Eupatorium maculatum	spotted Joe-Pye weed	3.00	15,000	3,000	10.0	1.50
Eupatorium perfoliatum	common boneset	3.00	15,000	7,000	4.2	1.50
Gentiana andrewsii	closed gentian	x	(280,000)	28,000	(10.0)	
Helianthus giganteus	tall sunflower	0.25	1,250	380	3.3	0.13
Helianthus grosseserratus	sawtooth sunflower	0.25	1,250	480	2.6	0.13
†Heracleum maximum	cow parsnip	0.50	2,500	85	29.4	0.25
†Hypericum ascyron	great St. John's wort	3.00	15,000	7,700	3.0	1.50
Iris virginica shrevei	blue flag iris	1.00	5,000	50	100.0	0.50
Liatris pycnostachya	prairie blazing star	4.00	20,000	420	47.6	2.00
Liatris spicata	marsh blazing star	4.00	20,000	420	47.6	2.00
Lilium superbum	Turk's cap lily	0.50	2,500	240	10.4	0.25
Lobelia cardinalis	cardinal flower	5.00	25,000	10,000	5.0	2.50
Lobelia siphilitica	great blue lobelia	5.00	25,000	16,000	3.0	2.50
Monarda fistulosa	wild bergamot	1.00	5,000	2,700	4.5	0.50
Physostegia virginiana	obedient plant	1.00	5,000	440	11.4	0.50
Rudbeckia laciniata	golden glow	2.00	10,000	520	19.2	1.00

Scientific Name	Common Name	% of Mix	# Seeds Needed	Seeds/Gram	# Grams	Seeds/Sq Ft
Rudbeckia subtomentosa	sweet black-eyed Susan	2.00	10,000	1,600	6.3	1.00
Rudbeckia triloba	brown-eyed Susan	1.00	5,000	1,100	4.5	0.50
Silphium perfoliatum	cup plant	0.25	1,250	50	25.0	0.13
Silphium terebinthinaceum	prairie dock	0.50	2,500	40	62.5	0.25
Thalictrum dasycarpum	purple meadow rue	2.00	10,000	490	20.4	1.00
Verbena hastata	blue vervain	3.00	15,000	3,500	5.8	1.50
Vernonia fasciculata	common ironweed	2.00	10,000	700	14.3	1.00
Veronicastrum virginicum	Culver's root	x	(260,000)	26,000	(10.0)	
Zizia aurea	golden Alexanders	3.00	15,000	420	35.7	1.50
32 Total Forbs		60.00	300,000		692.9	30.00

Grasses & Sedges	Common Name	% of Mix	# Seeds Needed	Seeds/Gram	# Grams	Seeds/Sq Ft
Andropogon gerardii	big bluestem	6.00	30,000	285	105.3	3.00
Calamagrostis canadensis	blue joint grass	14.00	70,000	5,000	14.0	7.00
Carex bicknellii	prairie sedge	2.00	10,000	1,234	8.1	1.00
Carex prairea	fen panicled sedge	3.00	15,000	3,527	4.3	1.50
Carex scoparia	pointed broom sedge	3.00	15,000	4,233	3.5	1.50
Elymus canadensis	Canada wild rye	5.00	25,000	145	172.4	2.50
Panicum virgatum	switch grass	2.00	10,000	635	15.7	1.00
Spartina pectinata	prairie cord grass	5.00	25,000	140	178.6	2.50
8 Total Grasses and Sedges		40.00	200,000		501.9	20.00
40 Total Forbs, Grasses, and Sedges		100.00	500,000		1,194.8	50.00

x Denotes species that will be successively planted in the fall of the second or third year.

† Precedes scientific names cross-references in Appendix C.

10
Seed Treatment and Propagation Methods

James F. Steffen

Restorationists who grow their own plants learn quickly that different species have different germination requirements. This chapter will outline some of the different processes used to propagate prairie, savanna, and woodland species. In general, seeds must be encouraged to imbibe water, be exposed to proper temperatures, and have proper ventilation and adequate time in order to transform themselves into living plants. The processes discussed here include: 1) sowing fresh seed, 2) cold-moist stratification, 3) warm-moist stratification, 4) cold-dry stratification, 5) scarification, 6) inoculation, 7) providing hosts for parasitic species, 8) light treatment, and 9) no treatment. Vegetative propagation is also briefly discussed. Table 10.1, following the text, gives the appropriate germination treatment for a wide range of prairie and savanna species, using the abbreviations for methods from the following paragraphs.

Sowing fresh seed (FR). This method works well for most spring-flowering species, such as rue anemone and bloodroot. The seeds are sown in plug trays or flats immediately after collection. They should be lightly covered with vermiculite or, for those species requiring light to germinate or for very small-seeded species, left uncovered. However, lightly covering seed with vermiculite, which transmits light and helps maintain soil moisture, may benefit all species. Flats should be placed outdoors in the shade and kept evenly moist until the seeds germinate. Covering flats with window screen will help disperse water and prevent seeds from washing out of the flats. Although some species will germinate in a few weeks, others will wait until the following spring. Regardless of the germination rate of its contents, each tray should be kept outside over winter and protected against rapid freeze-thaw cycles. At the Chicago Botanic Garden, the flats are kept in 12-by-36-foot, unheated, plastic-covered Quonset huts. Another method involves covering the flats with a tarp and then a layer of leaf or bark mulch. Be aware, however, that mulches often attract seed-loving rodents. If mulch is used, I recommend setting traps and covering palatable seed flats with ¼-inch-mesh hardware cloth. Seedlings produced in this manner can be moved to heated greenhouses at any time after germination or left in place until after the last frost date in the spring.

Cold-moist stratification (CM). Seeds are mixed with damp (not wet) builder's sand, vermiculite, or old sawdust (fresh sawdust may contain toxic compounds) at a ratio of 1:1 or 2:1 stratifying material to seed (Hartman and Kester 1983). Use a ratio of 3:1 when stratifying asters, liatris, and goldenrods that have the pappus left on. The mixture is then placed in ziplock bags and stored in a refrigerator or other location where a temperature of 34–40° F can be maintained. Make sure the seed and stratifying materials are loosely packaged so the seed can obtain oxygen. Species differ in the length of time they require to stratify—some need as little as 10 days, others require 120 days. For most species 60 to 90 days is typical. While some species will germinate only after being moved to warmer conditions, most species will germinate at low (stratification) temperatures—check bags periodically for radicle (root) emergence and plant sprouted seeds as soon as possible.

After stratification, the seeds are placed in plug trays or flats in a heated greenhouse. If a greenhouse is not available, flats can be placed in a cold frame or directly outside if temperatures are warm enough. Seed sowing can take place in early spring (early April in Chicago) if a greenhouse is used; otherwise, mid-spring (early May in Chicago) is suitable for outdoor sowing. When flats are placed outside, they should be protected with window screening to prevent seeds from washing away in heavy rains. Species that require stratification can also be sown directly in the field during the fall.

Warm-moist stratification (WM). Species that do not respond to simple stratification may possess more complex dormancies. Species with double dormancy, those possessing both a seed coat dormancy and some type of morphological or internal dormancy, require two treatments such as scarification followed by cold-damp stratification. Another way of treating the seed of these species is with warm-moist stratification (68°F to 75°F) followed by cold-moist stratification (WM/CM). Meanwhile, those species that have different temperature requirements for different parts of the developing embryo (epicotyl dormancy) require a strategy of alternating cold-moist/warm-moist/cold-moist treatments (CM/WM/CM). Approximately three months should be allowed for each of the temperature periods. After these treatments, the seeds are sown as described in the section on cold-moist stratification.

Cold-dry stratification (CD). Cold-dry stratification is commonly used to prepare prairie seed for spring planting with a seed drill. However, it also works on some woodland seed. The procedure is fairly simple. Dried seed is placed in plastic or paper bags and then refrigerated at 34–40° F until planting. They can also be placed outside in an unheated, insect- and rodent-free building or container over winter. This treatment is often used for diverse seed mixes. But, because this is not a moist treatment, any species that requires damp stratification may remain dormant until it goes through a winter season.

Scarification (SC). Scarification is the process by which the seed coats of certain species are physically broken, thereby allowing the embryo to imbibe water. The seed coat can be scarified by using sandpaper attached to sanding blocks or by rotating seeds inside cans lined with sandpaper. Seeds with very thick seed coats must be scarified with concentrated sulfuric or nitric acid. This procedure mimics the conditions the seed might encounter while traveling through the digestive tract of a bird or mammal. Dry seed is placed in a dry glass or ceramic container and covered with twice the volume of acid. The mixture is stirred occasionally with a glass rod. Workers should wear protective clothing and goggles when performing this operation, and the work space should be well ventilated. Although Dirr and Heuser (1987) list prescribed soaking times for many species, it is necessary to examine the seed periodically to check seed coat thickness. Remove a sample, rinse with cold water for five or ten minutes, and then cut the seed in half to examine the seed coat thickness. When the seed coat has been removed or nearly removed, decant the acid and seeds through a screen and rinse thoroughly with water for five or ten minutes. The seed is then ready to sow or stratify unless it needs other treatments for additional dormancy mechanisms.

Still other species must be soaked in hot water (170–190° F) to break down their waxy cuticle. The water is heated to the proper temperature and removed from the heat; the seed is then added and allowed to soak for six to twenty-four hours. The degree of imbibition can be determined by the amount of swelling. Once a seed is fully imbibed, it should never be fully dried again. It can be partially dried, however, to avoid clumping when planted. Some species may require a shorter soaking time followed by a period of stratification.

Inoculation (IN). The growth of all legumes will be enhanced by inoculating them with nitrogen-fixing bacteria. In most cases the inoculant is applied to wet seed just prior to sowing. Although water is generally used to wet the seed, some propagators use soda pop because its stickiness helps the inoculant adhere to the seed.

Hosts for Parasitic Species (PA). Some species are parasitic or semiparasitic. For these species it is necessary to either sow their seed along with the seed of a host species or transplant seedlings into pots containing host species. Another method requires making 2-inch-deep cuts in the soil at the base of the host plant with a knife and then sowing seed in the cuts, making sure it is not more than ⅜ inch deep (Wade 1995). This latter method apparently takes advantage of the fact that the seed of some parasitic species, such as clustered broom rape, will germinate in response to substances exuded from the roots of the host. Injuring the roots may expedite the release of such exudates.

Light treatment (Light). Some seeds that are very small (*Lobeliaceae*) or that require light to break dormancy (sedges) should not be covered with soil when sown. Seed should be sown on top of a smooth, firm seedbed and kept moist until germination occurs.

No treatment (None). This no-action method refers to those species that do not require any treatment to germinate. Seed should germinate as soon as sown in a warm, moist location. This differs from "sowing fresh seed," described above, in which some seeds, especially the short-lived seed of the spring-ripening ephemerals, will lose viability, or go dormant (for example, sedges) if not planted immediately. The species requiring no treatment can be planted immediately or the following season with little effect on viability or dormancy.

Vegetative (Veg). Asexual propagation is an alternative method for propagating species that rarely produce viable seed (rhizomatous sedges), are difficult to germinate from seed (puccoons), or have long seedling periods (*Liliaceae*). These vegetative methods include root, rhizome, and shoot cuttings and use of bulb scales. Many prairie and savanna species can be easily propagated by vegetative means. Dividing plants works well for shooting star, wild geranium, blue flag iris, prairie smoke, violets, prairie blue-eyed grass, and many woodland species. Rhizomes of sedges, prairie cord grass, prairie coreopsis, and heath aster will produce new plants. Puccoon propagates readily from root cuttings. You can propagate many species of lilies by planting their bulb scales. Vegetative propagation provides a means of propagating species that have seeds that are hard to collect or difficult to germinate. However, it restricts genetic diversity, is slow and labor-intensive, and may injure roots and lead to disease. I advise using a rooting hormone with fungicide to encourage rooting and prevent rot.

Table 10.1.

Species	Common Name	Treatment	Comments
Acorus calamus	sweet flag	CM	
Actaea pachypoda	white baneberry	CM	Remove flesh
Actaea rubra	red baneberry	CM	Remove flesh
Agastache spp.	giant hyssops	CM	
†*Ageratina altissima*	white snakeroot	CM	Light
Agrostis spp.	bent grasses	CD	
Aletris farinosa	colic root	CM	
Allium spp.	onions	CM	
†*Ambrosia coronopifolia*	western ragweed	None	
Amorpha canescens	lead plant	CM,IN	Short CM storage, 10 days
Amorpha fruticosa	indigo bush	CM	
Amphicarpaea bracteata	hog peanut	CD,SC,IN	Sandpaper
Andropogon gerardii	big bluestem	CM	
Anemone spp.	anemones	CM	See exception below
Anemone quinquefolia	wood anemone	FR	
Antennaria spp.	pussy toes	CM	
Apocynum spp.	dogbanes	CM	
Aquilegia canadensis	columbine	CM	
Arabis spp.	rock cresses	CM	See exceptions below
Arabis canadensis	sickle pod	FR	
Arabis lyrata	sand cress	FR	Light
Arenaria spp.	sandworts	CM	
†*Arisaema triphyllum*	Jack-in-the-pulpit	WM/CM or CM/ WM/CM	
Aristida basiramea	fork-tipped three-awn grass	None	
†*Arnoglossum* spp.	Indian plantains	CD or CM	
Artemisia spp.	sages	CD	Light
Asclepias spp.	milkweeds	CM	See exception below
Asclepias verticillata	whorled milkweed	CD	
Aster spp.	asters	CM	See exceptions below
Aster drummondii	Drummond's aster	CD	
Aster ericoides	heath aster	CD	

†Precedes scientific names cross-referenced in appendix C.

continues

Table 10.1. (*Continued*)

Species	Common Name	Treatment	Comments
Aster laevis	smooth blue aster	CD	
Aster lateriflorus	side–flowering aster	CD	
Aster oblongifolius	aromatic aster	CD	
†*Aster oolentangiensis*	azure aster	CD	
Astragalus canadensis	Canadian milk vetch	CM	Short CM storage, 10 days
Aureolaria spp.	false foxgloves	CM,PA	Oak hosts
Baptisia spp.	wild indigos	CM,SC,IN	Short CM storage, 10 days; sandpaper
†*Besseya bullii*	kitten tails	CM	Long CM storage, 120 days
Blephilia ciliata	Ohio horse mint	CM	
†*Boltonia asteroides*	false aster	CM	
Bouteloua spp.	grama grasses	CD	
Brachyelytrum erectum	long-awned wood grass	CD	
†*Brickellia eupatorioides*	false boneset	CD	
Bromus spp.	brome grasses	CM	See exception below
Bromus kalmii	prairie brome	CD	
Calamagrostis canadensis	blue joint grass	CD	
Callirhoe triangulata	clustered puppy mallow	CM	
†*Calopogon tuberosus*	grass pink	None	
Calystegia spp.	bindweeds	CD	
Camassia scilloides	wild hyacinth	CM	
Campanula spp.	bellflowers	CM	Light
Cardamine spp.	bitter cresses	CM	
Carex spp.	sedges	FR	Light; see exception below
Carex bicknellii	prairie sedge	CM	
Castilleja spp.	Indian paintbrushes	CM,PA	Various herbaceous hosts
†*Caulophyllum giganteum*	blue cohosh	FR or WM/CM or CM/WM/CM	
Ceanothus americanus	New Jersey tea	SC,CM	Hot water (170° F)
Cephalanthus occidentalis	buttonbush	CD	
†*Chamaecrista fasciculata*	partridge pea	CM,SC,IN	Sandpaper

†Precedes scientific names cross-referenced in appendix C.

Table 10.1. (*Continued*)

Species	Common Name	Treatment	Comments
Chelone glabra	turtlehead	CM	
Cicuta maculata	water hemlock	CM	
Cinna arundinacea	common wood reed	CM	
Cirsium spp.	thistles	CM	
Claytonia virginica	spring beauty	None or FR	
†*Comandra umbellata*	false toadflax	None, PA	Various herbaceous hosts
Coreopsis spp.	coreopsis	CM	
Dalea spp.	prairie clovers	SC,CD,IN	Acid
Danthonia spicata	poverty oat grass	CM	
Delphinium carolinianum ssp. *virescens*	prairie larkspur	CD or CM	Seed germinates on cool soil
Desmodium spp.	tick trefoils	CD,SC,IN	Sandpaper
Diarrhena americana	beak grass	CM	
Dodecatheon meadia	shooting star	CM or Veg	Short CM storage, 21 days; Division
Draba reptans	common whitlow grass	FR	Light
Dryopteris spp.	wood ferns	Veg	Division
Echinacea spp.	coneflowers	CM	
Eleocharis spp.	spike rushes	None	
Elymus spp.	wild ryes, wheat grasses	CD or CM	
†*Elymus trachycaulus*	slender wheat grass	CD	
†*Enemion biternatum*	false rue anemone	FR	
Equisetum spp.	scouring rushes	Veg	Division
Eragrostis spectabilis	purple love grass	None	
Erigeron spp.	fleabanes	CD	See exception below
Erigeron pulchellus	Robin's plantain	CM	
Eryngium yuccifolium	rattlesnake master	CM	
Eupatorium spp.	bonesets	CD	Light; see exceptions below
Eupatorium altissimum	tall boneset	CM	Light
Euphorbia corollata	flowering spurge	CM	
†*Festuca subverticillata*	nodding fescue	CD or CM	
Filipendula rubra	queen of the prairie	CM	
Fragaria virginiana	wild strawberry	CD	
Galium spp.	bedstraws	None	
Gaura biennis	biennial gaura	CM	
Gentiana spp.	gentians	CM	Light

continues

Table 10.1. (*Continued*)

Species	Common Name	Treatment	Comments
Geranium spp.	geraniums	CM	
Geum spp.	avens	FR	
Glyceria spp.	manna grasses	CD or CM	
Hedeoma hispida	rough pennyroyal	None	
Helenium autumnale	sneezeweed	CD	
Helianthemum spp.	rockroses	CM	
Helianthus spp.	sunflowers	CD	
Heliopsis helianthoides	false sunflower	CM or CD	
Heuchera richardsonii	prairie alum root	CM or CD	Light
Hieracium spp.	hawkweeds	CM	
Hierochloe odorata	sweet grass	CD	
Houstonia spp.	bluets	CD	
Hypericum spp.	St. John's worts	CM	
Hypoxis hirsuta	yellow star grass	CM	
†*Ionactis linariifolius*	flax-leaved aster	CD	
Iris virginica shrevei	blue flag iris	CM	
Juncus spp.	rushes	FR or CM	Light
†*Koeleria macrantha*	June grass	CD or CM	
Krigia spp.	dandelions	FR	
Lactuca spp.	wild lettuces	CM	
Lathyrus spp.	vetchlings	CD,SC,IN	Sandpaper
Leersia virginica	white grass	CM	
Lespedeza spp.	bush clovers	SC,CM,IN	Short CM storage, 10 days; acid
Liatris spp.	blazing stars	CM	
Lilium spp.	lilies	WM/CM or FR	
Linum sulcatum	grooved yellow flax	CD	
Lithospermum spp.	puccoons	CM or Veg	SC may help, root cuttings
Lobelia spp.	lobelias	CM	Light
Lupinus perennis occidentalis★	wild lupine	SC,CM,IN	Short CM storage, 10 days; sandpaper
Luzula multiflora	wood rush	FR	
Lycopus spp.	water horehounds	CD	
Lysimachia spp.	loosestrifes	CM	
Lythrum alatum	winged loosestrife	CM	
†*Maianthemum* spp.	false Solomon's seals	CM/WM/CM or WM/CM/Veg	Root cuttings or division
Mimulus ringens	monkey flower	CM	

†Precedes scientific names cross-referenced in appendix C.

★Indicates nomenclature differs from Kartesz.

Table 10.1. (*Continued*)

Species	Common Name	Treatment	Comments
Monarda spp.	bee balms	CD	
Muhlenbergia spp.	satin grasses	CD	
†*Nothocalais cuspidata*	prairie dandelion	CM	
†*Nuttallanthus canadensis*	blue toadflax	CD	
Oenothera spp.	evening primroses	CD	
Onosmodium molle hispidissimum	marbleseed	CM	SC may help
Opuntia spp.	prickly pears	CD or Veg	Stem cuttings
Orbexilum spp.	French grass	CM,SC,IN	
Orobanche spp.	broom rapes	FR,PA	Oak hosts
Oryzopsis racemosa	black-seeded rice grass	CD or CM	
Oxalis violacea	violet wood sorrel	CM or Veg	Bulbs
Oxypolis rigidior	cowbane	None	
Panicum spp.	panic grasses	CD	FR for some
Parnassia glauca	grass of Parnassus	CM	
Parthenium integrifolium	wild quinine	CM	
Pedicularis spp.	louseworts	CM,PA	Short storage, 30 days; several herbaceous hosts
Pediomelum spp.	prairie turnips	CM,SC,IN	
Penstemon spp.	beard tongues	CM	Short CM storage, 30 days
Perideridia americana	thicket parsley	CM	
Phlox spp.	phlox	FR or CM	
Phryma leptostachya	lopseed	CM	
Physalis spp.	ground cherries	CM	
Physostegia virginiana	obedient plant	CM	
Poa spp.	bluegrasses	CM	
Polemonium reptans	Jacob's ladder	CM	
Polygala senega	Seneca snakeroot	CM	
Polygonatum spp.	Solomon's seals	WM/CM or CM/WM/ CM	
Potentilla spp.	cinquefoils	CM	
Prenanthes spp.	white lettuces	CM	
Psoralidium spp.	scurfy peas	SC,CM	Short CM storage, 10 days; sandpaper
Pteridium aquilinum	bracken fern	Veg	Spores, division
Pycnanthemum spp.	mountain mints	CD	

continues

Table 10.1. (*Continued*)

Species	Common Name	Treatment	Comments
Ranunculus spp.	buttercups	FR	
Ratibida spp.	coneflowers	CM or CD	
Rosa spp.	roses	SC/CM	Sandpaper; double dormancy
Rudbeckia spp.	black-eyed Susans	CM or CD	
Ruellia humilis	hairy ruellia	CM	
Rumex verticillatus	swamp dock	CM	
Salix humilis	prairie willow	FR or Veg	Root cuttings
†*Samolus valerandi* ssp. *parviflorus*	water pimpernel	CM	
Sanguinaria canadensis	bloodroot	FR or Veg	Root cuttings; double dormancy
Saxifraga pensylvanica	swamp saxifrage	CM	Light
†*Schizachyrium scoparium*	little bluestem	CM	
Scirpus spp.	bulrushes	FR	Light
Scleria triglomerata	tall nut rush	None	
Scutellaria spp.	skullcaps	CM or None	
Senecio spp.	ragworts	CM	
Silene spp.	campions	CM	
Silphium spp.	rosinweeds	CM	
Sisyrinchium spp.	blue-eyed grasses	CM	Seed germinates on cool soil
Sium suave	water parsnip	CM	
Solidago spp.	goldenrods	CM	
†*Solidago ptarmicoides*	stiff aster	CD	
Sorghastrum nutans	Indian grass	CD	
Spartina pectinata	prairie cord grass	CD	Natural low viability
Sphenopholis intermedia	slender wedge grass	CD or FR	
Spiraea spp.	spiraeas	CM	
Sporobolus spp.	dropseeds	CD or CM	
Stachys palustris	woundwort	CM	
Stipa spp.	needle grasses	CD or CM	
Taenidia integerrima	yellow pimpernel	CM	
Tephrosia virginiana	goat's rue	SC,CM,IN	Short CM storage, 10 days; sandpaper
Teucrium canadense	germander	CM	

continues

Table 10.1. (*Continued*)

Species	Common Name	Treatment	Comments
Thalictrum spp.	meadow rues	CM	
†*Thalictrum thalictroides*	rue anemone	FR	
Thaspium trifoliatum aureum	meadow parsnip	CM	
Tofieldia glutinosa	false asphodel	CM	
Tradescantia ohiensis	common spiderwort	CM	
†*Trichostema brachiatum*	false pennyroyal	None	
Triglochin maritimum	common bog arrow grass	CM	
Trillium spp.	trilliums	FR or CM/ WM/CM or WM/CM	
†*Triodanis perfoliata*	Venus' looking glass	CM	
Valeriana edulis ciliata	common valerian	FR	
Verbena spp.	vervains	CM or CD	
Vernonia spp.	ironweeds	CM or CD	
Veronica scutellata	marsh speedwell	FR or None	
Veronicastrum virginicum	Culver's root	CD	Light
Vicia spp.	vetches	SC,CD,IN	Sandpaper
Viola spp.	violets	CM or FR	Light
Zigadenus elegans	plains white camass	CM or Veg	
Zizia spp.	golden Alexanders	CM	Long CM storage, 120 days

†Precedes scientific names cross-referenced in appendix C.

REFERENCES

Bader, B. J. 1992. *Native Plant Propagation*. Madison: University of Wisconsin–Madison Arboretum. Unpublished.

Dirr, M., and C. Heuser. 1987. *The Reference Manual of Woody Plant Propagation*. Athens, GA: Varsity Press.

Greene, H.C., and J.T. Curtis. 1950. "Germination Studies of Wisconsin Prairie Plants." *American Midland Naturalist* 43:186–194.

Hartman, H. T., and D. E. Kester. 1983. *Plant Propagation*. Englewood Cliffs, NJ: Prentice-Hall.

Rock, H. W. 1977. *Prairie Propagation Handbook*. Wehr Nature Center, Whitnall Park, Hales Corners, WI: Milwaukee Co. Park System.

Smith, J. R. 1980. *The Prairie Garden*. Madison: University of Wisconsin Press.

Sullivan, G. A., and R. H. Daley. 1981. *Directory to Resources on Wildflower Propagation.* St. Louis, MO: National Council of State Garden Clubs, Inc., Missouri Botanical Garden.

Wade, Alan. 1995. Prairie Moon Nursery catalog and cultural guide. Winona, MN: Self-published.

11
Interseeding

Stephen Packard

Both gardeners and farmers normally plant seed into bare ground. However, the seeds of prairie and woodland species most often take root not on bare soil but among other established plants. Their ability to do this is the key to the restoration technique called interseeding, in which seed is sowed directly into an existing turf. Interseeding is a good way to restore remnants—for even in poor-quality remnants, the turf of existing vegetation is often a better starting place for seeds than tilled earth. Interseeding thus provides an alternative to the plowed-ground restoration techniques discussed in chapter 12.

Interseeding's primary benefit may be the relative ease with which it restores many conservative species and thus dramatically improves a site's quality and its potential contribution to biodiversity conservation. The conservative species, when restored using the techniques described in this chapter, should eventually outcompete most weedy native and non-native species that have invaded a disrupted community (see figure 11.1).

Interseeding reportedly was one of the techniques used in the early years of the very first prairie restoration at the University of Wisconsin Arboretum, but it has never been systematically studied and has been relatively little used until recent years. However, it is now increasingly replacing the plow in certain situations. It is a good approach for old pastures, steep slopes, and oak savannas, where plowing would destroy the native biota already present, cause erosion, or damage the roots of trees. Planting without plowing capitalizes on the existing diversity of the system; thus it can help avoid the takeover of a site by aggressive prairie or other species.

Most of the following discussion is directed at interseeding that introduces a rich mix of hard-to-get conservative seed into fair-quality sites.

Figure 11.1. Species succession with interseeding.

First summer. The old-field turf looks as it did before the planting. Interseeded plants are nearly invisible (⅛ to ½ inch high). The predominant exotic species, such as timothy, bluegrass, and daisy, are drawn with hatched lines.

Third summer. The original species are still dominant, although some exotics are much reduced in size. Interseeded species are mostly 2 to 6 inches tall. Original natives, such as early goldenrod, have increased at the expense of the fire-sensitive exotics.

Sixth summer. Exotics are almost gone. The nonconservative natives survive in reduced numbers and size. Seeded conservatives such as purple prairie clover, prairie dropseed, and rattlesnake master clearly dominate. Some slow-growing conservative species including lead plant, shooting star, and cream wild indigo will flower in two to four more years.

However, it is also possible, in fact rather easy, to restore an old field to a fair-quality prairie by, for example, interseeding a Eurasian-grass–dominated pasture with tall native grasses and a few aggressive and easily obtained forbs. If conservative seed is not obtainable, that approach may be desirable in some cases. For example, if a pasture that was acquired as conservation land is in danger of losing its turf to brush, it may be advisable to interseed the grasses. They will compete with the brush and provide fuel for fires, and the combination of burning and competition will keep the shrubs in check.

Although interseeding has been tested and used principally in degraded remnant prairies and woodlands, it can be used effectively in weedy but diverse, old weed fields and even in pure stands of aggressive non-native grasses such as smooth brome and quack grass. In this case not only burning but also mowing the existing vegetation may be necessary; strategic mowing for one to three years after planting keeps the existing turf from shading out the slow-growing young seedlings. Planted prairies that consist of over-dense stands of a few aggressive prairie species can be restored to higher quality in the same way.

In some habitats and for some species, seed may need to be added for two or even many years, since favorable conditions for seed-set, germination, and survival of certain species may not occur every year.

When planning for interseeding, consult chapter 4 to select a target community and a basic approach. Consult tables 11.1 and 11.2 to determine which species to include as you develop a site-specific seed mix. These tables generally will be applicable on sites with fertile soils in the central tallgrass region. For sandy, heavy clay, or other less fertile soils, for sites on the periphery of the tallgrass region, and for other special cases, a variety of related lists can be prepared by visiting sites with soils, hydrology, and openness of canopy that resemble the area to be interseeded. If no open canopy remnants can be located, possibly appropriate species for interseeding lists may by found surviving in (or at the edge of) artificial openings such as railroad, highway, or powerline rights-of-way, woodland or road edges, cemeteries, etc. Follow the steps summarized below and also consider the material at the end of the chapter on sand prairies, savannas, woodlands, and wetlands if it applies.

Evaluate the Ground

Some of the best land for interseeding is the open turf of a former pasture, often called an "old field." In many cases the structure of the vegetation is such that ample sunlight reaches the ground all summer long;

Table 11.1.

Interseeding Mixes for Prairie and Open Savanna

These planting lists, emphasizing conservatives, were designed for raking into an established turf of exotic grasses in the central tallgrass region. The mesic prairie turf (MPT) mix is used well away from trees. The mesic savanna turf (MST) mix is used near oaks.

Scientific Name	Common Name	MPT	MST
†*Agalinis auriculata*	eared false foxglove		x
Amorpha canescens	lead plant	x	x
Apocynum androsaemifolium	spreading dogbane		x
Arabis glabra	tower mustard		x
Aralia nudicaulis	wild sarsaparilla		x
†*Arnoglossum atriplicifolium*	pale Indian plantain		x
Asclepias purpurascens	purple milkweed		x
Asclepias tuberosa	butterfly weed	x	x
Aster laevis	smooth blue aster	x	x
†*Aster oolentangiensis*	azure aster	x	x
Astragalus canadensis	Canadian milk vetch		x
†*Aureolaria grandiflora*	yellow false-foxglove		x
†*Baptisia alba macrophylla*	white wild indigo		x
†*Baptisia bracteata leucophaea*	cream wild indigo	x	x
Bromus kalmii	prairie brome	x	x
Camassia scilloides	wild hyacinth		x
Ceanothus americanus	New Jersey tea	x	x
†*Comandra umbellata*	false toadflax	x	x
Coreopsis palmata	prairie coreopsis	x	
Coreopsis tripteris	tall coreopsis		x
†*Dalea candida*	white prairie clover	x	x
†*Dalea purpurea*	purple prairie clover	x	
†*Dasistoma macrophylla*	mullein foxglove		x
Desmodium canadense	showy tick trefoil		x
Desmodium illinoense	Illinois tick trefoil	x	
Dodecatheon meadia	shooting star	x	x
†*Elymus trachycaulus*	slender wheat grass		x
Erigeron pulchellus	Robin's plantain		x
Eryngium yuccifolium	rattlesnake master	x	
Euphorbia corollata	flowering spurge	x	x
Galium concinnum	shining bedstraw		x
†*Gentiana alba*	yellowish gentian		x
Gentiana puberulenta	downy gentian	x	
†*Gentianella quinquefolia*	stiff gentian	x	x
†*Helianthus pauciflorus*	showy sunflower	x	
Heuchera richardsonii	prairie alum root	x	x
Hieracium scabrum	rough hawkweed		x

†Precedes scientific names cross-referenced in appendix C.

Table 11.1. (*Continued*)

Scientific Name	Common Name	MPT	MST
Hypoxis hirsuta	yellow star grass	x	x
†*Koeleria macrantha*	June grass	x	
Krigia biflora	false dandelion	x	x
Lathyrus venosus	veiny pea		x
Lespedeza capitata	round-headed bush clover	x	x
Lespedeza violacea	violet bush clover		x
Liatris aspera	rough blazing star	x	
Liatris scariosa nieuwlandii	savanna blazing star		x
Lilium philadelphicum	prairie lily	x	x
Lithospermum canescens	hoary puccoon	x	x
Lobelia spicata	pale spiked lobelia	x	x
Luzula multiflora	wood rush		x
†*Moehringia lateriflora*	wood sandwort		x
Oenothera perennis	small sundrops		x
Oxalis violacea	violet wood sorrel	x	x
Panicum latifolium★	wide-leaved panic grass		x
Panicum leibergii★	prairie panic grass	x	
Parthenium integrifolium	wild quinine	x	x
Pedicularis canadensis	lousewort	x	x
Phlox pilosa fulgida	prairie phlox	x	x
Physostegia virginiana	obedient plant	x	x
Polemonium reptans	Jacob's ladder		x
Polygala senega	Seneca snakeroot	x	x
Potentilla arguta	prairie cinquefoil	x	x
Prenanthes aspera	rough white lettuce	x	
†*Schizachyrium scoparium*	little bluestem	x	x
Silphium integrifolium	rosinweed		x
Silphium laciniatum	compass plant	x	
Silphium terebinthinaceum	prairie dock	x	x
Sisyrinchium albidum	common blue-eyed grass	x	
Solidago speciosa	showy goldenrod		x
Sporobolus heterolepis	prairie dropseed	x	x
Stipa spartea	porcupine grass	x	
Taenidia integerrima	yellow pimpernel		x
Thaspium trifoliatum	meadow parsnip		x
Tradescantia ohiensis	common spiderwort	x	x
Veronicastrum virginicum	Culver's root	x	x
Vicia americana	American vetch		x
Viola pedatifida	prairie violet	x	x
Zizia aptera	heart-leaved meadow parsnip	x	
Zizia aurea	golden Alexanders	x	x

Note: This table was compiled by John and Jane Balaban and Stephen Packard.
★Indicates nomenclature differs from Kartesz.
†Precedes scientific name cross-referenced in appendix C.

seedlings of prairie species thrive in these conditions. These old fields are often dominated by exotic species such as Kentucky and Canada blue-grass, timothy, redtop, daisy, yarrow, and white or red clover, often mixed with the least conservative prairie species such as wild strawberry, black-eyed Susan, and various goldenrods and asters. In time these diverse grasslands degrade into brushlands, the grass frequently being replaced by tall goldenrod. It is best to catch these fields while the Eurasian grasses are still dominant. Many years may be necessary to restore a large area for which high-quality seed is in short supply. In such cases the old field may benefit from midsummer mowing, which reverses the advance of tall goldenrod and brush.

Certain highly aggressive species may be present in small numbers. Their numbers may expand dramatically once burning begins. On wet sites look particularly for reed canary grass, purple loosestrife, and teasel. On uplands watch for leafy spurge, common dewberry, and garlic mus-tard (in woodlands). These plants can become so dense that they exclude most other species. Infestations of these species should be mapped and completely eliminated before or as the restoration begins.

Rather aggressive Eurasian grasses may be so thick on some sites that by midsummer the ground layer becomes too dark for seedling survival. Such grasses may include meadow fescue, smooth brome, quack grass, and others. These areas will need mowing as described below.

Many restoration sites include former wetland areas that have been drained by ditches or subsurface drainage tiles. These may have altered the hydrology of adjacent uplands as well. If ditches or tiles can be removed to restore wetlands, that decision should be made and imple-mented before investing rare seed in the site.

In the case of a site containing oaks, the critical issue is flammability. Frequent fire is essential to the progress of the restoration. Grasses and oak leaves both carry fire well. In some areas brush may have killed off the grass but the overstory oaks are not dense enough to blanket the ground with sufficient leaf fuel to carry fire. These areas should be restored to savanna and open woodland, communities that are of high conservation priority. They should be mapped separately because they will require special efforts to restore flammability.

Prepare the Ground

Areas of sparse open turf need no preparation, although a burn wouldn't hurt.

If grass is dense enough to put the ground into deep shade during any part of the growing season, the site needs fire or mowing before planting. Several years of late spring fires will break down a dense Eurasian grass turf sufficiently for the survival of prairie seedlings. A single burn is often sufficient, especially if the sward is not too thick or if the planting can be mowed for the first year or two. If it is not possible to burn an area of dense dead thatch before a spring planting, it is sometimes possible to remove sufficient thatch by raking.

Some managers prefer to burn a site for several years before other restoration work begins, to determine whether any suppressed prairie plants will emerge on their own. This strategy may close an important window of opportunity for turf planting, since conservative prairie species can establish themselves particularly well in the weakened community that is present for only a few years after the resumption of burning. Burning breaks down the existing dominance patterns, and a new community structure begins to form. Within a few years, shrubs, briars, or fire-adapted herbs create new dominance patterns. Under these conditions, the prairie plantings may not compete as well. For this reason many managers start interseeding immediately after the first prescribed burn. They believe there is not sufficiently much to be gained by learning whether a reappearing species was planted or spontaneous, especially if seed can be gathered nearby. In cases where managers do desire to test for spontaneous recovery, it may be best to burn test plots. Thus, instead of burning the entire site, consider burning one or more test patches for two years to see if any hidden prairie species emerge. Then proceed with burning and interseeding the area to be restored.

Sow the Seed

Seed can be sown in spring or fall or as soon as ripe. It can be sown by hand or by machine. Stratification is not necessary if the seeds are planted in fall or early spring (which is very practical with interseeding because it involves no race with agricultural weeds). Stratification may be desirable with mid and late spring plantings. Immediately before sowing, the legumes should be inoculated. This stratification, inoculation, and other seed treatments are described in chapter 10.

Because interseeding often depends on very rare, precious seed, there are great ethical, practical, and financial incentives to get just the right amount of seed in just the right places, as described below.

Prepare as many separate mixes as there are distinct habitats on the area to be seeded. Some sophisticated restoration projects have used precisely targeted seed mixes modeled after the community composition lists in

John Curtis's classic, *The Vegetation of Wisconsin* (1959). Thus, rather than three prairie lists (wet, moist, and dry), restorationists divide the prairie spectrum into five (wet, wet-mesic, mesic, dry-mesic, and dry). Because less seed ends up in spots where it can't grow, such mixes make more efficient use of rare and costly seed, if the restorationist can recognize the corresponding substrate. Sample planting lists of this type for savanna and woodland are given in table 11.2. Precisely targeted mixes for all wetland and upland types of prairie and woodland can be constructed for any region. The best references for aiding this process are listed (by state and province) in appendix D.

Separate mixes should also be made if planting is to include communities such as deep marsh, rock outcrops, native shrub areas, and problem areas. Likely problem areas include those with difficult weed or brush infestations; often the solution here is to cut back on conservatives and go heavy on prairie aggressives. However, as we become more sophisticated at interseeding strategies, we may find that certain conservatives are particularly good at fighting certain weed or brush problems. The seed mixes can be as sophisticated as the managers' understanding of their sites or as simple as time and practicality demand. One solution to the complexity of getting started is to pick one or two high-priority types (say, mesic prairie or dry-mesic open woodland) and, for the first year, gather seeds for and burn and plant only those portions of the site.

How do you determine where to broadcast which mix? In time a careful observer can recognize communities of various types and qualities by a variety of clues. The easiest way to learn them initially is to memorize short lists of both dominant and characteristic species for each community (for example, wet prairie in a given area may have plentiful blue joint grass, iris, and swamp milkweed, while wet-mesic prairie may have big bluestem, prairie Indian plantain, and marsh blazing star). Such species may change from region to region. Local botanists are often the best sources of insight into local plant community composition. The best written sources of this information at the state and province level are listed in appendix D.

One little twist that makes community recognition more challenging is that the dried vegetation has often been burned off before the sowing. Normally the person in charge of sowing has walked the site repeatedly and carefully before and after the burn and can recognize the distribution of communities by features that survive burns such as streams, land topography, and paths.

Table 11.2.

Interseeding Mixes for Savanna and Woodland

These mixes were designed for sites in the central tallgrass region which lack existing turf, where brush control or the reintroduction of fire has opened the way for the reseeding of a moderately to severely degraded community. This list includes both pioneer and conservative species. Mixes are identified by initial letters indicating dry (D), mesic (M), or wet (W) habitats, with two such letters combined indicating intermediate conditions (e.g., "DM" indicates dry-mesic habitats). The last letter indicates whether the mix is for savanna (S), woodland (W), or open woodland (O). The open woodland mix is used in areas resembling the left half of the woodland drawing in figure 4.1.

Scientific Name	Common Name	DMS	MS	WMS	DMO	MO	WMO	WO	DMW	MW	WMW
Aconus calamus	sweet flag							x			
Actaea pachypoda	white baneberry									x	
†*Agalinis auriculata*	eared false foxglove		x	x							
†*Agalinis purpurea*	purple false foxglove		x	x			x				
†*Agalinis tenuifolia*	slender false foxglove		x	x			x				
Agastache nepetoides	yellow giant hyssop		x			x					
Agastache scrophulariifolia	purple giant hyssop		x			x					
Agrimonia parviflora	swamp agrimony			x							x
Agrimonia pubescens	soft agrimony					x					
Agrostis perennans	upland bent grass		x				x			x	
Alisma subcordatum	common water plantain							x			
Allium tricoccum	wild leek									x	
Amphicarpaea bracteata	hog peanut					x	x				x
Anemone canadensis	meadow anemone			x							
Anemone quinquefolia	wood anemone		x			x				x	
Anemone virginiana	tall anemone		x			x					x

†Precedes those scientific names cross-referenced in appendix C.

continues

Table 11.2. (Continued)

Scientific Name	Common Name	DMS	MS	WMS	DMO	MO	WMO	WO	DMW	MW	WMW
Antennaria plantaginifolia	pussy toes	x	x			x					
Apios americana	ground nut			x							
Apocynum androsaemifolium	spreading dogbane	x	x			x					
Apocynum sibiricum★	Indian hemp		x	x							
Aquilegia canadensis	columbine									x	
Arabis glabra	tower mustard		x			x					
Arabis laevigata	smooth bank cress					x				x	
Aralia nudicaulis	wild sarsaparilla		x			x				x	
Arisaema dracontium	green dragon									x	x
†Arisaema triphyllum	Jack-in-the-pulpit									x	x
†Arnoglossum atriplicifolium	pale Indian plantain		x	x		x					
Asclepias exaltata	poke milkweed					x			x	x	
Asclepias incarnata	swamp milkweed							x			
Asclepias purpurascens	purple milkweed		x			x					
Asclepias sullivantii	prairie milkweed			x							
Asclepias tuberosa	butterfly weed	x	x								
Aster furcatus	forked aster			x							x
Aster macrophyllus	big-leaved aster					x				x	
Aster praealtus	willow aster			x							
Aster shortii	Short's aster					x				x	
Aster umbellatus	flat-top aster			x				x			
Astragalus canadensis	Canadian milk vetch		x								
†Aureolaria grandiflora	yellow false-foxglove	x	x		x						

Scientific name	Common name								
†Baptisia alba macrophylla	white wild indigo	x							
Bidens cernua	nodding bur marigold			x	x		x		
Boehmeria cylindrica	false nettle						x		x
†Boltonia asteroides	false aster						x		x
Brachyelytrum erectum	long-awned wood grass				x				
Bromus kalmii	prairie brome	x							
Bromus latiglumis	ear-leaved brome		x		x		x		
†Bromus pubescens	woodland brome		x		x		x	x	
Caltha palustris	marsh marigold					x		x	
Camassia scilloides	wild hyacinth	x			x		x		x
†Campanulastrum americanum	tall bellflower				x	x	x		x
†Cardamine concatenata	toothwort					x		x	x
Cardamine douglassii	purple spring cress							x	x
Carex cristatella	crested sedge				x		x		
Carex crus-corvi	raven's foot sedge		x				x		
Carex davisii	Davis's sedge		x		x		x		
Carex formosa	awnless graceful sedge				x				
Carex gracillima	graceful sedge				x				x
Carex granularis	meadow sedge		x		x	x			
Carex grayi	bur sedge	x						x	x
Carex lupulina	hop sedge	x							x
Carex muskingumensis	swamp oval sedge	x							
Carex normalis	larger straw sedge		x					x	
Carex pensylvanica	Pennsylvania sedge	x			x				x

†Precedes those scientific names cross-referenced in appendix C.
★Indicates nomenclature differs from Kartesz.

continues

Table 11.2. (*Continued*)

Scientific Name	Common Name	DMS	MS	WMS	DMO	MO	WMO	WO	DMW	MW	WMW
Carex rosea	curly-styled wood sedge		x	x						x	x
Carex sparganioides	bar-reed sedge									x	
Carex sprengelii	long-beaked sedge			x			x			x	x
Carex squarrosa	squarrose sedge							x			
Carex stipata	sawbeak sedge			x							
Carex swanii	downy green sedge			x		x					
Carex tenera	slender sedge			x							
Carex vulpinoidea	fox sedge			x				x			
†*Caulophyllum giganteum*	blue cohosh									x	x
Ceanothus americanus	New Jersey tea	x	x		x	x					
Celastrus scandens	climbing bittersweet		x		x	x					
Cephalanthus occidentalis	buttonbush							x			x
Chelone glabra	turtlehead			x			x				x
†*Chenopodium simplex*	maple-leaved goosefoot					x	x			x	
Cicuta maculata	water hemlock							x			
Cinna arundinacea	wood reed			x		x	x	x		x	x
Cirsium altissimum	tall thistle					x				x	
Cirsium discolor	field thistle		x								
Claytonia virginica	spring beauty		x	x		x	x			x	x
†*Comandra umbellata*	false toadflax		x	x							
Coreopsis tripteris	tall coreopsis		x								
Corylus americana	American hazelnut	x	x		x	x					
Cryptotaenia canadensis	honewort					x					x

Danthonia spicata	poverty oat grass						x				
†*Dasistoma macrophylla*	mullein foxglove		x	x		x	x	x	x		x
Desmodium canadense	showy tick trefoil			x		x	x		x		x
Desmodium cuspidatum	hairy-bracted tick trefoil					x					
Desmodium glutinosum	pointed tick trefoil					x				x	
Desmodium paniculatum★	tall tick clover					x				x	x
Dioscorea villosa	wild yam					x				x	x
Dodecatheon meadia	shooting star		x			x	x	x		x	x
Elymus canadensis	Canada wild rye		x	x		x				x	x
†*Elymus hystrix*	bottlebrush grass		x		x	x	x			x	x
Elymus riparius	riverbank wild rye		x		x	x				x	x
Elymus trachycaulus	slender wheat grass	x	x			x					
Elymus villosus	silky wild rye		x			x	x			x	x
Elymus virginicus	Virginia wild rye		x			x				x	x
Enemion biternatum	false rue anemone			x			x			x	x
Epilobium coloratum	cinnamon willow herb				x						
Erigeron pulchellus	Robin's plantain	x					x				
Erythronium albidum	white trout lily										
Eupatorium maculatum	spotted Joe-Pye weed		x				x	x		x	x
Eupatorium perfoliatum	common boneset		x					x			
Eupatorium purpureum	purple Joe-Pye weed					x	x			x	x
†*Evonymus atropurpurea*	wahoo					x				x	x
†*Evonymus obovata*	running strawberry bush					x					
†*Festuca subverticillata*	nodding fescue					x				x	x
Galium circaezans	hairy wild licorice					x				x	x

continues

†Precedes those scientific names cross-referenced in appendix C.
★Indicates nomenclature differs from Kartesz.

Table 11.2. (*Continued*)

Scientific Name	Common Name	DMS	MS	WMS	DMO	MO	WMO	WO	DMW	MW	W/MW
Galium concinnum	shining bedstraw				x	x			x	x	
†*Gaura longiflora*	large-flowered gaura		x			x				x	x
†*Gentiana alba*	yellowish gentian	x	x			x					
†*Gentianella quinquefolia*	stiff gentian	x	x								
†*Gentianopsis crinita*	fringed gentian			x							
Geranium bicknellii	northern cranesbill	x	x		x	x			x	x	
Geranium carolinianum	Carolina cranesbill				x	x			x	x	
Geranium maculatum	wild geranium		x	x	x	x	x			x	x
Glyceria septentrionalis	floating manna grass							x			
Glyceria striata	fowl manna grass			x		x	x	x		x	x
Helenium autumnale	sneezeweed			x			x	x			x
Helianthus strumosus	pale-leaved sunflower		x			x				x	
Heliopsis helianthoides	false sunflower		x								
†*Hepatica nobilis acuta*	sharp-lobed hepatica								x	x	
†*Heracleum maximum*	cow parsnip					x	x			x	x
Heuchera richardsonii	prairie alum root	x	x	x	x	x					
Hieracium scabrum	rough hawkweed	x	x		x	x			x		
Hydrophyllum virginianum	Virginia waterleaf									x	x
†*Hypericum ascyron*	great St. John's wort			x			x				
Hypericum prolificum	shrubby St. John's wort		x	x		x	x				
Hypoxis hirsuta	yellow star grass	x	x	x	x	x			x		
Ilex verticillata	winterberry										x
Iodanthus pinnatifidus	violet cress			x		x				x	

Scientific name	Common name										
Iris virginica shrevei	blue flag iris						X				
Krigia biflora	false dandelion			X		X		X	X		
Lactuca canadensis	wild lettuce		X								
Lactuca floridana	blue lettuce		X		X	X					
Lathyrus ochroleucus	pale vetchling					X	X		X	X	
Lathyrus venosus	veiny pea			X		X	X				
Leersia oryzoides	rice cut grass					X		X			
Leersia virginica	white grass		X		X	X	X	X	X		
Lespedeza violacea	violet bush clover		X			X		X	X	X	
Liatris scariosa nieuwlandii	savanna blazing star	X	X			X					
Lilium michiganense	Michigan lily				X		X			X	
Lithospermum latifolium	broad-leaved puccoon					X		X	X	X	X
Lobelia cardinalis	cardinal flower			X		X		X	X		
Lobelia siphilitica	great blue lobelia		X		X	X	X		X	X	X
†*Lonicera reticulata*	yellow honeysuckle		X		X	X		X	X	X	X
Ludwigia palustris	water purslane					X	X				
Luzula multiflora	wood rush	X	X		X	X		X	X		
Lysimachia ciliata	fringed loosestrife	X		X		X	X		X		X
Lysimachia quadriflora	narrow-leaved loosestrife			X	X	X	X			X	
†*Maianthemum racemosum*	feathery false Solomon's seal				X	X	X		X	X	
†*Maianthemum stellatum*	starry false Solomon's seal		X		X	X					
Menispermum canadense	moonseed			X	X	X			X		
†*Mentha canadensis*	wild mint			X	X	X		X	X	X	
Mertensia virginica	Virginia bluebells									X	
Mimulus ringens	monkey flower		X	X	X	X	X		X	X	
†*Moehringia lateriflora*	wood sandwort		X	X	X	X			X	X	X

†Precedes those scientific names cross-referenced in appendix C.

continues

Table11.2. (Continued)

Scientific Name	Common Name	DMS	MS	WMS	DMO	MO	WMO	WO	DMW	MW	WMW
Monarda fistulosa	wild bergamot	x	x	x		x					
Muhlenbergia mexicana	leafy satin grass		x	x		x	x				x
Napaea dioica	glade mallow		x	x		x	x				
Oenothera perennis	small sundrops		x	x	x						
Onoclea sensibilis	sensitive fern			x				x		x	
Osmorhiza longistylis	smooth sweet cicely									x	
Oxalis violacea	violet wood sorrel	x	x		x						
Oxypolis rigidior	cowbane		x	x			x	x			x
†Panicum lanuginosum implicatum★	slender-stemmed panic grass	x	x								
Panicum latifolium★	wide-leaved panic grass		x	x		x					
Penstemon calycosus	smooth beard tongue		x	x		x					x
Penthorum sedoides	ditch stonecrop							x			
Perideridia americana	thicket parsley		x	x		x					
Phlox divaricata	woodland phlox					x	x			x	x
Phryma leptostachya	lopseed					x				x	
Physostegia virginiana	obedient plant		x	x		x	x				
Physostegia virginiana ssp. praemorsa	prairie obedient plant	x	x		x						
Physostegia virginiana ssp. speciosa	showy obedient plant			x			x				x
Polemonium reptans	Jacob's ladder		x	x		x	x			x	x

Scientific name	Common name										
Polygala senega	Seneca snakeroot					x	x				
†Polygonatum biflorum commutatum	smooth Solomon's seal					x				x	
Prenanthes alba	white lettuce				x	x				x	
Prenanthes altissima	tall white lettuce				x	x	x				x
Prenanthes racemosa	glaucous white lettuce				x	x			x		
†Ranunculus hispidus nitidus	swamp buttercup					x					x
Ratibida pinnata	grey-headed coneflower	x			x	x					
Rudbeckia laciniata	golden glow					x		x			x
Rudbeckia subtomentosa	sweet black-eyed Susan				x	x	x				x
Rudbeckia triloba	brown-eyed Susan				x	x					
Rumex orbiculatus	great water dock							x			
Sagittaria latifolia	common arrowhead							x			
Sambucus canadensis	elderberry				x	x					
†Samolus valerandi ssp. *parviflorus*	water pimpernel							x			
Sanguinaria canadensis	bloodroot				x	x	x	x			x
Saxifraga pensylvanica	swamp saxifrage					x	x	x			x
Scirpus cyperinus	wool grass							x			
Scrophularia lanceolata	early figwort				x	x					
Scutellaria lateriflora	mad-dog skullcap				x	x	x				x
Silene stellata	starry campion				x	x					
Silene virginica	fire pink				x	x					x

continues

†Precedes those scientific names cross-referenced in appendix C.
*Indicates nomenclature differs from Kartesz.

Table 11.2. (Continued)

Scientific Name	Common Name	DMS	MS	WMS	DMO	MO	WMO	WO	DMW	MW	WMW
Sisyrinchium angustifolium	pointed blue-eyed grass		x			x	x				x
Sium suave	water parsnip					x	x		x		x
Smilax ecirrata	upright carrion flower					x				x	
Smilax lasioneura	common carrion flower					x				x	
Solidago caesia	blue-stemmed goldenrod					x				x	
Solidago flexicaulis	broad-leaved goldenrod					x	x			x	x
Solidago gigantea	late goldenrod			x			x				x
Solidago juncea	early goldenrod	x	x		x						
Solidago nemoralis	old-field goldenrod	x	x		x						
Solidago patula	swamp goldenrod							x			x
Solidago speciosa	showy goldenrod	x	x		x	x			x		
Solidago ulmifolia	elm-leaved goldenrod		x			x				x	
Sphenopholis intermedia	slender wedge grass					x	x			x	x
Spiraea alba	meadowsweet			x			x	x			
Stachys tenuifolia	rough hedge nettle			x							
Taenidia integerrima	yellow pimpernel		x			x				x	
Thalictrum dioicum	early meadow rue					x				x	
Thaspium trifoliatum aureum	meadow parsnip	x	x		x						
Tradescantia ohiensis	common spiderwort		x	x		x	x				

Scientific name	Common name				
Trillium grandiflorum	large-flowered trillium				x
Trillium recurvatum	red trillium			x	
Trillium grandiflorum	large-flowered trillium			x	x
Trillium recurvatum	red trillium			x	x
Triosteum aurantiacum	early horse gentian			x	x
Triosteum perfoliatum	late horse gentian			x	x
Uvularia grandiflora	bellwort			x	x
Verbena urticifolia	hairy white vervain		x		x
Vernonia fasciculata	common ironweed		x		x
Veronica scutellata	marsh speedwell			x	
Viburnum acerifolium	maple-leaved arrow-wood				x
Vicia americana	American vetch		x	x	x
Viola conspersa	dog violet		x	x	x
Zizia aurea	golden Alexanders	x	x	x	x

Notes: Savanna seed mixes include, in addition to the species listed here, all those species from the equivalent prairie mixes (e.g., all mesic prairie species of table 12.1 and other prairie seed mix lists are to be included in the MS mix).

This table was compiled by John and Jane Balaban and Stephen Packard.

In the case of large areas (tens to hundreds of acres), seed may be sown by machine. Many factors will govern whether hand- or machine-sowing is best. Machines are required unless adequate time is available from highly trained and motivated volunteers or staff. Machines that broadcast or drill seed are discussed in chapter 12.

Ten good people can hand-sow forty easy acres in a couple of hours. If the terrain is complex (many different combinations of wetness, tree density, etc.), the job will take a bit longer, but the labor-intensive approach is particularly valuable in such cases. If, for example, you are seeding prairie ground ranging from wet to dry, one knowledgeable person with the wet-mesic mix can search out and sow in the right spots. A less knowledgeable crew can broadcast within areas marked ahead of time with color-coded stakes.

In order to know where seed has and has not been broadcast, seed is normally mixed with perlite, a white material of volcanic origin used in gardening. The perlite keeps the seeds separate from each other and, once seed is disbursed, marks the areas that have already been seeded. At the boundaries where two mixes (say, mesic prairie and dry-mesic prairie) come together, the broadcast patterns should overlap. The overlap between the two mixes reflects both the continuum present in nature and our limited ability to read the landscape accurately.

The most common mistake when broadcasting seed is putting too much in too small an area. A handful may contain twenty thousand seeds or a million. If they are cast all in one spot, there won't be room or resources for the many seedlings, and only one or two will survive. That same handful of seed diluted in ten gallons of perlite and other seeds and spread over ten acres may well produce five thousand or ten thousand plants. If there are only a few suitable microhabitats for any given plant on a site, spreading the twenty thousand seeds evenly over the area improves the odds for thousands of plants to find the perfect spots.

The density of seed sown at many restoration projects is one cup to 100 square feet, or one KGB (kitchen garbage bag) to 18,000 square feet (a bit less than half an acre). Such a seed mix consists of 50 percent seed (with the heads broken up but chaff retained) and 50 percent per-lite. To get a feel for spreading seed at this rate, broadcast one cup evenly in a 10x10-foot area.

If the site is too large to plant with this density of hard-to-find con-servative seed, one option would be to spread however much seed you can afford or can gather over the whole acreage and hope that the scat-tered plants will gradually fill in. One drawback to this approach is that you may waste a large portion of the rare seed of those species that need to be incorporated into the soil, as described below.

Another drawback is that widely scattered seed may ultimately not compete well. Some managers believe that, when interseeding an old field or badly degraded prairie, it is necessary for the conservatives to be sufficiently close together to provide a "critical mass." Without this, the brush or weeds may win. According to that thinking, it is best to plant high-quality patches only as fast as diverse high-quality seed can be obtained.

Very small-seeded species (e.g., gentians and orchids) may benefit from being treated separately. These seeds can be covered adequately with dirt by the splatter of raindrops; thus, they don't need your help to be incorporated into the soil. Most of these can be kept separate when the seeds are mixed. They can then be spread after raking and also broadcast widely in areas that will not be raked. (Of course, this seed should be subdivided into wet, mesic, and dry components and spread into the proper habitat.) Here again a restorationist with considerable expertise might invest the seed more effectively by making separate mixes for more specialized habitats, for example, north-facing slopes, banks, etc.

When planting subsections rather than the entire site, one approach is to start at one end of the preserve and plant a new area each year (perhaps for many decades) until the planting is completed. Another approach is to plant spots or strips widely scattered over the entire site. Such scattered plantings are harder to keep track of, but they have their advantages: The varied parts of the site likely have varied characteristics, which may make certain areas more hospitable to certain species; the scattered plantings approach provides many more chances for any species to find such favorable areas. In addition, in the long run, we can expect all species to spread without assistance, but conservatives will mostly spread only short distances. They will reach most parts of the preserve much more slowly from one concentrated area than from widely scattered spots or strips.

Don't waste your best seed mix in areas that are brushy or thick with aggressive weeds. Control these problem species before you begin, or plant an aggressive prairie mix so that the prairie front-line soldiers can subdue the weeds and brush.

Incorporate the Seed

This heading refers not to Seed, Inc., but to the very satisfying last step in planting, incorporating the seed into the soil, where it will feel so wonderfully at home, where it will interact with heat and cold, wet and dry, microbes, fungi, and soil chemistry and will in time germinate and grow. A seed lying on the surface is likely to be eaten by small animals, or it may sprout and desiccate, and die. In one spring-planting test, a "raked in" patch eight years later was thick with conservatives, while a similarly seeded, unraked area had few conservative species (and no individuals of many species).

Seeds may be incorporated into the soil by hand-raking, harrowing, disking, or drilling. To rake seed by hand into small areas of turf, use long-handled garden cultivators (either the four-prong rake or the revolving spiked-wheel type) or other tools that will break up much of the surface of the soil to an average depth of ½ to ¼ inch. The soil will need to be fairly dry in order to crumble appropriately to incorporate the seed. Various types of seed will survive best at various depths; a rule of thumb is to cover a seed with a layer of soil equal to twice the seed's thickness. Thus, ½ inch may be too deep for many seeds. However, the architecture of the existing turf will make the effects of the raking highly uneven. In practice there will be many parts of the soil surface where seed will end up ⅛ inch deep or even on the surface despite the most conscientious raking. Thus, adequate niches will remain for the small seeds.

In order to incorporate seed over tens or hundreds of acres, machines will be needed. This technology is only now being developed. Seed drills specially designed for turf can be used. Light disking has been tried, although it is difficult to achieve a sufficiently delicate touch. A variety of harrows and drags have been used. Flexible harrows (for example, the Furst harrow) seem promising. *Restoration and Management Notes* is likely to be the first place to read about new developments in the state of this art.

A preferred option in many cases, if the logistics work out, is to burn in fall and broadcast seed before winter sets in. Then frost and rain will often churn up the bared ground sufficiently, especially during the time when temperatures are daily oscillating above and below freezing. If this method is used, it may be wise to wait until the main migration of sparrows has passed, or your efforts may amount largely to bird feeding, at least for many of the larger seeds.

It is particularly unnecessary to rake seed into the bare loose earth of woodlands after matted dead leaves have been removed by fire. Ideally, broadcast seed in this case immediately before a rainstorm, to minimize the loss of seed to wind or birds. However, degraded slopes are likely to erode if leaf litter is burned off in fall; often the turf species have been shaded out and their roots no longer hold the soil. Therefore, slopes may best be burned and planted in spring.

Maintain the Restoration

Especially if the existing vegetation is dense it is very valuable to mow it for one to three years after interseeding. Mowing is critical if the vegetation will create sufficient shade at the soil surface to kill off the seedlings. One rule of thumb is that whenever the weedy vegetation has reached 12–18 inches, mow it back to 4–6 inches. But each site and each year are different. Study the ground carefully to assure that the seedlings have adequate light. Don't mow so late that the fallen vegetation will itself create dense shade.

Poor weather or other conditions may result in poor results in certain years. Certain species or certain areas may need to be replanted. Species or genetic strains not available when the original planting was done may be interseeded into the planting. However, as the planting matures, new seedlings will have an increasingly hard time surviving the fierce competition. If the most conservative species are poorly represented, interseeding followed by additional strategic mowing or haying for two or three years after any planting may help tip the balance in favor of new seedlings without harming the prairie any more than a bison herd would.

Once a full complement of species has been restored, long-term maintenance is simply what any fragment of high-quality prairie needs. Such maintenance includes the burning, weed control, and monitoring described in later chapters.

Special Considerations for Certain Communities

Sand Prairies

Most of the flora of the sand prairie is also found in classic black-soil prairie. But many species that are common in sand prairies are absent on heavy soils—and absent from planting lists designed for heavy soils. Therefore when planting on sand, follow an appropriate species list; consult the references in appendix D. Even in the case of species common to both sand and black-soil prairies, it may be best to seek special "sand ecotype" seed. Indian grass growing in sand, for example, may have specialized genetic abilities to handle the diseases, soil chemistry, droughtiness, and other characteristics of the sand community.

Savannas

In the most open parts of oak savannas, the vegetation, and therefore seed mixes, are very similar to the vegetation and seed mixes of prairies. But note the distinctive savanna species included in the lists given in tables 5.1, 11.1, and 11.2. As the trees get denser, plant species that predominate in varying amounts of shade form complex patterns. Because savanna seed is scarce, there are advantages in understanding those patterns well enough so that most seed falls more or less in the right spot. Probably the best way to get a feel for where to throw which type of seed is to spend a fair amount of time in a high-quality community that is as similar as possible to the area to be planted. Study the ground cover in relation to the patches of sunlight and the configuration of trees. Try to take into account the impact of the various trees that will shade a given spot as the sun moves across the sky each day. Because the sun angles from the south, the shadow of a tree canopy will be displaced to the north of where it would be if the sun were straight overhead.

As with prairies, the seed mixes of most value for conservation (and the most successful ones) are those that most accurately reproduce the species mix that would have grown on a site of that type for thousands of years or longer. The varied floristic compositions of the many types of savanna reflect such features as fire history, soil type, and wetness. Often the species of oak present are good indicators of the site's physical features. Examples from the central parts of the tallgrass region include black oak, which often grows in single-species stands on sandy or very dry soils. Bur oak is often the dominant oak on moist, fertile soils, particularly where fire was most severe. White oak often occupies somewhat poorer or drier soils. Swamp white oak and pin oak grow in wet savanna or on the edges of woodland ponds. Post oak characterizes areas of claypan soils known as "flatwoods." The faithfulness of certain oak species to certain conditions provides clues for the customization of seed mixes. Try to gather seeds for a site (or a part of a site) from an area with similar oaks. In other words, gather seeds at a site where the oak species match the oak species of the restoration site.

The most practical land for the restoration of the now very rare savanna communities is pasture land with scattered oaks. Commonly, when savanna pasture is acquired for conservation purposes, the livestock are removed, but little restoration is done. However, like the reintroduction of fire, the cessation of close, year-round grazing marks a major change and restructuring of the ecological community. Thus, the removal of livestock commences a period of disequilibrium that restoration might exploit. Savanna might also be restored on actively grazed sites. One scenario might involve interseeding the warm-season species and, until they become established, restricting grazing to spring and fall. Once the warm-season species are reestablished, the spring and fall savanna species could be interseeded, immediately after an early fall or late spring burn, which would have set back the exotic cool-season species. Subsequently, the savanna might be grazed in an intermittent pattern that emulates the impact of wandering herds of bison.

The most typical savannas available for restoration on conservation lands are former pastures in which the grazing ended some years ago. The fuels for the fires that maintained the savannas are mostly the grasses. But in many degraded savannas at the start of restoration, the grassy turf has largely been replaced by brush, which has shaded out the grasses. When brush barriers are sufficient to block the fires, the entire savanna, with all its plant and animal species, is lost. Because grassless brushy areas generally won't burn, there is no way to restore these areas gradually through fire and seeding. As a result, the only established route to restoration is to cut the brush and apply herbicide to the stumps. The bare ground in the former shade of heavy brush, after the brush has been removed, is a ready-made seedbed. The return of grasses then provides the grassy fuel on which the savanna dynamic depends. Farm weeds are not a problem, but brush regrowth is likely from seed, even if cut stumps have been carefully herbicided. Plant a sufficiently aggressive grass matrix so that the herb competition and fire will subsequently be able to keep the brush at bay.

Hazel is thought to have been a major component of the original savannas. Hazel and at least small populations of other native shrubs should be protected in the early stages of savanna restoration. After a healthy native turf has been established, the prescribed burns will be the principal determinant of what shrubs survive, and where. If the relatively mild fires prescribed by conservationists are sufficient to eliminate a shrub species, then there is probably no need to be concerned about that species' disappearance: it was probably not found in that type of savanna. Areas of shrub dominance can be expected to alternately expand and contract in response to changing patterns of weather and fire. Additional savanna species may be easily restored to the community by broadcasting seed wherever and whenever the fire has shrubs on the retreat.

Copses of brush that rarely burn were probably a regular part of both the savannas and the prairies. And some rare herb species (for example, the eared false-foxglove) seem to be associated with the irregularly burned zone between the copses and the grass. The copses that rarely burn were prevented from succeeding to forest by occasional catastrophic fires during severe burning conditions.

Woodlands

A woodland is shaded by trees more than a savanna but less than a forest. Woodlands are much easier to restore than open savanna because even without the grasses, they have sufficient oak leaf litter to carry a fire. Brush can thus be controlled by frequent fires fueled mainly by oak leaves. Woodland turf plants can be seeded in gradually over the years.

It may be difficult to determine whether a given site is a woodland that needs burning or a forest that needs to be protected from fire. The following features help differentiate the two. Woodlands usually have two principal layers (turf and trees) and are usually dominated by oaks. Most forests have four well-developed layers (herbs, shrubs, understory trees, and canopy trees). (The understory trees are of different species than the canopy trees, completing their entire life cycle in that shady understory.) Some woodlands may have had a substantial component of fire–resistant shrubs, but the subject is still poorly understood.

Today's mixed oak, maple, and basswood forests in most cases seem to be a temporary phenomenon caused by forest species invading oak wood-land. Without prescribed burning and its resultant reduction of shade, the entire community of plants and animals associated with these woodlands gradually vanishes from the landscape, along with the oaks themselves, which do not reproduce in deep shade. Particularly on the fertile Corn Belt soils, all our oaks appear headed for oblivion, except where ecolog-ical restoration or other intentional management protects them.

The good news is the relative ease and safety with which oak wood-lands are burned, seeded, and otherwise restored. The crisp oak leaves themselves are modest but sufficient fuel to drive out invading brush. The grasses and wildflowers of the herb layer are still relatively common in most regions, and they respond impressively to seeding by simple broadcast. No soil preparation is necessary after burning because rain quickly splashes the loose soil over seeds.

Some rich woodlands require no restoration beyond occasional burning. Most woodlands are best managed initially by regular burning, herb–layer reseeding, and weed control.

The burning needs to be relatively frequent, perhaps every one to three years, because the stands are now much denser than they once were and remedial burning is required to reverse the effects of decades of fire suppression. Infrequent fire may or may not be sufficient, in the very long run, to bring back our full continuum of oak woods. Because the biota of more open woodlands appears to be in short and dwindling supply, frequent fire is called for on many sites.

Girdling to eliminate invasive tree species may be desirable in addition to burning. Oak leaf fires have the advantage that they are easier to control under moderate conditions than the much more vigorous fires in dense grass, but their modest heat may not kill many of the larger invading trees soon enough to prevent serious degradation of the oak woodland community. Fire is likely to keep out new seedlings of invader species, but large maples and basswoods may survive for decades or longer. During that time other biota that is dependent on more sunlight may not survive. Therefore, girdling even large trunks of invading species of trees (and even some oaks if they are more numerous and thus produce more shade than what the rare biota of the site are adapted to) may be desirable to restore the long-term health of the woods. The standing dead trees that result from girdling are also valuable habitat for many species.

The fires may also burn back the seedlings of the oaks. But the young savanna oaks resprout vigorously after fires. These resprouting "oak grubs" are a regular feature of the savanna. During periods of less frequent or intense fire the trunks of the oak grubs grow large enough to withstand fire, thus becoming the new canopy trees.

Some woods may retain all their herb species, just waiting for release by fire. But many have lost large numbers of species as a result of prior livestock grazing and excess shade. Some woods have a deceptively rich spring flora (the species of which are able to complete their life cycles before the trees fully leaf out). But the species of summer and fall have often been largely lost. It is these species on which the restoration should concentrate. The seeds of early ripening species should generally be broadcast as soon as collected (see tables 7.1 and 10.1). But those of fall-ripening species may best be held until the mat of dead leaves has been burned off; the seeds are then broadcast on the bare dirt.

Most weeds won't compete well in a rich turf of woodland grasses and wildflowers, but weeds will often densely fill a disturbed woodland once burning opens up the ground, if a turf of conservative or relatively conservative herbs is not rapidly restored. Once burning has begun, there will likely be a race between exotics and natives to control the newly opened ground. Strategic weeding may be important to tip the balance in the direction of the natives. Any aggressive exotic weeds should be eliminated before the burning starts. Even certain native species are very aggressive in woodlands that are being opened up by burning; these include tall goldenrod and briars. Some of the worst problem weeds are such non-natives as burdock, alien thistles, garlic mustard, reed canary grass, and hedge parsley. Although many restorationists put a high priority on eliminating such species from woodlands in an early stage of restoration, others recommend letting succession eliminate these weeds over time. That route may be the only one available in many cases, especially for large sites. There is little information about the speed at which such succession would proceed, but some such experiments look promising.

Wetlands

The wetlands that are fire dependent (those treated by this book) are either prairie wetlands (marsh, sedge meadow, etc.) or wooded wetlands (wet woods, swamp, etc.). Most components of wetland interseeding seem to be similar to those discussed above.

Reintroduction of seeds may be less necessary in wetlands than in other types of communities. Wetland seed banks are thought to be much longer lived than those in prairie or woodland; thus many wetland species may come back on their own once natural water levels have been restored by blocking ditches or disabling drainage tile systems.

At some sites, however, broadcasting seed has been highly successful following brush removal or hydrologic restoration. Many species have shown up in such planted areas that were absent in unplanted areas. In wetlands, extremely dense stands of weedy annuals such as smartweeds or tickseeds are the regular first stage. But many relatively conservative species (including such important fuel species as blue joint grass and many rare sedges) seem to be able to survive in the shade of the weeds and replace them within a few years.

REFERENCES

Bronny, C. 1992. "Successional Restoration of an Oak Woodland (Illinois)." *Restoration and Management Notes* 10:77–78.

Curtis, J. 1959. *The Vegetation of Wisconsin.* Madison: University of Wisconsin Press.

Green, H.C., and J.T. Curtis. 1953. "The Re-establishment of Prairie in the University of Wisconsin Arboretum." *Wildflower* 29:77–88.

Packard, Steve. 1993. "Restoring Oak Woodlands." *Restoration and Management Notes* 11:5–16.

———. 1994. "Successional Restoration: Thinking Like a Prairie." *Restoration and Management Notes* 12:32–39.

Reinartz, James A. "Planting State-Listed Endangered and Threatened Plants." *Conservation Biology* 9, no. 4 (August 1995).

Ross, Laurel M., and Tom Vanderpoel. 1994. "Mowing Encourages Establishment of Prairie Species." *Restoration and Management Notes* 9, no. 1:34–35.

12
Plowing and Seeding

John P. Morgan

The single most important consideration in prairie restoration planting is site preparation. More restoration failures are due to poor site preparation than any other single factor.

This is somewhat like building a house. You can skimp and cut corners while laying the foundation, and few people will notice. You will save time and money, and the result will not look any different than that of your neighbor who put a lot of resources into a proper foundation. Very soon the difference will be apparent, however, as the house shifts, cracks, and falls apart. Repairing a faulty foundation after the fact is far more difficult, costly, and aggravating than doing the job properly in the first place. Sometimes it is easier to demolish the house and start again.

Proper site preparation is the foundation of any bare-soil prairie restoration. Skimp or cut corners here, and you risk considerably prolonging the restoration process. It may well fail altogether. Much valuable time, money, and work invested in collecting and processing scarce native seed, planting, management, and monitoring may all be for naught. It is much easier and more efficient to prepare a good site from the beginning than to attempt to fix it at a later date. Often it is easier to plow the whole area again, starting from scratch, a heart-rending process, to say the least.

Site Inventory

With what we now know about prairie restoration, this scenario need never happen. Good site preparation starts with a thorough knowledge of the area to be planted. This includes its present vegetative condition, past land use history, and soil characteristics. Once you know these, a plan can be formulated to assemble the equipment and expertise necessary to prepare the site properly.

You also will need to know the herbicide history of the field, as some chemicals have long-lasting residues that will inhibit the germination and growth of any prairie species you plant. This is particularly true of cornfields where Atrazine or grainfields where trifluralin-family chemicals (Treflan, Avadex) have been used within the past two to four years.

Site Preparation

The easiest site to prepare is an existing agricultural field. It will not be weed free, but much of the preparation will already have been done for you. If perennial weeds are present, they should be eliminated by spot spraying with appropriate herbicides before you go any further.

Starting as early in the spring as the ground can be worked, use a light-duty cultivator or harrow to till the ground no more than 2 inches deep. Deep tillage of an agricultural field is not advisable because it simply brings to the surface additional weed seeds. Repeated shallow tillage will exhaust the surface-weed seed bank and thus eliminate competition for your native seeds.

Frequency of tillage depends upon the annual weed population in the field. It should be done as often as a good crop of weed seedlings emerges, before the weeds get taller than 2 inches. This usually means at least every three weeks in April, May, and early June. The old farmer's adage "Keep it black!" is a very appropriate guideline here.

Next to adequate perennial weed control, soil packing is the most important factor in a restoration seeding. A well-packed soil eliminates air passages that can dry out and kill a newly emerging seedling before it ever appears above ground. By creating a crust at the soil surface, it prevents moisture that lies deeper in the soil from evaporating, keeping it just below the surface, where it is most needed by the seeds. It also ensures good seed-to-soil contact, which is vital to the germination of native species.

Packing with a water-filled roller creates an ideal seedbed before drill seeding. Use the largest and heaviest roller packer that you can pull with your tractor. Standard agricultural cultipackers are also often used. You cannot overpack; at least twice over a field is a minimum before drill seeding, with the second packing operation at right angles to the first. A good rule of thumb is that a field is ready to seed if your footprint barely registers. If it sinks in more than a ½ inch, pack again. When broadcast seeding, packing must be done after seeding.

Weed Control

The most difficult site to tackle in plowed-ground prairie restoration is the old field. It is usually full of perennial, non-native weeds such as smooth brome, quack grass, and Canada thistle. Control of these species requires persistence and may take several years. (See chapter 11 for a non-plowing approach.)

First, burn in late fall or early spring to remove the accumulated litter and surface seed bank. If a burn is not possible, then close mowing with a rotary, sickle, or flail mower, followed by raking off the litter, can be done. Allow the vegetation to regrow to about 8 inches in height. This should be followed by a series of herbicide applications using a mixture of 2 percent glyphosate to kill grasses, plus a broad-leaved weed killer such as 2,4-D and dicamba. Glyphosate by itself sometimes is a poor controller of perennial broad-leaved weeds and needs help. Start herbicide applications in late summer or early fall before killing frosts. At that time of year perennial weeds are much more susceptible to herbicides. Several applications at three- to four-week intervals during the following growing season may be necessary if perennial weeds persist.

Certain very tough weeds such as Canada thistle and leafy spurge may not be controlled even by this regime of herbicides. Specific control of these weeds using special herbicides with spot sprayers often is necessary. When using herbicides, it is imperative that properly licensed personnel with suitable equipment, training, and protective clothing be employed. Consult local weed control experts first and follow label directions carefully.

The alternative to chemical control of perennial weeds on large restoration sites is intensive tillage every few weeks over the course of several years, a method which does not provide as good a control of tough perennial weeds. Environmental costs of this approach include much increased fuel and oil usage with its attendant emissions, more wear on machinery, much greater risk of soil erosion, and less cover and habitat for wildlife. Those who automatically reject herbicide usage for ecological reasons should consider the true environmental costs and effectiveness of the alternative. We have come a long way from the days of DDT; most registered herbicides have far fewer unwanted side effects in the 1990s.

Once a season of chemical control has been carried out, the remaining above-ground vegetation must be removed either by fire or by mowing. After that the site should be cultivated in the fall with farm machinery. First, cultivate the site with a deep tiller down to about 6 inches. Cultivate a second time at right angles to the first. This will bring any remaining living roots to the surface to be killed by winter frosts. Follow this the next spring with a double-disk or field cultivator to break the soil into smaller chunks. Again cultivate twice, with the second tillage at right angles to the first. Harrowing (raking) the ground with diamond or spring-toothed harrows will then smooth any surface irregularities or ruts. A final round with a rototiller to finely pulverize the soil should then be undertaken. Allow the site to sit idle for about a month in the spring to encourage any weeds still present to germinate and grow. If perennial weeds still are present in high numbers, another herbicide application is necessary. Severe infestations may require two or more years of repeated treatments. Time spent early on in the restoration process will pay big dividends later. Once the weeds have been brought under control, the next step, seeding, can begin.

Annual weeds such as wild oats, foxtails, pigweeds, and mustards generally are not a problem on most sites. They often are present in very heavy infestations in the first year of a prairie restoration, as they thrive on bare soil. The control measures listed above for perennial weeds will also reduce the annual weed population significantly. In Manitoba, we have had prairies successfully reestablish despite first-year annual weed seedling densities as high as twelve hundred per square yard! Annual weed populations decline substantially over time as the cover of native forbs and grasses increases.

Often, an important factor in annual weed control is to mow the weeds off before they go to seed. This prevents weed contamination of surrounding lands and keeps your neighbors happy. It is best done with a tractor-mounted rotary or flail mower that mulches the cuttings. The height should be set at about 6 inches above the ground so that it misses most of the slower-growing perennial native seedlings. Annual weeds also may be of some value in acting as a cover crop for the prairie species.

Seeding Equipment

There are two methods of seeding a prairie. The first and most effective is with a specialized native-seed drill. The second method is with hand or mechanical broadcasters. Both have pros and cons for the restorationist. Basic seed mix lists for all types of plowed ground restorations are given in Table 12.1, with suggestions for variations for the western edge of the prairie region included in Table 12.2. (See also chapter 9, which describes a technique for designing mixes and includes additional seed mix lists.)

Seed drills are tractor-pulled farm implements that have a series of

small plows or disks that open furrows in the soil, then meter in a specified amount of seed from a top-mounted storage box down tubes into
the ground. After the seed is placed, soil falls back into the furrow and is
packed firmly by rubber press wheels. The most widely used and successful native-seed drill in North America is made by the Truax Company of Minneapolis, Minnesota. Other makes are the Tye, Nesbit, and
Great Plains native-seed drills, the John Deere rangeland drill, and the
John Deere power seeder. Based on our experience in Canada and con-
versations with restorationists across North America, Truax drills are the
most highly regarded.

Broadcast seeding may be as simple as scattering seed from a bag by
hand across the site. Mechanical broadcasters range in size and complexity. The simplest is one that straps across your chest and throws the
seed out in a regular pattern as you walk across the field turning a
hand crank. The next level up is a push- or pull-type fertilizer
spreader that has a hopper above a rotary shaft and meters seed
through a slot in the bottom from which it falls to the ground. The
most advanced broadcasters are tractor-pulled or three-point, hitch-
mounted, fertilizer spreaders.

Native-seed drills are the most efficient means of seeding a prairie. By
accurately placing seed at an exact depth at an even rate across the site,
they make the most efficient use of precious native seed. Grass and forb
germination of native seed on a properly packed, drilled site is twice as
good as with broadcasting. Drills also allow you to seed on a windy day.

The main drawback of native-seed drills is their initial expense, from
$5,000 to $10,000 or more, depending on size and options ordered.
Their payback period is short, however, if you consider your time and
dollar investment in collecting and processing native seed. The drill will
allow you to seed twice as much area more quickly with the same
amount of seed. If you are planning restorations larger than a few acres,
or multiple ones over a number of years, the expense of a native-seed drill
is justified.

In many areas of the United States, native-seed drills also can be borrowed or rented from the Natural Resources Conservation Service or
county agricultural offices. Rental of equipment means that you have to
wait your turn, however. Your optimal planting time will invariably be
the same as everyone else's in the area, sometimes leading to frustration
and missed opportunities.

Another drawback of native-seed drills is their need for clean seed.
Even small amounts of straw in the seed will plug up the drill, necessi-
tating frequent, time-consuming stops to clean out plugged seed tubes.

Table 12.1.

Seed Mixes for Plowed Ground

These species lists provide basic seed mixes for initial planting on plowed, black–soil, prairie restoration sites of variable moisture (wet, wet–mesic, mesic, dry–mesic, and dry). These lists include the predominant species for each habitat type within the central portion of the tallgrass prairie region (i.e., northeastern Missouri, eastern Iowa, northern and central Illinois, southern Wisconsin, and northwestern Indiana). Not all species listed will occur in all parts of this range. Consult local resources and remnants to tailor your seed mix to a specific site. Certain classic prairie species (e.g., prairie fringed orchid, false toadflax, and veiny pea) have been omitted intentionally because of their unsuitability to initial plantings or lack of commercial availability.

Wet Prairie

Allium canadense	wild garlic
Anemone canadensis	meadow anemone
†*Aster lanceolatus*	panicled aster
Aster novae-angliae	New England aster
†*Boltonia asteroides*	false aster
Calamagrostis canadensis	blue joint grass
Carex comosa	bristly sedge
Carex lacustris	lake bank sedge
Carex scoparia	pointed broom sedge
Carex stipata	sawbeak sedge
Carex vulpinoidea	fox sedge
Cicuta maculata	water hemlock
Eupatorium perfoliatum	common boneset
†*Euthamia graminifolia*	grass-leaved goldenroda
Galium boreale	northern bedstraw
Gentiana andrewsii	closed gentian
Helenium autumnale	sneezeweeda
Iris virginica shrevei	blue flag iris
Lilium michiganense	Michigan lily
Lobelia spicata	pale spiked lobelia
Lysimachia quadriflora	narrow-leaved loosestrife
Lythrum alatum	winged loosestrife
Oxypolis rigidior	cowbane
Pycnanthemum virginianum	common mountain mint
Saxifraga pensylvanica	swamp saxifrage
Scirpus cyperinus	wool grass

Table 12.1. (*Continued*)

Solidago riddellii	Riddell's goldenrod
Spartina pectinata	prairie cord grass
Thalictrum dasycarpum	purple meadow rue
Vernonia fasciculata	common ironweed
Veronicastrum virginicum	Culver's root
Zizia aurea	golden Alexanders

Wet-Mesic Prairie

Allium canadense	wild garlic
Allium cernuum	nodding wild onion
Andropogon gerardii	big bluestem
Anemone canadensis	meadow anemone*a*
Angelica atropurpurea	great angelica
†*Aster lanceolatus*	panicled aster
Aster novae-angliae	New England aster
Aster puniceus	bristly aster
Aster umbellatus	flat-top aster
†*Baptisia alba macrophylla*	white wild indigo
Chelone glabra	turtlehead
Cirsium discolor	field thistle
Dodecatheon meadia	shooting star
Elymus canadensis	Canada wild rye
†*Euthamia graminifolia*	grass-leaved goldenrod*a*
Galium boreale	northern bedstraw
Gentiana andrewsii	closed gentian
†*Hypericum ascyron*	great St. John's wort
Liatris pycnostachya	prairie blazing star
Liatris spicata	marsh blazing star
Lilium michiganense	Michigan lily
Lobelia spicata	pale spiked lobelia
Lysimachia quadriflora	narrow-leaved loosetrife
Lythrum alatum	winged loosestrife
Melanthium virginicum	bunch flower
Monarda fistulosa	wild bergamot
Phlox pilosa	sand prairie phlox
Physostegia virginiana	obedient plant
Pycnanthemum virginianum	common mountain mint
Rudbeckia hirta	black-eyed Susan
Rudbeckia subtomentosa	sweet black-eyed Susan

*a*Very aggressive; use very small amounts or add several years after initial planting.

†Precedes scientific name cross-referenced in appendix C.

continues

Table 12.1. (*Continued*)

Rudbeckia triloba	brown-eyed Susan
Senecio pauperculus	balsam ragwort
Silphium integrifolium	rosinweed
Silphium perfoliatum	cup plant
Silphium terebinthinaceum	prairie dock
Solidago riddellii	Riddell's goldenrod
Spartina pectinata	prairie cord grass
Sporobolus heterolepis	prairie dropseed
Thalictrum dasycarpum	purple meadow rue
Vernonia fasciculata	common ironweed
Veronicastrum virginicum	Culver's root
Zizia aurea	golden Alexanders

Mesic Prairie

Allium cernuum	nodding wild onion
Amorpha canescens	lead plant
Andropogon gerardii	big bluestem
Anemone canadensis	meadow anemone[a]
Anemone cylindrica	thimbleweed
Artemisia ludoviciana	white sage
Aster ericoides	heath aster
Aster laevis	smooth blue aster
Aster novae-angliae	New England aster
Astragalus canadensis	Canadian milk vetch
[†]*Baptisia alba macrophylla*	white wild Indigo
[†]*Baptisia bracteata leucophaea*	cream wild Indigo
Bromus kalmii	prairie brome
Ceanothus americanus	New Jersey tea
Coreopsis palmata	prairie coreopsis
Coreopsis tripteris	tall coreopsis[a]
[†]*Dalea candida*	white prairie clover
[†]*Dalea purpurea*	purple prairie clover
Desmodium canadense	showy tick trefoil
Desmodium illinoense	Illinois tick trefoil
Dodecatheon meadia	shooting star
Elymus canadensis	Canada wild rye
Eryngium yuccifolium	rattlesnake master
Euphorbia corollata	flowering spurge
[†]*Euthamia graminifolia*	grass-leaved goldenrod[a]
Galium boreale	northern bedstraw
Gentiana andrewsii	closed gentian
Helianthus mollis	downy sunflower[a]
[†]*Helianthus pauciflorus*	showy sunflower[a]
Heliopsis helianthoides	false sunflower[a]

Table 12.1. (*Continued*)

Heuchera richardsonii	prairie alum root
†*Hypericum ascyron*	great St. John's wort
Lespedeza capitata	round-headed bush clover
Liatris aspera	rough blazing star
Liatris pycnostachya	prairie blazing star
Liatris spicata	marsh blazing star
Lobelia spicata	pale spiked lobelia
Monarda fistulosa	wild bergamot
Panicum virgatum	switch grass[a]
Parthenium integrifolium	wild quinine
Penstemon digitalis	foxglove beard tongue
Phlox pilosa	sand prairie phlox
Polytaenia nuttallii	prairie parsley
Prenanthes racemosa	glaucous white lettuce
Pycnanthemum tenuifolium	slender mountain mint
Pycnanthemum virginianum	common mountain mint
Ratibida pinnata	grey-headed coneflower
Rosa arkansana	sunshine rose
Rosa carolina	pasture rose
Rudbeckia hirta	black-eyed Susan
Rudbeckia subtomentosa	sweet black-eyed Susan
Rudbeckia triloba	brown-eyed Susan
†*Schizachyrium scoparium*	little bluestem
Senecio plattensis	prairie ragwort
†*Senna hebecarpa*	wild senna
†*Senna marilandica*	Maryland senna
Silene regia	royal catchfly
Silphium integrifolium	rosinweed[a]
Silphium laciniatum	compass plant
Silphium perfoliatum	cup plant
Silphium terebinthinaceum	prairie dock
Sisyrinchium albidum	common blue-eyed grass
Solidago rigida	stiff goldenrod
Solidago speciosa	showy goldenrod
Sorghastrum nutans	Indian grass
Sporobolus heterolepis	prairie dropseed
Thalictrum dasycarpum	purple meadow rue
Tradescantia ohiensis	common spiderwort
Vernonia missurica	Missouri ironweed
Veronicastrum virginicum	Culver's root

[a]Very aggressive; use very small amounts or add several years after initial planting.

†Precedes scientific name cross-referenced in appendix C.

continues

Table 12.1. (*Continued*)

Viola pedatifida	prairie violet
Zizia aptera	heart-leaved meadow parsnip
Zizia aurea	golden Alexanders

Dry-Mesic Prairie

Allium canadense	wild garlic
Amorpha canescens	lead plant
Andropogon gerardii	big bluestem
Anemone cylindrica	thimbleweed
Artemisia ludoviciana	white sage
Asclepias tuberosa	butterfly weed
Asclepias verticillata	whorled milkweed
Asclepias viridiflora	short green milkweed
Aster ericoides	heath aster
Aster laevis	smooth blue aster
[†]*Aster oolentangiensis*	azure aster
Aster sericeus	silky aster
Astragalus canadensis	Canadian milk vetch
[†]*Baptisia alba macrophylla*	white wild Indigo
[†]*Baptisia bracteata leucophaea*	cream wild Indigo
Blephilia ciliata	Ohio horse mint
Bouteloua curtipendula	side-oats grama
Bromus kalmii	prairie brome
[†]*Brickellia eupatorioides*	false boneset
[†]*Chamaecrista fasciculata*	partridge pea
Coreopsis palmata	prairie coreopsis
[†]*Dalea candida*	white prairie clover
[†]*Dalea purpurea*	purple prairie clover
Desmodium canadense	showy tick trefoil
Desmodium illinoense	Illinois tick trefoil
Dodecatheon meadia	shooting star
Echinacea pallida	pale purple coneflower
Elymus canadensis	Canada wild rye
Eryngium yuccifolium	rattlesnake master
Euphorbia corollata	flowering spurge
Gaura biennis	biennial gaura
[†]*Gentianella quinquefolia*	stiff gentian
Geum triflorum	prairie smoke
Helianthus mollis	downy sunflower[a]
Helianthus occidentalis	western sunflower[a]
[†]*Helianthus pauciflorus*	showy sunflower[a]
Heliopsis helianthoides	false sunflower[a]
Hypericum punctatum	spotted St. John's wort

Table 12.1. (*Continued*)

Lespedeza capitata	round-headed bush clover
Liatris aspera	rough blazing star
Liatris cylindracea	cylindrical blazing star
Lilium philadelphicum	prairie lily
Lobelia spicata	pale spiked lobelia
Monarda fistulosa	wild bergamot
Oenothera biennis	common evening primrose
Panicum virgatum	switch grass[a]
Parthenium integrifolium	wild quinine[a]
Pedicularis canadensis	lousewort
Penstemon digitalis	foxglove beard tongue
Phlox pilosa	sand prairie phlox
Polytaenia nuttallii	prairie parsley
Potentilla arguta	prairie cinquefoil
Pycnanthemum tenuifolium	slender mountain mint
Ratibida pinnata	grey-headed coneflower
Rosa arkansana	sunshine rose
Rudbeckia hirta	black-eyed Susan
Ruellia humilis	hairy ruellia
[†]*Schizachyrium scoparium*	little bluestem
Senecio plattensis	prairie ragwort
[†]*Senna marilandica*	Maryland senna
Silphium integrifolium	rosinweed
Silphium laciniatum	compass plant
Silphium terebinthinaceum	prairie dock
Solidago nemoralis	old-field goldenrod
[†]*Solidago ptarmicoides*	stiff aster
Solidago rigida	stiff goldenrod
Solidago speciosa	showy goldenrod
Sorghastrum nutans	Indian grass
Sporobolus heterolepis	prairie dropseed
Stipa spartea	porcupine grass
Tradescantia ohiensis	common spiderwort
Verbena stricta	hoary vervain
Vernonia missurica	Missouri ironweed
Viola palmata	early blue violet
Viola pedatifida	prairie violet
Zizia aptera	heart-leaved meadow parsnip

[a]Very aggressive; use very small amounts or add several years after initial planting.

[†]Precedes scientific name cross-referenced in appendix C.

continues

Table 12.1. (*Continued*)

Dry Prairie

Amorpha canescens	lead plant
Andropogon gerardii	big bluestem
Anemone cylindrica	thimbleweed
†*Artemisia campestris caudata*	beach wormwood[b]
Asclepias amplexicaulis	sand milkweed[b]
Asclepias hirtella	tall green milkweed[b]
Asclepias tuberosa	butterfly weed
Asclepias verticillata	whorled milkweed
Asclepias viridiflora	short green milkweed
Aster ericoides	heath aster
†*Aster oolentangiensis*	azure aster
Aster sericeus	silky aster
Bouteloua curtipendula	side-oats grama
†*Brickellia eupatorioides*	false boneset
Calamovilfa longifolia	sand reed[b]
Callirhoe triangulata	clustered poppy mallow[b]
Ceanothus americanaus	New Jersey tea
†*Ceanothus herbaceus*	inland New Jersey tea
†*Chamaecrista fasciculata*	partridge pea
Coreopsis lanceolata	sand coreopsis[b]
Coreopsis palmata	prairie coreopsis
†*Dalea candida*	white prairie clover
†*Dalea purpurea*	purple prairie clover
Desmodium illinoense	Illinois tick trefoil
Echinacea pallida	pale purple coneflower
Elymus canadensis	Canada wild rye
Eragrostis spectabilis	purple love grass[b]
Euphorbia corollata	flowering spurge
Froelichia floridana	large cottonweed[b]
Gnaphalium obtusifolium	old-field balsam[a]
Helianthus mollis	downy sunflower[a]
Helianthus occidentalis	western sunflower[a]
†*Helianthus pauciflorus*	showy sunflower[b]
Heuchera richardsonii	prairie alum root
Hieracium longipilum	long-bearded hawkweed[b]
†*Koeleria macrantha*	June grass[b]
Lespedeza capitata	round-headed bush clover

Table 12.1. (*Continued*)

Liatris aspera	rough blazing star
†*Mimosa quadrivalvis nuttallii*	sensitive briar
Monarda fistulosa	wild bergamot
Monarda punctata	spotted bee balm[b]
Oenothera biennis	common evening primrose
Opuntia humifusa	prickly pear[b]
Panicum virgatum	switch grass[b]
Parthenium integrifolium	wild quinine
†*Paspalum setaceum*	hairy lens grass[b]
Pedicularis canadensis	lousewort
Penstemon pallidus	pale beard tongue
Phlox pilosa	sand prairie phlox
Polytaenia nuttallii	prairie parsley
Potentilla arguta	prairie cinquefoil
Rosa arkansana	sunshine rose
Rosa carolina	pasture rose
Rudbeckia hirta	black–eyed Susan
Ruellia humilis	hairy ruellia
†*Schizachyrium scoparium*	little bluestem
Senecio plattensis	prairie ragwort
Silphium laciniatum	compass plant
Sisyrinchium campestre	prairie blue–eyed grass
Solidago nemoralis	old–field goldenrod
†*Solidago ptarmicoides*	stiff aster
Solidago rigida	stiff goldenrod
Solidago speciosa	showy goldenrod
Sorghastrum nutans	Indian grass
Sporobolus cryptandrus	sand dropseed[b]
Sporobolus heterolepis	prairie dropseed
Stipa spartea	porcupine grass
Tephrosia virginiana	goat's rue[b]
Tradescantia ohiensis	common spiderwort
Verbena stricta	hoary vervain
Viola pedata	bird's foot violet

Notes: This table was compiled by James F. Steffen.

aVery aggressive; use very small amounts or add several years after inital planting.

bPrimarily species of sand prairies.

†Precedes scientific name cross-referenced in appendix C.

Table 12.2.

Although many of the species in table 12.1 are present throughout much of the tallgrass region, they are joined or supplanted by others in some areas, particularly to the periphery. The lists in this table highlight some of the distinctive species in the western part of the tallgrass region. These brief lists are meant merely to suggest some of the distinctive plants to be included in seed mixes in these areas. To construct full planting lists, compare lists in this handbook with those in the local literature, consult local experts, or visit high-quality remnants in the area.

Eastern Nebraska and Kansas

Dry Prairie

Andropogon hallii	sand bluestem
Bouteloua gracilis	blue grama
Buchloe dactyloides	buffalo grass
Callirhoe alcaeoides	pink poppy mallow
Delphinium carolinianum ssp. *virescens*	prairie larkspur
Echinacea angustifolia	narrow-leaved coneflower
Lactuca tatarica ssp. *puchella*	western blue lettuce
Nassella viridula	green needlegrass
Onosmodium molle hispidissimum	marbleseed
†*Pascopyron smithii*	western wheat grass
Stipa comata	needle-and-thread

Dry-Mesic to Mesic Prairie

Amorpha nana	dwarf wild indigo
Asclepias stenophylla	glade milkweed
Calylophus serrulatus	toothed evening primrose
Dalea candida oligophylla	western prairie clover
Dalea leporina	foxtail dalea
Dalea villosa	silky prairie clover
†*Elymus trachycaulus*	slender wheat grass
†*Eustoma russellianum*	prairie gentian
Gaura parviflora	small-flowered gaura
Glycyrrhiza lepidota	wild licorice
Helianthus maximiliani	Maximilian sunflower
Linum rigidum	stiff-stemmed flax
Ratibida columnifera	long-headed coneflower

Table 12.2. (*Continued*)

Rosa woodsii	western wild rose
Solidago mollis	soft goldenrod
Tradescantia bracteata	long-bracted spiderwort
Vernonia baldwinii	western ironweed
Zigadenus elegans	plains white camass

Wet-Mesic to Wet Prairie

Scirpus hallii	Hall's bulrush
Sisyrinchium montanum	mountain blue-eyed grass
Viola pratincola	blue prairie violet

Western Minnesota, South Dakota, North Dakota

Dry Prairie

Andropogon hallii	sand bluestem
Bouteloua gracilis	blue grama
Buchloe dactyloides	buffalo grass
Delphinium carolinianum ssp. *virescens*	prairie larkspur
Echinacea angustifolia	narrow-leaved coneflower
Liatris punctata	dotted blazing star
Penstemon gracilis	slender beard tongue
†*Psoralidium tenuiflorum*	scurfy pea
Stipa comata	needle-and-thread

Dry-Mesic to Mesic Prairie

Amorpha nana	dwarf wild indigo
Astragalus flexuosus	slender milk vetch
Dalea candida oligophylla	western prairie clover
Dalea leporina	foxtail dalea
Dalea villosa	silky prairie clover
†*Elymus trachycaulus*	slender wheat grass
Gaillardia aristata	northern blanket flower
Glycyrrhiza lepidota	wild licorice
Helianthus maximiliani	Maximilian sunflower
Helianthus nuttallii	Nuttall's sunflower
Ratibida columnifera	long-headed coneflower
Zigadenus elegans	plains white camass

Wet-Mesic to Wet Prairie

Juncus longistylis	large-flowered rush
Liatris ligulistylis	blazing star

Note: This table was compiled by Dave Egan.
†Precedes scientific name cross-referenced in appendix C.

The Truax drill handles fluffy or heavy seed well, but it must be clean. Most newer drills also require that your tractor have at least single hydraulic outlets.

Drills also seed in parallel rows, which can cause some aesthetic concerns. These usually are apparent only for the first few years after seeding, disappearing over time as the rows fill in. Seeding in two operations, the second pass at right angles to the first, creates a cross-hatched pattern of rows. This will fill in more quickly than parallel rows and look more natural in its early stages.

Hand broadcasters and small pull-type fertilizer spreaders are cheap, from $20 to $100. They also are available in most hardware stores. Tractor-pulled spreaders are more expensive, from $400 to $8,000. They can be rented at most agricultural fertilizer and fuel supply centers. Their main disadvantage is the inefficiency of seeding, requiring twice as much seed as a drill for the same area. This is because seed placement and rate are much less accurate. They also cannot be used on a windy day, as seed placed on the surface will blow away.

Most broadcasters also will not handle fluffy seed very well without modifying the agitator, distribution mechanism, and opening. They tend to plug up often, unless the seed is heavy and flows well. This can be overcome by mixing the seed with an inert, weed-free carrier such as cracked wheat, rice hulls, ground corn cobs, vermiculite, or coarse sand.

Broadcast seeding requires a mechanism for incorporating the seed shallowly into the soil. On small plots the seed can simply be raked in lightly by hand. We have used a heavy chain mounted at each end to a two-by-four to drag behind our broadcast seedings. This is a low-tech, inexpensive way of incorporating broadcasted seed. Following incorporation, the site must be roller packed.

One advantage of broadcast seeding is that the seed does not need to be free of straw. In fact, the presence of a certain amount of prairie straw can be useful in providing a mulch. Too much straw, however, can interfere with the important seed-to-soil contact. Seed cleaning is a time-consuming and often expensive task. If you plan to broadcast seed, don't waste a lot of time in getting the seed milled down to 100 percent purity.

Seeding Methods—Drill

The actual seeding should be done immediately after the last cultivation and roller packing. Try to anticipate the weather and seed before a rain. While it is hard to predict, you can increase your chances of getting a good rain on your plot if you know the long-term average time of maximum rainfall in your area. In most of the tallgrass prairie region, this is in late spring or early summer. A good natural rainfall does wonders for a prairie restoration seeding, far more than even the best irrigation system.

Start with a full seedbox, and keep it that way as much as possible. Native-seed drills do not seed as efficiently when the box is less than one-quarter full. Make rounds around the entire area, overlapping slightly on the corners to avoid gaps when turning. Ground speed should be two to three miles per hour. Seeding depth should be ½ inch in clay, silt, or loam soils and ¾ inch in sandy soils. Cover the site entirely once, then again at a right angle to the first pass if seed allows or you are concerned about the row effect.

Monitor the seed-tube windows continuously to ensure they do not become plugged. If one does, stop immediately, remove the occluded seed-tube, and clean it out. We always carry a screwdriver and piece of wire while seeding, specifically for that purpose. When finished, consult the sky and pray for rain!

Seeding Methods—Broadcast

Broadcast seeding should be done immediately after the final cultivation, rototilling, or harrowing, but *before* the site is roller packed. Mix your seed well and divide it into two equal parts. Mix each part with an equal volume of horticultural vermiculite or perlite (available at most garden centers), clean sand, or other inert carrier. Mixing with a carrier bulks up the seed, makes it easier to spread, and allows you to see where you have seeded. Without a carrier the seed often disappears as soon as it hits the ground, making it difficult to see missed spots.

Then start spreading the first lot of seed evenly over the site in a north-to-south direction, making regular transects. Once finished, spread the second lot of seed evenly in an east-to-west direction. This double seeding will ensure that you have covered the entire site without missing any areas. Rake or chain drag the seed in and roller pack immediately. Seeding depth is the same as for drill seeding: ½ inch for clay, silt, and loam soils, ¾ inch for sand. It is normal with broadcasting to have some seed left on the surface. Rains or irrigation will wash the remaining seed in.

Mosaic Seeding

This technique involves differential seeding rates and species mixes for different parts of a prairie restoration. For example, on a hilly site you should plant drier adapted species such as blue grama in greater quantities at the top of a slope. Mesic species such as big bluestem should go in mid-slope areas, with wet meadow plants such as prairie cord grass concentrated at the bottom. This reduces the chance of seeding failures due to incompatibility of the site with the seed. It also more accurately mimics the actual species continuum found along moisture and slope gradients in a real prairie.

Mosaic seeding also may be used to increase the visual diversity of a site. For example, a larger percentage of showy forbs may be planted along a walkway or road where the public is more likely to see them. Biological reasons for mosaic seeding include increasing habitat diversity and more accurately reflecting the unevenness of the original prairie. Planting larger quantities of forbs in some areas also may help some of the less competitive prairie species to hold their own against some of the more aggressive native grasses.

Cover Crops

The question of cover crop usage in prairie restoration seeding is controversial. On the one hand is a large body of practical, hands-on farm experience that indicates that whenever a perennial crop is planted, sowing a faster-growing annual crop as a companion is useful in a variety of ways. The cover crop shades the soil and helps it retain surface moisture, thus preventing sunscald of tender young perennial seedlings when they emerge. Cover crops also outcompete annual weeds. They provide quick soil-holding capabilities on slopes or in light soils where wind erosion can be a problem. A dense annual grass cover crop provides abundant fuel for a managed burn after the first year. It also can be harvested as hay or for grain, providing a source of income off the land for that year.

In contrast, most professional agrologists recommend against cover crops because they compete with your perennial crop for moisture, sunlight, and nutrients. Many agricultural fields have a plentiful seed bank of annual weeds that act as a cover crop without being asked.

If you use a cover crop, choose an annual grass like oats and seed it at a rate of twenty-five to fifty pounds/acre with the prairie seed. Be careful of fall rye and wheat. There is some evidence that they give off underground chemicals that may interfere with the germination of native seed, a process called allelopathy. Cut the cover crop down before it goes to seed, setting the mower higher than the prairie seedlings. Remove or bale off the clippings.

Canada wild rye, native to the tall- and mixed-grass prairie, is widely used in restoration plantings as a short-lived perennial cover crop. It establishes quickly, provides good soil cover, and competes well with weeds. Canada wild rye usually does not persist beyond the first five to eight years of the restoration planting and allows other slower-growing native species to fill in as it declines in dominance.

Summarizing from a restorationist's point of view, the cover crop jury is still out. It probably is of some significant value on light soils or erodible slopes, and in providing fuels for managed burns. Whether it controls weed growth and how necessary this might be is another question. Canada wild rye is a useful cover in the early successional stages of a prairie restoration.

Mulching

Adding a protective mulch to a planting conserves moisture, reduces soil erosion, and increases germination, especially in dry periods. It is difficult to do on a large scale, but most smaller plantings benefit from it. It should be weed free, biodegradable, and nontoxic. Common mulches include straw, cellulose fibre, sawdust, and other organic materials. Straw is readily available in most farming areas, but it is difficult to get it without a lot of unwanted weed seeds. Spreading it evenly over large areas also is hard, unless you have access to a bale buster or straw chopper. Mulch also tends to blow away after the first strong wind, a real problem on open prairie sites. An innovative machine for anchoring straw mulch is the straw crimper. This specially designed rolling drum actually pushes one end of the straw down into the soil and stands the pieces upright. This is very useful on slopes and exposed sites.

Post-Planting Management

Managing the emerging prairie begins with irrigation if possible and if rains are inadequate, regular inspection for perennial weeds, and mowing of annual weeds. Mature prairie plants are adapted to dry conditions, but their seeds will not germinate without sufficient water. In some cases, an entire planting may be lost if seeded just before a drought. On sites without irrigation capability, timing your seeding to coincide with the average period of maximum rainfall is crucial. On small sites where watering is possible, 1 to 2 inches every three days for the first month is ideal. Water as necessary in the second month. Use a rain gauge or common sense to judge how much to water: stop if standing water begins to form puddles on the surface or if soils start to erode. After a few months, the prairie should be able to take care of itself.

Perennial weeds may cause problems even on the best-prepared sites. Dormant seed of these species may germinate, or it may be blown in by wind or brought in by wildlife. Scrupulous eradication of noxious perennials such as Canada thistle, leafy spurge, quack grass, and smooth brome is absolutely imperative. Without quick and effective action, any one of these species could take over your planting with surprising speed.

Appropriate herbicides, applied selectively with a backpack sprayer or wick applicator, are one way of preventing these species from becoming a problem. The length of time needed to be vigilant against weed incursion is unknown, but it is especially important in the first few years. Some managers believe that fire and competition will gradually eliminate most weeds over the years. Once the prairie matures, perennial weed control should be less necessary.

Annual weeds are rarely a problem if managed properly. Mow with a flail, sickle, or rotary mower set high enough to miss most prairie seedlings but low enough to cut the weeds off before they go to seed. This may need to be done every few weeks in the first years, as the prairie plants do not show much above-ground growth. They prefer instead to put down a deep, extensive root system to help them survive in the long term. As the prairie closes in, reducing the amount of bare soil, annual weed populations will decline significantly. Although some managers simply ignore annual weeds, keeping them under control will reduce competition for your native species in their crucial first years and will keep your restoration from being a source of weed pollution to your neighbors.

Fire management also is crucial. The long-term health of a restored prairie ultimately is tied to the proper use of controlled burning. Unless a cover crop has been used, it usually takes two to three years before enough fuel accumulates to carry a fire. Burn as soon as fuel conditions allow. Early to mid-spring burns are the most effective, with fall burns acceptable after the first full year (see chapter 14).

Alternative Prairie Establishment Techniques

The foregoing discussion has set out the most accepted, successful, and predictable means of restoring a plowed-ground prairie. If followed to the letter with no environmental catastrophes, it will result in a successful establishment of a native prairie community in five to ten years. There is more than one way to plant a prairie, however. Some promising but less proven techniques have emerged recently that have considerable potential.

Zero till seeding means using no cultivation or tillage to prepare the site. Existing vegetation is sprayed with herbicides, then burned off. A second, nonchemical method on smaller sites is to cover them with black plastic for one growing season. This kills all underlying vegetation and seeds. A native-seed till drill equipped with zero till coulters plants the seed directly into the killed sod. This method has the advantage of considerably reducing the cost and time for site preparation, reducing moisture loss by using the killed sod as a mulch, improving soil conservation by not laying the soil bare for long periods, increasing the chances of retaining valuable soil mycorrhizae, decreasing weed problems by not bringing additional buried weed seed to the surface, and eliminating the bare-soil surface that many weeds need to germinate.

A nonherbicidal alternative is to cultivate in the fall if the soil is clay, or in the spring if the soil is sandy. Then in the spring plant buckwheat to smother annual weeds. Mow the buckwheat when in flower, let dry, and then till in as a green manure crop. Plant winter wheat in the fall, then cultivate it in before flowering the next spring to prepare the site for a prairie restoration seeding.

Hydroseeding involves suspending the seed in a water-mulch mix and spraying it onto a site with a special high-pressure pump. Conventional bare-soil site preparation usually precedes the hydroseeding. A serious drawback here is getting good seed-to-soil contact, as the seed is suspended above the surface. Using a chain drag after seeding to incorporate the seed is recommended. Cover crops applied with the seed also may have some merit. Then a second application of mulch with no seed should be made. Hydroseeding is widely used by landscapers to seed fast-growing cultivars of introduced lawn grasses. It is useful on steep slopes where regular farm machinery cannot safely travel. The machinery is expensive to buy but usually can be rented from large landscape firms.

Soil impoverishment or reverse fertilization has been used in the forestry industry for many years to promote the growth of certain trees over others. It involves incorporating large amounts of organic matter such as sawdust into the soil. This subsequently decays, promoting substantial increases in soil microbes that temporarily tie up immense amounts of nitrogen. This nitrogen is unavailable for plant growth for one to two years.

Native prairie plants have an innate ability to do well in conditions of low nitrogen, having evolved in soils with limited amounts of this important nutrient. Annual weeds, however, have not. They require large amounts of nitrogen to prosper. These high levels of nitrogen and annual weeds are commonly found in agricultural cropland. Taking advantage of prairie species' ability to tolerate and do well in low-nitrogen soils has potential for giving them a competitive edge over annual weeds. This is especially true in the first few years of a restoration when prairie species are growing slowly and annual weed levels can be nearly astronomical.

To try exploiting this advantage in your own prairie seeding, have your soil nitrogen tested at a soils lab. With the soil test results in hand, consult with a soil scientist to determine the amount of organic matter needed to add to the soil to tie up the available nitrogen for at least one, and preferably two, growing seasons. Apply the recommended amounts of the impoverishing substance, then incorporate into the soil by rototilling. The substance can be any high-carbon-content organic matter such as sugar/sawdust, oat hulls, rice hulls, clean straw, peat moss, or any other clean, weed-free organic matter available.

Conclusion

Restoring native prairies from seed on plowed ground requires careful planning and suitable equipment. Proper site preparation, especially perennial weed control, is the biggest single factor in ensuring the success of your planting. Packing the soil to maintain good seed-to-soil contact also is essential. Drill seeding is the most efficient but also the most costly. Broadcast seeding is easier and cheaper; however, it requires much more seed and is less predictable. Adequate moisture from natural rainfall and/or irrigation after seeding is essential to the success of a prairie restoration. Cover crops and mulching may be helpful in certain circumstances. Followup management with fire and selective perennial weed control is necessary for continued success and the healthy development of your prairie.

REFERENCES

Armstrong, P.K. 1990. "Three No-Till Methods of Establishing Prairie on Small Sites (Illinois)." *Restoration and Management Notes* 8:33.
Betz, R.F. 1986. "One Decade of Research in Prairie Restoration at the Fermi National Accelerator (Fermilab), Batavia, Illinois." In G.K. Clambey and R.H. Pemble (eds.), *The Prairie: Past, Present and Future—Proceedings of the Ninth North American Prairie Conference,* pp. 179–185. Fargo, ND, and Moorehead, MN: Tri-College University Center for Environmental Studies.
Collicutt, D.R., J.P. Morgan, and J.D. Durant. 1994. "Tallgrass Prairie

Experiment Underway in Manitoba." *Restoration and Management Notes* 21, no. 1:74.

Duebbert, H.F., E.T. Jacobson, K.F. Higgins, and E.F. Podoll. 1981. *Establishment of Seeded Grasslands for Wildlife Habitat in the Prairie Pothole Region.* Washington, DC: U.S. Fish and Wildlife Service Special Scientific Report #234.

Howell, E.A., and V.M. Kline. 1994. "The Role of Competition in the Successful Establishment of Selected Prairie Species." In R.G. Wickett, P.D. Lewis, A. Woodliffe, and P. Pratt (eds.), *Proceedings of the Thirteenth North American Prairie Conference,* pp. 193–198. Windsor, ON, Canada: Department of Parks and Recreation.

Johnson, J.R., and M.K. Butler (eds.). 1988. *Proceedings of the Northern Plains Grass Seed Symposium.* Pierre, SD: U.S. Soil Conservation Service.

Morgan, J.P. 1994. "Soil Impoverishment." *Restoration and Management Notes* 12, no. 1:55–56.

Morgan, J.P., D.R. Collicutt, and J.D. Durant. 1995. *Restoring Canada's Native Prairies—A Practical Manual.* Argyle, MB, Canada: Prairie Habitats.

Schramm, P. 1992. "Prairie Restoration: A Twenty-Five-Year Perspective on Establishment and Management." In D.D. Smith and C.A. Jacobs (eds.), *Proceedings of the Twelfth North American Prairie Conference,* pp. 169–177. Cedar Falls: University of Northern Iowa.

13
Hand-Planted Prairies

Peter Schramm

The hand-planted seedling prairie represents the ultimate quality control in prairie restoration. It is the most labor intensive of all prairie planting procedures but on a small scale can be done by anyone in a location that has full sunlight. The process does require total commitment to weeding and watering the first growing season and possibly the second, but it is almost totally carefree thereafter. This process entails the use of selected seedlings set out in a predetermined arrangement and spacing. The following discussion details a procedure for establishing a small, circular prairie garden with a core of mixed grasses and taller forbs, surrounded by a random mix of medium to short forbs combined with the lower-profile quality grasses.

Attempt to obtain the greatest diversity of species, appropriate for your area, that you can get. The bulk of the planting will be based on showy forbs (see table 13.1), the species varying with your specific location. A few seedlings of the taller species such as big bluestem, Indian grass, compass plant, and prairie dock will go in the plot's center hub but should not be overdone. Certain key low-profile grasses—most significantly little bluestem and prairie dropseed—will be part of the spacing structure of the garden and will later provide the fuel matrix for burning, which is crucial to the garden's development and maintenance. Be sure to have extra seedlings of those two species.

Allow six to eight weeks to raise seedlings. The growing process ideally will be started some time in March in mid-latitudes of the prairie region. Using properly conditioned seed, sow pinches of seed in flats of commercial potting soil. If the seed is good, a very small quantity will establish dozens of seedlings. A small greenhouse is ideal for this initial work, but a kitchen window or grow light in a basement also will work. After the seedlings are up, in three or four weeks, gently pry them from the flat with a kitchen knife and transplant them into more potting soil

Table 13.1.

Forbs for Hand-Planted Prairies

Scientific Name	Common Name
Amorpha canescens	lead plant
Asclepias tuberosa	butterfly weed
Aster laevis	smooth blue aster
Aster novae-angliae	New England aster
†*Baptisia alba macrophylla*	white wild indigo
†*Baptisia bracteata leucophaea*	cream wild indigo
Ceanothus americanus	New Jersey tea
Coreopsis palmata	prairie coreopsis
†*Dalea candida*	white prairie clover
†*Dalea purpurea*	purple prairie clover
Dodecatheon meadia	shooting star
Echinacea pallida	pale purple coneflower
Echinacea purpurea	purple coneflower
Eryngium yuccifolium	rattlesnake master
Heliopsis helianthoides	false sunflower
Heuchera americana	alum root
Liatris aspera	rough blazing star
Liatris pycnostachya	prairie blazing star
Monarda fistulosa	wild bergamot
Parthenium integrifolium	wild quinine
Physostegia virginiana	obedient plant
Potentilla arguta	prairie cinquefoil
Pycnanthemum virginianum	common mountain mint
Ratibida pinnata	grey-headed coneflower
Silphium integrifolium	rosinweed
Solidago rigada	stiff goldenrod
Tradescantia ohiensis	common spiderwort
Veronicastrum virginicum	Culver's root
Zizia aurea	golden Alexanders

†Precedes scientific names cross-referenced in appendix C.

in individual cups or the plastic compartmentalized flats used for vegetables. Grow them for another three or four weeks, during which they will become somewhat root bound and crowded. They can remain in a greenhouse during this time, but if they were started in a kitchen window, move them into full sunlight in April. Cover them if frost is predicted and beware of squirrels and birds damaging these precious young plants. Transplant the seedlings into the garden in early to mid-May. This entire process can be started later and seedlings transplanted into the garden in midsummer or even later, as long as the garden is properly watered and weeded throughout the summer.

A circular plot in the middle of a lawn is ideal for such a prairie garden. Full sunlight is a must, and the plot must be kept away from buildings and fences and out from under trees, where it can be burned easily. Start small, so that planting and weeding the first season are easier; a basic circular plot can always be enlarged with concentric circles of additional plants.

As our example, let's start with a circular plot 15 feet in diameter. The simplest preparation is to remove the sod, till shallowly, water well, and place black plastic over the site to kill all the weeds. This is done in April and May, while the seedlings are growing in their individual containers. Controlling the weeds to the maximum extent at this stage will make hand weeding much easier later on.

Six- to eight-week-old or older seedlings are planted in a carefully spaced configuration and arrangement. Get the desired 9- to 12-inch spacing by using a planting board with large nails or bolts attached in the chosen grid configuration. The board can be padded on the other side and used to kneel on. Place it on smooth soil bolt side down and then move it aside and plant the seedlings into the pattern of marks left by the bolts or nails.

First, randomly plant taller grasses and forbs in a 3- to 4-foot core in the center of the 15-foot circle. Then plant the main bulk of the plot, again in a random manner, using various showy forbs interspersed with little bluestem and prairie dropseed. These two grasses should be interspersed throughout the remainder of the planting, in a ratio of roughly one-third grasses to two-thirds forbs, the proportions varying according to individual preference. The carefully spaced seedlings, once released from their root-bound environment, grow down more than up, at an enormous rate the first growing season. The more conservative species remain small for one to several seasons, while the successional prairie species develop more quickly and may even bloom the first, certainly the second, season.

The first growing season entails the most labor. Seedlings must be watered thoroughly and regularly throughout the summer. The garden must also be hand weeded regularly, eliminating *all* weed competition. A regular and dedicated effort is required to keep the plot weed free. Watering and weeding right to the end of the growing season will assure a remarkable result. Some followup weeding the second year may be desirable. And of course that all-important first burn during early spring of the second year will assure that the garden will continue to develop at the maximum rate possible. A bit of little bluestem hay cut in the fall, after the seeds have blown away, can be bagged, stored, and then spread over the plot in early spring to aid this first burn. Burning should be continued annually to maximize the garden's rapid development. By the third year, there will be plenty of fuel in the plot to carry the annual spring burn.

Hand-planted and hand-weeded prairies are labors of love and result in some of the most spectacular achievements in prairie restoration. Through this process you can establish a wonderful mix of even the most competition-sensitive species. In just a few years, the assemblage becomes totally weed free as the below-ground complex becomes a closed system to alien invaders. The hand-planted seedling prairie is truly the ultimate in prairie restoration, creativity, and achievement.

PART IV

Management and Monitoring

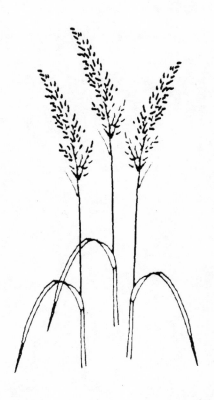

Conducting Burns

Wayne R. Pauly

This chapter describes one style of conducting small prairie fires using hand-held equipment. It is aimed at the novice who has seen a few controlled burns and wants to know a little more. Obviously, just reading this chapter will not qualify you to conduct a controlled burn. Sign up for the prescribed burn courses offered by conservation groups and governmental agencies, and get practical experience by volunteering on burn crews. Burn leaders learn their craft through years of field experience.

A prairie fire burns in a long, narrow line of flames moving quickly through the grass. It is possible to walk several feet behind the flames without discomfort from heat or smoke because flames quickly consume dry grass and move forward for more fuel. Usually a line of fire carried with the wind (head fire) is 5–15 feet deep with flames that leap 8 feet or more, while fire burning into the wind (backfire) is only a foot deep with flames a foot high. But the description of a prairie fire varies considerably, depending on the kind and amount of fuel, height and moisture content of grasses, topography, slope, wind speed, humidity, etc.

The typical prairie fire doesn't exist because there are too many variables. The same prairie will not burn the same way twice, and the way it burns will change from morning to afternoon. Under proper conditions, a grass fire looks tame, but it reacts swiftly to change in wind direction, wind speed, and humidity. A change in wind direction will transform a creeping backfire into a blazing head fire, a doubling of wind speed will quadruple the rate of spread of the fire, and a reduction in relative humidity as a day warms makes a fire burn hotter and faster.

Never take fire for granted, because the worst danger is overconfidence. Under proper conditions of moisture and wind, fire can be controlled, but it is always dangerous. During a few seconds of inattention a fire can change from a safely controlled burn to a racing wall of flames.

There is no substitute for experience when working with fire. If you have never worked on a prairie fire, get experienced people to work with you. Contact local conservation organizations for permission to watch a controlled burn, or volunteer to help. Above all, start small. Your first burn should be no more than a fraction of an acre and planned with as much attention to detail as possible.

Fire History and Effects

Fire has influenced plant communities for millions of years. Furthermore, Native Americans increased fire frequency during the past five or six thousand years, especially in the eastern half of the United States, where lightning fires occur less often than in the West. Early inhabitants burned for many reasons, including improved game habitat, greater nut and berry production, and easier traveling.

Prairies exist in central North America because of the dry climate and periodic drought; along the more rainy eastern edge of the prairie (e.g., Illinois and Wisconsin) fires tip the balance toward prairie and away from forest. Savannas and open oak forests survive because of fire, without which brush and shade-tolerant trees would quickly invade. On the other hand, maple forests are damaged by the coolest ground fire. During a spring woodland walk, notice the dry, crinkled oak leaves ready to burn, while the maple leaves are wet, matted together, quickly decomposing, and ready to resist fire. Today fire is used as a management tool in part due to its historical role, but also because of low cost relative to other habitat management techniques such as mowing, herbicides, and chain-saw work.

The most obvious effects of a burn are easily seen. Fire rejuvenates a prairie; more plants flower, produce seed, grow taller, and are generally more robust than the previous year. Fire lengthens the growing season for most native prairie plants and shortens it for many Eurasian weeds. Fire increases available nutrients through indirect stimulation of microbial activity in the soil and by releasing a small amount of nutrients from the ash. Fire also controls the invasion of shrubs and trees.

Fire lengthens the growing season for warm-season native plants by burning off accumulated leaf litter in the spring and exposing a darkened soil surface to the warming rays of the sun. Without fire, the light-colored leaf litter reflects the sun's rays, insulates the ground like a blanket, and slows the soil-warming process. Most prairie plants grow best in warm soil, and the sooner the soil warms up, the sooner plants start growing. This may extend the growing season by as much as four weeks. Prairie plants are not damaged by a spring fire because most have buds that lie just beneath the soil, where they are protected.

In contrast, fire shortens the growing season for many Eurasian weeds (cool-season plants that originated in the meadows of Europe). Blue-grass, quack grass, and brome grass are examples of cool-season plants that are serious weeds in some prairies. These grasses are usually dormant during the heat of summer, and studies have shown that warm soil causes the roots of some cool-season grasses to stop growing.

As a result, the same fire that encourages warm-season plants discourages cool-season invaders by advancing the onset of warm soil temperatures. In addition, fire may induce water stress on drier prairies, and since prairie plants are better adapted to drought, they compete favorably with the cool-season meadow plants of Europe. Finally, a late-season prairie fire can burn off 3 to 8 inches of growth on the cool-season plants before prairie plants have even started growing.

These factors combine to shorten the growing season for cool-season weeds and give a competitive edge to prairie plants. Unfortunately, late-season burns also shorten the growing season for native cool-season grasses such as porcupine grass, June grass, and Canada wild rye. Although fire may reduce the dominance of these cool-season native plants, it will probably not eliminate them.

Fire controls woody invasion in two ways. First, fire stimulates prairie plants to form a vigorous sod, which prevents establishment of woody seedlings. Second, fire kills the above-ground parts of invading shrubs and trees. Deciduous trees and shrubs resprout from the roots, but red cedar and some pines are killed by fire. Repeated fires are needed to keep resprouting brush under control. Fire weakens brush but rarely eliminates it completely.

Almost any area that has prairie plants will benefit from a burn. Burn a planted prairie as soon as enough plant material has accumulated to carry a fire, which may take two or three years. Prairie seeds added to an old field or prairie planting often grow and flower if encouraged with fire and are most successful on drier sites. Increasingly, oak openings and oak woods are burned to increase light penetration, which seems to stimulate reproduction of wildflowers and oaks. The cool ground fire top kills young saplings of buckthorn, box elder, honeysuckle, etc., whose shade reduces reproduction of desirable species.

There are many plant species, kinds of prairies, and environmental factors that influence a prairie's response to fire, and therefore there is no precise answer to the question of how often a site should be burned—only suggestions. The greater the litter cover, the more positive the response to fire, and since mesic prairies accumulate litter faster than dry prairies, mesic prairies respond better to frequent burning. On average, mesic prairies need between one and three years to accumulate preburn levels of leaf litter (i.e., where leaf litter production equals decomposition). Dry prairies may need four to six years to reach preburn levels. These intervals are adequate for burning healthy prairies with no serious weed problems.

Annual burns are recommended to improve prairies infested with cool-season grasses and will control these weeds more quickly on a dry site than a mesic one because of water stress. Three or more years of successive fires are recommended to begin controlling alien cool-season grasses and woody vegetation. If cool-season grasses are not a problem, then burn every three or four years at irregular intervals. Annual burns can increase the dominance of prairie grasses to the detriment of forbs, and burning at regular intervals can favor certain weeds. In a reasonably good-quality oak opening dominated by brush and saplings, a single fire can increase light penetration enough to improve wildflower growth and reproduction. The second and third consecutive years of fire may double and double again the percent of light reaching the ground.

Most prairie burns are conducted in late March, April, or early May. Dry prairies are usually burned on the earlier dates, because they start blooming several weeks earlier than moist prairies, and a late fire can damage early wildflowers such as violets and shooting stars, although another early wildflower, pasque flower, readily reblooms after a fire. Weedy prairies are burned on the later dates.

Fall fires are sometimes difficult to set up because cool temperatures, absence of killing frosts, and short days keep vegetation too moist to burn. Fall fires destroy winter food and shelter for wildlife, may induce erosion on steep hill prairies, and might escape into the crops adjacent to many prairie remnants. Spring fires are often easier to control because the vegetation has been packed down by snow; the fire moves slower, and flame height is reduced.

Whenever possible, though, degraded oak openings are burned in November and December when the leaves of non-oak species (e.g., common buckthorn, box elder, black cherry) provide effective fuel, instead of the soggy, decomposing leaf mat of spring. In contrast, oak leaves remain crisp and flammable well into spring.

Many ecologists are concerned about the negative impact of fire on insect populations, and recommend leaving half to two-thirds of large remnant prairies unburned each year so the insects can reinvade the burned portion.

Equipment and Its Use

A fire rake is an iron garden rake used to spread fire. (See appendix E for sources of this and other fire equipment.) Check that the metal rake head is bolted on, lest it fall off when heated by the fire. Specially designed fire or asphalt rakes have a 12-inch metal extension between the wooden handle and the rake head, which keeps the worker a foot farther away from the fire and keeps the wooden handle out of the flames. To start the fire, rake up a small bundle of dry grass, light it, and drag it along the ground, exerting a slight downward pressure. It will bounce along, dropping small bits of burning grass and picking up more dry grass for fuel. When dragging the fire rake, there is a tendency to go slower than necessary. Experiment with dragging the fire rake at different speeds. Notice that several seconds after passing over an area, fires start from pieces of burning grass that fall off the fire rake—as though dropping a hundred matches. If the rake is moved too slowly, the handle could burn and the rake head fall off. When necessary, an experienced person can set a line of fire while dragging the fire rake at a jog. Use extra rakes to clear fuel from firebreaks, from around wooden posts and specimen trees, and from any spots benefited by reducing fire intensity.

A wholly different type of fire rake has four sharp triangular teeth (sickle bar teeth) and is ideal for clearing narrow firebreaks in wooded areas. It cuts through small vines, roots, and saplings and does not get clogged with leaves as does the garden rake.

The drip torch is the professional's tool of choice for starting fires. It contains about one gallon of a three-to-one mix of fuel oil and gasoline, which drips out at a controlled rate past a flaming wick that ignites the fuel as it drips to the ground. The volatile gasoline ignites the fuel oil. As the wick heats, its ability to volatilize and ignite the fuel oil increases, becoming less prone to blow out on windy days. Do not increase the percentage of gasoline past 35 percent, and reduce the percentage on warm days. Never use 100 percent gasoline, which would be explosive. Control the drop rate by loosening or tightening the vent screw.

A major advantage of drip torches over fire rakes is the ability to quickly kindle continuous lines of fire, so your crew can immediately put out one edge of a firebreak's fire line. Rakes make interrupted lines of fire, which take several minutes to coalesce into contiguous fire lines. In addition, this increased efficiency gives the torch handler free time to set the torch down and become an extra pair of eyes or hands for fire control. A drip torch is particularly effective for setting fires through the oak openings, where a garden rake gets caught in the vines and saplings. Blow out the torch each time you set it down, and do not drip on your pants or shoes.

A fire swatter is a 12-by-18-inch piece of reinforced rubber attached to a 5-foot handle. It is used to smother small grass fires, and in tall grass it can extinguish the backfire. Swatters alone are useless against a head fire. Swatters are most effective when teamed up with a backpack pump;

the pump operator knocks down the hot fire, and swatters follow behind mopping up.

To use the swatter, raise it 1 or 2 feet and strike at the base of the flames. Do not strike with excessive force, or flaming debris will scatter, starting new fires. When striking the ground, pause momentarily to smother the fire. If the fire is stubborn, like a clump of burning bunch grass, then place the swatter over the fire and step on it to suffocate the flames. Pause occasionally to let the swatter cool since rubber can burn, or ask someone to spray it with water.

A backpack pump is a tank with a five-gallon capacity and a slide-action pump that can shoot a stream of water 20 feet. It is the most valuable piece of hand-held fire-control equipment. The empty tank weighs about 12 pounds, and water weighs about 8.5 pounds per gallon; a full tank weighs over 50 pounds. But tanks are not filled to the top because the water in the top 3 inches splashes out and down your back when you bend over!

Backpack pumps usually have both a single-hole and a two-hole nozzle. The two-hole nozzle produces a spray for working close to the fire and for wetting down areas before they catch fire. This spray nozzle is particularly useful in putting out backfires that are less than a foot deep. The closer the spray is to the fire, the better, so when extinguishing a backfire, work with the nozzle 2 or 3 feet above the base of the flames if the heat allows.

Head fires are 5 to 15 feet deep and hot enough to keep you 10 to 15 feet away. For hot fires use the single-hole nozzle aimed at the base of the flames. Fan the pump side to side so the stream of water covers a wider area. Sometimes in putting out a line of flames, especially backfires, you can stand at one end of a line of flames and lay a stream directly on 20 feet of flames.

Use water efficiently. Very little water is needed to cool a large volume of fuel below the kindling point, especially if a spray is used. With a hot fire, you must use the straight stream, but you can still create a spray. With practice you can use your index finger to create a wide variety of sprays with the single-hole nozzle. Keep the knuckle straight, and hold the fingertip about a half inch in front of the nozzle, so water strikes the fingertip and breaks into large droplets. By moving the fingertip in and out of the water stream, you can adjust the distance and intensity of the spray, or even direct the spray upward to extinguish the underside of logs. Commonly, beginners place a finger directly over the nozzle, as is done with a garden hose, and get more water on themselves than the fire.

Usually, two or more tanks are needed to control a fire. Keep track of how much water you've got left and work with a buddy—one person watches the fire, while the other refills a tank. Take along a bucket and strainer for getting water from lakes, rivers, and ditches.

If your tank goes dry, drop the strap off the left shoulder; this tips the tank, so remaining water pools over the intake hole of the pump hose. You'll get a few extra squirts this way. A few drops of detergent added to each tank breaks water surface tension and makes it spread on the vegetation. Practice so you can hit the target and experiment with the best way to hold the pump to deliver a powerful stream. Remember, the hose must always point down, so the ball valve at the base of the pump works properly.

Take the pump apart and learn how it works so you can fix it during a fire. Most can be taken apart with the fingers. Keep the pump slide well oiled, which reduces water leaking past the gland nut and soaking your hands and clothing. If water continues to leak after oiling, replace the rubber gasket in the gland nut. Occasionally, a tarnish builds up on the sliding brass cylinder, causing the pump to stick. Polish it with a very fine steel wool and it will work like new. Do not allow water to freeze in the tank. Empty the tank, and pump all water out of the hose—pumps are destroyed when water left in the mechanism freezes and expands. Galvanized tanks will rust, and flakes of rust will clog the nozzle; so thoroughly dry out the tank before storing it for the season, or store it upside down.

Sometimes you can borrow equipment from the fire department or from the state conservation department fire-control office. Also, check with local conservation organizations for leads on where to borrow, rent, and buy equipment

Finally, a few comments on clothing. If you can afford it, fireproof Nomex pants and shirts are hard to beat, but those of us on tight budgets can get by with a little common sense. Avoid synthetics such as nylon coats, which burn and melt, and avoid clothing with frayed edges. Wool coats and pants are quite fire resistant, insulate you from the heat, and keep you warm when the fire is finished. Gloves and a long-sleeve shirt protect your arms from radiant heat, which can cause first-degree burns, and a hat keeps embers from your hair. Pull down the brim to help protect your face from sudden flare-ups.

Weather Conditions and Planning

Selecting a day to burn can be discouraging. Spring weather is variable, and there may be only a few days in April when weather is not too windy, wet, dry, calm, or humid for burning. Therefore, plan to burn as early as possible, unless you require a late burn for weed control.

Relative humidity is the most important factor influencing the behavior of a grass fire. Relative humidity is a percentage comparing the actual quantity of water vapor in the air to the maximum quantity of water vapor air can hold at a given temperature. For example, a 60 percent relative humidity at 50° F means that the air contains only 60 percent of the total water vapor it can hold at that temperature. As temperature increases during the day, the quantity of moisture the air can hold also increases, and therefore the quantity of moisture creating 60 percent relative humidity at 50° F will yield only 30 percent relative humidity at 70° F.

As air cools, its ability to hold water vapor is reduced. At night the temperature often falls past the point where relative humidity is 100 percent, and excess water vapor is deposited as dew, which has the same effect as light rain. Relative humidity determines how hot a grass fire will burn. Dry air (low relative humidity) absorbs dampness from dead grass, whereas damp air (high relative humidity) returns moisture to the grass, and dead grass can adjust within minutes to a change in relative humidity. High relative humidity and moist fuel slow a fire because heat is wasted drying the grass before it will burn. In fact, at dusk the falling temperature and rising relative humidity can extinguish a grass fire.

A relative humidity between 25 percent and 60 percent is appropriate for a controlled fire; below 20 percent is hazardous, and above 70 percent grass burns poorly if at all. Above 50 percent there is little chance of spot fires starting from embers carried in the wind, but a fairly brisk wind (10 mph) is needed to drive the fire. The effect of wind is to deflect the angle of the flames and to drive drying heat into the vegetation ahead.

A useful rule of thumb to predict changes in relative humidity during a midwestern spring day is: relative humidity will drop to one-half of its previous value as temperature increases 20° F and will double as temperature decreases 20° F. For example, if the early morning temperature is 40° F, with an 84 percent relative humidity and an expected high for the day of 80° F, as the temperature increases to 60° F, the relative humidity will drop to 42 percent, and at 80° F the relative humidity will be about 21 percent. In another example, if the midafternoon temperature is 70° F with a 33 percent relative humidity, as the temperature drops to 50° F, the relative humidity will double to 66 percent.

The lowest relative humidity of the day is usually between 3:00 P.M. and 5:00 P.M. Therefore, early evening is a good time to burn firebreaks because the falling temperatures cause increased relative humidity and the grass absorbs moisture, burns cooler, and makes fire easier to control. But burning firebreaks in the morning can be tricky, because rising temperatures, decreasing humidity, and increasing winds make fire increasingly difficult to control as the day progresses. Remember, weather conditions affecting a fire can change dramatically in a few hours. You must stay aware of those changes and adapt fire-control techniques accordingly.

Air temperature primarily influences fire behavior by the associated changes in relative humidity, and direct sunshine speeds the drying process. It is hazardous to conduct a prescribed fire above 80° F, and from 70° F to 80° F the rate of spread of fire increases exponentially. Below 32° F light fuels do not burn, although a heavy mat of grass can burn well. Prolonged high temperatures coupled with a lack of rain will dry out heavier fuels like brush and dead wood. This increases the chance that these larger fuels will flare up. Bright sun multiplies the effect of temperature; a south-facing slope will warm up and dry out much faster than a level area. On a partly sunny day, a fire moderates when a cloud blocks the sun and quickens after it passes.

In the evening there can be a temperature inversion, which will hold smoke near the ground. Inversions occur on calm evenings as the sun disappears below the horizon. Air near the ground cools rapidly, but the upper air continues to be warmed by the setting sun. The interface between cold air below and warm air above traps smoke near the ground.

A steady breeze of 3 to 15 mph is ideal for burning because it carries fire in a definite direction, while gusts or steady winds over 15 mph make fire difficult to control. Do not burn on a calm day, when breezes can come from unexpected directions and take fire out of control. It is interesting to note that although wind speed has a marked effect on a head fire, it has little effect on the speed of a backfire. Wind speeds above 15 mph are appropriate for oak opening fires where trees diminish the wind needed to drive fire through sparse fuel. Nonetheless, burning at wind speeds above 15 mph is exclusively for managers experienced in the fire hazards of a particular site. In general, wind is calmer in the morning, picks up during the day, and falls off at dusk. You may choose to burn firebreaks during the morning and evening hours, avoiding the winds of midday.

Fires create their own thermal winds when the quick rise of hot air causes the inrush of cooler air to take its place. A steady breeze moderates the thermal updraft's tendency to take fire in erratic directions and also inhibits the formation of small fire whirlwinds. Whirlwinds form most often while burning grassland on rolling terrain and behave like dust devils you may have seen on dusty ball diamonds. Whirlwinds can pick up a piece of burning debris and carry it several dozen feet.

On the day of the burn, walk over the site and observe wind shifts and gusts. As you walk, throw small pieces of dry grass into the air to see how far they blow and in what direction. Do this several times in different locations. You cannot predict good burning weather more than a few hours ahead of time, so check weather reports the night before, and again on the morning of the fire. There is no substitute for experience in deciding what combination of weather conditions is appropriate for safe burning, so consult with someone who has had experience. For the inexperienced crew, it may be best to start when conditions favor control—45 percent to 60 percent relative humidity, wind around 3 to 10 mph, and air temperature 40° F to 60° F. Burn in late afternoon to early evening, when you know relative humidity is on the rise. Experiment with a few small burns and learn about the fire's behavior and the combustibility of various fuels.

Firebreaks

A firebreak is anything that will stop a fire and contain it in a controlled area. It could be a plowed field, a road, a mowed path, or a burned strip of land. The mowed trail is the most frequently used firebreak; however, sometimes fire is used to widen existing firebreaks or make them where none exist.

A minimum of three to four people is necessary to burn firebreaks. Equipment should include at least two fire backpacks, a fire rake or drip torch, extra water, and a few swatters. Often the person in charge of a crew lights the fire and drags the fire no faster than the crew can handle. One person walks back along the burned firebreak extinguishing smoldering areas that could flare up, while the other crew members work with the individual lighting the fire.

In the spring, you can cut the tall grass before burning a firebreak to make fire easier to control. On the other hand, grass mowed once in the fall at the end of the growing season mats down and is difficult to burn in spring. Grass mowed once in early summer grows enough to carry a fire the following spring, and the reduced fuel load makes fire easier to control.

The following describes how to burn a firebreak at right angles to the wind. With wind from the north, use this method to burn firebreaks on the south and north borders. Make the first firebreak in an east–west direction at the south end of the prairie by starting a fire at the southwest corner and dragging it 5 to 10 feet eastward. Quickly extinguish flames carried with the wind on the south side of the line of fire, because an unexpected gust of wind can fan it into a racing head fire. Allow the fire to slowly back into the wind on the north side. Set fire slowly enough so the crew can keep up.

Allow the backfire to burn until the firebreak is 3 to 20 feet wide, then extinguish it and drag the fire another 10 to 40 feet east. Again, quickly extinguish the south side of the flames carried with the wind and allow the backfire to burn north against the wind. Repeat this process until you have a firebreak the length of the area to be burned. Keep that backfire to a manageable length, usually 40 feet or less, because a wind shift can quickly transform that slow backfire into a blazing head fire. If you need to speed things up, light a second line of fire 5 to 10 feet upwind (north) and parallel to the first line of backfire, and the wind will drive this second line into the backfire of the first line, quickly widening the firebreak.

Some people prefer to rake a scratch line before they burn out the fire-break. They rake away as much litter as possible in a narrow line as wide as the rake along the downwind side of the proposed firebreak. Then they light a backfire along this scratch line. A good scratch line will significantly reduce the amount of water and work required to control a fire.

The following describes how to put in a firebreak by burning directly into the wind. With wind from the north, this is a technique to make firebreaks along the east and west borders. For this firebreak along the east border, start at the south end (downwind), and drag a 3- to 20-foot line of fire at right angles (east-west) to the wind. Put out the flames on the downwind (south) side and allow the fire to back into the north wind, making a firebreak 3 to 20 feet wide. Control the fire by putting out the edges of the line of fire, and allow it to burn into the wind, forming a firebreak along the east (or west) border of the prairie.

To burn firebreaks on steep slopes, burn the first break along the crest, so if fire escapes while burning the other firebreaks, it will burn uphill and stop at the top firebreak. To burn firebreaks down the side of a hill, use a modified version of the technique for burning firebreaks into the wind. Start a 5- to 20-foot line of fire at the top of the hill and parallel to the crest. Extinguish fire on the uphill side and allow it to creep downhill. Control the width of the firebreak by extinguishing the sides of the fire. Fire usually burns slowly downhill and quickly uphill, regardless of wind direction.

Conducting a Simple Burn

For this imaginary burn, we will use one acre of prairie surrounded by old fields of quack and brome grass. Wind is from the north, shifting northeast and then back north.

Some things to consider include: 1) where to get equipment, 2) whether the local municipality or fire department requires a permit, 3) having several plans for wind from different directions, 4) what to do if the wind shifts direction during the fire, 5) how to respond to an escaped fire, 6) what time of day you will burn, and 7) where you will put the primary firebreaks, and whether you can locate any secondary firebreaks that could contain an escaped fire.

Contact the fire department and sheriff on the day of the fire and explain your plans. Talk with the neighbors, since a fire department may be required to respond to a call despite prior assurance that it is a properly supervised fire. Take copies of any permits, write down the phone number of the nearest fire department, locate the nearest telephone or take along a cellular phone, and encourage the fire dispatch to call if any concerns arise during the fire.

Plan the sequence of burning firebreaks so that each completed firebreak reduces the risk of an escaped wildfire when the next firebreak is burned. Therefore, if wind is out of the north, burn the first firebreak on the south side at a right angle to the wind. If fire escapes while burning the other firebreaks, the north wind will drive the fire toward the south firebreak.

Burn the second firebreak on the west border using one of two methods; either a 10-foot-wide line of backfire burning at right angles (east–west) to the north wind, or a north–south line of fire burning to the east, while extinguishing flames burning on the west side of the proposed firebreak. This line of fire parallel to the wind is a flank fire, and since wind is shifting to the northeast, the flank fire burns as a backfire into the shifting northeast wind.

Flank fire is tricky to manage because a slight wind shift can transform it into a head fire. Remember, have no more than 40 feet of backfire burning at one time, lest an unexpected northwest wind transform it into a racing head fire. If a wind shift does bring about a racing head fire, it should burn out at the south firebreak if it's wide enough, while crew members put out the backfire to the north and east. Watch for patches of heavy fuel where fire can surge ahead, forming a bulge that the north wind could fan into a mini head fire. Strive to keep the fire line straight.

Make the third firebreak along the eastern border with either a 10-foot-wide fire burning northward into the wind, or a flank fire burning to the west. If fire escapes, it should burn out against the firebreaks on the south and west sides. If winds are variable, you may choose to burn a fourth break on the north end to encircle the site.

Now we're ready to burn the prairie. Walk the firebreaks to check for unburned fuel. In thickly matted grass, check by raking off the ashes to reveal either bare dirt or partially burned grass and burn the leftover fuels.

Gather the crew, explain the plan, and describe where each member should be. Station several people downwind and on the flanks to watch for spot fires started by glowing embers. Since people tend to stare at the main fire, remind them to look away toward the unburned areas. Review the fallback plan in case of an escaped fire and designate a person to phone the fire department. Remind the spotters that if enveloped by thick smoke, they should crouch down where air is cleaner and move to a safe location. Never get in front of an escaped head fire.

Review current weather conditions, especially the relative humidity, and conduct a small head-fire test along one of the firebreaks to see if you think conditions are appropriate for the larger fire.

There are three basic patterns of ignition: ring fire, backfire, and strip head fires. With a ring fire the prairie is encircled with fire, which sweeps across the area (see figure 14.1). But first, firebreaks are widened with backfires. Two people drag fire along the inside edge of the north fire-break in opposite directions from the center. They continue dragging the fire along the inside perimeter of the east and west firebreaks, and halt at the southern end of the firebreaks. If wind is shifting south to southeast, the person dragging fire up the east border should stay several dozen feet behind the equivalent position of the person on the west border, so as to prevent smoke and fire from engulfing crew members on the west border.

Make sure the downwind firebreak is wide enough to contain blown embers. You may want to use a couple of strip head fires to quickly widen it before starting to encircle the site with fire.

Now the crew leader must determine if the firebreaks are wide enough to contain a head fire set along the southern border. Finally, a head fire is dragged across the south end, and crew members put out the backfire burning southward. Be sure that everyone is ready for the head fire because it can burn with incredible speed and heat that will keep everyone dozens of feet away. Station people around the perimeter to watch for fires creeping across partially unburned portions of the fire-break and for spot fires ignited by airborne embers.

A ring fire gets the job done quickly, creates a strong, hot updraft that disperses smoke, and burns areas of sparse fuel where fire must jump from clump to clump. However, once the head fire gets a good start, it is a power unto itself, and only wide firebreaks will stop it. The strong updraft can carry glowing embers farther than a backfire. So watch for spot fires downwind of the head fire, especially in brushy areas where glowing wood embers persist longer than grass embers.

A second technique is to backfire the entire area (figure 14.2). It's a relatively easy type of fire for inexperienced crews to control, but watch for 180° wind shifts that would fan creeping backfire into running head fire. A disadvantage involves the slow progress of backfire, which might travel 30 feet in ten minutes while a head fire could travel 200 feet. This added time for backfire increases the chance of a wind shift before you're through. The advantage is a reduction in the density of smoke released at any one time, although a disadvantage is that smoke tends to stay near the ground because there isn't a strong thermal updraft to disperse it.

Figure 14.1. Ring fire.

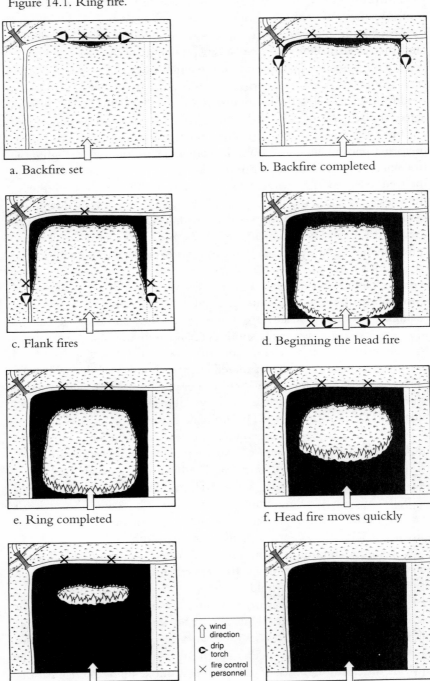

a. Backfire set

b. Backfire completed

c. Flank fires

d. Beginning the head fire

e. Ring completed

f. Head fire moves quickly

g. Head fire meets backfire

h. Fire completed

⇧ wind
direction

◖ drip
torch

✕ fire control
personnel

The third technique (figure 14.3), strip head fires, is probably the most versatile method of prescribed burning. The downwind firebreak is widened with the backfire so the first strip head fire won't jump across, and then each strip head fire is set upwind and at a distance chosen to keep flame length and fire intensity at a comfortable level. The strips can vary from 20 to 150 feet wide, and you adjust fire intensity by varying the width with changing weather or fuel conditions. Small areas of heavy fuels can be backfired.

The person igniting the strip fire should discontinue each strip well before it reaches the oncoming firebreak, especially if fuel is heavy near the break. The drip torch should then be tipped up (or extinguished) and carried to the point where the backfire from the previous strip meets the firebreak. Here the person carrying the drip torch begins a flank fire that will burn a necessary break up to the point where the next strip will start (see figure 14.3c). The reason for this practice is that otherwise the suppression crew would have to control a head fire immediately adjacent to the firebreak, an unnecessarily difficult and risky challenge except under very mild conditions. Normally the suppression crew controls only backfires and flank fires. Head fires are controlled by backfires or wide firebreaks.

Figure 14.2. Backfire.

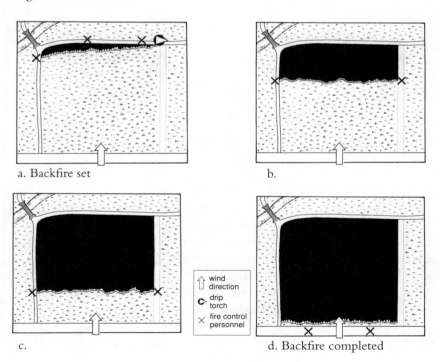

a. Backfire set

b.

c.

d. Backfire completed

↑ wind direction
C drip torch
× fire control personnel

Figure 14.3. Strip head fires.

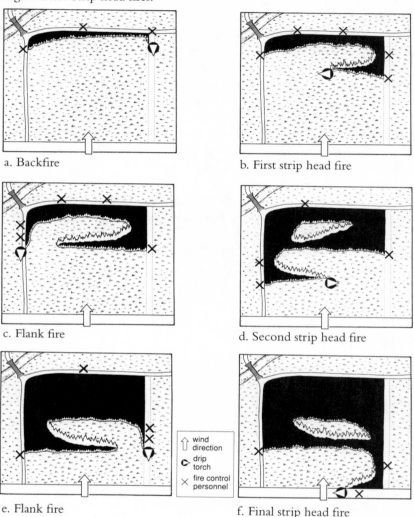

a. Backfire

b. First strip head fire

c. Flank fire

d. Second strip head fire

e. Flank fire

f. Final strip head fire

The greatest fire intensity occurs at the convergence of a head fire with backfire of the previous strip, where they interact to produce the largest flames, highest intensity, and greatest thermal updrafts. When three or more strips are burning, interaction can create unexpectedly fierce fires, especially when fuels are heavy, winds are light, and strips are closely spaced. Keep fire lines relatively straight and at a right angle to the wind, because a deep curve in the line allows fires on either side of the curve to come together and produce intense local fires.

With thorough planning and an experienced crew, there is no reason why a prescribed burn need ever escape. But planning for escaped fires is part of good preparation. All burn plans should locate all hazards near the site (fuel storage areas, homes, adjacent areas of dense fuel, roads where drifting smoke would be a problem etc.) At the beginning of each burn determine which of such hazards would be in the path of an escaped fire during that day's burn, and alert the crew to any special considerations. Determine under what conditions it would be necessary to call the fire department or police, and designate a person to do so.

In the case of an escaped fire, determine where that day's wind would take it, and locate the nearest natural firebreak like a road, river, or plowed field that might stop a racing fire. Then divide into two groups and work on opposite flanks of the escaped fire. Extinguish the edges, and work toward the middle so as to narrow the line of fire, while the leading edge of the head fire burns toward the natural firebreak. Be alert for burning debris blown across the firebreak, starting new fires.

A backfire set along the edge of a narrow firebreak like a small stream, ditch, or trail might widen it enough to halt a wildfire. But usually a backfire is a last resort to limit an out-of-control fire, because you must race to the area selected for the backfire, work directly in the path of the racing wildfire, and then get out of the way. And because you're working fast, there are more chances for mistakes. Worst of all, flames from the backfire could creep across a small, natural firebreak, creating two fires out of control. A partial solution is for two people to stay at the natural firebreak and set the backfire if needed.

Do not get directly in front of the head fire, because a gust of wind could cause flames to leap ahead, engulfing you in the heat and smoke. Wind-driven embers could start another fire dozens of feet beyond the main fire, trapping you in between.

Finish up by extinguishing the smoldering hot spots. Turn over logs to check the undersides, because wind can fan smoldering wood into flames hours after you're gone. Check for fire at the base of wooden fenceposts, trees, railroad ties, and poles. Conserve water; get it directly on the hot spot. Work in pairs; one person rakes away ashes or turns a log, while the other wets it down. Look for smoking clumps of bunch grass because these plants may die if fire in the center is not put out. It may not seem necessary to extinguish all the little smoldering fires, but it is good public relations to be thorough.

Finally, inventory equipment so nothing is lost.

Hazards

This final section introduces an assortment of difficulties that could arise on a controlled burn.

Overconfidence is always the number-one hazard. A controlled burn can change into a wildfire in less than a minute, and the typical reason is inattention and inadequate planning. People take their skill in handling fire for granted if they work with it for several hours, but conditions change during the day. An unexpected gust combined with lower relative humidity can dramatically change fire behavior, and the crew must be ready to respond instantly. Everyone must bear in mind that fire is a dangerous tool. It can be controlled but not tamed. *Every fire is a potential wildfire.*

Pines are often found near remnant dry prairies, and the pitch exuding from wounds is easily set ablaze and difficult to extinguish. On the other hand, many pines are surprisingly well adapted to fire. Needles may scorch and wither, but new ones emerge each spring from buds that seem immune to all but the hottest fires. Late spring fires after new needles emerge are sometimes hazardous because the high resin content of fresh needles is quite flammable. Also, ground fires often smolder under the surface of the needle duff and flare up several minutes after you're sure it's all out.

Fire and cutting are ways to control brush, but only the tops are killed and the brush resprouts. Burning through brushy grasslands causes problems, because embers from dead branches are carried by hot thermals across firebreaks. This is an increasing hazard as relative humidity drops below 50 percent, because above 50 percent spot fires rarely occur. Burning embers may travel 10 to 100 feet or more depending on wind speed and fire intensity, so plan your ignition pattern and firebreaks accordingly. By cutting down sparse patches of brush ahead of time you can deter embers from rising on hot air currents. However, if the brush is thick, you'll want to burn brush piles when there is snow or wet conditions. Another factor to consider is that the multiple resprouts of cut brush are often more heavily damaged by fire than single stemmed saplings. The leaf litter trapped in the center of the multiple stems burns hot, and thin-barked young growth is easily damaged by the heat.

The renewed vigor shown by some woody invaders after a fire can be discouraging, because it often takes three consecutive years of fire to significantly reduce the density and vigor of many woody species. A relative humidity around 30 percent is considered ideal to inflict maximum damage, but sometimes experienced managers can conduct safe low-humidity fires (below 25 percent) in brushy prairies. Keep in mind that the moisture content of woody material reacts more slowly than grass to relative humidity and rainfall, so fire safety and intensity are influenced by moisture conditions in the days preceding the fire in addition to current conditions. A succession of windy days with exceptionally low humidity coupled with no rain makes for extreme burning conditions. Burning at such times should be avoided by anyone without extensive experience.

Because oak leaves persist through the winter without decomposing, a breeze can carry burning leaves across firebreaks. The solution is wide firebreaks and alert crew members around the perimeter. Black oaks often hang on to their leaves all winter, and so a tongue of flame can ignite the leaf-laden branches, making for a good deal of excitement.

Fire whirlwinds can transport burning material and ignite new fires. The solution is alert crew members and the knowledge that whirlwinds happen most often when winds are light (3–8 mph), fuel concentrations are heavy, and head fires meet backfires. Whirlwinds also occur when fire burns up a lee slope and over a ridge into the wind.

A hollow or cracked wooden pole (e.g., a telephone pole) or tree (dead or alive) can ignite, creating a chimney fire, in which fire in the base creates a draft up the hollow center that burns like fire in a fireplace. Even a hollow log on the ground can act as a horizontal flue and send embers several hundred feet. A surprisingly small flame licking punky wood can start it smoldering, often not noticeably for fifteen or twenty minutes, and smoldering rotten wood is extremely difficult to extinguish. Cutting a tree down is about the only really effective way to stop a chimney fire; otherwise, you'll need lots of water and maybe a ladder. Hollow-tree fires can sometimes be moderated or extinguished by sealing the base with moistened dirt, which is most effective for hollow trees with no opening at the top. Therefore, create firebreaks around problem trees by raking away excess grass, wetting down the trunk, and burning a firebreak around the base.

Some people recommend removing hollow trees before conducting a prescribed burn, but these trees are homes for flying squirrels, raccoons, woodpeckers, bluebirds, and many other animals. Alternatively, you could deal with chimney fires as a natural phenomenon, particularly because some plant species reproduce best on ground scorched by hot fires. Allowing logs to burn out naturally also reduces future fire management problems. Watch for burning timber that might fall across firebreaks or roll down slopes, and remember that fires that die back in the evening may smolder and revive dramatically the next morning as temperatures rise.

Low telephone lines can be damaged by the heat of a head fire, so burn under lines with a backfire. Use caution around power lines because the carbon in a thick blanket of smoke billowing through the lines can allow bolts of electricity to arc across.

In a dry year, organic marsh soil can catch fire, so don't burn in a marshy area if the soil is dry. Peat fires are extremely difficult to put out and can burn for months. Be aware of sphagnum in certain wet prairie marshes which could be destroyed by fire in a dry year.

Fire in a thick mat of Eurasian old-field grasses is difficult to put out, because it smolders under the surface. When you use a fire swatter on a backfire in the thick mat, embers fly out from under and spread the fire (this is a particular problem with reed canary grass). A fire broom is especially effective on a backfire in matted grass, because it sweeps under the edge of the mat and gets directly at the hot spot. Water from a backpack pump is deflected by the dense mat, and fire beneath will continue to smolder. Water is most effective if you work from within the burned-out area and spray it back beneath the mat, directly on the hot spot. However, the burned-out area of a backfire is very smoky.

A hazard with burning firebreaks in matted grass moistened by dew or rain is that the dry upper layer burns off while the unburned moist grass beneath is exposed to the drying action of wind and sun. Later on, flames can creep across the firebreak, using these patches of partially dried grass.

It is hazardous to burn through areas of poison ivy, because smoke particles carry the irritating oil from dead leaves and woody stems. Contact with this smoke causes a rash on sensitive people, and if inhaled, causes serious complications in the lungs. This appears to be more of a problem with summer and fall fires and when burning brush piles containing poison ivy debris.

Burning late in the spring season when vegetation is green will produce lots of smoke. Avoid breathing this smoke, because it can make you sick. Often you can attack a smoky head fire from inside the burned area, and from that position wind carries smoke and heat away from you. If you get caught in a cloud of smoke, crouch down where air is cleaner and move to a safe area.

Extremely low relative humidity (less than 20 percent) makes for very hazardous fire conditions. A light gust of wind can take a small fire raging out of control, because there is so little moisture in the grass to slow ignition. Remember, moisture contributed by humidity slows a fire because some heat is used up drying out the grass before it will ignite.

Roads and trails are excellent firebreaks, but beware of bridges and leaf-filled culverts, where soggy leaves can smolder overnight until a fresh breeze spurs the fire through it and out the other side, creating a horizontal chimney fire.

A fence line of brush with too little litter to maintain a backfire cannot be trusted to stop a head fire, which can generate sufficient heat to ignite the tips of dead branches and send burning debris across the break.

As you gain experience with prescribed burns, you learn that there isn't one single best way to conduct one. Instead, you learn the basics of fire behavior, just as you might learn human behavior, and then treat each fire as an individual.

REFERENCES

Collins, S.L., and D.J. Gibson. 1990. *Fire in North American Tallgrass Prairies.* Norman: University of Oklahoma Press.

Henderson, Richard A., and Sandra H. Statz. 1995. *Bibliography of Fire Effects and Related Literature Applicable to Ecosystems and Species of Wisconsin.* Madison, WI: Department of Natural Resources, Technical Bulletin No. 187.

Hulbert, L.C. 1988. "Causes of Fire Effects in Tallgrass Prairie." *Ecology* 69, no. 1:46–58.

Pyne, S.J. 1982. *Fire in America: Cultural History of Wildland and Rural Fire.* Princeton, NJ: Princeton University Press.

Wright, H.A., and A.W. Bailey. 1982. *Fire Ecology.* New York: John Wiley.

15
Summer Fires

Roger C. Anderson

In midwestern prairies, prescribed burning usually takes place in fall and spring. However, after working in Nebraska and consulting historical sources, Bragg (1982) indicated that prairies also were burned in the summer. I have reported experimental results from studies of prairies burned in summer when they supported green biomass (Anderson 1972a, Adams et al. 1982), and Howe (1994a, 1994b) has reported the results of studies of summer burns on experimental plots containing prairie species. These studies, and the historical records of summer burns, suggest that prairies are at least tolerant to summer burning and raise the question of whether or not summer burns should be used as a management tool on tallgrass prairies.

Often, dormant-season burns in tallgrass prairies do not control invading woody species; many such, including prairie willow, smooth sumac, and oaks, readily resprout. Summer burns may be more detrimental to woody plants than dormant-season burns. They kill the shoot after energy and inorganic nutrient reserves were invested in a mass of leaves, and the energy reserves may not have been replenished by the newly developed foliage. Also, some plants send inorganic nutrients from leaves to roots before senescence in late summer or early fall (Adams and Wallace 1985). If the burn precedes that nutrient transfer, those nutrients may be lost to the plant by a summer burn.

Adams et al. (1982) compared woody plant response to late-winter (mid-March) and summer (mid-July) burns in a south-central Oklahoma old field invaded by prairie species and weeds and dominated by little bluestem. Except for stems of the smallest size sampled, the density of most woody species was reduced to below preburn conditions by both burns, and some woody species were eliminated by fire. These species included poison ivy, rough-leaved dogwood, post oak, and winged sumac on the late-winter burn site and poison ivy, rough-leaved dogwood, green ash, winged elm, and cottonwood on the summer burn site.

Unexpectedly, the late-winter burn was more detrimental to woody species than the summer burn. This may have resulted from pronounced drought in the growing season following the late-winter burn (in 1980)—possibly more detrimental to woody species on the late-winter burn site than on the summer burn site. Regrowth of vegetation after the summer burn in 1979 left litter on the surface that could have reduced soil moisture loss in 1980. In contrast, on the late-winter burn site the absence of the litter layer would have resulted in higher rates of soil moisture evaporation and heating than on the summer burn site. This would have accentuated the effect of the drought and contributed to woody plant mortality.

The regrowth of herbaceous vegetation following a summer burn can be quite rapid. For example, in 1972 I reported that following a summer burn in southern Illinois, the prairie began to resprout within a few days in spite of a severe drought (1972a). Many species had shortened life cycles and completed vegetative growth and flowered within a much shorter period than normal. For example, flowering spurge flowered within two weeks after the fire, and wild quinine after about five weeks. By the end of the growing season, about 84 percent of the ground surface was covered with vegetation.

Following the previously described summer burn in Oklahoma, herbaceous prairie species resprouted in about ten days to two weeks. Two woody species, winged sumac and peppervine, also resprouted during the growing season in which the summer burn occurred. Similarly, herbaceous prairie species resprouted following a prescribed burn in late June 1973 at the University of Wisconsin–Madison Arboretum. At the arboretum, a small portion (about 0.6 acre) of the Curtis Prairie was burned to control quaking aspen that was vigorously invading the east end of the prairie. Although the prairie species regrew during that season, aspen did not resprout that year or the next (Anderson 1982).

Dormant-season burns favor native C4 plants (warm-season plants) by increasing the rate of soil warming in the spring (Anderson 1972b, 1982) and the availability of inorganic nutrients and soil moisture (Knapp and Seastedt 1986, Gilliam et al. 1987), and by creating a favorable temperature for net primary production through litter removal (Old 1969, Peet et al. 1975, Knapp 1984). Often, prescribed prairie burns are conducted when native and exotic C3 plants (cool-season plants) are actively growing in the spring or fall and C4 plants are dormant. These burn conditions retard the growth of C3 plants and enhance the growth of the dominant C4 prairie plants. Because the current climatic conditions of the midwestern tallgrass prairie appear to favor C3 plants over C4 plants, most managers of prairies would accept this management scheme as being desirable (McClain 1986, Schramm 1990).

Recently, Howe (1994a, 1994b) proposed summer burning as a way of enhancing the grass and forb diversity of prairies. By burning in July and August when C4 plants are actively growing and C3 species have completed their period of most active growth, the growth of the dominant C4 plants is discouraged and the C3 plants are favored. Examination of the data presented by Howe, however, indicates that C3 species that had a positive response to fire included an exotic species—quack grass, an early successional prairie species—black-eyed Susan, and two native weeds—annual fleabane and horseweed. The only native C3 prairie grass included in the study was Canada wild rye, and it did not display a positive response to the growing-season burn compared to its response to a dormant-season burn.

The summer burn conducted by Howe occurred on July 15, 1989, following the extreme drought of 1988 that extended into the growing season of 1989. Droughty conditions may have influenced the response of the C4 plants to the burn. Following the summer burns I have seen in southern Illinois (July 1970), Wisconsin (late June 1973), and Oklahoma (July 1979), the prairie regrew during the growing season of the burn, as previously noted. The more northerly location of Howe's study site, or the later burn date, may have prevented the regrowth of prairie on his site. However, the drought conditions may have been responsible for the lack of regrowth. For example, McNaughton (1985) reported that in the Serengeti of Africa, grass will regrow following intensive grazing if there is excess soil moisture. Summer burns, if conducted early enough in the growing season, and intensive grazing may be similar in that both can stimulate regrowth.

The tallgrass prairie of the Midwest is a recent phenomenon (less than 10,000 years old), and this prairie was historically exposed to a fire regime of dormant-season burns that were mostly set in the fall by Native Americans (Axelrod 1985, Pyne 1986, Anderson 1990, Brown 1993, and McClain 1994). There is little evidence that lightning-caused fires were of frequent occurrence in the tallgrass prairie of the Midwest (McClain 1994). This is in contrast to the grasslands of the Great Plains, where summer fires caused by lightning strikes apparently occurred more frequently (Howe 1994a, 1994b). In this regard, it is of interest that the northern portions of the mixed-grass prairie of the Great Plains are dominated by C3 grasses (e.g., western wheat grass, thickspike wheat grass, and porcupine grass), whereas the southern mixed-grass prairie is dominated by C4 grasses (e.g., little bluestem and grama grasses) (Risser et al.

1981). This suggests that temperature is an important component in determining the relative abundance of C3 and C4 grasses even in areas where presumably summer burns occurred.

Growing-season burns may enhance the diversity of tallgrass prairie grasses and forbs and assist in controlling the invasion of woody species. Nevertheless, there is insufficient scientific documentation and historic evidence to propose widespread use of growing-season burns as a management procedure in midwestern tallgrass prairies. I strongly recommend that research on the effect of summer burns on prairie ecosystems, including studies of animal populations, be continued. We should not forget that only a few decades ago there was widespread opposition to the use of any prescribed burning as a management procedure. Other management practices, such as varying the length of time between prescribed burns (Kucera and Koelling 1964), increasing the ratio of forb seed to grass seed in planting mixtures for prairie restorations, and establishing prairie forbs before grasses are introduced in restored prairies, may increase diversity and abundance of C3 plants and forbs in Midwest tallgrass prairies.

REFERENCES

Adams, D., R. Anderson, and S. Collins. 1982. "Differential Response of Woody and Herbaceous Species to Summer and Winter Burning in an Oklahoma Grassland." *Southwestern Naturalist* 27:55–61.

Adams, D. E., and L. L. Wallace. 1985. "Nutrient and Biomass Allocation in Five Grass Species in an Oklahoma Tallgrass Prairie." *American Midland Naturalist* 113:170–181.

Anderson, R. C. 1972a. "Prairie History, Management and Restoration in Southern Illinois." In *Proceedings of the Second Midwest Prairie Conference, Madison, Wisconsin,* J. Zimmerman, ed., pp. 15–21.

———. 1972b. "The Use of Fire as a Management Tool on the Curtis Prairie." *Proceedings Annual Tall Timbers Fire Ecology Conference.* Tall Timbers Fire Ecology Research Station, Tallahassee, Florida.

———. 1982. "An Evolutionary Model Summarizing the Roles of Fire, Climate, and Grazing Animals in the Origin and Maintenance of Grasslands: An End Paper." In *Grasses and Grasslands: Systematics and Ecology,* J. Estes, R. Tyrl, and J. Brunken, eds., pp. 297-308. Norman: University of Oklahoma Press.

———. 1990. "The Historic Role of Fire in the North American Grassland." In *Fire in North American Tallgrass Prairies,* S. Collins and L. Wallace, eds., pp. 8-18. Norman: University of Oklahoma Press.

Axelrod, D. 1985. "Rise of the Grassland Biome, Central North America." *Botanical Review* 51:164–196.

Bragg, T. B. 1982. "Seasonal Variation in Fuel and Fuel Consumption by Fires in a Bluestem Prairie." *Ecology* 63:7–11.

Brown, D. A. 1993. "Early Nineteenth-Century Grasslands of the Mid-continent Plains." *Annals of the Association of American Geographers* 83:589–612.

Gilliam, F. S., T. R. Seastedt, and A. K. Knapp. 1987. "Canopy Rainfall Interception and Throughfall in Burned and Unburned Tallgrass Prairie." *Southwestern Naturalists* 32:267–271.

Howe, H. F. 1994a. "Managing Species Diversity in Tallgrass Prairie: Assumptions and Implications." *Conservation Biology* 8:691–705.

———. 1994b. "Response of Early- and Late-Flowering Plants to Fire Season in Experimental Prairies." *Ecological Applications* 41: 121–133.

Knapp, A. K. 1984. "Post-Burn Differences in Solar Radiation, Leaf Temperature and Water Stress Influencing Production in a Lowland Tallgrass Prairie." *American Journal of Botany* 71:220–227.

Knapp, A. K., and T. R. Seastedt. 1986. "Detritus Accumulation Limits Productivity of Tallgrass Prairie." *Bioscience* 36:662–667.

Kucera, C. L., and M. Koelling. 1964. "The Influence of Fire on Composition of Central Missouri Prairie." *American Midland Naturalist* 72:142–147.

McClain, W. E. 1986. *Illinois Prairie, Past and Future: A Restoration Guide.* Springfield: Illinois Department of Conservation, Division of Natural Heritage.

———. 1994. "Occurrence of Prairie and Forest Fires in Illinois and Other Midwestern States, 1679–1854." *Erigenia* 13:79–90.

McNaughton, S. J. 1985. "Ecology of a Grazing Ecosystem: The Serengeti." *Ecological Monographs* 55:259–294.

Old, S. M. 1969. "Microclimate, Fire and Plant Production in an Illinois Prairie." *Ecological Monographs* 39:355–384.

Peet, M., R. Anderson, and M. S. Adams. 1975. "Effect of Fire on Big Bluestem Production." *American Midland Naturalist* 94:15–26.

Pyne, S. J. 1986. "Fire and Prairie Ecosystems." In *The Prairie: Past, Present, and Future,* G. Clamby and R. Pemble, eds., pp. 131–137. Proceedings of the Ninth North American Prairie Conference, Tri-College University Center for Environmental Studies, North Dakota State University, Fargo.

Risser, P., E. C. Birney, H. Blocker, W. Parton, and J. Weins. 1981. *The True Prairie Ecosystem.* Stroudsburg, PA: Hutchinson Ross Pub. Co.

Schramm, P. 1990. "Prairie Restoration: A Twenty-Five-Year Perspective on Establishment and Management." In *Proceedings: Thirteenth North American Prairie Conference,* R. Wickett, P. Lewis, A. Woodliffe, and P. Pratt, eds., pp. 169–177. Department of Parks and Recreation, Windsor, Ontario, Canada.

16
Controlling Invasive Plants

Mary Kay Solecki

Prairies and savannas face a growing threat from aggressive exotic plants and animals. In addition, certain aggressive native plants can become so abundant that they degrade or slow recovery of native communities. By forming large monocultures, such problem species can significantly reduce the diversity and complexity of prairies and savannas.

Exotic plant species (also known as alien or introduced species) have become problematic for several reasons. First, a large number have become abundant and widespread in this country. Second, the disturbed nature of much of today's landscape provides growing conditions that are more suitable for a variety of exotic, distur-bance-adapted plants than for the native species that originally inhabited the land. Anything that damages a healthy ancient natural community—whether it be plowing, trampling, or less obvious disturbances such as lack of fire—is likely to open the way for invasive species.

Third, the small size (often under forty acres) and isolation of many prairie and savanna remnants or restorations, and their accompanying high proportion of edge, leaves them very susceptible to invasion by aggressive exotic and native plants.

This chapter details control methods for twenty plants that invade native prairies and savannas as well as established restorations. Herbicides recommended to control these plants are summarized in table 16.1. These problem species typically differ from those that farmers and gar-deners cope with. The latter species often affect prairie restorations during their first season after sowing and are combatted through soil preparation and burning, activities discussed elsewhere in this book.

Preceding the species-by-species listing of control guidelines is a dis-cussion of control principles and methods, which details the recom-mended control techniques. The restorationist should skip none of this introduction and may need to reread it with successive forays into

Table 16.1.

Herbicides: Use and Application

Alien or Aggressive Plant	Recommended for High-Quality Natural Areas, Restorations, and Degraded Areas	Recommended for Restorations and Degraded Areas
autumn olive	Roundup—cut surface	Garlon 4—basal bark; 2,4-D or dicamba—foliar spray
black locust	Roundup—cut surface	Garlon 3A—cut surface; Garlon 4—basal bark; Roundup or Krenite—foliar spray
buckthorns (alien species)	Rodeo, Roundup, or Trimec (not near desirable trees)—cut surface	Garlon 3A—cut surface; Garlon 4—basal bark; Rodeo—foliar spray
Canada thistle	2,4-D amine—foliar spray	Roundup—foliar spray
crown vetch	None	2,4-D amine, Mecamine, or Roundup—foliar spray
cut-leaved and common teasel	Garlon 3A, Roundup, or 2,4-D amine—foliar spray	Same as for high-quality natural areas
garlic mustard	Roundup—foliar spray	Roundup, 2,4-D amine, or Mecamine—foliar spray
honeysuckles—shrubby	Roundup or Rodeo—cut stump	Roundup, Rodeo, or Krenite—foliar spray
Japanese honeysuckle	Roundup or Crossbow—foliar spray	Same as for high-quality natural areas

Species		
Johnson grass	Roundup—foliar spray	Same as for high-quality natural areas
leafy spurge	None	2,4-D, Roundup, or picloram—foliar spray
meadow fescue	Roundup or Fusilade 2000—foliar spray	Same as for high-quality natural areas
multiflora rose	Roundup or Garlon 3A—cut stump	Roundup or Garlon 3A—cut stump; Krenite, Roundup, or Banvel—foliar spray
purple loosestrife	Garlon 3A—foliar spray	Rodeo or Roundup—foliar spray
quaking aspen	Garlon 3A or Roundup—cut stump	Roundup—cut stump; Krenite—foliar spray
reed canary grass	None	Rodeo, Roundup, or Amitrol—foliar spray
smooth sumac	Garlon 3A or Roundup—cut stump	Garlon 3A or Roundup—foliar spray
white poplar	Garlon 3A—cut stump	Garlon 3A—cut stump; Garlon 4—basal bark; Roundup—foliar spray
white and yellow sweet clover	None	2,4-D amine or Mecamine—foliar spray
wild parsnip	Roundup or 2,4-D amine—foliar spray	Same as for high-quality natural areas

See text for detailed information on appropriate use, including restrictions and warnings concerning use and time of application.

control work. Guidelines vary in effectiveness according to local conditions, and they carry no guarantees.

Approaches to Control

The invasion or increase of aggressive exotic and native plants usually results from disturbance or degradation of a natural system, for example, through cattle grazing or altering the hydrology. Aggressive plants are typically not a problem in a healthy, well-managed system. Many exotic plants can be controlled in prairies and savannas by restoring natural processes such as fire and the natural hydrological regime. Attempts to control problem species without restoring such natural processes may offer merely short-term relief.

The amount of control required depends on the nature of the invading plant and the degree to which it displaces other species. Although complete eradication may be the ideal, it can be difficult to achieve due to labor and resource limitations. Reducing a problem plant's density and population size to low levels may be more practical than complete eradication.

Most control measures, including herbicides and mowing, can be harmful to nontarget plants and animals. Consider the potential risks and alternatives and use the least damaging approach given your resources. Often, herbicide use is justified where labor is unavailable for mechanical control, and where difficult land conditions or large infestations prevent use of mechanical control. However, it rarely is desirable to risk degrading ecosystem health and diversity by using herbicides to eliminate an exotic species completely. Rather, one may use herbicides to reduce the population size of an aggressive species and then use less risky measures such as fire, cutting, or hand pulling to eliminate or further reduce the problem species. Avoid herbicides when natural (e.g., fire) or mechanical (e.g., cutting, girdling, mowing) control measures are feasible. Use chemicals only when their benefits exceed their risks. A combination of controls is often superior to a single method.

Eradication of native opportunistic plants (e.g., smooth sumac, quaking aspen, black cherry, gray dogwood, some sunflowers and goldenrods) usually is undesirable if the native species is a natural component of the community. However, if it has overpopulated due to changed conditions such as infrequent fire, then decreasing the population size of that plant is often recommended. The decision about whether to do that depends on the presence of rare or sensitive species that may require special protection and on the extent to which the opportunistic species displace other native species or disrupt ecological functions. For example, if a prairie is sufficiently large to provide refuge for grassland birds that require large treeless expanses, then complete removal of aggressive shrubs or trees to eliminate edge habitat may be desirable. However, if a prairie is very small and of high quality, it may be more important to preserve rare species or species diversity than to eradicate aggressive native plants.

Should you control native shrubs or not? Sometimes yes, and sometimes no. It depends on whether native shrubs were an integral part of the original community, and whether they occur at densities approximating original conditions. Accounts from early travelers at the time of European settlement in the Midwest indicate that the presence and density of shrubs in savannas and prairies varied. Some prairies and savannas were striking for their lack of shrubs or underbrush. Others contained dense shrub thickets within or at their borders. These shrubby areas were at times extensive, covering a square mile or more of land. When historic evidence indicates that a particular savanna or prairie had fewer shrubs than currently present, most restorationists are comfortable reducing the native shrub population. Before reducing native shrubs though, pay attention to which animals utilize the shrubby areas and consider providing for their habitat needs on-site or elsewhere when undertaking restoration work.

The time needed to control exotic species varies with the methods used. Some exotics gradually yield to native plants once natural ecological processes, such as fire or hydrology, return and native plants have had several years to compete under the restored conditions.

Where native plants can outcompete exotics in the long term, patience may be preferable to use of herbicides or limited labor resources. It can be satisfying to eradicate a species in one year but may be more realistic, more resource efficient, and better for ecosystem health to consider a three-, five-, ten-, or twenty-year time frame. However, aliens that spread very rapidly, such as purple loosestrife, leafy spurge, and garlic mustard, are best controlled or eliminated as soon as identified.

Once begun, control measures may be needed for many years, for example, when a persistent seed bank results in the appearance of new plants each year. Vigilant monitoring of prairies and savannas can result in detection of invasive species while they can be readily controlled. Once control measures are implemented, continued monitoring can detect new infestations or increases of exotic species.

After control measures are taken, reseeding with appropriate native plants is necessary in heavily degraded areas where the native seed bank is gone, because aggressive native or exotic weeds are poised to rapidly invade the newly opened areas.

Control Methods—Trees and Brush

Prescribed Fire. Burning stimulates prairie plants to form a vigorous sod, which hinders establishment of woody seedlings, and kills the above-ground parts of certain invading shrubs and trees. Most deciduous trees and shrubs resprout from the roots, but conifers such as eastern red cedar and some pines are killed by fire that burns all of the above-ground stem. Repeated fires are needed to keep resprouting brush under control.

Restored Hydrology. In wetlands where the water table has been artificially lowered, restoration of water levels usually kills certain trees or shrubs such as glossy buckthorn. Care should be taken not to flood sensitive communities by raising water levels higher than occurred historically.

Hand Pulling. Young seedlings and sprouts can be hand pulled when adequate ground moisture is present to allow removal of the root system along with above-ground growth. If possible, hand pull when the target plant is clearly visible. For instance, autumn olive is easily seen in early spring because its leaves appear while most native vegetation is still dormant.

Stem Cutting. Cut shrubs or trees off at or near ground level. Loppers or a hand saw can be used for small stems (under about 2 inches diameter) and small areas; a gas-powered brushcutter and/or chain saw is more efficient for larger stems and larger acreages. Many deciduous trees and shrubs resprout if an herbicide is not applied after cutting (see herbicides section below). If herbicide use is not desired, resprouts should be cut until food reserves are depleted. This may take numerous cuttings and many years.

Girdling. Girdling will kill most species of trees without herbicide. However, it does not work well for certain problem species, including white poplar and black locust, which respond by vigorous resprouting from the roots.

Girdling involves cutting the phloem (inner bark) but leaving the xylem (sapwood) intact. (See figure 16.1.) Then the roots busily nourish the top, but the top sends no nourishment to the roots, which die out. Girdling may be done any time of year but is easiest and most effective in late spring or early summer. The tree takes a year or two to die slowly. Leaves stay green and look healthy but gradually die.

Here's how it is done: Using an ax or saw, surround the trunk with two parallel cuts 3 to 6 inches apart. These cuts should be just a bit deeper than the cambium layer just inside the phloem. To determine where the

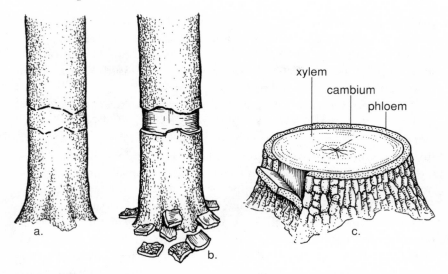

Figure 16.1. Girdling a tree. *a.* Tree with two rows of cuts about 4 inches apart. *b.* Tree with bark and phloem knocked off. *c.* Stump showing parts of the trunk. A bit of the bark and phloem is peeled back.

cambium is, make two lines of sample cuts to start a girdle. Then whack the bark between them sharply with the back of your ax. After a couple of whacks, you'll notice that the outer bark and phloem tend to pop off in one piece, leaving a smooth area where they separated from the wood of the trunk. This smooth wood is the most recent ring of the xylem.

The cambium, which is too thin to see easily, is a weak, actively growing layer (it produces new wood and bark) where the tree naturally breaks when you whack it. When you know approximately how thick the phloem is, try to make your initial parallel cuts just that deep. For aesthetic reasons and to minimize resprouting below the girdle, trees can be girdled (a bit less comfortably for the girdler) at or near ground level. Then, using a blunt object, knock out all of the bark and phloem from between the cuts. Or else peel away the bark and phloem using a blunt ax blade. Phloem should be removed without damaging the xylem. Girdles should be checked after a few weeks to make sure that bark does not develop over the cut area. All suckers below the girdle should be cut.

Control Methods—Herbaceous Plants

If a dandelion shows up in a prairie, an experienced prairie manager hardly notices. Fires and the competition of native prairie plants will gradually eliminate it and many other Eurasian invaders. But many herbaceous species can become serious problems in a prairie, outcompeting and replacing large parts of the native vegetation. These troublesome species include leafy spurge, white sweet clover, Korean bush clover, cut-leaved teasel, and purple loosestrife.

What control measures are appropriate depends on size and condition of the site, characteristics of the problem species, and available resources. Hand pulling (as described earlier) may be the best choice when the site is small and committed workers are available. Herbicide application (discussed below) is the only known effective control for substantial populations of leafy spurge and purple loosestrife, although biological control (insects) of the former shows promise. Stems of broadleaf plants can be cut near ground level at or near the time of flowering but before fruits develop on the plant; cut stems must be removed if flowers on the stem threaten to produce viable seeds. Rootstocks, however, may respond by sending up new shoots. Some weeds can be controlled by strategically timed burning or mowing, but during certain times of the growing season either technique can be hard on some of the plant or animal species we want to protect. Thus, choice of control methods represents tradeoffs. Managers analyze and discuss alternatives and then get on with the work.

Herbicide Control of Woody and Herbaceous Plants

Herbicides are applied to leaves with a hand-held or power-driven sprayer, and to the bark or stump of woody species with a wick applicator, hand-held sprayer, or other type of hand-held applicator. (See appendix E for equipment sources.) Some herbicides are so nonselective that they kill virtually any green plant touched (e.g., the glyphosates Roundup and Rodeo). Some kill only broadleaved plants (e.g., Garlon 4, 2,4-D). Others kill not only by touching leafy vegetation, but also by moving through the soil to reach and poison tree roots (e.g., the picloram, Tordon); these types are not appropriate for natural areas. Some restoration managers refuse to use herbicides except as a last resort, where difficult terrain or dense and extensive exotic plant populations defy other controls. Only use an herbicide after considering all alternatives.

Follow these precautions whenever using herbicides:

1. Federal and state laws provide that herbicides may be applied only as directed on the container label, and that various herbicides may be applied only by certified or licensed people. When using an herbicide, be sure to mix and apply it according to label

instructions. The label will state whether or not to dilute the herbicide and the type of liquid to dilute it with (e.g., water, herbicide oil). Follow all applicable federal, state, and local regulations.

2. Careful identification of the unwanted species is the first step in control. If a plant's identity is in doubt, consult a knowledgeable person or appropriate literature before applying herbicides.

3. To minimize damage to nontarget species, do not spray herbicide so heavily that it drips off the target vegetation. Take precautions to minimize herbicide drift: do not spray herbicides under windy conditions, and release the spray as close to the target plant as possible.

4. Apply spray while moving backwards, if possible, to avoid walking through contaminated foliage.

5. If there is a choice among forms of an herbicide, choose the form that is least volatile and presents the least danger to nontarget species (e.g., check the chemical formulation on the label for the amine form of 2,4-D rather than the ester form).

6. Use the minimum effective concentration of an herbicide, but do not use concentrations too low to be effective. This could result in greater overall herbicide use if you must apply the herbicide more than once because the first application was ineffective.

7. Proper spray equipment is essential. Appropriate orifice size, pressure, and choice of carrier can markedly reduce overspray and collateral damage. Use of a quality backpack sprayer with a gun jet and interchangeable orifices will result in less operator fatigue and fewer spills.

8. Wear appropriate protective clothing. At a minimum, wear rubber gloves, goggles, a long-sleeve shirt, long pants or a coverall, socks, boots (rubber boots are best), and a hat.

Applying Herbicides to Woody Plants

Frilling. This is a means of killing a standing tree by using herbicide. The tree is gashed with an ax or chain saw so that herbicide can be applied directly to the growing parts of the standing trunk. With an ax or chain saw, make a sharp stroke at a downward 45° angle, leaving pockets in the bark where herbicide can be deposited. This method has much in common with girdling, the differences being that surrounding vegetation may be damaged by herbicide and the tree dies immediately instead of over a number of years. Frilling works on many species for which girdling is ineffective, such as white poplar and black locust. Special injection equipment can be used to cut into the plant and inject the herbicide all in one procedure. Usually herbicide is injected at 1- to 3-inch intervals around the tree trunk and as close to the root crown as possible.

Cut Stump Treatment. Roundup herbicide (a formulation of glyphosate) effectively controls woody plants when applied directly to the cut stump. The Roundup label specifies a 50–100 percent concentration for cut-stump application, but a 10-20 percent solution has proven effective for many woody species (see "Species-Specific Control Recommendations" below). Roundup can be applied either by spraying individual stumps with a low-pressure hand-held or backpack sprayer or by wiping each stump, using a sponge applicator. Although sponge-type paint applicators can be used, spills can occur when herbicide is applied from an open container with paint applicators. As an alternative, securely wire a sponge to the end of a wand extension of a backpack sprayer. Use a plastic bag to catch all drips when not in use. With cut-stump treatment, herbicide is applied specifically to the target plant, reducing the possibility of damaging nearby, desirable vegetation. Cut-stump treatment is particularly effective late in the growing season (July-September) but is also effective during the dormant season. Glyphosate is a nonselective herbicide that can potentially kill any plant with green leaves that it contacts, so care should be taken to avoid contacting nontarget species. In wetland areas, a 50 percent solution of Rodeo (a formulation of glyphosate approved for use in wetlands) can be used for cut-stump treatment. To be effective, Roundup and Rodeo must be applied immediately after cutting.

Garlon 3A (an amine formulation of triclopyr) is a selective translocated herbicide that provides a high level of control of tree root systems when applied to cut stumps, especially those of suckering species such as black locust. Undiluted or 50 percent solutions of Garlon 3A can be sprayed or wiped onto stumps. Cut-surface application can be made during any season of the year, but application during the dormant season reduces the potential for drift injury. Application should be within a few hours of cutting, adhering closely to label precautions and directions and avoiding any exposure of nontarget plants. Garlon 4 (an ester formulation of triclopyr, discussed under "Basal-Bark Treatment" below) is an effective treatment for cut stumps, but it should be applied to the bark remaining on the stump below the cut surface. Avoid using triclopyr if rain is forecast for the following one to four days; runoff will harm nontarget species.

Alternatively, cut stumps in prairies can be treated with Trimec (a formulation of 2,4-D, MCCP, and dicamba). Trimec should not be used in savannas or woodlands because it moves readily in soil and can kill nearby trees. Do not apply Trimec within a distance three times the drip line (edge of the tree's canopy projected onto the ground) of any woody plant you want to save. Trimec, an herbicide specifically for broadleaf plants, should be diluted with an equal portion of water and applied according to label instructions. This herbicide effectively controls buckthorn.

Basal-Bark Treatment. Certain herbicides can penetrate the bark of some tree species, especially saplings. These are simply sprayed on the bark. This process is called basal-bark application.

Dormant-season basal-bark treatment using Garlon 4 herbicide is effective on trees and resprouts less than 6 inches in diameter. However, this treatment is not labeled for use in wetlands. Mix Garlon 4 with a nonpetroleum-based herbicide oil (e.g., a citrus or soy-based herbicide oil; several types are manufactured) according to label instructions. Garlon 4 may be mixed with diesel fuel instead of a nonpetroleum-based herbicide oil; but the diesel fuel has far greater potential for damaging nontarget plants. A concentration of three ounces Garlon 4 to one gallon nonpetroleum-based herbicide oil has proven effective on several tree species, although the Garlon 4 label specifies a higher concentration. The higher, labeled concentration is more effective on plants that resprout vigorously. Thoroughly spray the basal portion of the trunk to a height of 12–15 inches.

Thin-line basal-bark treatment with Garlon 4 is a treatment in which herbicide is applied only in a thin line surrounding the tree trunk, rather than a broad band. Undiluted Garlon 4 (or Garlon 4 diluted 50:50 with diesel fuel) should be applied in a pencil-point line around the base of the plant 6–12 inches above the ground and completely around the stem. Apply herbicide with a hand-held plant sprayer equipped with a nozzle that produces a straight-stream spray pattern. Do this during the dormant season to minimize risk to nontarget species. Neither basal-bark treatment should be used in high-quality natural areas because the diesel fuel may kill vegetation around the tree.

Foliar Treatment. Krenite (a formulation of fosamine ammonium) is a nonvolatile, contact herbicide that affects woody plants (and bracken fern). When applied as a spray to leaves between July and September (the few months before fall coloration), Krenite kills by inhibiting bud expansion the following spring. Although slight regrowth may occur, saplings will die the summer following application. Complete coverage is required; incomplete coverage can result in regrowth. A nonionic surfactant will improve results. The Krenite S formulation contains the appropriate amount of surfactant to improve results. Because of its selectivity, Krenite is a preferred foliar spray treatment for woody plants.

Foliar application of dicamba herbicides (available under the tradename Banvel) and 2,4-D herbicides (available under a variety of brand names, including Crossbow) is effective against all broadleaf plants, woody as well as herbaceous. A dicamba herbicide should not be used in savannas or near woody plants you want to save because of its mobility. These herbicides generally kill all broadleaf plants, and there are problems with drift, especially in hot weather. During the growing season (April to September) they should be used only in lower-quality areas. In high-quality areas, they should be used only during the dormant season to control aliens that remain green while native vegetation is dormant. Treatment is especially effective during the summer when plants are actively growing and flowering. One hundred percent of the foliage should be sprayed.

When brush is young, many species are most safely and effectively controlled by mowing or cutting and spraying the resprouts. Less herbicide is needed and off-target application is reduced because spray is directed downward. First-year growth is tender, and herbicide penetrates the bark as well as the leaves.

Applying Herbicides to Herbaceous Plants.

Several herbicides effectively control invasive herbaceous plants when sprayed on the green foliage. In general, this method should not be used in high-quality prairies and savannas during the growing season because of potential damage to nontarget plants. In high-quality areas, foliar spraying can be used to carefully spot treat individual alien plants if done during the spring or fall when native vegetation is dormant and the alien plants remain green.

Glyphosate (trade name Roundup or Rodeo), one such nonselective herbicide, can be sprayed on leaves using a hand sprayer. Spray coverage should be uniform and complete. Because this herbicide kills all nontarget plants it contacts, extreme care is needed when spraying to avoid nontarget plants.

Spot application of the amine formulation of 2,4-D (which has less vapor drift than the ester formulation) can control several broadleaf invaders such as Canada thistle. Green leaves of individual plants should be treated with a wick applicator or hand sprayer used according to label instructions. The herbicide 2,4-D amine will not harm most monocots. Crossbow, a formulation of triclopyr and 2,4-D, very effectively controls broadleaf plants, Japanese honeysuckle in particular. Crossbow should be applied as a foliar spray.

Spot application of Fusilade 2000 selectively kills grasses and effectively controls exotic grasses such as meadow fescue. Poast, another grass-specific herbicide, also is useful in controlling exotic grasses.

Species–Specific Control Recommendations

Autumn olive

Autumn olive is a nonleguminous, nitrogen-fixing woody shrub that is widely distributed in open and semi-wooded sites. Plants flower and annually produce up to eight pounds of fruit after reaching three years of age. Seed dispersal appears to be mainly by falling fruit and birds. Once established, this species is highly invasive and difficult to control. Burned, mowed, and cut plants resprout vigorously.

CONTROL TECHNIQUES:
- hand pull young seedlings and sprouts from moist soil in early spring
- cut stem, apply Roundup
- apply thin-line basal-bark treatments of Garlon
- apply dicamba herbicides (in prairies only) or 2,4-D (provides complete kill)
- mow or cut stems and then spray resprouts (leaves and stems) with Garlon 4

INEFFECTIVE:
- repeated cutting without herbicide stump treatment
- burning (does not control mature trees)

Black locust

Black locust, found in a variety of disturbed habitats, has become naturalized in midwestern prairies, savannas, and woodlands and throughout much of the world. This aggressive tree (including its many cultivated forms) is a potential threat to upland prairies and savannas and is an especially serious management problem on hill prairies, sand prairies, and savannas.

Black locust produces seed prolifically, but most natural reproduction is vegetative by stump sprouts and root suckers that arise spontaneously from the extensive root system.

Black locust is difficult to control due to its rapid growth and clonal spread. Mowing and burning have proven only temporarily effective. As a result, management has concentrated on chemical control with variable success. Whatever control measure is adopted, a followup treatment is usually necessary.

CONTROL TECHNIQUES:
- cut stems and apply Garlon 3A or Roundup to stump
- girdle stems, apply Garlon
- basal-bark treatment with Garlon 4 (may lead to resprouting)
- mow or cut, then spray resprouts with Garlon 4
- apply Krenite or Roundup as foliar spray (with Roundup, treat all leaves); may require followup applications

INEFFECTIVE:
- girdling or cutting stems without herbicide
- cut-surface application of Tordon RTU

Buckthorns (alien species—common buckthorn, glossy buckthorn, Dahurian buckthorn):

Common and glossy buckthorn readily invade unburned or degraded prairies and savannas. Once established, exotic buckthorns shade out native herbs and shrubs. Glossy buckthorn is found most frequently in wetland communities such as fens, wet prairies, and sedge meadows. However, it also invades mesic upland sites, including prairies, roadsides, and old fields. Dahurian buckthorn invades woodlands and savannas but is not as widespread as the other exotic buckthorns.

All exotic buckthorns produce a fruit that is eaten by birds, and the severe laxative effect of these fruits distributes the seeds. These shrubs prolifically resprout from cut or damaged stems.

CONTROL TECHNIQUES:
- repeated hot fire; for complete control, burning yearly or every other year may be needed for five or six or more years; initially, one or two burns stimulate resprouts
- in wetlands, restore natural water levels
- cut or girdle large trees and clip resprouts as they occur
- cut stems, apply Garlon 3A or Roundup (50 percent Roundup concentration) to stumps; in wetlands use Rodeo for cut-stump treatment; autumn is best time to cut and treat stumps
- on disturbed or buffer sites, as a supplemental method, use Garlon 4 as a dormant-season basal-bark treatment, cut stems, and then spray resprouts with Garlon 4 or spray foliage with Rodeo

Canada thistle

Canada thistle crowds out native grasses and forbs. Prairies, barrens, savannas, and glades that have been disturbed or are undergoing manipulative restoration are susceptible to invasion, as are sedge meadows and wet prairies.

This dioecious, weedy, alien perennial occurs in patches and thrives in sunny disturbed areas. Seed, which remains viable in soil up to twenty years, is dispersed mostly by wind. Once introduced, this species spreads rapidly by rhizomes or root segments with aerial shoots produced at 2- to 6-inch intervals.

CONTROL TECHNIQUES:
- perform late spring burns (May to June in Illinois) annually for first three years of control effort
- hand cut or pull plants at least three times each season, in June, August, and September
- spot apply 2,4-D amine to foliage; in high-quality areas, applying with gloved hands and a sponge or wick applicator just before flowering is relatively safe; spring burning before herbiciding makes thistle visible for easier spraying
- apply Roundup to foliage in spring when plants are 6-10 inches tall
- in heavy infestations on disturbed sites, mow close to ground when plants are in full bloom; remove cut flowerheads from site; repeat annually as needed

INEFFECTIVE:
- early spring fires, which increase sprouting and reproduction
- grazing (livestock generally do not eat this plant)

Crown vetch

Crown vetch spreads rapidly by seed and through its multibranched creeping roots. This aggressive, perennial alien is a serious management threat to prairies and savannas, which it invades from widespread roadside plantings.

Little control information is available. The following methods have met with some success, but field research is badly needed.

CONTROL TECHNIQUES:
- late-spring burning; controls seedlings but only top-kills mature plants, which then resprout
- mow in late spring for several consecutive years
- in disturbed areas, apply 2,4-D, Mecamine (2,4-D plus dicamba), or Roundup to foliage in early spring when plant is actively growing; or apply Garlon 4 to foliage of mature plants; repeat

application in following years as needed; area should be spring-
or fall-burned before spraying to remove litter and ensure good
foliar coverage

Cut-leaved and common teasel

These exotic teasels, left unchecked, can quickly form large monocultures in prairies and savannas that exclude most native vegetation. Cut-
leaved teasel is more aggressive than common teasel. The teasels are
monocarpic perennials that grow as basal rosettes for one year or longer,
send up a flowering stalk, flower, and die. Each plant produces thousands
of seeds, which can remain viable for at least two years and typically don't
disperse far. Immature seed heads of cut-leaved teasel are capable of producing viable seed.

CONTROL TECHNIQUES:
- dig rosettes with dandelion digger, removing as much root as
  possible to prevent resprouting
- cut flowering stalks at ground level after flowering begins but
  before seeds ripen; remove cut stalks from area
- late spring burns may control sparse populations; once teasel is
  dense, fire does not spread well
- spot apply Garlon 3A, Roundup, or 2,4-D amine to foliage of
  individual plants in spring or fall when teasel is green but most
  native plants are dormant

Garlic mustard

Garlic mustard can invade upland and floodplain savannas in the upper
Midwest. It typically invades shaded areas, especially disturbed sites, but
occasionally occurs in areas receiving full sun. This biennial herb spreads
rapidly and excludes other herbs, often dominating the ground layer.
Seeds germinate in early spring and young plants overwinter as basal
rosettes. Adults bloom the following May and June and die after producing seeds.

CONTROL TECHNIQUES:
- perform intense fall or spring fires that thoroughly burn site,
  repeat for several years as needed; remove unburned plants by
  hand before flowering
- cut flowering stems at ground level (scythe works well on dense
  populations); plants cut near ground level when in full flower

usually do not resprout; remove cut stems, which may produce viable seed
- combination of spring burning, hand pulling, and cutting flowering stems works well
- for light infestations, hand pull plants, including roots, and remove; roots of nonflowering plants left in ground may resprout; minimize soil disturbance, tamp soil firmly to avoid bringing more seed to soil surface
- spray foliage of individual plants with 2 percent Roundup, an amine formulation of 2,4-D, or a 1 percent solution of Mecamine during spring or fall when most native vegetation is dormant but garlic mustard remains green; do not use 2,4-D or Mecamine in high-quality natural areas

INEFFECTIVE:
- low-intensity fires that leave unburned areas

Honeysuckles (shrubby—Tartarian, Morrow's, belle, and Amur honeysuckle):

These shrubby honeysuckles have a broad tolerance of various moisture regimes and habitats and thus can invade a wide array of native habitats. Invasion from nearby plantings or disturbed areas is stimulated by habitat disturbance such as grazing.

Seeds are widely spread by birds; thus plants commonly grow under tall shrubs or trees that serve as perches. Shrubby honeysuckles may produce allelopathic chemicals that inhibit growth of surrounding native competitors. Shade from these honeysuckles also suppresses surrounding shorter plants. Shrubby honeysuckles leaf out before many native species and hold their foliage until November.

CONTROL TECHNIQUES:
- burn repeatedly in spring; annual or biennial burning for five or more years may be needed
- hand pull from moist soil, remove all of root; do not do this in sensitive habitats where aliens would reinvade open soil
- cut stem, apply Roundup or Rodeo to stump; may require followup applications to control resprouts
- apply Roundup or Rodeo as foliar spray just after flowers bloom (usually in June)
- apply Krenite as foliar spray

INEFFECTIVE:
- Garlon 3A (seems to be inadequate)

Japanese honeysuckle

Japanese honeysuckle readily invades open natural communities, often by seed spread by birds. This semi–evergreen, aggressive vine seriously alters or destroys understory and herbaceous layers of prairies, barrens, glades, flatwoods, and savannas. Japanese honeysuckle climbs and drapes native vegetation, shading it out. Vegetative runners are most prolific in open sun and will resprout where touching soil, forming mats of new plants. Under moderate shade, little growth occurs. In deep shade, runners develop but often die back.

CONTROL TECHNIQUES:
- repeated spring burning, which greatly reduces cover, followed by herbicide treatment, if needed; apply Roundup or Crossbow to foliage after surrounding vegetation is dormant in autumn and before a hard freeze (25° F); herbicide retreatment may be needed in dense growth

INEFFECTIVE:
- mowing (stimulates stem production)
- grazing

Johnson grass

Johnson grass invades riverbank communities and disturbed sites, particularly fallow fields and woodland edges, where it quickly dominates herbaceous flora and slows succession. This grass is a serious potential threat in old fields where restoration to prairie or savanna communities is desired.

A very aggressive perennial, Johnson grass grows in dense clumps that spread by seed and rhizomes to form nearly pure stands. Rhizome cuttings commonly form new plants, making eradication very difficult.

CONTROL TECHNIQUES:
- for small populations, hand pull during June when ground is soft; all plant parts should be removed from area
- for heavily infested restorations, apply 2 percent Roundup to foliage during June just prior to seed maturity; all nontarget species contacted will be killed
- for heavily disturbed sites, repeated and close mowing kills seedlings, prevents seed production, and reduces rhizome growth and regrowth of shoots

- sites may be tilled where practical (e.g., abandoned cropland) and exposed roots left to winter kill; repeated tillage (e.g., six times at two-week intervals during the growing season) prevents rhizome development and reduces populations; tillage is seldom effective by itself
- grazing can reduce populations but may introduce other exotic plants and damage native species

INEFFECTIVE:
- limited early-season tillage (spreads pieces of the rhizomes)
- mowing
- spring burning (may encourage regrowth)
- single applications of herbicide

Leafy spurge

Leafy spurge is a deep-rooted perennial adapted to moist to dry soils. Especially aggressive where extreme dryness reduces competition from native species, leafy spurge invades disturbed open areas, disturbed and undisturbed mesic to dry prairies, and savannas. Leafy spurge is well established in the central plains, where much time and effort is spent on control.

Leafy spurge emerges in early spring, and flowers may appear by May. Although it produces abundant seed with a high germination rate, its key reproductive capabilities remain underground. Even if foliage is removed, the extensive root system generates new shoots from buds located anywhere along the root. Invading populations should be treated immediately and vigorously—the sooner the better.

CONTROL TECHNIQUES:
- combine prescribed burning with herbicides (burning stimulates vegetative growth, making spurge more vulnerable to herbicides); spray plants with 2,4-D amine in September, burn the following April. Again apply 2,4-D amine the following June, then burn in October. The June herbiciding and fall burning may have to be repeated many times
- apply picloram (trade name Tordon) to foliage when true flowers (not yellow bracts) begin to appear; this is not recommended for high-quality natural areas
- for top-growth control, spray a 2 percent solution of 2,4-D amine on foliage in mid- to late June when true flowers appear, and again in early to mid-September when fall regrowth has begun but before killing frost
- spray a 5 percent Roundup solution on foliage; this provides

80–90 percent top control if applied between mid–August and mid–September; follow with a 2 percent solution of 2,4-D amine between mid-June and mid-July the following year to control seedlings

INEFFECTIVE:
- mowing or hand cutting (roots vigorously resprout)
- hand pulling, digging, or tilling (usually leaves root portions that resprout)

Meadow fescue

Meadow fescue can become a significant problem because of its adaptability to open areas, allelopathic character, and tenaciousness. Found in a variety of disturbed habitats, this grass does well in open sunlight on poor acid soils and where there is little competition from other species. It can tolerate a wide range of moisture conditions and is often planted along levees and stream banks.

Meadow fescue spreads primarily by seed to form dense stands with thick mats of roots that defy hand pulling. Although it becomes established slowly, once the solid clumps are formed, fescue is difficult to eradicate.

CONTROL TECHNIQUES:
- burn in late spring for several consecutive years; if ineffective, apply 1–2 percent Roundup to foliage in fall when fescue is 8–12 inches tall and actively growing; if desirable plants are present, apply Roundup after frost causes their dormancy
- for light infestations, spot apply Fusilade 2000 after a burn
- eliminate surrounding fescue seed sources to prevent reinvasion
- exclude livestock that feed on fescue; seeds are spread in manure

INEFFECTIVE:
- grazing (usually eliminates other plants first and encourages spread of fescue)
- mowing

Multiflora rose

Multiflora rose is a thorny shrub that invades prairies, savannas, and disturbed areas. It can form impenetrable thickets or "living fences" and smother out other vegetation. Flowers borne in May or June develop into small, hard fruits that remain through winter. Most seeds germinate close to parent plants, although birds and mammals disperse some greater distances. Seeds may remain viable in soil for ten to twenty years. This rose also spreads by layering, by which cane tips touching the ground form roots.

CONTROL TECHNIQUES:

- for light infestations, hand pulling or grubbing, if all roots are removed
- prescribed burning; slows invasion
- three to six cuttings or mowings per growing season, repeated for two to four years; achieves high plant mortality; increased mowing rates (more than six per season) do not increase mortality; in high-quality areas, cut individual plants rather than mow (fill mower tires with foam to avoid flat tires)
- cut stems during dormant season, apply Garlon 3A or Roundup solution to stump
- for degraded areas, mow or cut in late summer or fall, then spray resprouts in spring with Garlon 4; or spray Krenite (must treat all foliage; lanky canes are easily missed), Banvel (less preferred; kills all broadleaves), or a 1 percent solution of Roundup (least preferred; kills all plants) on foliage
- rose rosette disease, a sometimes fatal disease of multiflora and other roses. This may be a potential biological control agent in some regions

Purple loosestrife

This herbaceous perennial is widely spread among wet habitats, including wet prairies and savannas, where it quickly crowds out most native wetland vegetation, creating a monoculture.

Each plant produces enormous numbers of seeds that can remain viable after twenty months in water and may be dispersed by water, wind, and mud attached to animals. Root and stem segments can form new flowering stems, a process stimulated by muskrat cuttings and mowing. Seed and plant segments float to new locations, which causes rapid spread. Thus early detection and treatment is critical.

Current research is focusing on biological control, but in the meantime, try the following.

CONTROL TECHNIQUES:

- in small infestations, hand-pull plants one to two years old before flowering; dig out older plants; bag and remove plants, burn where possible; apply followup treatments for three years
- apply Garlon 3A to foliage before seed sets, but only where surface water is absent (e.g., summer drying of wetlands); apply

again a few weeks later to plants missed initially; Garlon 3A is selective for broadleaf and woody plants but may not be used over open water; Roundup is nonselective but an effective foliar spray when surface water is absent

- if surface water is present, spot apply Rodeo when flowering has just begun; timing is important, seed can set if plants are in mid-late flower; where feasible, cut flower heads, bag, and remove them before application to prevent seed set; if needed, apply Rodeo again two or three weeks later to missed plants; since purple loosestrife is usually taller than the surrounding vegetation, application to plant tops alone can be effective and limit nontarget exposure; re-treat annually until control is achieved; if unable to apply Rodeo during flower initiation, application between flowering and first frost is effective
- for large monocultures, spray Garlon 3A (but not over water) or Rodeo (okay over water) using a vehicle-mounted sprayer; begin treatment at the margin and work toward the center in successive years—this allows peripheral native vegetation to reinvade treated areas
- cut purple loosestrife and subsequently flood the area so that cut plant stalks are completely immersed; however, if seed is present in soil, flooding may encourage its spread; not recommended for high-quality communities with intact natural flooding regime

INEFFECTIVE:
- mowing, burning, and flooding (can stimulate spread of seed and rootable plant segments), except for cutting followed by flooding as described above

Quaking aspen

Quaking aspen is one of the most aggressive pioneer trees. It quickly colonizes recently burned or bare areas, grows rapidly, and can soon establish dense clones. This tree grows in diverse soils and is a problem in some disturbed prairies. It tends to exclude prairie species and provides favorable conditions for other trees and shrubs to become established. Quaking aspens can reproduce sexually by seeds, but most reproduction occurs asexually by suckering.

CONTROL TECHNIQUES:
- girdle main stem, cut any small stems, and apply Garlon 3A
- late spring burning (one to two weeks after aspen flowering) approximately every other year is said to control aspen within a few decades

- cut stumps and treat with Garlon 3A, or with Roundup
- for disturbed sites, spray foliage of small saplings and root suckers with Krenite

INEFFECTIVE:
- cutting down trees without applying herbicide to stump (results in numerous resprouts)

Reed canary grass

The Eurasian ecotype of reed canary grass is a major threat to natural wetlands because of its hardiness, aggressive nature, and rapid growth. This alien ecotype occurs in a variety of wetlands, including wet prairies, where it can quickly replace native species. The native ecotype of reed canary grass is not believed to be as aggressive as the Eurasian ecotype.

A coarse, sod-forming, cool-season, perennial grass adapted to much of the northern United States, this species grows in wet to dry habitats with best growth on fertile and moist or wet soils. Reproduction of both ecotypes is from seed and vegetatively by stout, creeping rhizomes.

CONTROL TECHNIQUES:
- burn annually in late autumn or late spring up to five or six years
- hand chop culms at flowering time (may kill small clones)
- for disturbed areas, spray Rodeo or Roundup on foliage in spring when reed canary grass is green and most other vegetation is dormant; burning before spraying removes litter and makes grass more visible; re-treat the following spring
- restore water levels to artificially drained wetlands

INEFFECTIVE:
- mowing
- grazing (not practical in wetlands)

Smooth sumac

Smooth sumac, a native shrub, is usually found on disturbed sites but also occurs in prairies, glades, and savannas. It is a primary woody invader of midwestern hill prairies, where its dense clones shade and replace other native species. This sometimes aggressive shrub occurs in clumps and spreads by seeds and rootstocks. It sprouts easily and grows rapidly. Above-ground stems are relatively short lived, but the roots persist and continually produce new stems.

It should not be eliminated totally from prairies or savannas where it occurred in presettlement times but should be controlled where it has spread to the detriment of other native vegetation. In general, some sumac should be left in ravines and draws within prairie communities.

CONTROL TECHNIQUES:
- cut stems in July or shortly after flowering; cut sprouts in August; cutting at the appropriate time is crucial, fall or winter cutting has little effect; repeat July and August cuttings for consecutive years as needed; stump treatment with Garlon 3A, Garlon 4 (treat bark remaining below cut surface), or Roundup minimizes resprouting
- burning in August often kills mature plants, but sprouts must be cut; dormant-season fires do not control sumac and early spring fires can actually increase sprouting and encourage spread
- midsummer (July or August) mowing or cutting reduces sumac vigor
- for restoration sites, foliar applications of Garlon 3A, Garlon 4, or Roundup

INEFFECTIVE:
- grazing (encourages sumac growth and spread)

White poplar

White poplar is an aggressive exotic tree that dominates prairie or savanna communities, shading out native vegetation. It easily escapes cultivation and forms dense groves that are hard to eradicate. White poplar grows in open sunny habitats and in most soil types.

In the Midwest, white poplar appears to reproduce primarily by suckers that arise from adventitious buds on the extensive lateral root system. Profuse suckers from the "mother" plant form large vegetative colonies, a primary threat to prairies and savannas. Suckering can be enhanced by top removal, fire, or other disturbance to the plant.

Little research has been done on white poplar control; control methods listed are those successful with aspen species.

CONTROL TECHNIQUES:
- girdle main stem and cut sprouts
- cut stems and apply Garlon 3A to stump
- burn annually for three or more years; top-kills plants and controls spread
- in dense clones, prescribed burning is most effective when combined with cutting; cut poplars for one or two years before a burn to allow herbaceous fuels to accumulate; if clone is very large, cut and burn around the edges; each year cut and burn further into clone

- apply Garlon 4 as a thin-line basal-bark treatment
- in restoration areas, apply Roundup on foliage

White and yellow sweet clover

White and yellow sweet clover invade open habitats and successfully exploit native prairies and unflooded savannas. These sweet clovers are adapted to a variety of conditions and climates. They grow well in direct sunlight and partial shade but do not tolerate dense shade. Sweet clovers apparently prefer calcareous or loamy soils.

Sweet clover is an obligate biennial; the plant develops roots and leaves the first year, flowers the second, sets seed, and dies. Seeds may remain viable in the soil over thirty years. Because sweet clover dies the second year, seed production is critical for its continued existence and is the key to control. If flowering is halted, so is the plant's spread—as long as management procedures continue long enough to deplete seeds in the soil.

CONTROL TECHNIQUES:
- hand pulling; easiest in fall, after first-year plant root-crown buds have developed, or early in spring, before second-year plants develop flower buds; effective in summer if done when ground is moist
- for large colonies, cutting stems close to ground with a hand-held scythe after lower leaves have died (before flowering occurs) and up to early stages of flowering (before seeds form); usually no resprouting occurs when cut this way
- burning sequence: a hot, complete, April burn the first year scarifies sweet clover seeds, stimulating them to grow; a late fall burn also has this effect; a hot, complete, May burn the next year kills emerging shoots before they go to seed. This sequence can eradicate an even-aged stand. Heavily infested stands are best controlled with the above sequence twice, separated by two years without burning. Problems may arise if the burn is patchy, leaving viable seeds or second-year shoots unscathed
- in an even-aged stand, mowing can speed up the two-year burn program: burn in April; mow first-year plants in August, leaving the stems behind to dry; burn again in mid-late September
- in an uneven-aged stand, spring burns could be later (after shoots emerge, but before second-year plants set seed), or an early spring burn can be followed by hand pulling or clipping plants at base before seeds form
- for degraded sites, after a fall burn, hand spray seedlings with

2,4-D amine or Mecamine in spring, before native prairie vegetation emerges—effective when cotyledons (first pair of leaves)
appear and subsequently; or hand wick with Roundup on small
populations

Wild parsnip

Wild parsnip is a serious problem in some mesic prairies and savannas. It
thrives in rich, alkaline, moist soils but can survive under most open conditions. This Eurasian perennial exists as a basal rosette for at least one
year. It often flowers and sets seed during its second year, sometimes in
subsequent years, and then dies.

Many people are sensitive to this plant and develop a rash upon contact with leaves or plant sap in the presence of sunlight. Sometimes a very
painful rash develops that leaves scars that persist for several months.
When undertaking control measures, avoid skin contact by wearing
gloves, sleeves, and long pants.

CONTROL TECHNIQUES:
- in high-quality prairies, native species sometimes outcompete and
  eventually displace wild parsnip
- for best control, hand pull and remove plants, including roots
  (may resprout if root crown is not removed); easiest right after
  rain, or during drought when roots shrink; seeds in ground not
  viable after four years, which eases control attempts
- cut plant below root crown during spring of the second year
  when flowers appear but have not matured; repeat after several
  weeks as other plants flower
- after a spring burn, rosettes emerge rapidly and are easily detected
  and dug out
- mow or cut base of stem with scythe while plant is flowering but
  before seeds set; parsnip must be removed or recut often and
  checked later for small flowering shoots near the ground
- spot apply 2 percent Roundup solution to rosettes
- apply 2,4-D amine to rosettes between March and May or
  August and October; repeat early spring applications before the
  flower stalk begins to elongate

INEFFECTIVE:
- poorly timed mowing, as is likely along roadsides (may increase
  number and survival of seedlings; probably favors parsnip matura-
  tion by increasing sunlight to immature rosettes and reducing
  competition)

- burning (removes litter, providing favorable conditions for parsnip rosettes); however, periodic burning increases competition from native plants
- parsnip webworm (damages some plants severely but is not known to eradicate whole patches; probably not a useful biocontrol agent)

ACKNOWLEDGMENTS

This chapter has been adapted with permission from the Illinois Nature Preserves Commission's *Vegetation Management Manual,* 1990, cooperatively written by staff of the Illinois Nature Preserves Commission, Illinois Department of Natural Resources, Division of Natural Heritage, and Natural Land Institute. The manual is available from the Illinois Nature Preserves Commission, 524 South 2nd Street, Springfield, IL 62701-1787. Lengthier species descriptions, guidelines, and literature references are included there and reprinted in the *Natural Areas Journal* 11, nos. 2–4, and 12, nos. 1, 3, and 4 (1991–1992).

The Illinois chapter of the Nature Conservancy graciously shared certain information and materials. I greatly appreciate the useful ideas provided by William Glass, Randy Heidorn, Ken Fiske, and Loren Lown.

REFERENCES

Apfelbaum, S., and C. Sams. 1987. "Ecology and Control of Reed Canary Grass (*Phalaris arundinacea* L.)." *Natural Areas Journal* 7: 69–74.

Elton, C. 1958. *The Ecology of Invasions by Animals and Plants.* London: Butler and Tanner.

Evans, J. E. 1983. "A Literature Review of Management Practices for Multiflora Rose." *Natural Areas Journal* 3:6–15.

Glass, S. 1994. "Experiment Finds Less Herbicide Needed to Control Buckthorn (Wisconsin)." *Restoration and Management Notes* 12:93.

Kline, V. 1981. "Control of Honeysuckle and Buckthorn in Oak Forests. (Wisconsin)." *Restoration and Management Notes* 1:18.

———. 1986. "Response of Sweet Clover (*Melilotus alba* Desr.) and Associated Prairie Vegetation to Seven Experimental Burning and Mowing Treatments." *Proceedings of the Ninth North American Prairie Conference*, pp. 149–152. Moorehead, MN: Moorehead State University.

Lorenz, R. ed. 1986. *Leafy Spurge News* 2 (Mandan, ND: Land Reclamation Research Center).

McKnight, B. M., ed. 1993. *Biological Pollution, the Control and Impact of Invasive Exotic Species.* Indianapolis: Indiana Academy of Science.

Mooney, H., and J. Drake, eds. 1986. *Ecology of Biological Invasions of North America and Hawaii.* New York: Springer-Verlag.

Nixon, P., C. Anderson, N. Pataky, R. Wolf, R. Ferree, and L. Bode. N.d. *Illinois Pesticide Applicator Training Manual: General Standards.* Urbana-Champaign: University of Illinois.

U.S. Congress, Office of Technology Assessment. 1993. *Harmful Non-Indigenous Species in the United States.* OTA-F-565. Washington, DC: U.S. Government Printing Office.

U.S. Department of Agriculture. 1977. *Response of Selected Woody Plants in the United States to Herbicides.* Agricultural Handbook No. 493. Washington, DC: USDA, Agricultural Research Service.

Weed Science Society of America. 1989. *The Herbicide Handbook of the Weed Science Society of America.* Champaign, IL: Weed Science Society of America.

White, D., E. Haber, and C. Keddy. 1993. *Invasive Plants of Natural Habitats in Canada.* Ottawa: Canadian Museum of Nature.

Restoration and Management Notes (published twice yearly by the University of Wisconsin Press) has a section on control of pest species that routinely has useful information.

17
Monitoring Vegetation

Linda A. Masters

Most restorationists need to answer a simple but very important question: Should their current management or restoration practices be continued or should they be modified? The best way to answer this question is by monitoring the changes that happen during restoration. Monitoring data should allow the restorationist to evaluate movement toward or away from the restoration goals and thus help revise restoration priorities. However, monitoring programs take time and resources, neither of which restorationists have in unlimited amounts. It is important to choose strategically a few factors to measure rather than trying to monitor everything. So, what should we monitor and how should we do it?

While there are some highly specialized monitoring challenges, such as legal requirements in mitigation or problems that need state-of-the-art research, they are relatively rare and are addressed in growing bodies of technical literature. It is important to recognize that, while you will often learn a lot about your site during your monitoring efforts, these efforts are not research in the narrow sense and will not necessarily demonstrate cause and effect. If, for example, you want to compare the effectiveness of several different management techniques, you would be well advised to consult with someone well qualified in experimental design and analysis.

For most restoration efforts, relatively simple monitoring programs yield all the information required to gauge success. This chapter discusses several techniques restorationists can use to design effective monitoring programs to get the feedback they need to make sound management decisions. This chapter also provides, as examples, five case studies that examine some common monitoring questions:

1. Are current management techniques effective in reducing non-native brush patches in a prairie?

2. Is a certain endangered species increasing or decreasing?
3. What is the effect of burning on an aggressive woodland exotic?
4. What species of plants have been successfully reseeded in a new restoration?
5. How does a certain management regime change the vegetation in a restoration, and is the change good?

Some readers may be uncomfortable with the value-judgment question, "Is it good?" Yet, accomplishing something of ecological value is what restoration is all about. The discussion of these questions will suggest ways of thinking that may help in the creation of monitoring plans, and the list of references at the chapter's end will provide access to many variations and alternatives.

Designing a Monitoring Program

First, identify your restoration goals clearly. Restoration implies that an area is going to change from what it is now to what the restorationist has determined is best for the site. You need to state, with some detail, what you mean by success, or you will not be able to develop a method to assess whether you are getting there. Stating the restoration goals and the monitoring study's objectives clearly and concisely will help determine monitoring methods and set work priorities. It is terribly frustrating, after several years of monitoring, to realize that the information gathered does not tell you very much about the progress toward your restoration goal.

The time and effort needed to pursue a productive monitoring program is dependent on a couple of factors. First, how large a population, or an area, are you interested in tracking? If, for example, you want to follow a rare species and there are only fifty individuals on your site, it is most effective to census the entire population. You then will know, with great precision, how the population is changing. Alternatively, if you need to track the decline of an invasive weed over several hundred acres, you will need to collect some samples that are (as a group) representative of the entire area. Using appropriate monitoring techniques and analyses, you will be able to say something about the entire population.

You also need to determine how much change is important to you. If your goals are quantitative—e.g., if you want to see a hundredfold increase in a certain species—you needn't collect data that enable you to detect a change in abundance as small as 5 percent. Unfortunately, most monitoring programs fail in the other direction. Often, restorationists want to be able to detect relatively small changes (e.g., 10 percent change), yet they collect only the coarsest information, leaving them unable to detect the desired changes.

In summary, you need to answer four questions prior to undertaking your monitoring—and your restoration: 1) What is the species or area that you are interested in? 2) What are your restoration goals for that species or area, and what does success look like? 3) What are the indicators of change that can be measured? and 4) What kind of change and how much of it needs to occur (over what period) before you consider your program successful?

Once you have answered these questions, prepare a map of the site showing streams, lakes, topography, roads, and the like. Additional maps showing watersheds, trails, drainage tiles, and events such as controlled burns will add to your information base. Aerial photographs can be helpful in delimiting plant communities. Visual changes over time can be recorded by establishing permanent photographic stations. For the most part, the only sampling tools you will need will be your map, a quadrat frame, a measuring tape, a compass, data recording supplies, and a guide to the plants in your area. Prairies, savannas, and woodlands contain the bulk of their vegetative species richness in the ground–cover layer. The sampling techniques discussed below concentrate on the measurement, frequency, and quality of the ground cover. This is where you will get the most sensitive measurements for both quantitative and qualitative vegetation changes in your restoration.

For an overall picture of the plant community, start with a complete inventory. Plants should be recorded at least twice during the growing season, once early enough for the spring flora and a second time late enough for the fall flora. Be sure to record as many species as possible over the entire site so that you capture the full floristic variety.

Inventories are useful; however, they do not show which species are increasing and decreasing, or which are common and which are rare. Measuring such floristic changes over time can best be achieved through quantitative sampling repeated at various intervals. Sampling is done when the population or area of interest is too large to census in its entirety. When done efficiently, sampling provides a picture of the entire population or area with a minimum of time and effort. However, when done poorly, sampling can lead to inaccurate conclusions. There are two types of errors that can occur with monitoring, sampling errors and non-sampling errors. Nonsampling errors are the result of human activity, such as flawed transcription and recording of data, or incorrect and inconsistent plant identification. It is very important that the sampling methods be clearly defined, so that they can be repeated not only by you but also by others. Defining the methods clearly will help reduce non-sampling errors and problems due to changes in monitoring personnel.

Sampling errors result from chance and are inevitable in all sampling studies. Such errors result from the heterogeneity of the natural world. Any small plot cannot truly represent all the variability found within a much larger area. As a result, the information from a single sample can be far from representative of the larger population. However, a collection of these samples can, when analyzed appropriately, give a very accurate picture of the population as a whole. One thing is certain about the gathering of data and subsequent analysis: Differences in sampled units will occur. You will have to decide whether these differences are significant, informative, or merely reflective of sampling error.

When to sample depends largely on the questions being asked. If you are interested in monitoring the recovery of the fall flora in a degraded savanna, sample in the fall. If you are interested in the recovery of a sedge meadow, sample in late spring or early summer when the sedges are easily identifiable. How often to sample also depends on the questions being asked. A plant community that changes slowly does not need to be sampled as often as one that changes more quickly. For example, you may want to sample the ground cover in a savanna every year or two, but sampling of the trees needs to be done no more than once every five to ten years. It will also be valuable to conduct baseline (prerestoration) sampling to document the condition of the site before restoration begins.

Three types of samples are commonly used to monitor the composition of the vegetation and its changes with restoration: plots, quadrats, and transects. Plots are usually larger sampling areas (e.g., one hectare, one-quarter acre, or 100 by 100 feet) that are often permanently marked. They can be placed randomly but are often purposely placed in an area judged to be representative of the site to be monitored. They are frequently used in woodlands to sample trees. Plots can be further subdivided into subplots to monitor different size classes, such as saplings, seedlings, and herbaceous ground layer plants.

Quadrats are typically much smaller than plots. They can range in size from $1.16m^2$ to $1m^2$; the recommended size is $1/4m^2$. They can be arranged regularly in transects or scattered randomly over the site through the use of a grid system and a random number table. Transects are usually lines of quadrats, which may or may not be randomly placed (see discussion below). One simple form of sampling is to select arbitrarily one or more lines that pass through all of the important vegetative features of the site. If you want to resample the same transect later to detect changes through time, you should permanently mark the transect.

One way to locate transects randomly is to measure any edge of the site, use a random number table to select points along the measured edge, and then run transects perpendicular from the edge starting at those points. If you want to be sure to sample certain parts of the site, treat those parts as separate monitoring projects. Or divide the site into strips and then place the transects randomly within the strips (stratified random sampling). The number of samples needed is proportional to the size of the site, variability of the vegetation, and the level of certainty desired.

Samples should be sufficiently numerous so as to achieve a representative amount of plant frequency and coverage data. Too few quadrats can result in a large sampling error from year to year, and some of the more subtle floristic changes may be missed. Too many quadrats make the sampling too burdensome to continue on a regular basis. You might start with a greater number of quadrats for the initial baseline sampling, such as seventy-five or more, and then take random subsets of fifty, or forty, or thirty, etc., to determine when the measurements of interest begin to differ significantly from the larger baseline sampling. There are simple equations that allow you to assess the adequacy of the chosen number of samples needed to detect the amount of change you feel is important (Krebs 1989 and others).

Placement of quadrats along a transect can be determined by randomly selecting a point within a predetermined pacing interval. For example, you decide that fifty quadrats are sufficient to sample a particular prairie. The sampling interval selected is one to ten paces and a random number between one and ten is chosen, such as seven; the first quadrat is then placed seven paces from the start of the transect. The next random number is chosen—six—placing the next quadrat six paces from the first. The third random number is four, and the quadrat is placed four paces later, and so on until fifty quadrats have been sampled.

There may be times when regular spacing of quadrats gives more helpful feedback. A fixed spacing between quadrats works best if you want to map changes in plant communities across a shade gradient, detail the coverage of a particular disturbance, or correlate vegetation to soil moisture or some other factor. For example, if you want to detect changes in the extent of a community or encroachment, place quadrats in a line that extends from one area into another. Spacing and number of quadrats are especially important in this instance because too few quadrats widely spaced may fail to detect any change in the community soon enough. To incorporate randomness into a method using regular spacing, place the first quadrat randomly along the transect and then proceed using fixed spacing. This will give the same results as random spacing of quadrats, as long as there is not a regular pattern to the variation in the vegetation, which is generally true for midwestern grasslands.

Plot and quadrat shapes are usually round or quadrangular. Plots commonly range from 0.1ha to 1ha. Sizes of quadrat frames typically range from $0.1m^2$ to $1m^2$. For prairie systems, the most efficient quadrat is a square, 0.5m on a side ($0.25m^2$). This size is small enough that all the plants in the quadrat can be seen in one field of vision, and thus more samples can be established per unit time. The larger the quadrat frame, the more difficult it becomes to see all the plants at once, the harder it is to determine an accurate cover value, and the more time it takes. Quadrats that are too small will require an excessive number of samples to describe the variability present in most grassland systems. A $0.25m^2$ square quadrat frame can be constructed from ½-inch by ½-inch wood or ½-inch PVC pipe, 0.5m on a side. One side of the quadrat can be left off so that it will fit easily around bulky plants; and if the joints are hinged, the quadrat can be folded for easy carrying (figure 17.1). A $0.25m^2$ hoop can be made by buying a 1.57m length of stiff, flexible tubing (e.g., PVC pipe), putting a snugly fitting dowel in one end, bending it into a circle, and pushing the two ends together over the dowel. The hoop can be opened to fit around bulky plants. The choice of plot and quadrat size and shape is up to you, but it is important to stay with whatever method you begin with if you want to make meaningful comparisons.

When monitoring a natural community, record a complete list of all species present in each quadrat and, if desired, their estimated cover. "Cover" is defined as the ground area covered by the vertical projection of the above-ground plant parts. It is important to consider what is included in the cover estimate. For example, will you include plants not rooted in the quadrat, but that arch over it, such as vines or saplings? Record in your methods what is to be included as part of the cover estimate so it can be estimated consistently with repeated sampling.

Percent cover is the estimated percent of cover for each species in the quadrat, while cover classes lump percent cover estimates into broader measures such as: 1 = 1–10%, 2 = 11–30%, 3 = 31–50%, and 4 = 51–100%. If the abundance of the species is to be integrated, a cover-abundance coefficient can be assigned that combines an estimated cover with an estimated distribution and abundance within the quadrat. For example, give each species in a quadrat a cover-abundance coefficient from 1 to 5 as follows:

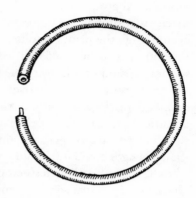

Figure 17.1. Frames for sampling 0.25 m² quadrats. For a square frame, sides should be ½ meter long. For a circular frame, tubing should be 1.57 meters long.

1 = species consisting of one to a few stems in only one quarter of the quadrat.

2 = species occupying 1 to 2 quarters and numbering several stems.

3 = species occupying 2 to 3 quarters with cover and density notable in each.

4 = species occupying 3 to 4 quarters with a regular density throughout.

5 = restricted to species that dominate the entire quadrat.

Do not get bogged down trying to be extremely precise with the cover values. As long as the values are applied consistently, the results will be useful and generally repeatable.

Cover estimate is one measure used to determine a species' importance relative to all other species in the sample area. Another measure of importance is derived from a species' frequency, which is the number of quadrats in which a particular species occurred. Relative frequency is calculated by dividing the frequency of one species by the total frequency of all species. Relative cover is calculated by dividing the total cover of one species by the total cover of all the species. The relative importance value (RIV) of a species is figured by adding the relative frequency (RFRQ) and relative cover (RCOV) together (RIV 200). Some people find it clearer to divide this number by two (RIV 100) (figure 17.2).

An important thing to remember about a table of relative importance values is that the rank of a species will not remain the same throughout the growing season or from year to year. Rank is, in part, a factor of the plant's structure and is influenced by the year's weather, herbivory, mortality, reproduction, etc. The relative importance of a certain plant species may drop when more species are added, or rise if species drop out, even though the plant's absolute cover and frequency remain the same. If vegetation is to be evaluated based on changes in the cover of certain species, it is important to sample the plots or transects at the same time of the year, using the same cover value guidelines. Remember, the RIV rankings are like a snapshot of the restoration at the time of sampling. It is difficult to categorize changes in cover, frequency, or importance values as positive or negative unless you have a hypothesis about what these changes could or should be at a particular site.

As discussed earlier, restorationists must make value-based decisions concerning the management and floristic direction of their work. It is

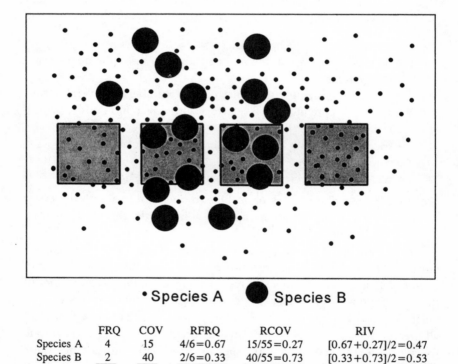

	FRQ	COV	RFRQ	RCOV	RIV
Species A	4	15	4/6=0.67	15/55=0.27	[0.67+0.27]/2=0.47
Species B	2	40	2/6=0.33	40/55=0.73	[0.33+0.73]/2=0.53
Total	6	55	1.00	1.00	1.00

Figure 17.2. Sampling of two plant species. The following calculations show how the relative importance of a plant species is affected by its size and distribution. Abbreviations: Frequency (FRQ), cover (COV), relative frequency (RFRQ), relative cover (RCOV), and relative importance value (RIV) of two species. Species A has a higher RFRQ; species B has a higher RCOV. Overall, species B has a higher RIV.

not sufficient to know that the numbers of certain plants are increasing or decreasing; you must also be able to evaluate whether those changes are positive or negative. Nor is it sufficient merely to distinguish between native and exotic species. It is crucial to know whether these are the native species that can coalesce into functioning communities that will form a part of a sustainable ecosystem. If certain native plant species can be correlated with ecological integrity, then their presence would be an indicator of system health or quality. How can changes in quality be measured quantitatively?

An approach to vegetational monitoring in northeastern Illinois was developed in 1979 by Gerould Wilhelm. Previously known as the Natural Area Rating Index (NARI), the system has been updated and published in the book *Plants of the Chicago Region* by Floyd Swink and Gerould Wilhelm (Indiana Academy of Science, Indianapolis, 1994); it is now known as floristic quality assessment (FQA). This approach helps to answer some of these questions and specifically addresses the question of natural system quality. Floristic quality assessment is based on the concept of species conservatism. Conservatism represents the degree to which an experienced field botanist has confidence that a given species is representative of high-quality remnant habitat. High-quality remnants are those with intact presettlement structure, composition, and processes. Native plants of an area exhibit an observable range of conservatism. Some are ubiquitous and commonly found in degraded or ruderal conditions. Others are restricted to highly specific remnant habitats such as marl flats, bogs, or sedge turfs in savannas.

A range of conservatism can be demonstrated by considering three plants from a tallgrass prairie: common ragweed, pale purple coneflower, and prairie lily. There is little disagreement among botanists concerning the level of conservatism these plants exhibit. The ragweed can be found in all types of degraded sites, from roadsides and vacant lots to disturbed areas in high-quality prairies. You would have no confidence that the presence of this plant would indicate a remnant habitat; it would not be considered at all conservative. The coneflower, on the other hand, is fairly sensitive to habitat degradation and is restricted to sites with at least some natural-remnant quality; therefore, compared to ragweed, coneflower is considered a relatively conservative plant. The lily is considered a highly conservative plant because it is narrowly restricted (in Illinois) to high-quality prairie, savanna, or fen remnants. Note that a plant's conservatism is described by its restrictedness not to specific plant communities but rather to high-quality remnants in a particular region.

To assess floristic quality quantitatively for monitoring purposes using

FQA, native plants are given coefficients of conservatism that range from 0 to 10. When analyzing an inventory the mean C of the entire list of native plants will be informative about the floristic quality of the site. If your site has a large proportion of conservative plants, the mean C is higher; if it is degraded, the mean C will be lower. Often in relatively high-quality plant communities that are being managed, the mean C will tend to remain stable, while the total number of species may increase, decrease, or remain the same. What a change in species richness means in terms of floristic quality is measured by calculating a floristic quality index (FQI). The FQI is calculated by multiplying the mean C by the square root of the total number of native species recorded (FQI = $C\sqrt{n}$). Because the FQI takes into account the number of species along with the mean C, it incorporates species richness and quality so that floristic diversity is integrated as a qualitative measurement. As management causes change to take place, the mean C and the FQI will reflect the extent to which conservative species are being recruited and floristic quality is improving.

Only the native plants of an area are assigned C values, because these native species represent the distillation of thousands of years of local natural selection. These species reflect the effects of sustained inhabitancy at a particular site, with its individual variations of substrate, moisture, slope, aspect, and vicissitudes of seasonal and yearly fluctuations. Communities consisting of a high ratio of conservative to nonconservative plants reflect relative stability within the natural fluctuation that is characteristic of healthy biological systems. The presence of a large proportion of adventive species and nonconservative natives suggests an area that has been degraded—for example, by overgrazing, plowing, soil removal, or fire suppression.

Coefficients of conservatism are available for many parts of the tallgrass region: Illinois (Taft et al. 1996), Missouri (Ladd 1996), Michigan (Herman et al. 1996), thirty-one counties in northern Ohio (Andreas and Lichvar 1995), southern Ontario (Oldham et al. 1995), and a twenty-two county region surrounding Chicago (Swink and Wilhelm 1994). For the coefficients of conservatism assigned to prairie plants in these areas, refer to appendix A. Coefficients for conservative savanna and woodland species are included in table 5.1. If rankings are not available for your area, it is possible to improvise, basing your values on lists of nearby regions, realizing that the farther you are from an evaluated area, the less likely it is that the conservatism values will reflect local conditions. Coefficients of conservatism should be tailored to the state or region in which the system will be used. Any person (or even better, group of people) with a thorough knowledge of a region's native flora and its ecology can derive a spectrum of conservatism rankings. Coefficients are assigned by an experienced botanist to each native taxon using the guiding philosophy that the assignments reflect only the relative conservatism of each species to remnant habitats within the context of the region under consideration, and without specific regard to rareness, showiness, wildlife amenities, etc. When two or more experienced botanists have assigned values for a given area, an averaging of their values may provide improved precision. If you would like to monitor vegetation quality but work in an area without assigned coefficients, you may assign coefficients yourself. It is possible to begin with a simplified conservatism scale of 0, 5, and 10. A zero would indicate native species most commonly found in recently disturbed areas; ten would apply to species restricted to high-quality remnants; and five would cover all the rest. Referring to our previous example, common ragweed would rate 0, pale purple coneflower 5, and prairie lily 10.

If you attempt to assign coefficients in this way, you will quickly discover that there are species with conservatism values intermediate between 0 and 5, and between 5 and 10. With observation of the plants in your area, continue to fine-tune the coefficients until you have a full range of C values from 0 to 10.

In theory, C values could be objectively determined by sampling in areas of varying quality (as determined by some objective method). Such an ambitious task, however, has not yet been carried out. Thus, the existing FQA systems all depend on the subjective judgment of independent, experienced botanists who assigned the coefficients. However, the FQA process has an advantage over most other community quality assessment methods in that, once the numbers are assigned, subsequent use of the system, including the qualitative comparisons between areas or within areas over time, is entirely objective and repeatable.

Floristic quality assessment can be used to analyze both site inventory lists and samples. It allows anyone with the requisite botanical experience to obtain similar results. Essentially, it allows the restorationist to reduce a complex pattern of change to a few key statistics that are sensitive enough to codify responses indicative of the plant community or ecosystem as a whole.

Monitoring Case Studies

Five specific case studies are presented in this section. Each study addresses a different type of management question. There are many variations and alternative methods for finding the answers to these questions, but these examples can provide a starting point in planning a monitoring program at your particular site.

Are current management techniques effective in reducing non-native brush patches in a prairie?

A certain prairie contained six patches of non-native brush patches. The brush patches did not appear on a 1938 aerial photograph, and they were considered a symptom of degradation resulting from decades of fire suppression. Management consisted of burning one-third of the site each year. The edges of the patches contracted in the years of burns, but expanded during the years without burns. The interiors of the patches did not burn because of a complete lack of grassy fuel in the shade of the shrubs. Fire management had been initiated in 1980 after three species of prairie birds that formerly nested there abandoned the site. The management goal was to diminish significantly the extent of the patches.

The circumference of every patch was measured every three years and recorded along with the specifics of how measurements were made: for example, "We walked around the patch and placed stakes at points where the prairie grass stopped. A tape measure was stretched from stake to stake to form a polygon. We recorded the circumference of each patch."

The data in table 17.1 show that there was a variation from year to year, and although patches 2 and 4 were getting smaller, the overall trend did not look good. The prairie was usually burned with the prevailing wind from the southwest, and the fire could not build up enough heat to control the brush in the patches near the south and west edges. At least in the case of four patches (1, 3, 5, and 6) a reevaluation of the management regime seemed necessary. After analyzing the data, the manager convinced her supervisor to appropriate funds to have the shrubs removed manually, to treat the stumps with herbicide, and to reseed the open ground with prairie grasses.

Is a certain endangered species increasing or decreasing?

A proposed federal-endangered plant species thrives on a five-acre, high-quality hilltop within a fifteen-hundred-acre prairie preserve. The preserve managers are removing 5 percent of the plant's seed each year in an attempt to establish new populations on eight other hilltops within the preserve. An endangered species recovery team has recently begun to study the demographics and genetics of the plant under various management regimes at several different sites, but the results are not expected for ten years or more.

Table 17.1.

	Circumference of Brush Patches				
Brush Patch	Circumference in Meters				
	1980	1983	1986	1989	1992
1	20	18	22	26	24
2	14	10	11	11	8
3	16	14	20	25	23
4	14	9	11	12	9
5	21	25	23	27	29
6	46	52	48	53	56
Total	131	128	135	154	149

Local volunteers had "adopted" the site before it was purchased for conservation. They had been carefully censusing the population by recording the number of blooming plants for five years. The managers asked the volunteers to continue their monitoring for two reasons. First, there was some concern about removing even so small an amount of seed, because each plant dies after flowering and this population may need all the seed it produces just to maintain its current numbers. Second, the plant appeared to be thriving under a regime of light grazing, and when the site was acquired for conservation, the cows were removed. It was not known how the plant would respond to the new situation. The managers would have liked to have a count of juvenile and nonflowering plants as well, but such plants can be hard to find and neither the managers nor the volunteers felt they had the time. It is anticipated that the recovery team study will eventually provide information on seedling recruitment.

When analyzing the results, the managers noted that the number of individuals varied radically from year to year (table 17.2). In order to detect more easily the long-term trends, a three-year average was computed and graphed (figure 17.3). As of 1995, the managers saw no reason to be concerned about the collection of seed, nor did they see the need to change their management practices. Small numbers of blooming plants were appearing on three of the eight hilltops where their seed was broadcast.

What is the effect of burning on an aggressive woodland exotic?
In 1977 a forty-acre remnant woodland was dedicated as a nature preserve. During an early walk-through, the volunteer science and management team noticed that small numbers of the opportunistic weed garlic mustard was growing throughout the woods. As part of the assessment

Linda A. Masters

Table 17.2.

Numbers of Individuals of an Endangered Plant													
Year	83	84	85	86	87★	88	89	90	91	92	93	94	95
Individuals	42	8	19	22	3	32	6	14	51	6	7	59	15
3-year average		23	16	15	19		14	17	24	24	21	24	27

★Grazing halted.

for setting management priorities, the managers decided to track the population of garlic mustard in this woodland and an adjacent woodland of similar size and quality. Neither woodland was managed for the first six years. In 1984 a burn program was initiated in the nature preserve. Since then, management in the preserve has consisted of either a spring or a fall burn as well as the reseeding of herbaceous species. The garlic mustard received no weeding or other special management. The other woodland continued to receive no management.

The sampling consisted of recording presence and absence of any garlic mustard plant within one hundred randomly selected 1m² circular quadrats. The volunteer scientists divided the entire forty acres of each woodland into ten 10-meter-wide strips running north and south. Along the south border, within each strip, one randomly selected point located the beginning of each transect. The first quadrat of each transect was placed by randomly selecting a number between one and ten. The sampler walked that many paces north, and put down the 1m² hoop directly in front of him, touching the tip of his shoe. He recorded presence or absence of garlic mustard plants within the hoop. Then he continued to pace due north and, at ten-pace intervals, repeated the sample, until reaching the north border. He continued such transects until he had one hundred samples from each forty acres. These transects were repeated every two years for eighteen years.

The volunteer scientists were asking a simple question: Is the current management program controlling the spread of garlic mustard? In order to be confident of the answer, they also needed to determine whether any differences between the treated and untreated areas were significant. When the frequency of garlic mustard for each woodland was plotted on a graph (figure 17.4), it was clear that the garlic mustard increased in the unmanaged woodland and decreased in the managed woodland. However, skeptics pointed out that sometimes changes can be the result of chance variation or sampling error. The managers consulted with a volunteer statistician, who, after performing the appropriate analyses, confirmed that, indeed, the difference between the two sites had become

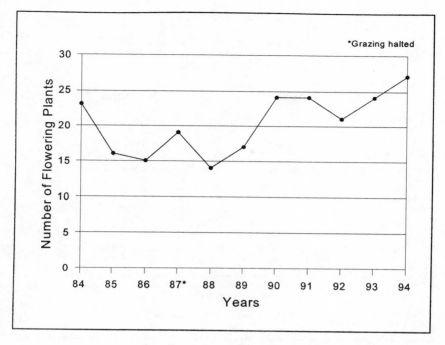

Figure 17.3. Population size changes in an endangered plant. Three-year averages of the numbers of flowering individuals.

significant by 1989. With this and other information, the Nature Preserves Commission staff convinced the owner of the adjacent woods to dedicate that land as a preserve as well, with restoration to begin in 1996.

What species of plants have been successfully reseeded in a new restoration?
As part of the mitigation agreement for the development of nearby land, an attempt was made to restore a forty-acre agricultural field to its original wet-prairie condition. The field was part of a larger preserve, but had been leased to a farmer until six years before. In 1990, the field was left fallow, and many of the drain tiles were blocked or removed to restore the original hydrology. The preserve manager and the restoration contractor agreed upon a seed mix that was installed in the spring of 1991.

As part of the monitoring program, the manager wanted to know which of the planted species germinated and persisted. Volunteers inventoried the site several times a year for five years, noting every plant species they saw. They compared the seed list with these inventories to evaluate the success of the planting (table 17.3). After five growing seasons, nine

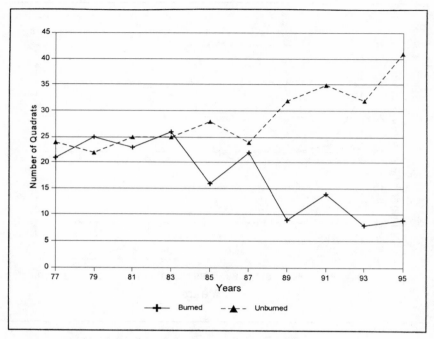

Figure 17.4. Garlic mustard in burned and unburned woodlands.

of the twenty-five planted species had not appeared, and four previously recorded species were not seen in 1995.

The manager was concerned that the numbers of individuals of many of these species remained low and that weedy vegetation seemed to be increasing. As a result, a new study was planned for 1996. Additional seed of an expanded list of wet-prairie species would be broadcast over the entire site each fall from 1996 to 1998. To compare two management techniques, the site was divided into four similar plots of equal size. In two plots, the weedy vegetation would be mowed once a year to a height of 6 inches whenever the soil was dry enough to support a tractor. In the other two, the plots would not be mowed. Twenty random quadrats would be sampled in each of the four plots each year from 1999 to 2002. The average FQI for the forty quadrats in the mowed area would be compared with the average in the unmowed area to determine whether mowing helped in the establishment of the conservative wet-prairie species. The quadrat data would also show whether the more conservative plants were replacing less conservative weedy species, as one would expect.

Table 17.3.

Species Success in a Planted Wetland.   List of species planted, along with their coefficients of conservatism (C) and the year in which they were first recorded (x).

Planted Species	Common Name	C	1991	1992	1993	1994	1995
Acorus calamus	sweet flag	7					
Angelica atropurpurea	great angelica	7				x	x
Asclepias incarnata	swamp milkweed	4	x		x		x
Aster novae-angliae	New England aster	4			x	x	x
Aster puniceus firmus	shining aster	7					
Calamagrostis canadensis	blue joint grass	3	x				
Carex lacustris	lake bank sedge	6					
Carex stricta	tussock sedge	5		x	x	x	
Carex vulpinoidea	fox sedge	2			x	x	x
Elymus canadensis	Canada wild rye	4	x	x	x	x	x
Eupatorium maculatum	spotted Joe-Pye weed	4		x	x	x	x
Gentiana andrewsii	closed gentian	8					
Helenium autumnale	sneezeweed	5		x	x	x	
Iris virginica shrevei	blue flag iris	5					
Leersia oryzoides	rice cut grass	4		x	x	x	
Liatris pycnostachya	prairie blazing star	8				x	x
Liatris spicata	marsh blazing star	6			x		
Lobelia cardinalis	cardinal flower	7					
Lobelia siphilitica	great blue lobelia	6			x	x	x
Panicum virgatum	switch grass	5	x	x	x	x	x
Physostegia virginiana	obedient plant	6					
Pycnanthemum virginianum	common mountain mint	5					x
Solidago riddellii	Riddell's goldenrod	7					
Spartina pectinata	prairie cord grass	4					
Zizia aurea	golden Alexanders	7			x	x	
Total Species (25 planted)			4	5	11	12	12
Mean C (Planted = 5.4)			4.0	4.4	4.5	5.1	5.1
Percent Recruitment			16	20	44	48	48

How does a certain management regime change the vegetation in a restoration, and is the change good?

A prairie supported a state-endangered sedge, the numbers of which had dropped discouragingly low. Eurasian brush and weeds had become a problem throughout the prairie, probably because it had not been burned in many years. The managers decided to initiate a burn program to help revitalize the sedge population and to improve the overall floristic quality of the site. An existing trail system divided the prairie into two plots that had generally similar vegetation. In 1977, thirty $0.25m^2$ quadrats were sampled along a permanently marked random line through the center of each plot. Beginning in 1979, plot A was burned every six years and plot B was burned every two years. The transects were repeated every two years. In order to test the effect of the two burn regimes on the quality of vegetation, a quadrat average for both the mean C and the FQI were computed for each transect (table 17.4).

The managers noted that in the frequently burned plot (B) the mean C and FQI steadily increased, while the less frequently burned plot (A) continued to lose conservative species slowly. They also noted an interesting trend in plot B. The total number of native species initially rose and then fell (figure 17.5). If only the number of native species was considered, one might conclude that essentially no net change had occurred. However, the data showed that in plot B both the mean C and the FQI values had been rising steadily, an indication that the less conservative species were dropping out, while the system was gaining a higher proportion of conservative species (figures 17.6 and 17.7). From looking at the graph, this trend is clearly apparent and was confirmed by statistical analysis.

The more subtle trends shown in figure 17.5, measured using the floristic quality assessment method, suggest strongly that floristic quality is steadily improving in the frequently burned plot (B) and remaining essentially the same in the infrequently burned plot (A). These trends give the managers confidence that their restoration activities are effectively

Table 17.4.

Eighteen Years of Community Monitoring Data from a Tallgrass Prairie					
	Total Native Species		Mean C/Quadrat		FQI/Quadrat	
Year	Plot A	Plot B	Plot A	Plot B	Plot A	Plot B
1977	25	24	2.5	2.4	7.0	7.1
1979	26	29	2.6	2.6	6.9	6.6
1981	24	30	2.3	2.5	7.2	8.0
1983	22	33	2.4	2.5	6.5	7.8
1985	23	31	2.3	2.8	5.9	10.1★
1987	20	30	2.2	2.9	5.7	9.7★
1989	22	26	2.1	3.1	6.0	11.2★
1991	23	28	2.2	3.0	5.6	12.4★
1993	20	27	1.9	3.5★	4.9	14.3★
1995	19	27	2.0	3.4★	5.1	15.2★

★The yearly mean is significantly different from the baseline 1977 mean, $p < 0.05$.

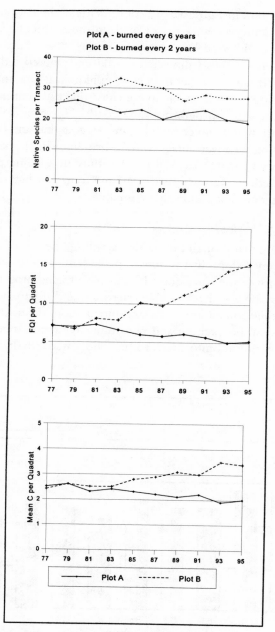

Figure 17.5. Changes in floristic quality under two burn regimes. C = coefficient of conservatism, FQI = floristic quality index.

driving the system in a positive direction. With all the data and statistical analyses taken into account, the changes in the frequently burned plot can be considered "good."

Their monitoring also showed that the endangered sedge is flourishing in plot B but continues to decline in plot A. Based on the vegetation monitoring, it is reasonable to conclude that the prairie represented by plot A should be burned more frequently. However, some preliminary observations on insect populations suggest that the burn regime may be stressing the invertebrate community. Since little is known about the life history of many native insects, a study now being planned will compare the effect of annual, two-year, and four-year burn rotations on butterflies, spiders, ants, and other animals.

What Does It All Mean?

After spending many, often hot, hours sampling, the monitoring process is only half finished. Now it is time to make sense of all that good information to answer your questions. If your monitoring program had clear objectives, if you asked answerable questions, and if you collected your data so that they contain the necessary information, the next part of your monitoring will be exciting and rewarding. Remember, an important goal in restoration monitoring is to find those items that can help con-

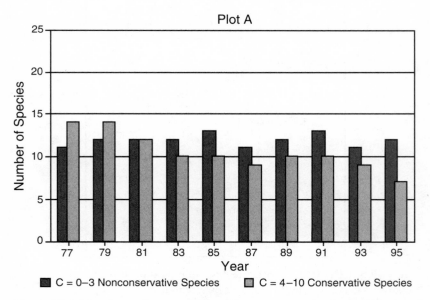

Figure 17.6. Numbers of conservatives and nonconservatives in an infrequently burned plot. Plot A, represented here, is burned on a six-year rotation.

firm that you are on the right track, or that will cause you to change your restoration techniques. You can also use your data to look for trends and make sense of relationships and variations in your ecosystem. Scrounging through data, looking for unanticipated trends is a good way to look for new questions. But keep in mind that long-term directional changes will be complicated by seasonal and annual variations and sampling error, and that the ecosystem, with its resident species, is adjusting in many complex ways to changed management.

Monitoring data often show no statistically significant differences between years even though subtle long-term trends seem quite apparent. In other cases, restoration produces changes that are so dramatic that you will not even need to sample to know that positive change has occurred. But when you need monitoring data to help determine whether your efforts are effective, you may want to learn to use statistics in order to objectively analyze the changes. It is important to remember that ecological knowledge, statistical inference, and informed intuition also play a role in the interpretation of the changes that take place in the management of restoration areas. We are able to measure only those things in the ecosystem that we have the technology, labor, time, and money to measure. There are many ecosystem properties that we are unable to measure at the moment that are just as important to the overall successful functioning of

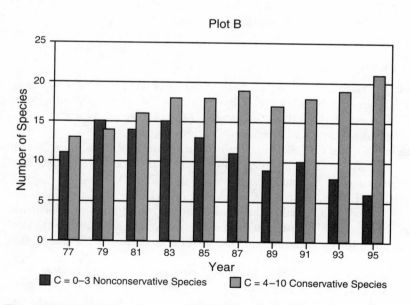

Figure 17.7. Numbers of conservatives and nonconservatives in a frequently burned plot. Plot B, represented here, is burned on a two-year rotation.

the system. The goal for restorationists and land managers should be to design monitoring programs that will best help them track the progress of restoration toward a dynamic, diverse community in which as many as possible of the resident native plants and animals are able to flourish and reproduce indefinitely.

SOURCES OF STATE AND REGIONAL FLORISTIC QUALITY ASSESSMENT INFORMATION

Herman, K.D., L.A. Masters, M.R. Penskar, A.A. Reznicek, G.S. Wilhelm, and W.W. Brodowicz. 1996. *Floristic Quality Assessment System with Wetland Categories and Computer Application Programs for the State of Michigan*. Michigan Department of Natural Resources, Wildlife Division, Natural Heritage Program, Lansing, Michigan.

Ladd, D.M. 1996. "The Missouri Floristic Quality Assessment System." *Nature Conservancy*. St. Louis: The Nature Conservancy.

Oldham, M.J., W.D. Bakowsky, and D.A. Sutherland. 1995. *Floristic Quality Assessment for Southern Ontario*. Ontario Ministry of Natural Resources, Peterborough, Ontario: Natural Heritage Information Centre.

Swink, F.S., and G.S. Wilhelm. 1994. *Plants of the Chicago Region*. Indianapolis: Indiana Academy of Science. Covers parts of Illinois, Indiana, Michigan, and Wisconsin.

Taft, J. B., G. S. Wilhelm, D. M. Ladd, and L. A. Masters. 1996. "Floristic Quality Assessment for Illinois." *Erigenia* 15, no. 1.

REFERENCES

Andreas, B.K., and R.W. Lichvar. 1995. *Floristic Index for Establishing Assessment Standards: A Case Study for Northern Ohio*. Technical Report WRP-DE-8. Vicksburg, MS: U.S. Army Corps of Engineers Waterways Experiment Station.

Baskin, J.E., and C.C. Baskin. 1986. "Some Considerations in Evaluating and Monitoring Populations of Rare Plants in Successional Environments." *Natural Areas Journal* 6, no. 6:26–30.

Brower, J.E., J.H. Zar, and C.N. Von Ende. 1990. *Field and Laboratory Methods for General Ecology*, 3rd edition. Dubuque: Wm. C. Brown.

Davis, G.E. 1989. "Design of a Long-Term Ecological Monitoring Program for Channel Islands National Park, California." *Natural Areas Journal* 9, no. 2:80–89.

Goldsmith, F.B., ed. 1991. *Monitoring for Conservation and Ecology*. New York: Chapman and Hall.

Green, R.H. 1979. *Sampling Design and Statistical Methods for Envronmental Biologists*. New York: John C. Wiley.

Greig-Smith, P. 1964. *Quantitative Plant Ecology.* London: Butterworths.

Kershaw, K.A. 1973. *Quantitative and Dynamic Plant Ecology,* 2nd edition. New York: American Elsevier Publishing.

Krebs, C.J. 1989. *Ecological Methodology.* New York: Harper and Row.

Mueller-Dombois, D., and H. Ellenburg. 1974. *Aims and Methods of Vegetation Ecology.* New York: John C. Wiley.

Myers, W.L., and R.L. Shelton. 1980. *Survey Methods for Ecosystem Management.* New York: John C. Wiley.

Noss, Reed, and A.Y. Cooperrider. 1994. *Saving Nature's Legacy.* Washington, DC: Island Press.

Nuzzo, V.A., and E.A. Howell. 1990. "Natural Area Restoration Planning." *Natural Areas Journal* 10, no. 4:201–209.

Pickart, A.J. 1991. "The Evolution of a Rare Plant Monitoring Program: A Case Study at the Lanphere-Christensen Dunes Preserve." *Natural Areas Journal* 11, no. 4:187–189.

Smith, R.L. 1980. *Ecology and Field Biology,* 3rd edition. New York: Harper and Row.

Travis, J., and R. Sutter. 1986. "Experimental Designs and Statistical Methods for Demographic Studies of Rare Plants." *Natural Areas Journal* 6, no. 3:3–12.

Wilhelm, G.S., and L.A. Masters. 1994. "Floristic Changes After Five Growing Seasons in Burned and Unburned Woodland." *Erigenia* 13:141–150.

PART V

Protecting, Restoring, and Monitoring Animals

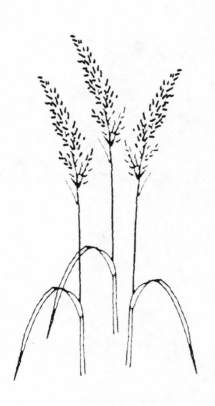

18
Insects

Douglas J. Taron

Prairies That Buzz

Few people today are fortunate enough to have visited Healey Road Prairie, a small but high-quality, gravel-hill prairie just north of Elgin, Illinois. Gravel mining destroyed the prairie in 1990. Much has been written about the vibrant prairie that grew there, and about the heroic efforts to rescue much of that community by transplanting the prairie sod to Bluff Spring Fen, six miles away. What I will always remember most about Healey Road Prairie, however, is its insect community. I first visited Healey Road Prairie on a warm afternoon in June of 1986. The then-abundant lead plant was attended by hundreds of fat yellow and black bumblebees, their pollen baskets the vivid orange of the lead plant stamens. The entire prairie buzzed—the effect of the gentle droning in the warm sunshine was almost hypnotic. It remains one of my most vivid memories of experiencing a prairie primarily by hearing it.

In 1990, just before the sod transplant, I was one of about twenty-five volunteers who attempted to rescue some of the Healey Road Prairie insect community. We crisscrossed the hillside with sweep nets, periodically transferring the contents to an ice-filled cooler. Looking back on that day, I realize that the contents of our nets were nothing short of astonishing. With only a couple of dozen sweeps, the nets filled with scores of insects from many diverse taxa. When we opened our nets, the effect was similar to removing the lid from a popcorn popper. Leafhoppers, froghoppers, and treehoppers ricocheted off the sides of the net. Grasshoppers, beetles, and katydids clambered over each other as we poured the contents into the cooler. By the end of the day, we had transferred over ten thousand insects to Bluff Spring Fen.

Today, five years later, native vegetation has largely knit together the scarred surface of the gravel hill where the Healey Road sod was transplanted. Most of the plant species have successfully transferred to their new home; some even flourish. The insects have not fared so well. Sweeping the vegetation reveals lower numbers and fewer species than we found at Healey Road Prairie. Standing before the hill on a warm afternoon in June is again becoming a treat for the eyes, but it is no longer a spectacle for the ears. This is one prairie that no longer buzzes.

The experience at Healey Road Prairie mirrors that of invertebrates on many remnants and restorations. Just as many plants recovered from the trauma of relocation, many prairie plant species in northern Illinois still hold their own on tiny hospitable prairie remnants. In contrast, the situation of prairie insects is more precarious. On many sites, healthy, diverse plant communities contain few prairie insect species.

The Teeming Millions:
Managing for Insect Species Diversity

By now, the statistics on insect species abundance are well known. Animals constitute between 75 and 80 percent of all species on earth. Insects and other arthropods represent from 75 to 80 percent of all animal species. With such diversity, it follows that insects play a wide variety of ecological roles: as herbivores, predators, scavengers, parasites, parasite hosts, and agents of seed dispersal, among others. Edward Wilson vividly illustrates this point in his 1992 book *The Diversity of Life:*

> So important are insects and other land-dwelling arthropods that if all were to disappear, humanity probably could not last more than a few months. Most of the amphibians, reptiles, birds, and mammals would crash to extinction about the same time. Next would go the bulk of the flowering plants and with them the physical structure of most forests and other terrestrial habitats of the world. The land surface would literally rot. As dead vegetation piled up and dried out, closing the channels of the nutrient cycles, other complex forms of vegetation would die off, and with them all but a few remnants of the land vertebrates. The free-living fungi, after enjoying a population explosion of stupendous proportions, would decline precipitously, and most species would perish. The land would return to approximately its condition in early Paleozoic times, covered by mats of recumbent wind-pollinated vegetation, sprinkled with clumps of small trees and bushes here and there, largely devoid of animal life.

Remnant-Reliance

Given the bewildering array of insect species, and their importance in maintaining the health of prairies and savannas, stewards can feel overwhelmed when faced with the prospects of managing for insects. Fortunately, the idea of separating insect species into remnant-reliant and remnant-independent categories, described by Ron Panzer of Northeastern Illinois University, offers some hope in dealing with this daunting problem. Whereas remnant-reliant species require relatively intact natural areas to survive, remnant-independent species are able to adapt to a wide range of natural and altered landscapes. Panzer et al. (1995) surveyed a variety of natural-area remnants and degraded habitats for their insect fauna and identified roughly 1,100 species from 9 orders and 60 families. Only 257 species (fewer than 25 percent) were scarce or absent from degraded habitats. These were termed remnant-reliant. Significantly, this finding suggests that the majority of insects inhabiting prairies and savannas are remnant-independent. Because the study stressed groups expected to depend on high-quality areas, the figures for frequency of remnant-reliance may be somewhat inflated. Panzer discovered that certain groups tend to be rich in remnant-requiring species, whereas others do not. For example, remnant-reliance among grouse locusts, carrion beetles, stink bugs, and treehoppers ranged from zero to 2 percent of the species studied. In contrast, 75 percent and 83 percent of the species in the moth genera Papaipema (root-boring moths) and Schinia (flower moths) showed remnant-reliance.

Implications for Management

Remnant-independent species, which comprise the majority of insects found in prairies and savannas, also thrive on developed and agricultural lands. These species do not require that any particular management efforts be directed toward their well-being. The idea of remnant-reliance allows stewards to focus their insect management activities on those groups most likely to be significantly impacted. Thus, the problem of managing prairies and savannas for insects is more tractable than the large number of species might suggest. The diversity of remnant-reliant species remains a nontrivial problem, however. Hundreds of species of insects, many of which remain difficult to identify, are likely to be reliant on prairies and savannas. The concept of remnant-reliance has the benefit, however, of reducing the problem to the same order of magnitude as that of the vascular plants.

Restoration Type

There are three fairly discreet types of restoration activities: creation of new prairies where native prairies were destroyed, creation of new prairie habitats adjacent to remnants of original prairie, and restoration of portions of highly degraded prairies. These activities create different challenges for the conservation of imperiled prairie insects.

Creating New Prairies. Newly created prairies are unlikely to be home to a potential reservoir of prairie invertebrate species. Remnant-reliant insects, which are usually endowed with poor dispersal ability, are unlikely to colonize highly isolated new prairies. Although these new prairies may buzz with insects, they are likely to be the same species that dominate surrounding pastures, woodlots, and backyards. To serve an ecological role as habitat for prairie invertebrate species, created prairies must be "stocked" with species, an activity beyond the scope of current translocation techniques (described below) and an opportunity for research.

Restoring Adjacent to High-Quality Remnants. Of all the activities likely to help imperiled prairie insects, this presents the best options. Most surviving prairie remnants are small and, if unmanaged, composed of a mosaic of low- to high-quality habitats. The insect populations present are often small and highly vulnerable to random extinction events due to weather, fire, or stochastic population fluctuations. Many existing prairie remnants therefore risk slowly losing their complement of species, one by one. Creating new prairie adjacent to existing remnants provides additional habitat for some remnant-reliant species, allowing populations to expand and microhabitat diversity to increase, thereby providing buffering capacity against localized extinction. This practice can reduce costs associated with establishing insects on a one-by-one basis, by passively tapping a source population for all the remnant-reliant species present (including unknown species) and allowing them to expand into restored habitats as they become suitable.

Restoring Larger but More Degraded Prairies. Many degraded prairies are much larger than those with the highest-quality plant communities. Such prairies may have retained a greater portion of their remnant-reliant insect species than the small prairies rated as high quality on the basis of their plants. Restoring the plant communities on such sites while maintaining and increasing the numbers of remnant-restricted invertebrates is a high priority for conservation.

Food Plants

Many insects are remnant-reliant because they depend on conservative species as food plants. Conversely, most wide-ranging species feed on abundant horticultural, agricultural, or exotic plant species. For example, the black swallowtail (*Papilio polyxenes*) uses the non-native Queen Anne's lace; the eastern tailed blue (*Everes comyntas*) and silver spotted skipper (*Epargyreus clarus*) use non-native legumes. The baptesia dusky-wing skipper (*Erynnis baptisiae*) has recently made the transition from remnant-reliant to wide-ranging species by adopting crown vetch as a larval food plant.

The patterns of plant use by remnant-dependent and wide-ranging insect species suggest strategies of plant management that stewards can use for managing their remnant-dependent insects:

- Maintain healthy populations of food plants. When restoring an area adjacent to a high-quality area, it may be possible to favor food plants needed by species or groups that currently survive in precariously small numbers in the remnant prairie.
- When planning a prairie reconstruction, consider what insect species should eventually be on the site. Include food plants in the seed mixes as early as possible.

Two important butterfly food plant groups, sedges for skippers and prairie and bird's foot violets for fritillaries, may deserve more attention than most restorationists have devoted to them. Improvements are needed in our ability to expand populations of such hard-to-grow plant species.

Nectar Sources

Insects that require nectar- or pollen-producing plants, such as bees, flies, beetles, wasps, and butterflies, tend to be less specific in their requirements than those species that consume other plant parts. Thus, detailed, species-oriented management of nectar sources is unnecessary. Instead, attempt to recreate the "waves of bloom" characteristic of healthy prairie to furnish dense stands of blooming nectar plants. Many of the prairie plants that serve well as nectar sources are some of the more easily restored species, such as prairie coreopsis, pale purple coneflower, lead plant, blazing stars, and goldenrods. Although augmenting particular species as nectar sources does not appear critically important, managers might consider activities such as trying to minimize periods during the growing season when little is in bloom. Species such as lead plant and the various blazing stars serve both as excellent nectar sources and as food

plants for one or more important remnant-requiring insect. Remember
that many wetland insects can use nectar sources on adjacent uplands and
vice versa.

The Flames of Controversy

Prescribed burning has provoked more questions and criticism than any
other management practice. Critics have vehemently proclaimed that
burning damages or even eliminates populations of rare insects. Unfortunately, little peer-reviewed literature considers the effects of fire on insect
communities. Thus, site managers must balance the essential effects of fire
on native plant communities with the undocumented but potentially dev-
astating impact of excessive burning on prairie insects. The current range
of burn policies reflects the uncertainty surrounding this issue. Some
managers have recommended that burning be eliminated in favor of alternative practices such as mowing or grazing. Others recommend burning
everything annually. Between these extremes, burn rotations of three, five,
ten, or even thirty years have been proposed. The following guidelines
represent the current best wisdom used by most prairie managers:

- No more than one-third to one-half of any given habitat type
  (e.g., sedge meadow, wet savanna, dry prairie) on a site should be
  burned in any given year.
- Brushy or weedy areas should be burned on a two- to three-year
  rotation schedule.
- Prairie reconstructions can be burned annually.
- A patchwork of burned and unburned sections may leave important refugia for fire-sensitive species; therefore, do not return to
  re-light unburned patches that the fire has skipped over.
- Large portions of the best areas should be left unburned as long as
  practical, consistent with protecting them from overgrowth by
  brush or non-native weeds. Concentrate burning in low-quality
  areas that need it most. This approach protects critical microhabitats, while gradually creating more available high-quality habitat
  for insects.

Restocking the Ark:
Restoring Prairie and Savanna Insect Communities

In Illinois, estimates indicate that at least 95 percent of the original presettlement insect species still exist. The story of species abundance, however, is not so cheery. Remnant-reliant species are confined overwhelm-

ingly to relatively intact remnants of native vegetation, which have been reduced to approximately 0.07 percent of their original area statewide. Worse yet, many prairie and savanna remnants do not contain anywhere near the full complement of appropriate reliant species.

Insect surveys in Illinois have revealed three important patterns in the distribution of prairie- and savanna-requiring species. First, remnant-reliant species of uplands are faring more poorly than those of wetlands. Many of the smaller upland sites (up to about seventy acres) contain few remnant-reliant species. Those few species tend to be wetland species hanging on in tiny wet pockets of a predominantly upland site. In contrast, wetland sites of even just a few acres are usually home to at least five remnant-reliant species. Second, missing remnant-reliant species do not spontaneously appear on prairies during the course of management unless the site is next to a colony from which founders can easily migrate. Third, remnant-reliant species do not appear spontaneously on prairie reconstructions. For example, the thousand-acre prairie reconstruction at FermiLab is home to only nine remnant-reliant species—as few as would be expected on a five- to six-acre prairie. All are either species from surviving wetlands or leafhoppers that can hang on in the tiniest remnants of native grasses.

Taken together, these observations suggest the need for active management, including species translocations, of remnant-reliant species. Translocations make restorations more biologically authentic and increase the number of colonies of species with perilously restricted distributions. Remnant-reliance simplifies the restoration of insect communities: the majority of species are wide ranging and therefore not important candidates for restoration.

Methods for Insect Translocation

In contrast to the variety of methods available for restoring plant species, few methods are available for insect translocation. This emerging field is still undergoing extensive experimentation. There are four general approaches to translocation as a tool for insect restoration:

Translocating through Sod Transplant. Translocating insects associated with transplanted prairie sod has been tried once, as part of the Healey Road Prairie sod transplant described above. Before the removal of sod from the donor site, between ten thousand and fifteen thousand insects were captured with sweep and aerial nets, placed in a chilled cooler to quiet them during transport, and released on the recipient site. This translocation was substantially a failure, probably because of the prompt dieback of above-ground portions of the newly transplanted sod. No species was conclusively transferred. Two important remnant-requiring species, a moth (*Schinia lucens*) and a froghopper (*Lepyronia gibbosa*), did not survive the transplant; however, eggs of the lead plant leaf beetle (*Ammoea lacti-clava*) apparently survived the move in fragments of the transplanted sod. The species continues to be found five years after the transplant. Had the transplant occurred during the season of dormancy, a larger number of buried eggs, larvae, and pupae might have successfully colonized the new site.

Translocating Large Numbers of Adults. This method requires a large population of the species of interest on the donor site. From fifty to several hundred individuals are collected by sweeping or aerial netting, and placed in plastic containers on ice. At the recipient site the containers are opened. For butterflies, sugar water may be provided. The recruits warm slowly, and thus disperse without panic flight and departure from the site.

Between 1988 and 1992, this method was used to transfer three species from a threatened site to the Nachusa Grasslands, an eleven-hundred-acre mosaic of remnant prairie, savanna, and reconstructed prairie in north central Illinois. Approximately 300 individuals of the bunchgrass grasshopper (*Pseudopomala brachyptera*), more than 1,000 Great Plains froghoppers (*Lepyronia gibbosa*), and approximately 350 gorgon checkerspot (*Chlosyne gorgone*) butterflies were transferred. Preliminary success has been achieved with all three species, which have been seen one or more growing seasons after they were translocated. Populations remain small for all three species. Followup surveys are needed to determine the long-term viability of these newly established populations.

Unfortunately, this technique requires large numbers of individuals for transfer. These large numbers may be difficult to obtain. Colonial species present at low densities are poor candidates for this technique: it is at least theoretically possible to eliminate the donor population.

Translocating Captively Reared Larvae. This method has been used most widely for moths in the genus Papaipema. Adults of this genus are nocturnal and difficult to obtain in sufficient numbers for translocation. In contrast, larvae are easily obtained by searching patches of the host species for damaged plants, many of which contain larvae boring into the stem or roots.

Papaipema larvae were reared in carrots. One-quarter-inch holes were drilled into 2- to 3-inch segments of the carrots, the larvae were coaxed inside, and the carrots were placed in dry cages. The larvae were transferred to fresh carrots weekly. Upon pupation, the pupae were removed from the cages, placed on moist soil or sphagnum moss, and misted lightly every other day. When the adults emerged, they were transferred to the recipient site in groups of six or more. Because adults are inactive during the day, they are best transferred outdoors late in the afternoon to early evening. At that time of day, they are not yet sufficiently active to leave the site in a panic flight. Furthermore, they are not exposed to possible predation for a long period of time.

This method has been used with three species: *Papaipema silphii,* which has been translocated to the Nachusa Grasslands; *Papaipema eryngii,* which has been translocated to Gensburg-Markham Prairie; and *Papaipema cerina,* which has been translocated to Bluff Spring Fen. The transfers have all involved forty to fifty individuals and have all been successful to some degree. At Nachusa, over a dozen Silphiums were found with *P. silphii* larvae bored into them. At Gensburg-Markham, *P. eryngii* larvae were found in over one hundred rattlesnake master plants. Six larvae were removed and reared in captivity to confirm the identification. Results at Bluff Spring Fen have been more modest, with *P. cerina* larvae found in six Mayapple plants.

The main advantage to this technique is its reliability. All attempts to date have succeeded. The main limitation is the narrow range of species for which the technique is appropriate.

Translocating Captively Bred Insects. This method has not yet been widely attempted. A current project involves the regal fritillary. David Wagner of the University of Connecticut and John Elkington of the University of Massachusetts at Amherst have joined with George Leslie of the Butterfly Place in Massachusetts. This team has induced regal fritillaries to mate in captivity in Leslie's butterfly museum and atrium. They plan to use this method to begin a captive breeding program in New England, where the regal fritillary's decline has been even more precipitous than in midwestern prairies.

A Cautionary Note

The art of insect translocation is still in its infancy. For the examples cited here, almost all of the donor populations were on unprotected sites threatened with destruction. Thus, attention to the continued health of the donor population has been unnecessary. Some species, such as the gorgon checkerspot and Great Plains froghopper, remain abundant on their donor sites after several years of fairly intensive harvest. Species that inhabit very small colonies may not share this resilience.

Tranlocations will remain beyond the scope of most management for the near term. Work on insect translocations is focused on improving the efficiency of transfer so that smaller numbers of insects can be removed from the donor site. This development is essential for translocations involving species normally present in small numbers, and for translocations from protected sites where an intact donor population must be maintained. Only when these methods are more fully developed should translocations become a widespread feature of prairie and savanna management.

Monitoring

Insect species may be more easily eliminated from a site than plant species. In contrast to most prairie plants, which are perennial, most prairie insects must complete their entire life cycle annually. Whereas perennial plants can persist for decades without setting viable seed, a colony of insects that fails to reproduce for just a single season will perish. Insects also have no long-term repository of reproductive potential similar to a seed bank that might allow them to reappear after an extended period of unsuitable conditions. By revealing trends in the population size, insect monitoring can reduce the risk that management practices will inadvertently displace species from a site. Monitoring is also an essential followup to translocations.

Monitoring Techniques

Various monitoring techniques provide different kinds of information. Species surveys allow managers to know which remnant-requiring species are present and absent on their sites, and may give information about distribution within a site. This information can guide burn strategies and can suggest candidate species for translocation. Censuses can detect changes in population size during the course of management. Mark and recapture approaches involve capturing a sample of the population, marking these individuals, and releasing them. The population is then re-sampled and the fraction of marked individuals in the second sample is used to calculate the population size. Annual census methods determine relative abundance from year to year. Count circles, such as those used by the Fourth of July Butterfly Count, census insects within a specified radius of a defined central point. Transect corridors, often called Pollard transects for their inventor, repeatedly census insects over the same defined transect. Pollard transects can be especially useful in detecting long-term population trends.

The Butterfly Advantages

Butterflies represent an ideal group for insect population study for the following reasons:

- Because a high percentage (about 30 percent) of midwestern butterflies is remnant-reliant, they are a good model for the health of the insect community as a whole.
- Butterflies are conspicuous, easily observed, and easily identified.
- Butterflies are a sufficiently small group (about one hundred species in Illinois) to be learned by nonprofessionals.
- Butterfly monitoring can be performed without expensive equipment and with minimal impact on the study site.
- An enormous body of readily available literature, including numerous excellent field guides, is available.
- Because of their beauty, butterflies are a popular group with the public. This popularity facilitates the recruitment of volunteers for monitoring, and helps to focus public attention on the need for insect conservation.

The Illinois Butterfly Monitoring Network

Since 1987, the Butterfly Monitoring Network (BMN) has monitored butterfly populations in north and central Illinois. The Volunteer Stewardship Network of the Illinois chapter of the Nature Conservancy oversees the BMN. A Pollard transect traversing all major habitat types and management units is established on each site in the program. Each volunteer monitor walks the transect a minimum of four to six times during the summer. All butterflies seen within 30 feet of the route are identified and counted. At the end of each season, the data are entered into a computer database.

The BMN has flourished, growing from seven sites in 1987 to forty-two sites in 1994. Others who wish to set up similar insect-monitoring programs may wish to consider guidelines that have contributed to the success of the BMN:

- Keep the method simple. BMN monitors are not expected to gather complex data. The vast majority of monitors' questions concern problems in identification rather than methods or design.
- Provide continuing training and education. The BMN offers a winter indoor workshop with mounted specimens and a summer outdoor workshop that stresses field identification.
- Recruit actively. A BMN slide lecture travels to schools, garden clubs, and libraries. The lecture discusses the ecology of prairie butterflies, describes the monitoring program, and invites audience members to become monitors.
- Plan for computer data storage. Some monitoring programs have

failed because the data end up on hundreds of sheets of paper in someone's filing cabinet.

- Release monitors into the field to collect data as early as possible. The BMN requires attendance at a single workshop before monitors begin data collection. The monitors identify only those species that they can, and list others as unidentified species (or unidentified skippers). Most monitors master nonskippers in their first year and begin skipper identification in their second year.

Interpreting the Data

Early in the process of data collection, programs such as the BMN gave information about regional distribution of species. The data have confirmed the three patterns described above for distribution of remnant-reliant butterflies in northeastern Illinois. Conclusions about changes in population size have been harder to come by. Changes observed over just a few years are likely to represent the large year-to-year fluctuations typical of butterfly populations rather than genuine results of management. This problem and a possible solution are illustrated in figure 18.1, which depicts observations of the eyed brown (*Satyrodes eurydice*) at Bluff Spring Fen, a site that has received heavy burn management. Because of the annual variance in population size, it was impossible to draw conclusions about population changes over just a few years. Only after many years of data collection (eight in this case) did the trend reach a sufficient magnitude to be detectable over the variance, and the increase in population size became apparent. This increase correlates with the increase at Bluff

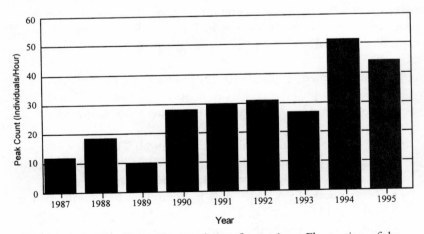

Figure 18.1. Graph of butterfly population fluctuations. Fluctuation of the peak count (individuals/hour) of *Satyrodes eurydice* at Bluff Spring Fen.

Spring Fen of open wetland areas with appropriate larval food plants observed by Stoynoff and Hess (1986). Data collected from the BMN may demonstrate long-term effects of management on butterflies but cannot be used for short-term fine-tuning of management practices.

The Future

Restoring and managing prairie and savanna insect populations are still little tested, especially when compared with plant restoration. Many research opportunities are available, particularly those that augment the current inventory of remnant-requiring species. Advances are also needed in monitoring methods, husbandry techniques, and coordination between plant and insect restoration. As the opportunities for more active management of insect communities increase, avocational and professionally trained volunteers will be needed to supplement the activities of members of staffs that have traditionally performed these tasks. Dr. T.R. New discusses this need for collaboration in his 1991 book *Butterfly Conservation:*

> In an age of increasing "professionalism" in biology, it is worth emphasizing once again that much conservation biology stems from good natural history as a foundation, and that there is abundant need for more of this. The amateur naturalist still has a very real role to play in documenting our natural world.

In the future, management of insects will be a growing part of restoration activities. Site evaluation will consider fauna more fully—some sites with high-quality vegetation may be candidates for insect restoration, whereas others with lower-quality vegetation may be accorded a higher preservation priority. Prairie reconstruction plans will go beyond the matrix of vegetation to include plans to reconstruct insect and other animal communities. As the restoration efforts of the last decade have already increased rare plant populations, efforts of the next decade should similarly increase rare insects.

REFERENCES

Gall, L.F. 1985. "Measuring the Size of Lepidopteran Populations." *Journal of Research on the Lepidoptera* 24:97–116.
New, T.R. 1991. *Butterfly Conservation.* New York: Oxford University Press.
Otte, D. 1981. *The North American Grasshoppers,* 2 vols. Cambridge, MA: Harvard University Press.

Panzer, R. 1988. "Management of Prairie Remnants for Insect Conservation." *Natural Areas Journal* 8:83–90.

Panzer, R., D. Stillwaugh, R. Gnaedinger, and G. Derkovitz. 1995. "Prevalence of Remnant Dependence among the Prairie and Savanna-Inhabiting Insects of the Chicago Region." *Natural Areas Journal* 15:101–116.

Pollard, E. 1977. "A Method for Assessing Changes in the Abundance of Butterflies." *Biological Conservation* 12:115–133.

Stoynoff, N.A., and W. J. Hess. 1986. "Bluff City Fen: Communities, Vegetation History and Management." *Transactions of the Illinois Academy of Sciences* 79:53–58.

Swengel, A. 1990. "Monitoring Butterfly Populations Using the Fourth of July Butterfly Count." *American Midland Naturalist* 124:395–406.

Wilson, Edward O. 1992. *The Diversity of Life.* Cambridge, MA: Harvard University Press.

19
Amphibians and Reptiles

Kenneth S. Mierzwa

Amphibians have been in the popular and scientific press recently, due to reported declines in the number of individuals of some species. Members of the Central Division of the Declining Amphibian Population Task Force are monitoring at least eighteen sites in the midwestern United States. At the 1994 meeting of that group, amid the doom and gloom of successive reports of habitat destruction and population loss, a few members reported that there are success stories, too. Most successes are occurring where the natural landscape is being restored.

On such restoration sites as well as in remnant natural areas, amphibians and reptiles can be useful indicators of ecosystem health. Many mammals and birds are able to travel considerable distances, but most terrestrial amphibians and reptiles are less mobile, at least in the short term. Where relatively undisturbed core areas remain, sensitive species associated with those habitats may persist.

Monitoring the status of amphibians and reptiles at a restoration site can provide valuable information on trends over time, particularly when this information is analyzed along with data on plants and other groups of animals.

Site Inventory

Some amphibian and reptile species, such as bullfrogs or ornate box turtles, are conspicuous and easily observed. Others, including most terrestrial salamanders, are nocturnal or remain underground most of the year. Some species simply occur at such low densities that they are difficult to sample. Surface activity also varies seasonally and from year to year. Thus, to census most amphibian and reptile species actually present on a site, an intensive multiseason effort is usually required. (See appendix B for a listing of tallgrass biome species.)

Inventories may be qualitative and intended only to compile a site species list, or they may be quantitative, using drift fences or other means to measure catch per unit of effort. Quantitative results are useful for monitoring faunal response to site management over time, or for comparing different sites or communities. Detailed descriptions of sampling methods can be found in Heyer et al. (1994). The methods discussed for amphibians, with a few exceptions such as breeding call surveys and larval sampling, are also valid for reptiles.

Identification requires care because of the occasional presence of cryptic varieties. However, the number of species present in any one region is usually not overwhelming. Many amphibians and reptiles can be easily approached and observed, and the devoted nonspecialist armed with a good field guide can learn quickly.

A current reference is an important tool. Taxonomy and nomenclature are constantly changing as a result of genetic investigations and application of phylogenetic classification methods, and new species are still occasionally described from the continental United States. At this writing, the only reasonably up-to-date field guide is Conant and Collins (1991). Avoid guides with lots of glossy photos; all too often these pretty pictures are of individuals atypical of the species. Good state and regional accounts are also available for many areas, including Collins (1993), Dixon (1987), Christiansen and Bailey (1991), Johnson (1992), Vogt (1981), Smith (1961), and Oldfield and Moriarty (1994).

Managing Restoration Sites and Natural Areas

The best way to manage for amphibians and reptiles is simply to restore, on a large scale, elements of the presettlement landscape. Big sites are better, because they are likely to include more diverse habitat, more core areas retaining some level of natural quality, metapopulations (distinct populations connected by dispersal and gene flow) of individual species, and greater species richness. I have yet to see a site much less than two hundred acres that retains more than moderate herpetofaunal species richness, and the best sites cover several thousand acres. Some of these consist mostly of restored habitat.

I have been monitoring amphibians and reptiles at Glacial Park, a McHenry County Conservation District site near Richmond, Illinois, for seven years. The three thousand-acre site is large by Illinois standards. It is also diverse, with considerable topographic variation and multiple core areas including both upland and wetland habitats. As overgrown oak savannas have been cleared of brush and burned, wetlands restored, and former farm fields planted to prairie, the annual catch of amphibians and reptiles has increased tenfold. One restored pond and adjacent marsh helped amphibians survive the 1988–89 drought, and another was used for breeding by four types of frogs the first year after hydrology was restored. The native herpetofauna is evidently well adapted to frequent fire, since multiple management units on the preserve are burned each year. Most of the eighteen kinds of amphibians and reptiles at Glacial Park are more easily found today than they were a few years ago.

Restoration plans should address all significant upland and wetland habitats on a preserve. When designing burn regimes, avoid predictable rotations. That is, don't burn the same management unit every other spring, but vary the season and length of time between burns. The prairie-savanna ecosystem developed in response to thousands of years of stochastic disturbance, and too much predictability may favor one set of plants and animals over others.

Translocations

Approaches to translocating animals seem to fall into three distinct schools of thought. One group, which includes several prominent biologists and policy makers, feels that translocations should never be done under any circumstances. Another feels that it must be done quickly; in a few cases action has already been taken, sometimes illegally. Both groups make compelling arguments for their case. A third group feels that translocations are justified under certain circumstances, with careful preparation and documentation and within all existing regulations.

Some people want to reestablish the rare and glamorous species first. Unfortunately, the sometimes marginal populations of these species are frequently in no condition to withstand collecting pressure at the few surviving sites. In some cases, it is not even possible to collect enough individuals to establish a genetically viable population. Metro Toronto Zoo and a few other institutions are looking into the feasibility of using captive-bred offspring in such cases. Amphibians have been translocated successfully by moving freshly laid eggs into recently restored ponds. The New York Department of Environmental Conservation used this technique to return tiger salamanders to a historic Long Island locality. In Missouri, Owen Sexton of Washington University moved wood frog eggs into four St. Louis area ponds; one of the translocations was successful, and this population later dispersed to nearby ponds. However, the best hope for most rare species is habitat preservation and restoration. We simply don't know enough about most rare species, and we cannot afford to make mistakes.

Often a habitat restoration site has lost a certain amphibian or reptile species that occurred there historically and that is still common not far away. This situation is an opportunity for translocation that should be explored. It is important, but often difficult, to maintain objectivity. Is the proposed action really good for the ecosystem or just so new and exciting that critical judgment is suspended? The North American landscape is already populated by too many troublesome weeds, both native and alien, released in the wrong places by well-intentioned individuals. Also, would-be developers are increasingly proposing to translocate animals off their sites and justifying this eviction by citing the translocation efforts of others. The checklist below can help evaluate translocation proposals by suggesting ways of answering two basic questions.

1. *Does the species belong there?*

- Did the species occur at the site historically? Are there specimens from the area in museum collections or documented in the scientific literature?
- Is appropriate habitat available at the site? Keep in mind that habitat needs are poorly understood for some species, and that they may vary across the range. Check the literature but also determine if the species occurs in similar habitat at a nearby site. For amphibians consider both larval (usually aquatic) and adult (usually semi-aquatic or terrestrial) habitat needs. Consultation with a recognized authority on the species is advised.
- Is the site large enough? For most species, forget about sites under 150–200 acres. Consider the home range of the species. For some small salamanders it may be less than 100 yards; for large active snakes it could extend for miles. Also remember that some species are thought to have homing abilities.
- Has a detailed baseline inventory been done? Maybe the species is already present but has yet to be found.

2. *Is a translocation feasible?*

- Will you have access to one or more large, stable host population within a reasonable distance? Is it possible to collect enough individuals to establish a viable population without damaging the source population? Has a population viability analysis (PVA) been conducted on the species of interest? See Meffe and Carroll

(1994) for a detailed but understandable discussion of population
viability analysis and minimum viable population size.

- Can you tell males from females? Remember that some species
  have temporal differences in surface activity peaks for males and
  females. It is important to avoid a severely skewed sex ratio.

- How will the animals be transported? Moving large quantities of
  animals may not be easy. Overcrowding or excessive heat or cold
  can result in mass mortality. Crowded animals are under stress and
  are more prone to disease and parasites—things you really don't
  want to release into your favorite natural area. Can the animals be
  transported the same day? If some must be held for long periods,
  is a helpful veterinarian available?

- Can all of the necessary permits and clearances be obtained for
  both the source and release sites? Most states now regulate the
  collecting of amphibians and reptiles in some way, and managing
  agencies responsible for public land generally enforce additional
  restrictions. Under some circumstances, moving animals across
  state lines without proper permits could be a federal offense.
  Complying with laws and regulations is important: screw up and
  get caught, and it will be a lot harder for the next person.

- Are you willing to monitor the release site for up to several years?
  A translocation is not successful until reproduction has been documented. Lack of monitoring is one of the most frequent criti-
  cisms of past release efforts.

- Are you willing to publish the results, successful or not? If you
  don't publish, future workers may be confused and the status,
  distribution, or in extreme cases even taxonomy of the species
  may be obscured by false or incomplete information. If you do,
  someone finding the species in the future will know where it
  came from, and someone contemplating another translocation
  can learn from experience.

At Glacial Park, efforts have been made to translocate two species into
restored habitat, and a third is planned. Several specimens gathered in the
1940s are in the collection of the Field Museum of Natural History in
Chicago and document that cricket frogs (*Acris crepitans*) once occurred
at the site. However, this species has now disappeared from much of
northern Illinois. A large source population is available seventy miles
away at the Joliet Army Ammunition Plant, so a carefully planned and
fully permitted effort was made in 1993 to move tadpoles into a restored
wetland. Tadpoles were chosen because they are easily collected in large

numbers, and because removal of individuals in that stage of the life cycle was judged unlikely to harm the source population, which is only one of many populations on the source site.

Moving large numbers of tadpoles seventy miles is no simple logistical task, especially in hot midsummer weather. Keeping the tadpoles cool and not overcrowded required quite a bit of advance thought and effort. Gallon containers filled with pond water were used to hold thirty to fifty tadpoles each. Multiple containers were placed inside each of several large plastic storage bins with lids. Ice on the bottom of each bin, covered by thick layers of insulating newspaper, kept the tadpoles cool but not cold. The route was planned in advance, and enforcement personnel at both the collecting and release sites were notified. The release was made about two hours after collection, with no mortality in transit.

However, it is impossible to control all factors influencing the potential for success or failure of such a translocation. Several months after the tadpoles were moved, an unexpected diversion of the water source on adjacent private property lowered the pond level. The result of the translocation effort is unknown at this writing, and followup monitoring is planned.

The second translocation effort apparently was more successful. Plains garter snakes (*Thamnophis radix*), a mesic prairie species, had been almost eliminated at Glacial Park because almost all of the level grasslands had been farmed. The savanna and wetland core areas on the preserve do not provide suitable plains garter snake habitat, and those areas instead support healthy populations of a related species, the common garter snake (*Thamnophis sirtalis*). Only two plains garter snakes had been captured on the preserve in several years of intensive monitoring. With the original habitat now restored, pregnant female plains garter snakes were collected in the summer of 1993 from nearby railroad right-of-ways where the species is common, uniquely marked by clipping corners of ventral scales, and released the same day in restored grasslands. One of the marked adults was seen a quarter mile from the release point late that fall, and in 1994 a few yearling plains garter snakes were captured in drift fences. A success? We think so, but more monitoring will be necessary.

REFERENCES

Christiansen, J. L., and R. M. Bailey. 1991. *The Salamanders and Frogs of Iowa*. Des Moines: Iowa Department of Natural Resources.
———. N.d. *The Snakes of Iowa*. Des Moines: Iowa Department of Natural Resources.

Collins, J. T. 1993. *Amphibians and Reptiles in Kansas,* 3rd edition. Lawrence: University of Kansas Museum of Natural History.

Conant, R., and J. T. Collins. 1991. *Field Guide to Reptiles and Amphibians, Eastern and Central North America,* 3rd edition. Boston, MA: Houghton Mifflin.

Dixon, J. R. 1987. *Amphibians and Reptiles of Texas.* College Station: Texas A&M University Press.

Heyer, W. R., M. A. Donnelly, R. W. McDiarmid, L. C. Hayek, and M. S. Foster. 1994. *Measuring and Monitoring Biological Diversity: Standard Methods for Amphibians.* Washington, DC: Smithsonian Institution Press.

Johnson, T. 1992. *The Amphibians and Reptiles of Missouri.* Springfield: Missouri Department of Conservation.

Meffe, G. K., and C. R. Carroll. 1994. *Principles of Conservation Biology.* Sunderland, MA: Sinauer Associates.

Oldfield, B., and J. Moriarty. 1994. *Amphibians and Reptiles Native to Minnesota.* Minneapolis: University of Minnesota Press.

Smith, P. W. 1961. "The Amphibians and Reptiles of Illinois." *Illinois Natural History Survey Bulletin* 28, no. 1:1–298.

Vogt, R. C. 1981. *Natural History of Amphibians and Reptiles in Wisconsin.* Milwaukee: Milwaukee Public Museum.

Victoria J. Byre

Populations of many birds that forage, find shelter, and nest primarily in grasslands have suffered serious declines during the last half century (Knopf 1994). Habitat loss, mainly to agriculture, urban development, and recreational use, is often cited as the major cause of this decline (Goriup 1988, Smith 1991). The restoration and careful management of prairies and other grasslands can be of great benefit to grassland birds. Whenever possible, our efforts to preserve and restore grasslands should include practices that enhance grassland bird habitats.

Grassland Habitat

Not all grasslands are equal in a bird's eyes. Birds have subtle differences in their needs and in their responses to disturbances. Different species are naturally attracted to different types of grassland, and some grassland bird species may occur in only one prairie type (Sample and Hoffman 1989). Birds of taller grasslands, especially, seem to differentiate among sites on the basis of vegetation height and density (Cody 1985). Other characteristics such as the amount and type of ground cover and litter, availability of singing posts, topography, and total size of the area also determine a grassland's suitability to certain species (Wiens 1969, Rotenberry and Wiens 1980). Sometimes, even within sites that appear to have uniform vegetational structure, subtle differences from place to place may be significant in determining the site's suitability to certain species (Cody 1985).

Table 20.1 lists selected grassland bird species of North American tallgrass and mixed-grass prairies, along with each species' preferred habitat, approximate territory size, and usual minimum habitat requirements. The list excludes brush/edge species such as the clay-colored sparrow

(*Spizella pallida*), common yellowthroat (*Geothlypis trichas*), and field sparrow (*Spizella posilla*), as well as prairie marsh species such as black-birds, ducks, shorebirds, and marsh-nesting sparrows. A more complete listing of birds of the tallgrass biome is included in appendix B.

Table 20.1 provides a general guideline only. The ranges, territory sizes, and minimum habitat requirements of grassland birds may vary at a site between years and among sites that differ in a variety of factors such as climate, food supply, and human modification (Cody 1985). Some dry-prairie species such as the vesper sparrow (*Pooecetes gramineus*), lark sparrow (*Chondestes grammacus*), and upland sandpiper (*Bartramia longi-cauda*), may at times require a minimum habitat size of 25–250 acres (Sample and Hoffman 1989). Horned lark (*Eremophila alpestris*) territory size has been shown to vary locally by factors of five to twelve, depending on habitat quality, with the largest territories found on recently plowed fields (Beason and Franks 1974). For other species, variability in territory size may be much less. Wiens (1973) found grasshopper (*Ammodramus savannarum*) and Savannah sparrow (*Passerculus sandwichensis*) territory sizes to vary only by about 25 percent. The smaller territories were those that were established earlier in the season, in more centrally located positions in higher-quality grasslands.

Much more research on specific habitat requirements is needed before completely effective management strategies can be developed for most grassland bird species. However, with the information already at hand much can be done to manage grassland habitat in a general way for the benefit of most species.

Management Objectives

Because of the wide variety of habitats required by grassland birds, it is usually impossible, unless working with areas of several hundred acres, to provide suitable habitat for more than four to six common passerine (songbird) species and possibly a few nonpasserines (e.g., hawks, owls, sandpipers) (Cody 1985). Both the diversity and the density of birds in grassland habitats are naturally lower than in most other habitats. An analysis of twenty-four censuses conducted in tallgrass prairies between 1975 and 1985 produced breeding bird estimates averaging 0.8 +/− 0.4 pairs/acre (Cody 1985). Breeding-bird densities in mixed-grass prairies are generally even lower, 0.59 +/− 0.29 pairs/acre. Therefore, most grass-land managers should attempt to restore and maintain high-quality habitat for the half dozen or so true grassland bird species for which an area is well suited, not try to attract as many species as possible.

Table 20.1.

Habitat Requirements of Selected Grassland Birds

Species	Preferred Habitat	Approximate Territory Size[1]	Minimum Habitat Requirement[2]
northern harrier *Circus cyaneus*	Open tracts of tall grassy fields and extensive undisturbed marshes.	Usually 200–600 acres for hunting and nesting.	25–250 acres (a)
greater prairie chicken *Tympanuchus cupido*	Tallgrass prairie and grasslands with a mixture of forbs. Open areas are needed for booming and mating.	About 300–400 acres for a booming ground and several nests. Females usually nest within a mile of booming ground.	Greater than 250 acres (a)
upland sandpiper *Bartramia longicauda*	Prairies, meadows, open hayfields, grazed grasslands; prefers short to medium height grass (less than 30 inches) and avoids dense tall grass.	2–12 acres per nest but will nest in loosely spaced colonies.	25–250 acres (a,b)
short-eared owl *Asio flammeus*	Open tall grass fields and meadows.	Nesting territory size of 30–40 acres but 200–600 acres for hunting.	Greater than 200 acres (c)
horned lark *Eremophila alpestris*	Thinly vegetated barren areas; short or mixed grass with bare ground, mowed grasslands, grazed lands, edges of agricultural fields including row crops.	Quite variable. As many as 20 nests on 90 acres. Other territory sizes include 100 yards square, and 300 yards long by 200 yards wide.	2.5–25 acres (a)

[1] Territory size is dependent on richness of habitat and density of the bird population; see text for further explanation. Sources include Bent 1968, Goriup 1988, Harrison 1975, Sample and Hoffman 1989, and Terres 1980.

[2] Habitat area requirements are usually somewhat larger than the actual territory size requirements. See (a) Samson 1980, (b) Herkert 1991, (c) Johnsgard 1988, (d) Byre 1989, (e) Bent 1968, vol. 2.

Table 20.1. (*Continued*)

Species	Preferred Habitat	Approximate Territory Size[1]	Minimum Habitat Requirement[2]
sedge wren *Cistothorus platensis*	Moist tallgrass prairies, meadows, drier marshes with mostly sedges, hayfields.	Usually 1.25–2 acres per nest. In prime habitat, as little as 0.25–0.3 acres per nest.	2.5–5 acres (d)
dickcissel *Spiza americana*	Medium to tall prairie grasses, open meadows, overgrown pastures, hayfields.	2–2.8 acres per nest.	2.5–25 acres (a,b)
vesper sparrow *Pooecetes gramineus*	Dry, sparsely vegetated, short-grass prairie, upland meadows, fallow fields, high perches.	Over 2 acres per nest.	25–250 acres (a,b)
lark sparrow *Chondestes grammacus*	Short grass with open barren patches of exposed sandy soil, dry treeless plains, brush-lined pastures with bare ground.	Weakly territorial and only until incubation begins. Male sometimes polygynous.	25–250 acres (a,b)
Savannah sparrow *Passerculus sandwichensis*	Very adaptable. Meadows, prairies, fields with medium to tall grass.	1.5–2 acres per nest.	2.5–75 acres (a,b)
Baird's sparrow *Ammodramus bairdii*	Native tall and mixed-grass prairies, dry prairies, weedy fields.	1–2 acres per nest.	10–20 acres (e)
grasshopper sparrow *Ammodramus savannarum*	Patchy mixed to tall grass, less than 35% scattering of shrubs; prefers previously burnt prairies where cover is light and open. Requires some dead ground vegetation for nesting.	Loosely colonial; territories about 2 acres; will inhabit very small (2–4-acre) fields.	2.5–75 acres (a,b)

Species	Habitat	Territory size[1]	Area requirements[2]
Henslow's sparrow *Ammodramus henslowii*	Rigid requirements; tall grass but with a dense groundcover or dead grass, usually in lower, less drained areas; burning grasslands prevents nesting for 2–3 years.	1 acre per nest; may nest in loose colonies.	25–250 acres (a,b)
chestnut-collared longspur *Calcarius ornatus*	Moist upland prairies and plains. Often where grass is sparse and less than 8 inches tall, also moderately grazed fields and hay meadows.	1–2 acres per nest.	10–20 acres (e)
bobolink *Dolichonyx oryzivorus*	Grain fields, meadows, medium to tall prairies, hayfields, cultivated grasslands.	5 acres per nest. May be polygynous at times.	25–75 acres (b)
eastern meadowlark *Sturnella magna*	Medium to tall grass, mixed grasses and forbs, quite dense vegetation.	4–5.5 acres per nest; sometimes as little as 2.5 acres per nest.	Less than 25 acres (b)
western meadowlark *Sturnella neglecta*	Shorter, more sparse vegetation than eastern meadowlark, and drier, more open situations.	4–5.5 acres per nest.	Less than 25 acres (d)

[1]Territory size is dependent on richness of habitat and density of the bird population; see text for further explanation. Sources include Bent 1968, Goriup 1988, Harrison 1975, Sample and Hoffman 1989, and Terres 1980.

[2]Habitat area requirements are usually somewhat larger than the actual territory size requirements. See (a) Samson 1980, (b) Herkert 1991, (c) Johnsgard 1988, (d) Byre 1989, (e) Bent 1968, vol. 2.

Most prairies and other grasslands need a certain amount of management if they are to be maintained as prime habitat for grassland birds. The key to effective management is to first determine what type of grassland is to be established or maintained, and which species of grassland birds will likely inhabit it. By understanding the changes and effects, both short and long term, caused by various management practices (fire, mowing, grazing, brushcutting, etc.), the manager can be more effective in meeting the habitat requirements of grassland birds.

Management Techniques

Edge effect, an increase in the diversity and density of species where the edges of two habitat types (e.g., grassland and woodland) meet, is a well-known but undesirable factor to contend with when trying to establish or manage grasslands. Prairie habitats less than 150 feet from a woody edge have reduced nest productivity due to increased predation and parasitism (Johnson and Temple 1986). This means that on prairies less than ten acres in size that are surrounded by woody edge, most or all grassland breeding birds are likely to be influenced by edge effect. It also follows that long narrow prairie plots would be much more influenced by edge effect than rectangular plots. Managers should minimize deleterious edge effects whenever possible by eliminating brushy edges and brushy areas within the grassland itself (usually through cutting or burning). Obviously, the larger and more expansive the grassland, the less important edge effect becomes to the survivorship and productivity of the birds inhabiting it. Much still needs to be learned about the effects of competition between edge species and true grassland species.

Forbs, nonwoody plants that grow in grasslands, are an essential component of good grassland habitat. They create a diverse, more heterogeneous structure, are an important food source, and attract a variety of insects, a vital source of protein for birds, especially during the nesting season. Therefore, native forbs should be restored or preserved along with native grasses.

Fire is a very effective means of controlling shrubby growth and revitalizing grasslands. The timing of prescribed burns, however, is a critical factor for nesting birds. Higgins (1986) found higher nesting success among upland sandpipers and northern harriers (*Circus cyaneus*) that nested in fall-burned fields than among those nesting in spring-burned fields. Fall burns allow for more cover to develop by the nesting season and, hence, provide more protection from predators. Spring burning may of course also destroy the nests of early nesters. When planning a spring burn for the site, be sure to check the records (usually available from the state Department of Conservation or local birding organizations) for earliest nesting dates of birds that may nest in a particular area.

Many studies have been done on bird densities and diversity before and after an area has been burned to determine bird sensitivities to changes in the vegetative structure, and to determine the foraging opportunities different structures control (Cody 1985). As might be expected, various grassland bird species react very differently to burned grasslands. Some species such as eastern meadowlarks (*Sturnella magna*), which require ample ground vegetation, are likely to avoid areas burned in the current growing season (Sample and Hoffman 1989). Other species with very rigid habitat requirements, such as Henslow's sparrow (*Ammodramus henslowii*), may not inhabit a grassland for two to three years after it has been burned (Zimmerman 1988). In a study done on four Kansas prairie sites, two of which were annually burned, Knodel (1980) found Henslow's sparrows only on unburned sites. On the other hand, birds that nest in more open habitat such as horned larks and lark sparrows will inhabit burned areas almost immediately and prefer them to more grassy fields for nesting (Sample and Hoffman 1989).

The effects of grazing on bird populations can be very complex (Ryder 1980). Grazing influences erosion, the amount and composition of plant cover, food supply, and species of plant growth, all factors that affect bird populations. In general, the number and diversity of bird species tend to increase with increased grazing in tallgrass regions and to decrease with increased grazing in mixed-grass regions. Moderate grazing in mixed-grass prairie areas, however, sometimes results in an increase in species, as dense, homogeneous grasslands become more open and provide a more diversified supply of food sources (Kantrud and Kologiski 1983). A study done in northeast Oklahoma showed that both eastern meadowlarks and dickcissels (*Spiza americana*) were much more common in grazed grassland, and ungrazed grassland was completely lacking in grasshopper sparrows (Risser et al. 1981). A mixture of grazed and ungrazed habitat will provide protection from predators and sheltered sites for nesting, in addition to more open areas in which to forage.

Mowing also creates habitat for species that require shorter grass and more open grasslands, such as the upland sandpiper, grasshopper sparrow, and western meadowlark (*Sturnella neglecta*). In a study done on prairie chicken (*Tympanuchus cupido*) sanctuaries in Jasper and Marion counties in Illinois, upland sandpipers chose fields of mixed grasses and forbs that had been high-mowed (6–12 inches) for weed control or burned the previous summer or fall, over fields consisting of tall, rank prairie grasses (big bluestem, Indian grass, and switch grass) (Westemeier 1989). In most areas, mowing should be delayed at least until after mid-July or later to prevent loss of nests and young.

Depending on the size and type of grassland involved, mowing every two to three years, combined with prescribed burns, may be effective in providing suitable nesting and brooding cover for the upland sandpiper and other species with similar requirements. And, although management for the upland sandpiper may not create the most suitable habitat for species such as the greater prairie-chicken, eastern meadowlark, and Henslow's sparrow, which require taller, more dense growth, a combination of mowed and burned areas interspersed with more dense stands of tall grass such as big bluestem may provide habitat for a wider range of species. Again, note that such options are usually feasible only when dealing with areas of several hundred acres or more.

Smaller prairie plots of various types, if managed in a general way to prevent woody growth and invasive weeds, will eventually attract the grassland birds that can adapt to them. Even very small remnant grasslands of a few acres in size may provide food and shelter for birds during times of dispersal and migration. In addition, these areas provide vegetative bridges or "stepping stones" to the larger, more expansive grassland areas that are scattered throughout the Great Plains, thereby helping to provide links between isolated breeding populations.

As a general rule, grasslands should be protected from disturbances during the entire nesting season. Care should be taken during brush cutting and other management practices not to disrupt species that may be nesting in the area. Birds nesting in smaller (less than fifty-acre) areas are extremely vulnerable to disturbances in and near the grassland. A well-informed and educated public can be an important factor in the ultimate success of a local prairie preservation or restoration effort. Grasslands viewed as nothing more than playgrounds or dumping grounds will not be suitable habitat for grassland birds.

Monitoring

An important but often neglected part of any management plan is the careful monitoring of changes in bird diversity and density as the grassland habitat is modified. The species that inhabit a grassland are important indicators of its quality and of the success of its management. Estimating numbers of grassland birds, especially the smaller species, can be difficult. Most grassland birds are inconspicuously colored and spend much time on the ground or hidden in the vegetation. Biases can be easily introduced, since those species that sing loudest or that are the most brightly colored are the most conspicuous, though not necessarily the most numerous. Measurements of the success of restoration and management may also be complicated by the adaptability of many species. For example, a grassland may be managed as perfect habitat for bobolinks (*Dolichonyx oryzivorus*), but red-winged blackbirds (*Agelaius phoeniceus*), which are starting to nest farther and farther from marshes, may become serious competition for them (Byre 1989).

To arrive at an accurate estimate of the breeding-bird population in a specific area, one of several census methods may be used. Spot-mapping, in which individual territories are noted on scale maps, is the most accurate, but also the most time consuming, and is usually feasible only in areas of less than fifty acres. In larger grasslands, point counts, in which an observer stands at a fixed point or station for a designated period of time (usually twenty minutes) and counts all birds seen or heard, are a very efficient way to obtain quantitative results. Point counts have evolved from the more traditional line-transect censusing techniques. See Ralph et al. (1993) and Franzreb (1981) for descriptions and comparisons of censusing methods. A series of censuses should be conducted every two to three years while a habitat is in transition, and at least every five years once the area is more stabilized.

Conclusion

Habitat preservation must be the main focus of our efforts to conserve and protect grassland birds. Agricultural practices in tallgrass prairies especially have led to increased fragmentation and isolation of native grasslands. The purchase and restoration of large tracts of land that will support viable populations of grassland birds must be a top priority. State and local governments as well as private landowners should be encouraged to preserve grasslands and especially native prairie habitat. Once habitat is preserved, management practices will, with time, restore the native vegetation and attract the grassland birds that are so superbly adapted to it.

REFERENCES

Beason, R.C., and E.C. Franks. 1974. "Breeding Behavior of the Horned Lark." *Auk* 91:65-74.

Bent, A.C. 1968. *Life Histories of North American Cardinals, Grosbeaks, Buntings, Towhees, Finches, Sparrows, and Allies,* 2 vols. Washington, DC: U.S. National Museum, Bulletin 237.

Byre, V.J. 1989. "The Birds of Fermi National Accelerator Laboratory: Their Seasonal Occurrence and Breeding Activity, Including an Annotated List of Species." *Bulletin of the Chicago Academy of Sciences* 14, no. 4.

Cody, M.L. 1985. "Habitat Selection in Grassland and Open-Country Birds." In *Habitat Selection in Birds,* M.L. Cody, ed., pp. 191–226. Orlando, FL: Academic Press.

Franzreb, K.E. 1981. "A Comparative Analysis of Territorial Mapping and Variable-Strip Censusing Methods." In *Estimating Numbers of Terrestrial Birds,* C.J. Ralph and J.M. Scott, eds. Studies in Avian Biology No. 6. Lawrence, KS: Cooper Ornithological Society.

Goriup, P.D., ed. 1988. *Ecology and Conservation of Grassland Birds.* International Council for Bird Preservation Technical Publication No. 7. Cambridge, England: International Council for Bird Preservation.

Harrison, H.H. 1975. *A Field Guide to Birds' Nests (Eastern Region).* Boston: Houghton Mifflin.

Herkert, J.R. 1991. "Prairie Birds of Illinois: Population Response to Two Centuries of Habitat Change." *Illinois Natural History Survey Bulletin* 34:393–399.

Higgins, K.F. 1986. "A Comparison of Burn Season Effects on Nesting Birds in North Dakota Mixed-Grass Prairie." *Prairie Naturalist* 18:219–228.

Johnsgard, P.A., 1988. *North American Owls.* Washington, DC: Smithsonian Institution Press.

Johnson, R.G., and S.A. Temple. 1986. "Assessing Habitat Quality for Birds Nesting in Fragmented Tallgrass Prairies." In *Wildlife 2000: Modeling Habitat Relationships of Terrestrial Vertebrates,* J.M. Verner, M.L. Morrison, and C.J. Ralph, eds., pp. 245–249. Madison: University of Wisconsin Press.

Kantrud, H.A., and R.L. Kologiski. 1983. "Avian Associations of the Northern Great Plains Grasslands." *Journal of Biogeography* 10: 331–350.

Knodel, J.J. 1980. "Breeding Bird Censuses #104–107: Annually Burned and Unburned Tallgrass Prairie, Kansas." *American Birds* 34:69–70.

Knopf, F.L. 1994. "Avian Assemblages on Altered Grasslands." *Studies in Avian Biology* 15:247–257.

Ralph, C.J., G.R. Geupel, P. Pyle, T.E. Martin, and D.F. DeSante. 1993. *Handbook of Field Methods for Monitoring Landbirds.* General Technical Report PSW-GTR-144. Albany, CA: Pacific Southwest Research Station, Forest Service, U.S. Department of Agriculture.

Risser, P.G., E.C. Birney, H.D. Blocker, S.W. May, W.J. Parton, and J.A. Wiens. 1981. *The True Prairie Ecosystem.* US/IBP Synthesis Series 16. Stroudsburg, PA: Hutchinson Ross.

Rotenberry, J.T., and J.A. Wiens. 1980. "Habitat Structure, Patchiness, and Avian Communities in North American Steppe Vegetation: A Multivariate Approach." *Ecology* 61:1228–1250.

Ryder, R.A. 1980. "Effects of Grazing on Bird Habitats." In *Management of Western Forests and Grasslands for Nongame Birds,* R.M. DeGraff and N.G. Tilghman, eds., pp. 51–66. General Technical Report INT–86. Washington, DC: USDA Forest Service.

Sample, D.W., and R.M. Hoffman. 1989. "Birds of Dry-Mesic and Dry Prairies in Wisconsin." *Passenger Pigeon* 51:195–208.

Samson, F.B. 1980. "Island Biogeography and the Conservation of Nongame Birds." *Transactions of the 45th North American Wildlife Conference,* pp. 245–251.

Smith, C.R. 1991. "Partners in Conservation." *Living Bird Quarterly* 10:16–20.

Terres, J.K. 1980. *The Audubon Society Encyclopedia of North American Birds.* New York: Alfred A. Knopf.

Westemeier, R.L. 1989. "Upland Sandpipers on Illinois Prairie-Chicken Sanctuaries." *Illinois Natural History Survey Report* 284, Champaign: Illinois Natural History Survey.

Wiens, J.A. 1969. *An Approach to the Study of Ecological Relationships Among Grassland Birds.* AOU Ornithological Monograph No. 8. Lawrence, KS: Allen Press.

———. 1973. "Interterritorial Habitat Variation in Grasshopper and Savannah Sparrows." *Ecology* 54:877–884.

Zimmerman, J.L. 1988. "Breeding Season Habitat Selection by the Henslow's Sparrow (*Ammodramus henslowii*) in Kansas." *Wilson Bulletin* 100:17–24.

21
Bison

Allen A. Steuter

 Bison (*Bison bison*) are members of the cattle family. They were closely associated with human cultures of prairie grasslands as these developed during the last ten thousand years. The Great Plains were the primary bison range at the time of European colonization. However, bison were reported from northern Florida to the Yukon River and from Maine to northern Mexico. Both Allen (1876, 1974) and Roe (1970) document the existence of large herds of bison on the Illinois and Indiana prairies and in the Ohio River valley during the early historic period. These animals were almost completely gone by the first decade of the nineteenth century. A rough estimate of bison numbers in the "wooded areas bordering the Plains" was suggested by Tom McHugh (1972) to be two million animals. This compares with his estimate of thirty million on the plains. Firsthand knowledge of bison in Midwest tallgrass and savanna is limited. However, recent experience with bison on tallgrass range is being gained at Konza Prairie in Kansas, Prairie State Park in Missouri, and the Tallgrass Preserve in Oklahoma. I will draw heavily on this work and on the Nature Conservancy's Mellon ecosystem project, now in progress, in the mixed-grass prairies of Nebraska and the Dakotas.

Although I have immense respect for bison, they will not promote the restoration of today's tall grasslands and savanna in all cases. But at appropriate stocking rates, and under conditions to which they are adapted, bison can sustain themselves and promote other species by interacting with a diverse grassland structure with minimal human input. The reestablishment and promotion of such dynamic interacting systems is one characteristic of a successful prairie restoration.

Useful Bison Adaptations

Bison thrive on a diet consisting almost exclusively of grasses and sedges. This is the most productive group of plants within a tallgrass prairie or savanna. When tall, warm-season grasses are burned while dormant and not subsequently grazed, they are capable of dominating the light, moisture, and space resources of an area. Under these conditions a few tallgrass species flourish, while a diverse group of forbs, mid, and short grasses is suppressed. Bison forage selectively on grasses, thus reducing grass dominance and increasing the representation of other plant species. Diet comparison studies between cattle and bison in a wide variety of grassland types consistently show bison to choose less forb and shrub forage than cattle. Bison select a diet consisting of 90 percent to 95 percent grasses and sedges. Bison also create disturbances by wallowing, trampling, defecating, urinating, and rubbing, which provide establishment sites for a wide array of plant species. This tends to increase plant species richness.

Bison Social and Foraging Behaviors

Bison efficiently utilize open grasslands that concentrate most annual production during a few summer months. However, bison social and foraging behaviors change in response to seasonal changes in climate, forage quality, and animal physiology. We can expect bison to use the highest-quality forage available to them within restrictions imposed by their fixed behavior patterns. Group size in bison herds is largest during the breeding season and in open habitats during the growing season when forage quality is high. Bison herd size tends to be smallest during winter, in closed habitats, and when forage quality is low. Bison social behavior, habitat selection, and foraging ecology will be significantly modified by diet supplementation. Indeed, it is my experience that bison behave increasingly like cattle as they are more intensively managed like cattle.

The above characteristics apply to bison in relatively large and heterogeneous prairie landscapes. Whether in large or small groups, bison remain grass and sedge eaters throughout the year. However, they shift between warm-season and cool-season grasses depending on which have the highest nutrient levels in a given season. If, for example, a tallgrass restoration has areas of the exotic smooth brome or Kentucky bluegrass along with reseeded areas of native warm-season grasses, bison will selectively graze the brome and bluegrass areas during the fall, winter, and spring. During the summer the warm-season reseeded areas will be selected, especially if they were recently burned. This is because bison consistently choose areas with younger regrowth over areas with a buildup of old growth. Fire is a very useful tool in manipulating the amount of old growth and thus the intensity and location of bison grazing. In the confined landscapes of a prairie restoration, bison will continue to graze burned patches until other parts of the landscape become more attractive based on forage quality. Therefore, sufficient area will need to be burned to prevent overgrazing. Also, additional burned patches will need to be provided each year to prevent annual heavy use of the same parts of a restoration.

The interactions among habitat openness, seasonal changes in forage quality, and bison social group size result in a dynamic set of space and time patterns imposed by bison grazing. This complexity is part of the evolutionary history of tallgrass and savanna ecosystems. Conventional grazing methods (whether with cattle or bison) control where, when, and to what intensity grazing occurs by subdividing a given area with fences and prescribing a grazing sequence among the different pastures. This may be the more appropriate method when plants that are easily damaged by grazing are clumped within a restoration area that would otherwise benefit from a large grazer. However, in this situation, cattle would probably be the more practical animal to use since they have less restrictive social requirements and are easier to handle.

Bison and Continental Winters

Bison are well adapted to the extreme cold of continental winters. However, because they have cloven hooves and relatively short legs, they are less well adapted to deep snows than horses and moose. This, along with their preference for grass forage, is thought to have limited their populations in the mountains to the west and forests to the east of the Great Plains. Windswept grasslands and those subject to regular midwinter thaws are the most appropriate bison habitat.

Bison develop a dense winter coat with extra growth in the vital chest and head regions, which protects them against the most extreme cold. As do other wild ungulates, they develop fat reserves during the summer and fall and conserve energy during winter months by restricting their activity, including forage intake. The quality of native tallgrass forages is below maintenance requirements for bison in the winter. Under those conditions, bison may lose 15 percent of their body weight. However, they recover rapidly when green-up begins in the spring and can maintain high reproductive rates even with pronounced annual swings in body condition.

Bison and Disease Resistance

When managed in large landscapes and at low animal densities, bison are remarkably disease resistant. They are susceptible, however, to brucellosis and bovine tuberculosis, which they can get from, and transmit to, cattle.

Female bison can be vaccinated against brucellosis between three and twelve months of age. Also, a blood test reliably determines bison exposure to brucellosis. There is no vaccination against bovine tuberculosis, and the widely used sensitivity test is not always reliable.

In addition to reducing herd productivity and vigor, brucellosis and bovine tuberculosis can be transmitted to humans. Most states require a current negative test for both brucellosis and bovine tuberculosis prior to interstate shipment. If bison are included as part of a restoration project, develop a working relationship with a local large-animal veterinarian interested in your work.

Pneumonia is probably the most common disease in physically or environmentally stressed bison. When confined for extended periods in dense groups, small pens, and humid climes, bison may also develop high levels of internal and external parasites. Parasites can be controlled using commercially available cattle medications. Bison will be more susceptible to other infectious bovine diseases when in close confinement. Anaplasmosis, which infects many ungulates, has not been a serious problem for bison. However, some states require a recent negative test for anaplasmosis prior to admitting bison.

Bison and Water Use

If water is available, bison will drink daily. However, they are known to go without water for a day in the summer if there are long distances between sources. During the winter, bison remain healthy by utilizing snow for long periods as their only water source. This adaptation has significant ecological and economic implications for a restoration project.

Bison do not loaf around water sources, preferring instead to move in, drink, and move back away. When watering along wooded stream bottoms or lakes during the summer, they will intensely disturb the watering site but will graze little in the surrounding wooded habitats. In the prairie region, bison graze woodland riparian areas primarily during the fall and spring. At those times of the year, bison congregate in small social groups and select for cool-season grasses and sedges.

Bison Limitations

Bison prefer large, open grasslands with diverse plant communities and require the least management input in these types of restorations. Under these conditions, bison meet their seasonally changing social and nutrition needs by moving among various habitats. However, even large restorations are far smaller and more confining than the grasslands that bison roamed in presettlement times. Thus bison inhabiting today's restorations always will be facing important limitations in distribution, herd size, and population dynamics. Small numbers of bison (fewer than twelve) maintained on small overstocked grasslands surrounded by developed lands will be difficult to confine and expensive to handle. Their social requirements will not be satisfied. Also, genetic management will be required to avoid deleterious inherited traits. Here bison will be a species out of place. If the impact of a large grazer is needed to improve this type of restoration, cattle would be the more useful species.

An exhaustive treatment of bison management is beyond the scope of this chapter; more information is available through the National Bison Association in Denver, Colorado. However, there are no substitutes for experience when it comes to practical aspects of bison management. Any costs associated with selecting and training staff will be well spent, as those people will determine the safety and effectiveness of a bison restoration project.

Confining and Handling Bison

Bison are obviously large and very mobile animals. It has been said that you can make bison go anywhere and do anything—that they want. This suggests a philosophy of "working with bison," which can form a sound basis for confining and handling the animals.

Perimeter pasture fencing for bison will usually consist of woven wire topped by one or two strands of barbed wire with a total height of at least 5 feet. Steel or wooden posts should be spaced no more than 16 feet apart. New costs for this type of fence may range from $6,000 to $10,000 per mile. In areas with few people and similar on both sides of a bison forage, barbed wire (five or six strands, 5–6 feet tall) or smooth electrified fence may be an acceptable lower-cost alternative. Regardless of the setting, it is difficult to maintain two separate groups of bison on opposite sides of a fence. If one is attempting to do so, a 6- to 7-foot heavy woven-wire fence will be required. As bison operations multiply, this will be an increasingly common situation.

Stronger and taller fences are required as bison are forced into smaller and more dense groups in holding areas and handling corrals. Solid walls (wood, metal, concrete) 7–8 feet tall are recommended in the narrow pens and alleyways leading to restraining chutes. Many successful designs for corrals and handling equipment have been developed. Visit several successful bison operations and incorporate those features most appropriate for your situation. When handling bison, a quiet, calm, and organized approach is more successful than noisy confusion.

Determining Bison Stocking Rates

The impact of bison on a restoration project will be largely determined by the number of animals, the season, and the length of time that they use the area. Bison utilize forage at a predictable daily rate based on their body size. Estimating liberally, a 1,000-pound bison will eat and trample about thirty air-dry pounds of forage per day. Smaller and larger animals will use proportionally more or less. For example, a 600-pound yearling bison will use about 18 pounds of air-dry forage per day. Adult female bison generally weigh between 900 and 1,200 pounds, while adult males range from 1,500 to 2,000 pounds, and yearlings from 600 to 800 pounds.

Annual forage production is less easily estimated, especially on prairie restorations. Total herbage (grass, sedge, and forb) production on mesic, deep-soil, tallgrass prairie sites may range from five thousand to ten thousand pounds/acre. On dry- or shallow-soiled sites, annual herbage production is more likely between twenty-five hundred and five thousand pounds/acre. The proportion of annual herbage production that is actually bison forage (grass and sedge) may range from less than 10 percent on recently restored sites dominated by weeds, to over 90 percent on late successional sites. A moderate bison stocking rate would allocate 25 percent of the annual forage production to bison, while a light stocking rate would allocate 10 percent and a heavy stocking rate, 40 percent of the annual forage production to bison.

The information required to calculate the bison stocking rate for a given area includes: 1) number of acres available; 2) average annual forage (grass/sedge) production per acre; and 3) the number of bison animal units (AUs). (1 AU = a 1,000-pound animal; a 600-pound yearling would be 0.6 AU, while a 1,700-pound bull would be 1.7 AUs.) The following example demonstrates how to determine the number of year-round bison required to conservatively stock a thousand-acre tallgrass restoration producing on average four thousand pounds of forage per acre per year:

1,000 acres × 4,000 pounds/acre × 25% (conservative stocking) = 1,000,000 pounds of bison forage available per year

1,000,000 pounds of available forage ÷ 30 pounds of forage required per AU ÷ 365 days per year = 91 bison AUs on a year-round basis

The actual number of bison that make up these 91 AUs will depend on the age and sex ratio of the herd. The mixture could be, for example, fifty 1,000-pound cows, fifteen 1,500-pound bulls, twenty 600-pound year-lings, and eight 800-pound two year olds.

Bison Productivity

In unsupplemented herds, female bison breed first as two year olds and calve nine and a half months later as three year olds weighing 800 to 1,000 pounds. Newborn calves weigh about 50 pounds, a weight re-sulting in relatively easy births. However, bison herds that are supple-mented to maintain a high-quality diet year-round will have many year-ling females reaching sexual maturity, breeding, and then calving as two year olds. Though these females may still weigh 800 to 1,000 pounds, more calving problems may occur under this type of management, be-cause the bison, although sexually mature, are not yet physically mature.

Bison are promiscuous breeders. Although bison sex ratios are 1:1 at birth, managing for adult sex ratios of 1 male : 10 females greatly reduces the amount of male fighting during the breeding season. Mature bulls are the most difficult bison to confine and handle. They form small groups or are solitary during the nonbreeding season. Small herds of mature bulls are very different in social and grazing behavior from herds dominated by cows and young bulls. Mature bulls tend to use smaller patches of high-quality forage and more wooded habitats and do more physical damage by rubbing woody plants, wallowing, and pawing the ground—activities that may be important to maintaining small-scale heterogeneity within a prairie.

The seasonality of breeding and calving depends on the physiological condition of mature females. The highest nutrient quality in native tall-grass and savanna forage occurs from June through August. Mature female bison reach a body condition that triggers their reproductive cycle during this time. As a result, most calves are born in April, May, and June—the beginning of the next "good forage" cycle. However, depending on the individual female and her diet, calves can be born throughout the year, since male bison two years and older are fertile and potent year-round (unlike members of the deer family, in which the breeding season is controlled by the male's seasonal potency). If a bison herd is supplemented to provide a high-quality diet throughout the year, calving season is less distinct, with calves being common even in winter.

At birth, a few calves may be in a backwards, upside-down, or leg-back position, making delivery difficult or impossible, especially for heifers (females having their first calf). As in the case of a diseased or injured animal, a restoration manager will need to decide how to respond. The bison may be euthanized or assisted through recovery, or time may provide the solution. It is my philosophy that ecological restorations should attempt to embrace ecological processes, and that managers should focus on populations rather than individuals. Individuals should be treated with respect but with the objective of doing what is most effective for the overall restoration.

Bison herds in good habitat and without predators can be expected to grow by an annual increment of 80 percent to 90 percent of the number of mature females (less than twelve years old) in the population. Once the stocking rate desired for restoration objectives has been achieved, the annual population growth will need to be removed. Removed bison usually should be the oldest and the youngest. Bison herds on grassland range without supplement should generally be restricted to age classes less than ten years old. Animals twice this old may remain healthy when fed high-quality feed; however, the teeth of bison over ten years old will be wearing out, vigor will be declining and disease increasing, especially during winters on native grasslands. Surplus animals removed from restoration projects are attracting high prices in an expanding market. Thus removing such bison may help achieve both ecological and economic objectives.

When Will Bison Benefit My Restoration?

Bison will benefit tallgrass and savanna restorations that are relatively large, grass-dominated, surrounded by other low-intensity land use, and lacking rare or sensitive species that require protection from bison grazing. In 1993, Plumb and Dodd reported that cattle can have many of the same ecological benefits as bison. Indeed, cattle may be more appropriate than bison when a restoration's size, facilities, management, and economics are limiting. Yet bison grazing, especially in combination with prescribed burning, has the potential for inducing a much more complex set of local interactions and spatial and temporal patterns than cattle grazing or fire or mowing alone. Matching the number of bison and prescribed fire regime with the biology of other species (e.g., plants, insects, birds) on appropriate sites will induce a wide range of beneficial habitat opportunities.

REFERENCES

Allen, J.A. 1876. *The American Bisons, Living and Extinct.* Mem. Mus. Comp. Zool., Harvard College. 1974. New York: Arno Press.

American Bison Association. 1993. *Bison Breeders Handbook,* 3rd edition. Denver, CO: American Bison Association.

Collins, S.L. 1987. "Interactions of Disturbances in Tallgrass Prairie: A Field Experiment." *Ecology* 68:1243–1250.

Jennings, D.C., and J. Hebbring. 1983. *Buffalo Management and Marketing.* Ft. Pierre, SD: National Buffalo Association.

McHugh, T. 1972. *The Time of the Buffalo.* Lincoln: University of Nebraska Press.

Milchunas, D.G., O.E. Sala, and W.K. Lauenroth. 1988. "A Generalized Model of the Effects of Grazing by Large Herbivores on Grassland Community Structure." *American Naturalist* 132:87–106.

Pfeiffer, K.E., and A.A. Steuter. 1994. "Preliminary Response of Sand-hills Prairie to Fire and Bison Grazing." *Journal of Range Management* 47:395–397.

Plumb, G.E., and J.L. Dodd. 1992. *A Bibliography on Bison* (Bison bison). University of Wyoming, Agricultural Experiment Station Publication MP-71.

———. 1993. "Foraging Ecology of Bison and Cattle on a Mixed Prairie: Implications for Natural Area Management." *Ecological Applications* 3:631–643.

Roe, F.G. 1970. *The North American Buffalo: A Critical Study of the Species in Its Wild State,* 2nd edition. Toronto, Ontario: University of Toronto Press.

Skarpe, C. 1991. "Impacts of Grazing in Savanna Ecosystems." *Ambio* 20:351–356.

Steuter, A.A., C.E. Grygiel, and M.E. Biondini. 1990. "A Synthesis Approach to Research and Management Planning: The Conceptual Development and Implementation." *Natural Areas Journal* 10:61–68.

Steuter, A.A., E.M. Steinauer, G.L. Hill, P.A. Bowers, and L.L. Tieszen. 1995. "Distribution and Diet of Bison and Pocket Gophers in a Sandhills Prairie." *Ecological Applications* 5:756–766.

Vinton, M.A., and D.C. Hartnett. 1992. "Effects of Bison Grazing on *Andropogon gerardii* and *Panicum virgatum* in Burned and Unburned Tallgrass Prairie." *Oecologia* 90:374–382.

Vinton, M.A., D.C. Hartnett, E.J. Finck, and J.M. Briggs. 1993. "Interactive Effects of Fire, Bison (*Bison bison*) Grazing and Plant Community Composition in Tallgrass Prairie." *American Midland Naturalist* 129:10–18.

Appendixes

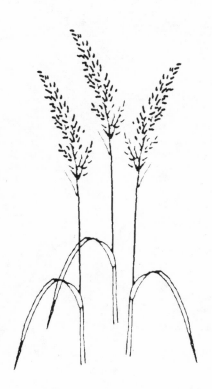

Appendix A
Vascular Plants of
Midwestern Tallgrass Prairies

Douglas Ladd

This appendix lists 988 taxa of native vascular plants occurring in tallgrass prairies in the midwestern United States and adjacent Canada. This area includes all of Minnesota, Iowa, Missouri, Illinois, Wisconsin, Indiana, Michigan, and Ohio, as well as eastern portions of Kansas, North Dakota, South Dakota, Nebraska, and Oklahoma, Arkansas prairies north of the Arkansas River, and Ontario south of the Canadian Shield. Plants included in this list are those that occur or formerly occurred regularly in tallgrass prairies somewhere in the biome, and also have native ranges that are at least partially east of the western edges of Minnesota, Iowa, Missouri, and Arkansas.

Selection of taxa for inclusion on the list is necessarily arbitrary. Tallgrass prairies grade imperceptibly into marshes, sedge meadows, mixed-grass prairies, glades, and savannas. This list encompasses the characteristic flora of sites in the midwestern tallgrass region that are not excessively wet or shaded. Included are prairies on sites ranging from wet to xeric, on soils ranging from sterile sands to deep, organic loams, including sites classified as sand prairies, wet prairies, mesic prairies, dry prairies, and hill prairies on substrates ranging from gravel to loess. Plants restricted to communities with extensive bedrock exposures, such as glades and cliffs, are not included here, although species of those sites that also inhabit prairies are included.

This list is intended to circumscribe roughly the universe of prairie flora in the main part of the tallgrass region. Many plants included here, while regularly occurring in prairies, may be modal in nonprairie habitats over much of their range. Other taxa of vascular plants not included here may appear in prairie sites but are not regular components of prairie vegetation. While all taxa on the list are species native to the Midwest, some of them also occur as introduced weeds in other parts of the region.

Inclusion of native weeds is based largely on the field experience of several prairie biologists and is predicated on perceptions of whether the plant is ever a component of native prairie systems, or appears only in sites with a history of severe post-settlement anthropogenic perturbation. Thus, plants such as horse nettle, believed to be native in parts of the southeastern United States, are omitted from the list, although they may regularly occur in degraded or overgrazed sites.

This list was compiled from state floras, natural area reports, site flora summaries, ecological sampling data, and consultation with biologists. Each entry provides the scientific and common name of the plant, its physiognomy, and its wetness rating as expressed by a numerical coefficient. Here as throughout the book, plants are arranged alphabetically by genus, generally following the nomenclatural concepts of Kartesz (1994).

Wetness ratings are included for each plant as a guide for ecologists and restorationists. As discussed by Wilhelm (1992), these ratings are derived by assigning a numerical coefficient of wetness (CW), ranging from −5 (obligate wetland) to +5 (upland), for each of the wetland indicator categories used in Reed (1988). Lower numbers indicate greater wetland affinities. Wetness ratings used in this list are generally those assigned to the plant in region 3 of Reed; if no value for region 3 is available, the values from region 4 or 5 are used. In several instances the modified values of Swink and Wilhelm (1994) are used to reflect more accurately the wetland affinities of the plant in the Midwest.

The distribution of wetness ratings among the tallgrass prairie flora is shown in table A.1. The largest category of the tallgrass prairie flora has upland affinities, as would be expected since the species of the wettest phases of prairie biome vegetation, including marshes, fens, sedge meadows, etc., are not included here. The pattern of distribution of wetness categories among the flora suggests that there may be biases against assigning "+" or "−" ratings to plants: in every case, the percent of the flora receiving such designations is lower than that of the parent category. Interestingly, when the "+" and "−" designations are lumped with their parent categories, the proportion of the flora in each category (obligate wetland, facultative wetland, facultative, facultative upland) is essentially equal.

Plants on this list are divided into physiognomic classes of forb, grass, sedge, vine, tree, shrub, and vascular cryptogam (abbreviated "crptgm"). Vines are codified as woody (W) or herbaceous (H). Nonwoody plants are identified as annual (A), biennial (B), or perennial (P). In some cases,

Table A.1.

Distribution of Wetness Ratings among
Tallgrass Prairie Vascular Flora

	Wetness Rating (CW)	Number of Taxa	% of flora
Upland	5	445	44.9
Facultative Upland −	4	45	4.5
Facultative Upland	3	74	7.5
Facultative Upland +	2	14	1.4
Facultative −	1	37	3.7
Facultative	0	67	6.8
Facultative +	−1	32	3.2
Facultative Wetland −	−2	19	1.9
Facultative Wetland	−3	80	8.1
Facultative Wetland +	−4	37	3.7
Obligate Wetland	−5	138	14.0

a species may be a combination of annual, biennial, or perennial in different parts of its range. In these cases, the category assigned is that thought to best represent the physiognomy of the plant in midwestern tallgrass prairies.

Table A.2 provides a summary of the flora by physiognomic classes. These data reinforce the concept that the flora of midwestern tallgrass

Table A.2.

Summary of Physiognomic Classes of Tallgrass
Prairie Vascular Flora

Physiognomy	Number of Taxa	% of flora
Annual Forb	141	14.2
Biennial Forb	31	3.1
Perennial Forb	514	52.0
Annual Grass	14	1.4
Perennial Grass	94	9.5
Annual Sedge	5	0.5
Perennial Sedge	105	10.6
Herbaceous Vine	4	0.4
Woody Vine	3	0.3
Shrub	46	4.7
Tree	16	1.6
Cryptogam	15	1.5

prairies is prevailingly perennial: almost 73 percent of the flora are herbaceous perennials, and another 7 percent are woody plants. The largest single physiognomic category is perennial forbs, which account for 52 percent of the total vascular diversity. Despite their prevalence in most prairie systems, graminoids contribute a disproportionately low proportion of the total vegetational diversity, with only about a quarter of the total species richness contributed by grasses, sedges, and rushes.

Following the physiognomy column in table A.3 in the list is a series of fifteen columns, each labeled with the abbreviation of a state or province. These columns show the distribution for each taxon by political unit, including which taxa are of special status or concern. These data are compiled largely from literature reports and are intended to provide general patterns of distribution. A dot (•) in the appropriate cell indicates that the plant occurs in that state or province, while an empty cell indicates that there is no documentation of the plant occurring there. Inclusion of a plant for a particular state indicates only that the taxon has been documented from the state, not necessarily within tallgrass prairies in the state. If a species is considered to be introduced in a state or province, this is indicated by a sunburst (✻) in the appropriate cell. The discrimination of introduced taxa is of varying accuracy from state to state, and in some states introduced taxa are not elucidated.

For four states and southern Ontario (ON), a numerical coefficient of conservatism is provided for the native flora instead of a dot, applying the rationale outlined in chapter 17 of this volume. Coefficients are provided for Illinois (Taft et al.), Michigan (Herman et al. 1996), Missouri (Ladd 1993), northeastern Ohio (Andreas and Lichvar 1995), and southern Ontario (Oldham et al. 1995). In these areas, for the few cases where a coefficient of conservatism cannot reliably be assigned because of nomenclatural problems or differences in species concepts, a dot is used.

Additional symbols are used to indicate taxa of special concern from a state perspective, as summarized below. These symbols are included in place of dots in the appropriate cells, or appended as superscripts in areas with conservatism coefficients. Kansas, Oklahoma, and South Dakota do not have any listings or designations for plant species of special concern from a conservation standpoint. Other states and provinces and the categories they employ are:

- Arkansas (Arkansas Natural Heritage Commission 1987)—
  Endangered (E) and Threatened (T).
- Illinois (Herkert 1991, 1994)—Endangered (E) and Threatened (T).
- Indiana (Indiana Department of Natural Resources 1993, aug-

mented working list dated December 1994)—Endangered (E), Threatened (T), Rare (R), Watch List (W), and Extirpated within the state (X).

- Iowa (Iowa Department of Natural Resources 1994)—Endangered (E), Threatened (T), and Special Concern (S); note that a few Iowa plants listed as S are now considered to be introduced in the state (Eilers and Roosa 1994) and are asterisked in this list.
- Michigan (Michigan Natural Features Inventory 1992)—Endangered (E), Threatened (T), Special Concern (S), and Extirpated within the state (X).
- Minnesota (Coffin and Pfannmuller 1988)—Endangered (E), Threatened (T), and Special Concern (S); note that for some taxa the listings are proposed but not official.
- Missouri (Missouri Department of Conservation 1992)—Endangered (E), Rare (R), Status Undetermined (S), Watch List (W), and Extirpated within the state (X).
- Nebraska (as discussed in Nebraska Game and Parks Commission 1992)—Nebraska plants are classified as Endangered (E) or Threatened (T) according to their federal designation (U.S. Fish and Wildlife Service 1994); only a single threatened species occurs in the tallgrass prairies.
- North Dakota (North Dakota Game and Fish Department 1986)—Endangered (E) and Threatened (T).
- Ohio (Ohio Division of Natural Areas and Preserves 1994)—Endangered (E), Threatened (T), Potentially Threatened (P), and Presumed Extirpated within the state (X).
- Ontario (Ontario Ministry of Natural Resources 1994)—Endangered (E), Threatened (T), Rare (R), and Extirpated within the province (X).
- Wisconsin (Wisconsin Natural Heritage Program 1993)—Endangered (E), Threatened (T), Special Concern (S), and Apparently Extirpated within the state (X).

Data revealed by this list reinforce the need for active prairie conservation efforts. Slightly more than half (55 percent) of the tallgrass prairie flora is designated under one of these categories in one or more states in the region. Five tallgrass prairie plants are listed as federally threatened, and one is federally endangered.

Table A.3.

Vascular Plants of Midwestern Tallgrass Prairies, Their Distribution and Status

SCIENTIFIC NAME	COMMON NAME	CW	PHYSIOG	AR	IL	IN	IA	KS	MI	MO	MN	ND	NE	OH	OK	ON	SD	WI
Acalypha gracilens	slender mercury	5	A-Forb	•	4	•		•		3			•	•	•			☼
Acalypha gracilens monococca	one-seeded mercury	5	A-Forb	•	4	•	S	•		3				•	•			•
Acalypha virginica	Virginia mercury	3	A-Forb	•	2	•	•	•	☼	2				0	•	•	•	•
Acalypha virginica rhomboidea	rhombic copperleaf	3	A-Forb	•	0	•	•		0	0				0	0	0		•
Achillea millefolium	woolly yarrow	3	P-Forb	•	0	•	•		•	0	•	•	•	0	0	•	•	•
Aconus calamus[1]	sweet flag	-5	P-Forb	•	4	•	•	•	6	4	T	•	6	8		•	•
Agalinis aspera	rough false foxglove	5	A-Forb	•	10	E	•	•		10	•	•				•	•
†*Agalinis auriculata*	eared false foxglove	5	A-Forb	•	9^T	E	S	•	10^X	10^R	•	•	8^E			•	X
Agalinis fasciculata	fascicled agalinis	5	A-Forb	•	6	W	•	•		7							
Agalinis heterophylla	prairie false foxglove	0	A-Forb	•					10^E	10^E							
†*Agalinis purpurea*	purple false foxglove	-3	A-Forb	•	6	•	•	•	7	10^W		•	8^E	10	•	•
Agalinis skinneriana	pale false foxglove	5	A-Forb	•	10^T	E	E	•	10^T	7^W	•	•	10^E	10	•	E
†*Agalinis tenuifolia*	slender false foxglove	-3	A-Forb	•	5	•	•	•	5	4	•	•	5	7	•	•
Agalinis viridis	green false foxglove	5	A-Forb	•			•		10^E	10^E							
Agoseris glauca	pale mountain-dandelion	3	P-Forb	•			•		10^T							•	•
Agrimonia parviflora	swamp agrimony	-1	P-Forb	•	5	•	•	•	4	6	•	•	6	4	•	S
Agrostis elliottiana	awned bent grass	5	A-Grass	•	5	•	•	•		3		•	X		•	•
Agrostis hyemalis	tickle grass	1	P-Grass	•	1	•	•	•	4	3		•	2	4	•	•
Agrostis perennans	upland bent	1	P-Grass	•	2	•	•	•	5	3		•	4	5	•	•
Aletris farinosa	colic root	0	P-Forb	•	9	•	•		10	10		•	8	10^T	•	•
Allium canadense	wild garlic	3	P-Forb	•	2	•	•	•	4	1	T	•	3	8	•	•
Allium canadense mobilense	glade onion	5	P-Forb	•	3	•	S	•	•	1						
Allium cernuum	nodding wild onion	5	P-Forb	•	7	•	T	•	5	8	•	•	5	9		•

continues

Scientific name	Common name	C	Form												
Allium stellatum	prairie onion	5	P-Forb	•	10	•	•	10	•	•		•	10	6	•
Allium textile	textile onion	5	P-Forb	•	•	•	•	•	•	•		•	•	6	•
Ambrosia bidentata	southern ragweed	4	A-Forb	•	0	S	•	0	•	•	☼	•	0	0	•
†*Ambrosia coronopifolia*	western ragweed	5	P-Forb	•	2	☼	•	2	•	•	☼	•	☼	2	•
Amorpha canescens	lead plant	5	Shrub	•	8	•	•	8	•	•	•	•	8	8	10
Amorpha fruticosa	indigo bush	−4	Shrub	•	6	T	•	6	•	•	2	•	☼	5	5
Amorpha nana	dwarf wild indigo	5	Shrub	•			•			•		•			•
Amphiachyris dracunculoides	broom snakeroot	5	A-Forb	•	☼	☼	•	☼	•	•	☼	•		3	•
Amphicarpaea bracteata	hog peanut	0	A-Forb	•	5	•	•	5	•	•	5	•	5	4	5
Anagallis minima	chaffweed	4	A-Forb	•	5	•	•	5	•	•	6	•	5	5	•
Andropogon gerardii	big bluestem	1	P-Grass	•	5	•	•	5	•	•	6	•	5	5	7
Andropogon gyrans	Elliott's broom sedge	5	P-Grass	•	3	•	•	3	•	•	•	•	3	3	•
Andropogon hallii	sand bluestem	5	P-Grass	•	☼	S	•	☼	•	☼		•			•
Andropogon ternarius	splitbeard bluestem	3	P-Grass	•	8ᴱ	W	•		•	•		•	5	5	•
Andropogon virginicus	broom sedge	1	P-Grass	•	1	•	S	1	•	•	3	•	4	2	5
Andropogon virginicus	rock jasmine	4	A-Forb	•	4	T	•	4	•	•	10ᵀ	•	6ᵀ	3	6
Androsace occidentalis	meadow anemone	−3	P-Forb	•	4	•	•	4	•	•	5	•	4	6	3
Anemone canadensis	Carolina anemone	5	P-Forb	•	7	X	•	7	•	•		•	7	6	E
Anemone caroliniana	thimbleweed	5	P-Forb	•	8	•	•	8	•	•	9ᵀ	•	6	10ᵂ	•
Anemone cylindrica	windflower	5	P-Forb	•		•	•	•	•	E		•	10	10	E
Anemone multifida	wood anemone	0	P-Forb	•	8	•	•	8	•	•	5	•	5	10ᴱ	•
Anemone quinquefolia	tall anemone	5	P-Forb	•	4	•	•	4	•	•	3	•	3	4	•
Anemone virginiana	great angelica	−5	P-Forb	•	6	•	•	6	•	•	6	•	6	6	6
Angelica atropurpurea	wood angelica	5	P-Forb	•	8	•	•	8	•	•	8	•	8ˢ	7	10

[1]See Swink and Wilhelm (1994), p. 80.
*Indicates nomenclature differs from Kartesz.
†Precedes scientific name cross-referenced in appendix C.

Table A.3. (Continued)

SCIENTIFIC NAME	COMMON NAME	CW	PHYSIOG	AR	IL	IN	IA	KS	MI	MO	MN	ND	NE	OH	OK	ON	SD	WI
Antennaria microphylla[2]	pink pussy toes	5	P-Forb	•					10^T		•	•	•		•		•	
Antennaria neglecta[3]	field cat's foot	5	P-Forb	•	4	•	•	•	2	4	•	•	•	2	•	2	•	•
Antennaria parvifolia	plains pussy toes	5	P-Forb			•					•	•	•		•		•	•
Antennaria plantaginifolia	pussy toes	5	P-Forb	•	4	•	•	•	3	5	•	•	•	1	•	2	•	•
Apios americana	ground nut	-3	H-Vine	•	4	•	•	•	3	6	•	T	•	4	•	6	•	•
Apocynum androsaemifolium	spreading dogbane	5	P-Forb	•	6	•	•	•	3	5	•	•	•	6	•	3	•	•
Apocynum cannabinum	prairie dogbane	0	P-Forb	•	3	•	•	•	3	3	•	•	•	3	•	3	•	•
Apocynum sibiricum★	Indian hemp	-1	P-Forb	•	2	•	•	•	•	2	•	•	•	8^E		?		•
Apocynum × floribundum	intermediate dogbane	5	P-Forb	•	6	•	•	•		4	•	•	•	3	•		•	
Arabis drummondii	Drummond's rock cress	3	B-Forb	•	10	E	•	•	6		•	•	•	9^E	•	9	•	•
Arabis glabra	tower mustard	5	B-Forb	•	6	T	•	•	3	8^E	•	•	•	3	•	4	•	•
Arabis lyrata	sand cress	4	B-Forb	•	7	•	•	•	7	8	•	•	•	6^P	•	7	•	•
Argentina anserina	silverweed	-4	P-Forb	•	6	T	T	•	5		•	•	•	10^P	•	5	•	•
Aristida basiramea	fork-tipped three-awn grass	5	A-Grass	•	6	☆	•	•	3	4	•	•	•		•	10	•	•
Aristida dichotoma	poverty grass	3	A-Grass	•	2	•	•	•	5^X	3			•	2	•	10	•	S
Aristida longespica	slimspike three-awn	4	A-Grass	•	2	•	•	•	6^T	2			•	10	•	8	•	•
Aristida oligantha	plains three-awn grass	5	A-Grass	•	0	•	•	•	☆	1			•	0	•	☆	•	•
Aristida purpurascens	arrow feather	5	P-Grass	•	5	•	•	•	8	5			•	8^P	•	10	•	•
Aristida purpurea	purple three-awn	5	P-Grass	•	9	•	•	•	9		•	•	•		•			
Aristida tuberculosa	beach three-awn grass	5	A-Grass		5	•	•	•			•	•	•		•		•	•
†*Arnoglossum atriplicifolium*	pale Indian plantain	5	P-Forb	•	5	•	•	•	10	4			•	7	•			
†*Arnoglossum plantagineum*	prairie Indian plantain	0	P-Forb	•	10	•	•	•	10^T	8	T	•	•	P	•	10^R	•	T
†*Artemisia campestris caudata*	beach wormwood	5	B-Forb	•	5	•	•	•	5	5	•	•	•	10^T	•	8	•	•
Artemisia dracunculus	false tarragon	5	P-Forb	•	9^E	•	•	•	10^X		•	•	•		•		•	S

Species	Common name		Form									
Artemisia frigida	prairie sagebrush	5	Shrub	•	☆	•	☆	•	•	•	•	S
Artemisia ludoviciana	white sage	5	P-Forb	2	☆	•	3	•	•	•	☆	•
Artemisia serrata	saw-toothed sagebrush	5	P-Forb	10	☆	•	•	•	•	•	•	•
Asclepias amplexicaulis	sand milkweed	5	P-Forb	8	E	•	9	S	•	7^P	•	•
Asclepias engelmanniana	Engelmann's milkweed	5	P-Forb	•	E	•	10	T	•	•	•	
Asclepias hirtella	tall green milkweed	5	P-Forb	6	•	•	4	•	•	8	10	•
Asclepias incarnata	swamp milkweed	−5	P-Forb	4	•	•	5	•	•	5	6	•
Asclepias lanuginosa	woolly milkweed	5	P-Forb	10^E	T	•	•	•	•	•	•	T
Asclepias meadii[4]	Mead's milkweed	5	P-Forb	10^E	X	•	10^E	•	•	•	•	X
Asclepias ovalifolia	oval milkweed	5	P-Forb	10^E	•	•	10^E	•	•	8	8	•
Asclepias purpurascens	purple milkweed	3	P-Forb	7	•	•	6	•	•	•	10	E
Asclepias speciosa	showy milkweed	0	P-Forb	☆	•	•	☆	E	•	•	•	☆
Asclepias stenophylla	glade milkweed	5	P-Forb	10^T	•	•	9	T	E	•	•	T
Asclepias sullivantii	prairie milkweed	5	P-Forb	8	•	•	9	E	T	9	8	•
Asclepias syriaca	common milkweed	5	P-Forb	0	•	•	0	•	E	0	0	•
Asclepias tuberosa	butterfly weed	5	P-Forb	5	•	•	5	•	•	6	8	•
Asclepias verticillata	whorled milkweed	5	P-Forb	1	•	•	2	•	•	6	6	•
Asclepias viridiflora	short green milkweed	5	P-Forb	9	•	•	9	•	•	9^P	10	•
Asclepias viridis	green-flowered milkweed	5	P-Forb	6	E	•	6	•	•	P	•	•
Aster dumosus	bushy aster	−1	P-Forb	9	•	•	9	E	•	10^T	10	•
Aster ericoides	heath aster	4	P-Forb	4	•	•	4	•	•	3	4	•
Aster falcatus	curved aster	1	P-Forb	•	•	•	•	S	•	•	•	•
Aster fragilis subdumosus	small white aster	−2	P-Forb	3	•	•	6	•	•	2	2	•

[2]Including *Antennaria rosea.*
[3]Including *Antennaria neodioica.*
[4]Federally designed as Threatened (USFWS 1994).
*Indicates nomenclature differs from Kartesz.
†Precedes scientific name cross-referenced in appendix C.

continues

Table A.3. (Continued)

SCIENTIFIC NAME	COMMON NAME	CW	PHYSIOG	AR	IL	IN	IA	KS	MI	MO	MN	ND	NE	OH	OK	ON	SD	WI
Aster laevis	smooth blue aster	5	P-Forb	•	8	•	•	•	5	7	•	•	•	6	•	7	•	•
†Aster lanceolatus	panicled aster	-5	P-Forb	•	3	•	•	•	2	4	•	•	•	2	•	3	•	•
Aster lateriflorus	side-flowering aster	-2	P-Forb	•	2	•	•	•	2	3	•		•	2	•	3		•
Aster novae-angliae	New England aster	-3	P-Forb	•	4	•	•	•	3	4	•	•	•	3	•	2	•	•
Aster oblongifolius	aromatic aster	5	P-Forb	•	7	R	•	•	6		•	•		T	•	9	•	•
†Aster oolentangiensis	azure aster	5	P-Forb	•	8	•	•	•	4	7	•	•	•	7	•	9	•	•
Aster paludosus hemisphericus	southern prairie aster	2	P-Forb							9								
Aster parviceps	small-headed aster	5	P-Forb		3					3								
Aster patens	spreading aster	5	P-Forb		6					5				9				
Aster pilosus	hairy aster	4	P-Forb	•	0	•	•	•	1	0	•	•	•	1	•	4		
Aster praealtus	willow aster	-5	P-Forb	•	5	•	•	•	6	6	•	•	•	7	•	8	•	•
Aster puniceus	bristly aster	-5	P-Forb	•	8	•	•	•	5	10	•	•	•	6	•	6	•	•
Aster puniceus firmus	shining aster	-5	P-Forb	•	5	•	•	•	4		•	•		•		6	•	•
Aster sericeus	silky aster	5	P-Forb	•	10	R	•	•	10^T	8	•	T	•	•			•	•
Aster turbinellus	prairie aster	5	P-Forb	•	7	•	•	•	6	6	•		•	•				
Aster umbellatus	flat-top aster	-3	P-Forb	•	8	•	•	•	5		•	•	•	2	•	6	•	•
Aster umbellatus pubens	northern flat-top aster	-3	P-Forb	•			S			10^E	•			•		6		
Astragalus adsurgens	standing milk vetch	5	P-Forb				S				•	•					•	•
Astragalus agrestis	field milk vetch	5	P-Forb		☆						•	•						
Astragalus canadensis	Canadian milk vetch	-1	P-Forb	•	7	•	•		9^T	6	•	•	•	3	•	8	•	•
Astragalus crassicarpus	Indian pea	5	P-Forb	•		•	•			10	•	•	•	7			•	•
Astragalus crassicarpus trichocalyx	ground plum	5	P-Forb	•	8^E													E
Astragalus distortus	bent milk vetch	5	P-Forb	•	8		S			6				7				
Astragalus flexuosus	slender milk vetch	5	P-Forb	•			•				S	•					•	

continues

Scientific name	Common name	Physiognomy	C												
Astragalus lotiflorus	low milk vetch	P-Forb	5	•	•	•	•	•	•	•	•	•	•	•	•
Astragalus missouriensis	Missouri milk vetch	P-Forb	5	•	•	S	•	•	•	•	•	•	•	•	•
Astragalus neglectus	Cooper's milk vetch	P-Forb	4	10^E	X	•	9^S	S	•	9	•	S	•	•	E
Astragalus tennesseensis	Tennessee milk vetch	P-Forb	5	10^E	•	•	•	•	•	•	•	•	•	•	•
Astranthium integrifolium	western daisy	A-Forb	5	•	•	6	•	•	•	•	•	•	•	•	•
†*Baptisia alba macrophylla*	white wild indigo	P-Forb	3	6	•	10^T	6	•	8^P	•	•	•	•	•	•
Baptisia australis	blue wild indigo	P-Forb	5	☼	T	8	•	E	•	•	•	•	•	•	•
†*Baptisia bracteata leucophaea*	cream wild indigo	P-Forb	5	9	W	10^E	6	S	•	•	•	•	•	•	•
Baptisia tinctoria	yellow wild indigo	P-Forb	5	10	W	10	•	S	8	10	•	•	S	•	•
Beckmannia syzigachne	American slough grass	A-Grass	−5	10^E	•	4^T	☼	•	☼	4	•	•	•	•	•
†*Besseya bullii*	kitten tails	P-Forb	5	8^T	E	10^T	•	T	X	•	•	T	•	•	T
Betula pumila	dwarf birch	shrub	−5	10	T	8	•	T	10^T	9	•	•	•	•	•
Bidens aristosa	swamp marigold	A-Forb	−3	1	•	1	1	•	3	•	•	•	•	•	•
Bidens coronata	tall swamp marigold	P-Forb	−5	8	•	7	☼	•	3	9	•	•	•	•	•
Bidens frondosa	common beggar's ticks	A-Forb	−3	1	•	1	2	•	2	3	•	•	•	•	•
Blephilia ciliata	Ohio horse mint	P-Forb	5	6	T	7	5	•	4	10	•	•	•	•	•
†*Boltonia asteroides*	false aster	P-Forb	−3	5	•	5^S	5	•	8	8	•	•	•	•	•
Boltonia diffusa	doll's daisy	P-Forb	−3	4	•	•	7	•	•	•	•	•	•	•	•
Bothriochloa saccharoides	silver beard grass	P-Grass	5	☼	•	•	2	•	•	•	•	•	•	•	•
Botrychium campestre	prairie moonwort	Crptgm	5	•	S	10^T	•	S	T	3	•	E	•	S	•
Botrychium minganense	Mingan moonwort	Crptgm	−3	•	•	7	•	•	9	•	•	E	•	S	•
Botrychium simplex	dwarf grape fern	Crptgm	0	4^E	E	5	2	•	10	7	•	•	•	X	•
Bouteloua curtipendula	side-oats grama	P-Grass	5	7	•	5	•	T	10^T	10	•	•	7	•	•
Bouteloua gracilis	blue grama	P-Grass	5	5	•	8^X	•	•	10^T	☼	•	☼	•	☼	•

---

*Indicates nomenclature differs from Kartesz.

†Precedes scientific name cross-referenced in appendix C.

361

Table A.3. (*Continued*)

SCIENTIFIC NAME	COMMON NAME	CW	PHYSIOG	AR	IL	IN	IA	KS	MI	MO	MN	ND	NE	OH	OK	ON	SD	WI
Bouteloua hirsuta	hairy grama	5	P-Grass	E	9	•	•	•	•	10^R	•	•	•	☼	•	•	•	•
Brachyactis ciliata angusta	rayless aster	0	P-Forb	☼	☼	☼	•	•	☼	10^X	•	•	•	☼	•	•	•	☼
†*Brickellia eupatorioides*	false boneset	5	P-Forb	•	6	•	•	•	10^S	5	•	•	8	8	•	•	•	•
Bromus ciliatus	fringed brome	-3	P-Grass	•	10	•	•	•	6	•	•	•	7	7	•	6	•	•
Bromus kalmii	prairie brome	0	P-Grass	•	10	•	•	•	8	•	T	•	8	8	•	8	•	•
Bromus latiglumis	ear-leaved brome	-2	P-Grass	•	7	•	•	•	6	10^S	•	•	7	7	•	7	•	•
Buchloe dactyloides	buffalo grass	4	P-Grass	•	☼	•	S	•	5^R	S	•	•	•	•	•	•	•	•
Buchnera americana	blue hearts	1	P-Forb	•	10	E	•	•	10^X	10	•	•	8^T	8^T	•	10^T	•	•
Bulbostylis capillaris	hair sedge	2	A-Sedge	•	4	•	•	•	4	4	•	•	•	3	•	5	•	•
Calamagrostis canadensis	blue joint grass	-5	P-Grass	•	3	•	•	•	3	6	•	•	4	4	•	4	•	•
Calamagrostis stricta inexpansa	bog reed grass	-4	P-Grass	•	5	•	•	•	10^T	8	•	•	•	10^P	•	8	•	S
Calamintha arkansana	low calamint	-3	P-Forb	•	8	•	•	•	10	7	•	•	8^T	8^T	•	10	•	S
Calamovilfa longifolia	sand reed	5	P-Grass	•	8	•	T	•	10	10^X	•	•	•	•	•	10	•	T
Callirhoe alcaeoides	pink poppy mallow	5	P-Forb	•	5	•	S	•	•	5	•	•	•	•	•	•	•	•
Callirhoe bushii	Bush's poppy mallow	5	P-Forb	•	•	•	•	•	•	10	•	•	•	•	•	•	•	•
Callirhoe digitata	fringed poppy mallow	5	P-Forb	☼	☼	•	•	•	•	6	•	•	•	•	•	•	•	•
Callirhoe involucrata	purple poppy mallow	5	P-Forb	☼	☼	☼	•	•	☼	5	•	•	•	•	•	☼	•	•
Callirhoe triangulata	clustered poppy mallow	5	P-Forb	•	9	X	E	•	10^X	10^X	•	•	•	•	•	•	S	S
†*Calopogon tuberosus*	grass pink	-5	P-Forb	•	10^E	•	S	•	9	10	•	•	•	10^P	•	9	•	•
Caltha palustris	marsh marigold	-5	P-Forb	•	7	•	•	•	6	10^E	•	•	•	5	•	5	•	•
Calylophus serrulatus	toothed evening primrose	5	P-Forb	•	10	•	•	•	☼	4	•	•	•	•	•	☼	•	S
Calystegia sepium	hedge bindweed	0	H-Vine	☼	1	•	•	•	2	1	•	•	•	1	•	2	•	•
†*Calystegia spithamaea*	low bindweed	5	P-Forb	•	10	•	S	•	8	9	•	•	•	6	•	7	•	•
Camassia angusta	prairie hyacinth	5	P-Forb	•	10^E	E	•	•	•	10	•	•	•	•	•	•	•	•

Scientific Name	Common Name	C	Physiognomy							
Camassia scilloides	wild hyacinth	-1	P-Forb	• 7	6	9^T	•	5	•	E
Campanula aparinoides	marsh bellflower	-5	P-Forb	7	10^E	7	•	7	10^R	•
Campanula rotundifolia	harebell	1	P-Forb	8	10^E	6	T	8^T	7	•
Cardamine bulbosa	bulbous cress	-5	P-Forb	• 5	6	4	•	4	8	•
Carex aggregata	glomerate sedge	5	P-Sedge	4 S	6	1	•	2	5	•
Carex alata	winged oval sedge	-5	P-Sedge	10^E	10^W	10	•	8^P	10	•
Carex alopecoidea	brown-headed fox sedge	-4	P-Sedge	4 E	3	3	•	6	6	•
Carex annectens	yellow-fruited sedge	-3	P-Sedge	3	4	1	•	6	9	•
Carex aquatilis	water sedge	-5	P-Sedge	8	10^E	7 S	•	9	7	•
Carex arkansana	Arkansas sedge	-5	P-Sedge	10^E	10^R	•	•	•	•	•
Carex austrina	southern sand sedge	5	P-Sedge	•	6	•	•	•	•	•
Carex bebbii	Bebb's oval sedge	-5	P-Sedge	8 T	4	•	•	7^T	3	•
Carex bicknellii	prairie sedge	1	P-Sedge	8	10 8	•	•	T	10	•
Carex bicknellii opaca	southern prairie sedge	1	P-Sedge	E	9^S	10	•	•	•	•
Carex brevior	short-beaked sedge	0	P-Sedge	4	4 3	•	•	4	7	•
Carex bushii	Bush's sedge	-3	P-Sedge	3 E	3 ☀	•	•	•	•	•
Carex buxbaumii	brown bog sedge	-5	P-Sedge	10	10^R 10	•	T	10	10	•
Carex caroliniana	Carolina sedge	0	P-Sedge	7	7	•	•	6	•	•
Carex comosa	bristly sedge	-5	P-Sedge	5	10^R 5	•	•	2	5	•
Carex conjuncta	soft fox sedge	-3	P-Sedge	5	5	T	•	5	•	•
Carex conoidea	field sedge	-5	P-Sedge	10 E	10^E 10	•	•	8^T	9	•
Carex crawei	Crawe's sedge	-5	P-Sedge	9^T T	10 10	•	•	8^P	10	S
Carex crinita	fringed sedge	-5	P-Sedge	7 S	6 4	•	•	2	6	•
Carex cristatella	crested sedge	-4	P-Sedge	3 S	4 3	•	•	3	3	•
Carex crus-corvi	raven's foot sedge	-5	P-Sedge	6	5 10^T	E	•	10^E	10	E

continues

*Indicates nomenclature differs from Kartesz.
†Precedes scientific name cross-referenced in appendix C.

Table A.3. (Continued)

SCIENTIFIC NAME	COMMON NAME	CW	PHYSIOG	AR	IL	IN	IA	KS	MI	MO	MN	ND	NE	OH	OK	ON	SD	WI
Carex davisii	Davis's sedge	-1	P-Sedge	•	3	•		•	8^S	4	T	•	•	6	•	10		•
Carex douglasii	Douglas's sedge	0	P-Sedge	•			S			☼		•		•			•	•
Carex eleocharis	slender-leaved sedge	5	P-Sedge							☼		•					•	•
Carex emoryi	Emory's sedge	-5	P-Sedge	•	6	•		•	7	6	•	•	•	6	•	8	•	•
Carex festucacea	fescue sedge	0	P-Sedge	•	6	•		•	8^S	6	•		•	6	•	9		•
Carex filifolia	thread-leaved sedge	5	P-Sedge	•								•			•			
Carex fissa	hardpan sedge	-1	P-Sedge	•					9						•			
Carex frankii	Frank's sedge	-5	P-Sedge	•	4	•		4^S		5			•	5	•	7	•	•
Carex granularis	meadow sedge	-4	P-Sedge	•	3	•		2		4			•	3		3	•	
Carex gravida	heavy sedge	5	P-Sedge	•	4	E		10^S		5			•	T	•	10	•	•
Carex hallii	Hall's sedge	0	P-Sedge	•							T						•	
Carex haydenii	cloud sedge	-5	P-Sedge	•	8	•		8^S		10			•	10^X	8	9	•	•
Carex hyalinolepis	shoreline sedge	-5	P-Sedge	•	4	•		4^S		5			•	8	4		•	•
Carex inops heliophila[5]	yellow sedge	5	P-Sedge	•	7^E			•		7			•		•	10	•	•
Carex interior	interior sedge	-5	P-Sedge	•	10	•		3		10			•	8	•	6	•	•
Carex lacustris	lake bank sedge	-5	P-Sedge	•	6	•		6		10^E			•	5	•	5	•	•
Carex laeviconica	smooth cone sedge	-5	P-Sedge	•	10	•				9			•		•		•	
Carex leavenworthii	Leavenworth's sedge	5	P-Sedge	•	2	•		☼		3			•	6	•	8	•	
Carex leptalea	bristle-stalked sedge	-5	P-Sedge	•	10	W	S	5		10		T	•	5	•	8	•	•
Carex lupulina	hop sedge	-5	P-Sedge	•	5	•		4		6			•	3	•	6	•	•
Carex lurida	sallow sedge	-5	P-Sedge	•	7	•	S	3		6			•	3	•	6	•	•
Carex meadii	Mead's sedge	0	P-Sedge	•	8	•		8		8			•	7	•	9	•	•
Carex mesochorea	oval-headed sedge	3	P-Sedge	•				☼		5				E	•	8		
Carex microdonta	little tooth sedge	0	P-Sedge	•					10^S						•			

Scientific name	Common name																	
Carex molesta	troublesome sedge	0	P-Sedge	•	2	•	•	2	4	•	•	•	•	4	•	5
Carex muhlenbergii	sand sedge	5	P-Sedge	•	5	•	•	7	5	•	•	•	•	6	•	7
Carex normalis	larger straw sedge	-3	P-Sedge	•	4	•	•	5	4	•	•	•	•	4	•	6
Carex oklahomensis	Oklahoma sedge	0	P-Sedge	•		•	•		8R	•	•					
†*Carex pellita*⁶*	woolly sedge	-5	P-Sedge	•	4	•	•	2	5	•	•	•	•	6P	•	4
Carex pensylvanica	Pennsylvania sedge	5	P-Sedge	•	5	•	•	4	6	•	•	•	•	3	•	5
Carex praegracilis	expressway sedge	-3	P-Sedge	•	☼	☼	•	☼	☼	•	•	•	☼		☼	
Carex prairea	fen panicled sedge	-5	P-Sedge	•	10	•	•	10		•	•	•	•	9	•	7
Carex projecta	necklace sedge	-4	P-Sedge	•	4	•	•	3	5	•	•	•	•	8T	•	5
Carex richardsonii	prairie hummock sedge	5	P-Sedge	•	10	E	S	9S		•	T	•	•	10X	•	9
Carex sartwellii	running marsh sedge	-5	P-Sedge	•	5	•	•	5	10E	•	•	•	•	9P	•	9
Carex saxinontana	Rocky Mountain sedge	5	P-Sedge	•		•	S			•		•				
Carex scoparia	pointed broom sedge	-3	P-Sedge	•	5	•	•	4	4	•	•	•	•	4	•	5
Carex shortiana	Short's sedge	-4	P-Sedge	•	4	•	•	4	4	•	•	•	•	5	•	9
*Carex siccata*⁷	running savanna sedge	-1	P-Sedge	•	7	•	S	5		•	T	•	•	9	•	8
Carex sparganioides	bur-reed sedge	0	P-Sedge	•	4	•	•	5	6	•	•	•	•	3	•	5
Carex squarrosa	squarrose sedge	-5	P-Sedge	•	5	•	•	9S	6	•	•	•	•	5	•	8
Carex stipata	sawbeak sedge	-5	P-Sedge	•	2	•	•	1	4	•	•	•	•	2	•	3
Carex straminea	straw sedge	-5	P-Forb	•		T	•	10S	10S	•	•	•	•	9T	•	S
Carex suberecta	prairie straw sedge	-5	P-Sedge	•	7	•	•	8	10	•	•	•	•	9P	•	S
Carex tenera	slender sedge	-1	P-Sedge	•	5	•	S	4	5	•	•	•	•	6	•	4
Carex tetanica	rigid sedge	-3	P-Sedge	•	8	•	•	9	10S	•	•	•	•	8	•	8

continues

---

⁵See Swink and Wilhelm (1994), p. 212.

⁶=*Carex lanuginosa*; see Swink and Wilhelm (1994), p. 212.

⁷=*Carex foenea* of many midwestern authors (misapplied).

*Indicates nomenclature differs from Kartesz.

†Precedes scientific name cross-referenced in appendix C.

Table A.3. (Continued)

SCIENTIFIC NAME	COMMON NAME	CW	PHYSIOG	AR	IL	IN	IA	KS	MI	MO	MN	ND	NE	OH	OK	ON	SD	WI
Carex tonsa	deep green sedge	5	P-Sedge	•	10[E]	•	S	•	4	10[E]	•							•
Carex tribuloides	blunt broom sedge	-4	P-Sedge	•	3	•	•	•	3	3	•		•	4	•	5		•
Carex typhina	cat-tail sedge	-5	P-Sedge	•	6	•	•	9[T]	7	7				6		9		•
Carex umbellata	umbel-like sedge	5	P-Sedge	•	6	•	S	5	5	6	•		•	9	•	7	•	•
Carex utriculata	beaked sedge	-5	P-Sedge		9[T]	•			5		•			7[P]		7	•	•
Carex vesicaria	inflated sedge	-5	P-Sedge	•	10	•	•		7	9[S]			•	7		7	•	•
Carex vulpinoidea	fox sedge	-5	P-Sedge	•	2	•	•	1	1	4	•	•	•	3	•	3	•	•
Castilleja coccinea	Indian paintbrush	0	A-Forb	•	10	•	•	8	8	5	•			8		9		•
Castilleja sessiliflora	downy yellow painted cup	5	P-Forb	•	10[E]	•	•	10[W]		10[W]		•	•				•	
Ceanothus americanus	New Jersey tea	5	Shrub	•	7	•	•	8	8	7			•	6	7			•
†Ceanothus herbaceus	inland New Jersey tea	5	Shrub	•	10[E]	X	•	9	9	8			•	10[E]	9		•	•
Cephalanthus occidentalis	buttonbush	-5	Shrub	•	4	•	S	7	7	3	S		•	7	7			•
Cerastium arvense	prairie chickweed	4	P-Forb	•	4	•	•	6	6	4		•	•	2	8	8	•	•
Chaerophyllum tainturieri	southern chervil	5	A-Forb	•	1	•	•			3				3				
Chaetopappa asteroides	least daisy	5	A-Forb	•						10[S]								
†Chamaecrista fasciculata	partridge pea	4	A-Forb	•	1	•	•	2	1	1	•		•	3	☼			•
Chamaecrista nictitans	wild sensitive plant	4	A-Forb	•	2	W	•	3	3	2				•	•			
Chamaesyce geyeri	Geyer's spurge	5	A-Forb	•	10	•	•	☼		10[E]		•	•				•	
Chamaesyce missurica	Missouri spurge	5	A-Forb	•			S			8	T	•	•					
Chamaesyce serpyllifolia	thyme-leaved spurge	5	A-Forb	•	☼	•	☼	☼	☼	☼		•		☼		☼		☼
Chelone glabra	turtlehead	-5	P-Forb	•	7	•	•	7	7	7				8		7		•
Chloris verticillata	windmill grass	5	P-Grass	•	☼	☼	☼	☼		1			•				•	
Chrysopsis pilosa	soft golden aster	5	A-Forb	•					3	3								
Cicuta maculata	water hemlock	-5	B-Forb	•	4	•	•	4	4	5	•	•	•	3	•	6	•	•

Scientific name	Common name		Physiognomy
Cirsium altissimum	tall thistle	5	P-Forb
Cirsium carolinianum	Carolina thistle	5	B-Forb
Cirsium discolor	field thistle	5	P-Forb
Cirsium flodmanii	Flodman's thistle	5	P-Forb
Cirsium hillii	prairie thistle	5	P-Forb
Cirsium muticum	swamp thistle	-5	B-Forb
Cirsium undulatum	wavy-leaved thistle	1	P-Forb
Cladium mariscoides	twig rush	-5	P-Sedge
Claytonia virginica	spring beauty	3	P-Forb
Clematis fremontii	Fremont's leather flower	5	P-Forb
Clematis pitcheri	Pitcher's leather flower	3	W-Vine
Cleome serrulata	Rocky Mountain bee plant	4	A-Forb
Coelorachis cylindrica	joint grass	5	P-Grass
Collomia linearis	slender gilia	3	A-Forb
†*Comandra umbellata*	false toadflax	3	P-Forb
Commelina erecta	narrow-leaved day flower	5	P-Forb
Comptonia peregrina	sweet fern	5	Shrub
Conyza canadensis	horseweed	1	A-Forb
Conyza ramosissima	dwarf fleabane	5	A-Forb
Cooperia drummondii	rain lily	5	P-Forb
Coreopsis grandiflora	large-flowered coreopsis	5	P-Forb
Coreopsis lanceolata	sand coreopsis	3	P-Forb
Coreopsis palmata	prairie coreopsis	5	P-Forb
Coreopsis tripteris	tall coreopsis	0	P-Forb

continues

*Indicates nomenclature differs from Kartesz.

†Precedes scientific name cross-referenced in appendix C.

Table A.3. (Continued)

SCIENTIFIC NAME	COMMON NAME	CW	PHYSIOG	AR	IL	IN	IA	KS	MI	MO	MN	ND	NE	OH	OK	ON	SD	WI
Cornus amomum obliqua	pale dogwood	-5	Shrub	•	4	•	•	•	2	5	•	•	•	2	•	5	•	•
Cornus drummondii	rough-leaved dogwood	0	Shrub	•	2	•	•	•	6	1	•	•	•	4	•	4	•	•
Cornus racemosa	gray dogwood	-2	Shrub	•	1	•	•	•	1	3	•		•	2		2	•	•
Cornus sericea	red-osier dogwood	-3	Shrub	•	3	•	•	•	2	•	•	•	•	4		2	•	•
Corydalis aurea	golden corydalis	5	A-Forb		5^E	T	•	•	5	3	•	•	•	•		8	•	•
Corydalis crystallina	mealy corydalis	5	B-Forb	•						7								
Corydalis curvisiliqua grandibracteata	large-bracted corydalis	5	A-Forb	•	10^T	E												
Corydalis micrantha	small-flowered corydalis	5	B-Forb	•	2	•	•	•	•	4	•	•	•	•			•	•
Crotalaria sagittalis	rattlebox	5	A-Forb	•	3	•	•	•	☼	4	•	•	•	•	☼		•	•
Croton capitatus	hogwort	5	A-Forb	•	0	•	•	•	0	0	•	•	•					
Croton glandulosus septentrionalis	sand croton	5	A-Forb	•	1	•	•	•	☼	1				E				☼
Croton monanthogynus	prairie tea	5	A-Forb	•	2	S	S	•	☼	2								
Croton willdenowii	rushfoil	5	A-Forb	•	5	E	S			6								
Cunila origanoides	dittany	5	P-Forb	•	5	•				5				6				
Cuphea viscosissima	waxweed	3	A-Forb	•	4	S	•			4			•	6				•
Cuscuta cuspidata	cusp dodder	-4	A-Forb	•	5	X	•	•	10^S	6							•	•
Cuscuta glomerata	rope dodder	0	A-Forb	•	6	•	•	•	3	5	•	T	•	T		4	•	•
Cuscuta gronovii	common dodder	-3	A-Forb	•	2	•	•	•	3	4	•	•	•	3		2	•	•
Cuscuta pentagona[8]	prairie dodder	5	A-Forb	•	9	•	•	•	10^S	5	•	•	•	5^X		7	•	•
Cuscuta polygonorum	knotweed dodder	5	A-Forb	•	6	E	S	•	9^S	5	•	•	•	7		7	•	•
Cyperus echinatus	hedgehog club rush	0	P-Sedge	•	2	•	•			3			•	•				
Cyperus esculentus	chufa	-3	P-Sedge	•	0	•	•	•	1	1	•	•	•	2	•	1	•	•
Cyperus grayioides	Gray's sedge	5	P-Sedge	•	8^T	•		•	1	10^E				3	•		•	•
Cyperus lancastriensis	many-flowered flatsedge	1	P-Sedge	•	7	•				7				E				

Scientific Name	Common Name		Physiognomy																					
Cyperus lupulinus	slender flatsedge	4	P-Sedge	5	•	•	•	•	2	•	•	•	2	4	•	•	•	3	•	•		•
Cyperus pseudovegetus	green flatsedge	-3	P-Sedge	5	R	•	•	5	5	•	•	•	•		•	•		•
Cyperus schweinitzii	rough sand sedge	5	P-Sedge	5	•	•	5	6	•	•	9^P	9	•
Cyperus strigosus	straw-colored flatsedge	-3	P-Sedge	0	•	•	3	1	•	•	2	5	•
Cypripedium candidum	white lady's slipper	-5	P-Forb	10^E	R	S	10^T	10^E	T	10^T	10^E	T
Cypripedium parviflorum	small yellow lady's slipper	-1	P-Forb	10^E	R		7	8	T	10^E	7	S
Cypripedium pubescens	large yellow lady's slipper	-1	P-Forb	8	W		5	8	T	8^P	5	•
Cypripedium reginae	showy lady's slipper	-4	P-Forb	10^E	W	T	9	10^W	T	10^T	7	S
†*Dalea candida*	white prairie clover	5	P-Forb	10	•		8	•
Dalea candida oligophylla	western prairie clover	5	P-Forb	5	
Dalea enneandra	nine-anthered prairie clover	5	P-Forb	☼		•	10^W	T
Dalea foliosa[9]	leafy prairie clover	5	P-Forb	10^E			10^W	•
Dalea leporina	foxtail dalea	5	A-Forb	☼	☼	☼	4	☼	•
Dalea multiflora	round-headed prairie clover	5	P-Forb			10^X	8	X	•
†*Dalea purpurea*	purple prairie clover	5	P-Forb	9	E	10^X	8	•	X	•	S
Dalea villosa	silky prairie clover	5	P-Forb	E		•	•	•	•	•
Danthonia spicata	poverty oat grass	5	P-Grass	3	•	4	3	3	•
Daucus pusillus	small wild carrot	5	B-Forb	☼		4	•
Delphinium carolinianum	Carolina larkspur	5	P-Forb	10	S		7	3	5	•
Delphinium carolinianum ssp. *virescens*	prairie larkspur	5	P-Forb	10	•	6	•
Deschampsia cespitosa	tufted hair grass	-5	P-Grass	8	R		9	10^P	9	•	S
Descurainia incana	hoary tansy mustard	5	B-Forb			9	•	•	•

continues

---

[8] See Swink and Wilhelm (1994), pp. 281 and 283.
[9] Federally designated as Endangered (USFWS 1994).
*Indicates nomenclature differs from Kartesz.
†Precedes scientific name cross-referenced in appendix C.

Table A.3. (*Continued*)

SCIENTIFIC NAME	COMMON NAME	CW	PHYSIOG	AR	IL	IN	IA	KS	MI	MO	MN	ND	NE	OH	OK	ON	SD	WI
Descurainia pinnata brachycarpa[10]	tansy mustard	5	A-Forb	•	7	•	•	•	☼	3	•	•	•	7^T	•	4	•	•
Desmanthus illinoensis	Illinois bundleflower	1	P-Forb	•	4	☼	•	•	•	3	S	T	•	9	•		•	•
Desmodium canadense	showy tick trefoil	1	P-Forb	•	5	•	•	•	3	4	•		•	5	•	5	•	•
Desmodium ciliare	hairy tick trefoil	5	P-Forb	•	7	•	•	•	10	5			•	6	•	10		•
Desmodium illinoense	Illinois tick trefoil	5	P-Forb	•	5	•	•	•	6	4	•		•	10^E	•	10^X	•	•
Desmodium marilandicum	small-leaved tick trefoil	5	P-Forb	•	6	•			7	5				•		10		•
Desmodium obtusum	stiff tick trefoil	5	P-Forb	•	5	•			9	5				•				
Desmodium paniculatum[11]*	tall tick clover	5	P-Forb	•	2	•	•	•	4	3	•		•	4	•	6		•
Desmodium sessilifolium	sessile-leaved tick trefoil	5	P-Forb	•	6	•	S	•	8	5			•	8^E	•	10		
Digitaria cognata	fall witch grass	5	P-Grass	•	4	•	•	•	3	3	•		•	4	•	6	•	
Digitaria filiformis	slender crab grass	5	A-Grass	•	6	•	S	•	10^X	4			•	X	•		•	
Diodia teres	buttonweed	3	A-Forb	•	2	•	S	•	☼	2			•	•	•			•
Diospyros virginiana	persimmon	0	Tree	•	2	•				3				3	•			
Distichlis spicata	inland salt grass	5	P-Grass	•	☼	•	•	•		10	•		•			•	•	
Dodecatheon meadia	shooting star	4	P-Forb	•	6	•	•	•	10^T	5	S		•	10		•		•
Draba brachycarpa	short-fruited whitlow grass	5	A-Forb	•	2	•				0				E	•			
Draba reptans	common whitlow grass	5	A-Forb	•	3	•	•	•	8^T	2	•		•	7^E	•		•	
Dracopis amplexicaulis	coneflower	4	A-Forb	•	☼	•	•	•	☼	3^S			•	3	•			
Drosera intermedia	narrow-leaved sundew	-5	P-Forb		10^T	R	•		8		•		•	10^E		9		•
Echinacea angustifolia	narrow-leaved coneflower	5	P-Forb	•	•	•	•	•		10^S	•		•		•	•	•	
Echinacea pallida	pale purple coneflower	5	P-Forb	•	7	•	•	•	☼	7	•		•	E	•	9	•	T
Echinacea paradoxa	yellow glade coneflower	5	P-Forb	T						9								
Echinacea purpurea	purple coneflower	5	P-Forb	•	6	•	S	•	10	5			•	8	•	10	•	•
Eleocharis compressa	flat-stemmed spike rush	-5	P-Sedge	•	7	•	•	•	9^T	6	•		•	9^T	•	8	•	T
Eleocharis erythropoda	red-rooted spike rush	-5	P-Sedge	•	3	•	•	•	4	5	•		•	4	•	4	•	•

Scientific name	Common name	W	Phys													
Eleocharis palustris[12]	pale spike rush	−5	P-Sedge	•	8	•	•	•	5	•	•	•	•	4	•	•
Eleocharis smallii	Small's spike rush	−5	P-Sedge	•	5	•	•	5	5	•	•	5	•	4	•	•
Eleocharis tenuis verrucosa	slender spike rush	−3	P-Sedge	•	6	•	•	•	5	•	•	5	•	•	6	•
Eleocharis wolfii	Wolf's spike rush	−5	P-Sedge	•	10	S	•	5	10^E	E	T	E	•	E	•	X
Elymus canadensis	Canada wild rye	1	P-Grass	•	4	•	•	7	5	•	•	3	•	3	•	•
Elymus glaucus	blue wild rye	3	P-Grass	•	•	•	•	8^S	10	10	T	•	•	8	•	8
Elymus interruptus	wild rye	5	P-Grass	•	•	S	•	8	10	•	•	•	•	•	•	•
†*Elymus trachycaulus*	slender wheat grass	0	P-Grass	•	8	•	•	8	☼	•	•	8^T	•	•	7	•
Elymus trachycaulus subsecundus	bearded wheat grass	5	P-Grass	•	8^E	•	•	8	8	•	•	•	•	•	•	•
Elymus villosus	silky wild rye	3	P-Grass	•	4	•	•	5	4	•	•	4	•	4	7	•
Elymus virginicus	Virginia wild rye	−2	P-Grass	•	4	•	•	4	4	•	•	3	•	3	5	•
Epilobium coloratum	cinnamon willow herb	−5	P-Forb	•	3	•	•	3	6	T	•	2	•	2	3	•
Epilobium leptophyllum	fen willow herb	−5	P-Forb	•	9	•	•	6	10^E	•	•	7	•	7	7	•
Equisetum arvense	horsetail	0	Crptgm	•	0	•	•	0	0	•	•	0	•	0	0	•
Equisetum hyemale	scouring rush	−2	Crptgm	•	2	•	•	2	3	•	•	2	•	2	2	•
Equisetum laevigatum	smooth scouring rush	−3	Crptgm	•	4	•	•	2	4	•	•	8	•	8	7	•
Equisetum sylvaticum	wood horsetail	−3	Crptgm	•	10^E	T	•	5	4	T	•	7^P	•	7^P	7	•
Equisetum × ferrissii	intermediate scouring rush	0	Crptgm	•	2	•	•	•	3	•	•	4	•	4	•	•
Eragrostis spectabilis	purple love grass	5	P-Grass	•	3	•	•	3	3	•	•	4	•	4	2	6
Eragrostis trichodes	sand love grass	5	P-Grass	•	5	•	•	4	4	☼	•	2	•	2	•	•
Erechtites hieracifolia	fireweed	3	A-Forb	•	2	•	•	2	2	•	•	3	•	3	3	2
Erigeron annuus	annual fleabane	1	A-Forb	•	1	•	•	1	1	•	•	1	•	1	1	0

continues

10 Several recently discovered populations in Ohio appear to be introductions.

11 Included here *sensu lato*, conceptually encompassing material variously referred to as *D. dillenii*, *D. glabellum*, and *D. perplexum*.

12 See Gleason and Cronquist (1991).

*Indicates nomenclature differs from Kartesz.

†Precedes scientific name cross-referenced in appendix C.

Table A.3. (*Continued*)

SCIENTIFIC NAME	COMMON NAME	CW	PHYSIOG	AR	IL	IN	IA	KS	MI	MO	MN	ND	NE	OH	OK	ON	SD	WI
Erigeron glabellus	smooth fleabane	5	B-Forb								•		•				•	•
Erigeron philadelphicus	marsh fleabane	-3	B-Forb	•	3	•	•		2	3	•		•	2	1		•	•
Erigeron strigosus	daisy fleabane	1	A-Forb	•	2	•	•	•	4	3	•		•	1	0		•	•
Erigeron tenuis	slender rough fleabane	5	P-Forb	•						4								
Eriophorum angustifolium	narrow-leaved cotton grass	-5	P-Sedge		10	R	S		10				•				•	•
Eriophorum virginicum	rusty cotton grass	-5	P-Sedge		10^E	•	S		10				•	10	10		•	•
Eriophorum viridicarinatum	tall cotton grass	-5	P-Sedge		10^E	R			8				•	10^P	9		•	•
Eryngium leavenworthii	Leavenworth eryngo	5	A-Forb	•				•										
Eryngium prostratum	creeping coyote thistle	-5	P-Forb	•	5^E			•		6	•		•					
Eryngium yuccifolium	rattlesnake master	-1	P-Forb	•	8		•		10^T	8	S		•	10^P			•	•
Erysimum capitatum[13]	western wallflower	5	P-Forb	•	7		☼		☼	7	•		•	E		•	•	
Erysimum inconspicuum	small wormseed mustard	5	P-Forb	•	☼	☼	•		☼	☼	•		•	•		☼	•	☼
Erythronium mesochoreum	prairie dog-tooth violet	5	P-Forb		9^E		•		6	6								
Eupatorium altissimum	tall boneset	3	P-Forb	•	1		•		0	3	•		•	3	3		•	
Eupatorium maculatum	spotted Joe-Pye weed	-5	P-Forb	•	5		•		4	10^E	•		•	6	3		•	•
Eupatorium perfoliatum	common boneset	-4	P-Forb	•	4		•		4	5	•	T	•	3	2		•	•
Eupatorium serotinum	late boneset	-1	P-Forb	•	1		•		0	1	•		•	3		☼	•	
Euphorbia corollata	flowering spurge	5	P-Forb	•	3		•		4	3	•		•	4	7		•	•
Euphorbia dentata	toothed spurge	5	A-Forb	•	0		•		☼	0	•		•	☼		☼	•	
Euphorbia marginata	snow-on-the-mountain	3	A-Forb	☼	☼	☼	•		☼	3	•	☼	•	☼	☼	☼	•	☼
Euphorbia spathulata	prairie spurge	5	A-Forb	•	10^E		•			5								
†*Euthamia graminifolia*	grass-leaved goldenrod	-2	P-Forb	•	3		•		3	3	•		•	2	2		•	•
Euthamia gymnospermoides	Great Plains goldenrod	-1	P-Forb	•	5		•		8	3	•			T			•	
Euthamia leptocephala	western bushy goldenrod	3	P-Forb	•	5					8								

continues

Scientific name	Common name	Physiognomy	C
Evolvulus nuttallianus	Ozark morning glory	P-Forb	5
Festuca paradoxa	cluster fescue	P-Grass	0
Filipendula rubra	queen of the prairie	P-Forb	-5
Fimbristylis autumnalis	autumn sedge	A-Sedge	-4
Fimbristylis dichotoma	tall fimbry	A-Sedge	-5
Fimbristylis puberula	glade fimbry	P-Sedge	3
Fragaria virginiana	wild strawberry	P-Forb	1
Froelichia floridana	large cottonweed	A-Forb	5
Froelichia gracilis	small cottonweed	A-Forb	5
Fuirena simplex	umbrella grass	P-Sedge	-5
Gaillardia aristata	northern blanket flower	P-Forb	5
Galium boreale	northern bedstraw	P-Forb	0
Galium concinnum	shining bedstraw	P-Forb	3
Galium obtusum	wild madder	P-Forb	-4
Galium pilosum	hairy bedstraw	P-Forb	5
Galium tinctorium	stiff bedstraw	P-Forb	-5
Galium virgatum	dwarf bedstraw	A-Forb	5
Gamochaeta purpurea	early cudweed	A-Forb	3
Gaura biennis	biennial gaura	B-Forb	4
Gaura coccinea	scarlet gaura	P-Forb	5
†*Gaura longiflora*	large-flowered gaura	B-Forb	5
Gaura parviflora	small-flowered gaura	B-Forb	5
†*Gentiana alba*	yellowish gentian	P-Forb	3
Gentiana andrewsii	closed gentian	P-Forb	-3

---

13 *Sensu* Rollins (1993).

*Indicates nomenclature differs from Kartesz.

†Precedes scientific name cross-referenced in appendix C.

Table A.3. *(Continued)*

SCIENTIFIC NAME	COMMON NAME	CW	PHYSIOG	AR	IL	IN	IA	KS	MI	MO	MN	ND	NE	OH	OK	ON	SD	WI
Gentiana puberulenta	downy gentian	3	P-Forb	•	9	T	•	•	10^E	9	•	•	•	10^E		10	•	•
Gentiana saponaria	soapwort gentian	-2	P-Forb	•	9	•			10^X					10^E	•			•
†*Gentianella quinquefolia*	stiff gentian	0	A-Forb	•	7	•	•	•	9^T	10	•	T	•	9		9	•	•
†*Gentianopsis crinita*	fringed gentian	-4	A-Forb		10	•		•	8		•		•	8^P		8	•	S
Gentianopsis procera	small fringed gentian	-5	A-Forb		10	•	S		8		•		•	8^P		8	•	•
Geranium carolinianum	Carolina cranesbill	5	A-Forb	•	2	•	•	•	4	0	•		•	4	•	7	•	•
Geum triflorum	prairie smoke	5	P-Forb	•	10	•	•	•	10^T		•		•				•	•
Glandularia bipinnatifida	Dakota verbena	5	P-Forb	•	•	☼	•		☼	☼	•							
Glandularia canadensis	rose vervain	5	P-Forb	•	7	☼	•	•	4	5	•		•	2	•	3	•	•
Glyceria striata	fowl manna grass	-5	P-Grass	•	4	•	•		4	4	•		•		•		•	•
Glycyrrhiza lepidota	wild licorice	4	P-Forb	•	☼			•	3	3	•		•		•		•	S
Gnaphalium obtusifolium	old-field balsam	5	B-Forb	•	2	•			2	2	•		•	2		4		•
Grindelia lanceolata	spiny-toothed gumweed	5	P-Forb	•						3				☼				
Grindelia squarrosa	gum plant	3	B-Forb	☼	☼	☼		☼	1	1	•		•	☼	•		•	☼
Hedeoma hispida	rough pennyroyal	5	A-Forb	•	2	•	•	•	3	3	•		•	8^T		7	•	•
Hedyotis nigricans	narrow-leaved bluets	5	P-Forb	•	8	R	•	•	8	5	•		•	8^P			•	•
Helenium autumnale	sneezeweed	-4	P-Forb	•	3	•		•	3	5	•	•	•	4	•	7	•	•
Helenium flexuosum	purple-headed sneezeweed	-1	P-Forb	•	4	•		•	3	3	☼		•	☼			•	•
Helianthemum bicknellii	rockrose	5	P-Forb	•	7	•	•	•	10	6	•	E	•	9^T		9	•	☼
Helianthemum canadense	common rockrose	5	P-Forb	•	7	•			8	10^S	•			9^T		9	•	•
Helianthus angustifolius	swamp sunflower	-2	P-Forb	•	10^T	☼				7^E						☼			☼
Helianthus annuus	common sunflower	1	A-Forb	•	☼	☼	•	☼	5	0	☼		•	☼	•	4	•	☼
Helianthus decapetalus	pale sunflower	5	P-Forb	•	5	•			5	4	•		•	4	•	4	•	•
Helianthus divaricatus	woodland sunflower	5	P-Forb	•	5	•			5	6	•		•	5	•	7	•	•

Scientific Name	Common Name	C	Physiognomy					
Helianthus giganteus	tall sunflower	−3	P-Forb	9^E	5		6	6
Helianthus grosseserratus	sawtooth sunflower	−2	P-Forb	2	2	4	4	6
Helianthus hirsutus	oblong sunflower	5	P-Forb	5	10^S	4	5	☼
Helianthus maximiliani	Maximilian sunflower	5	P-Forb	☼	☼	5	☼	☼
Helianthus mollis	downy sunflower	5	P-Forb	7	9^T	6	8^T	☼
Helianthus nuttallii	Nuttall's sunflower	−3	P-Forb					☼
Helianthus occidentalis	western sunflower	4	P-Forb	7	8	5	7^P	
†*Helianthus pauciflorus*	showy sunflower	5	P-Forb	6	5	5	4	8
Helianthus petiolaris	plains sunflower	5	A-Forb	☼	☼	☼	☼	☼
Helianthus salicifolius	willow-leaved sunflower	5	P-Forb	☼		8		
Helianthus strumosus	pale-leaved sunflower	5	P-Forb	4	4	4	5	7
Helianthus tuberosus	Jerusalem artichoke	0	P-Forb	3	6	3	3	☼
Helictotrichon hookeri	spike oats	5	P-Grass					
Heliopsis helianthoides	false sunflower	5	P-Forb	5	5	5	5	3
Heliotropium tenellum	glade heliotrope	5	A-Forb	10^E (T)		6		
†*Heracleum maximum*	cow parsnip	−3	P-Forb	6	3	6	4	3
Heterotheca villosa	golden aster	5	P-Forb	5		1	☼	
Heuchera americana	alum root	4	P-Forb	7	8	7	6	9
Heuchera richardsonii	prairie alum root	1	P-Forb	7	8	5		
Hexalectris spicata	crested coral root	5	P-Forb	10^E (R)		8	E	
Hieracium canadense	canada hawkweed	5	P-Forb	5	3		10	7
Hieracium gronovii	hairy hawkweed	5	P-Forb	5	5	4	6	9
Hieracium longipilum	long-bearded hawkweed	5	P-Forb	6	6	5	7^E	10
Hieracium scabrum	rough hawkweed	5	P-Forb	5	3	6	5	7

continues

---

*Indicates nomenclature differs from Kartesz.

†Precedes scientific name cross-referenced in appendix C.

Table A.3. (Continued)

SCIENTIFIC NAME	COMMON NAME	CW	PHYSIOG	AR	IL	IN	IA	KS	MI	MO	MN	ND	NE	OH	OK	ON	SD	WI
Hieracium umbellatum	narrow-leaved hawkweed	5	P-Forb	•					7			•	•			☼	•	•
Hierochloe odorata	sweet grass	-3	P-Grass	•	7	•	•		9		•	•	•	8	•	5	5	S
Houstonia caerulea	bluets	0	A-Forb	•	7	•		•		6				4	•	10		S
Houstonia longifolia	long-leaved bluets	5	P-Forb	•	7	•	•	•	6	5	•		•	7	•	8	•	•
Houstonia pusilla	least bluets	4	A-Forb	•	3	•	•	•		3					•		•	
Hymenopappus scabiosaeus	old plainsman	5	B-Forb	•	9					7			•	6				
Hypericum drummondii	nits and lice	3	A-Forb	•	6	•	S	•	4	4				6	•			
Hypericum gentianoides	orange grass	3	A-Forb	•	6	•	E	•	6^S	5				4	•	10		•
Hypericum kalmianum	Kalm's St. John's wort	-2	Shrub		10^E	W			10		•			10^T		9		•
Hypericum majus	sand St. John's wort	-3	A-Forb	•	7	•	•		4	10^E	•	•	•	7^P	•	5	•	•
Hypericum mutilum	weak St. John's wort	-3	P-Forb	•	5	•	•	•	5	4	•		•	5	•	6		•
Hypericum punctatum	spotted St. John's wort	-1	P-Forb	•	3	•	•	•	4	3	•		•	3	•	5		•
Hypericum sphaerocarpum	round-fruited St. John's wort	3	P-Forb	•	5	•	•		8^T	5			•	7	•	6		T
Hypoxis hirsuta	yellow star grass	0	P-Forb	•	6	•	•	•	10	4	•		•	7	•	10	•	•
†*Ionactis linariifolius*	flax-leaved aster	5	P-Forb	•	10	T	S			10				7	•			•
Ipomoea lacunosa	small morning glory	-3	A-Forb	•	1	•	•	•		1			•	3				
Ipomoea pandurata	wild sweet potato	3	P-Forb	•	2	•	•	6^T		2			•	3	•	9		
Iris virginica shrevei	blue flag iris	-5	P-Forb	•	5	•	•	•	5	6	•		•	6	•	5		
Isoetes butleri	Butler's quillwort	-5	Crptgm	•	10^E					8								
Iva annua	marsh elder	0	A-Forb	•	0	•	S	•		0		•		☼				
Juncus acuminatus	sharp-fruited rush	-5	P-Forb	•	4	•	•	•	8	4			•	3	•	6	•	•
Juncus alpinoarticulatus fuscescens	Richardson's rush	-5	P-Forb	•	8^E	•	S	•	5	10^X	•	•	•	10^T		5	•	5
Juncus balticus	lake shore rush	-5	P-Forb	•	4	R	•	•	4	10^E	•	•	•	9^P	•	5	•	•
Juncus biflorus	two-flowered rush	-3	P-Forb	•	5	•	•		8^S	5				4	•	10		•

Scientific Name	Common Name	C	Physiognomy												
Juncus brachycarpus	short-fruited rush	-3	P-Forb	•	5	•	•	9^T	7	•	•	•	5	•	10	•
Juncus brachycephalus	short-headed rush	-5	P-Forb	•	9	•	•	7	7	•	•	E	6	•	7	•
Juncus brachyphyllus	small-headed rush	4	P-Forb	•		•	•	8	8	•	•	•	•	•	•	•
Juncus dudleyi	Dudley's rush	0	P-Forb	•	4	•	•	1	6	•	•	•	1	•	1	•
Juncus effusus	common rush	-5	P-Forb	•	4	S	•	3	5	•	•	•	1	•	4	•
Juncus greenei	Greene's rush	0	P-Forb	•	7	S	•	10		•	•	7^E	•	9	
Juncus interior	inland rush	-1	P-Forb	•	3	•	•		4	•	•	T	•	•	
Juncus longistylis	large-flowered rush	-3	P-Forb	•											
Juncus marginatus	grass-leaved rush	-3	P-Forb	•	5	S	•	8	5	T	•	6	•	9	
Juncus nodatus	stout rush	-5	P-Forb	•	6	•	•		6	•	•	•	•	•	
Juncus nodosus	joint rush	-5	P-Forb	•	6	•	•	5	10^E	•	•	4	•	5	
Juncus scirpoides	round-leaved rush	-4	P-Forb	•	10	T	•	9^T	9	•	•	7^T	•	9	
Juncus secundus	secund rush	1	P-Forb	•	6	E	•		4	•	•	1	•	0	
Juncus tenuis	path rush	2	P-Forb	•	0	•	•	1	0	•	•	1	•		
Juncus torreyi	Torrey's rush	-3	P-Forb	•	3	•	•	4	6	•	•	3	•	3	
Juncus validus	round-headed rush	-3	P-Forb	•		•	•		10^X	•	•				
Juncus vaseyi	Vasey's rush	-3	P-Forb	•	10^E	S	•	10^T	9	T	•			9	S
Juniperus virginiana	red cedar	3	Tree	•	1	•	•	3	2	•	•	3	•	4	•
†*Koeleria macrantha*	june grass	5	P-Grass	•	7	•	•	9	6	•	•	10^E	•	10	•
Krigia biflora	false dandelion	3	P-Forb	•	7	•	•	5	5	•	•	7	•	10	•
Krigia caespitosa	opposite-leaved dwarf dandelion	5	A-Forb	•	1	T	•	2	2	•	•	•			
Krigia dandelion	potato dandelion	3	P-Forb	•	6	•	☼	5	5	•	•	E	•		
Krigia occidentalis	western dwarf dandelion	5	A-Forb	•		•	•	7	7	•	•		•		
Krigia virginica	dwarf dandelion	5	A-Forb	•	4	E	•	4	3	•	•	9^T	•	•	•

---

*Indicates nomenclature differs from Kartesz.

†Precedes scientific name cross-referenced in appendix C.

Table A.3. (*Continued*)

SCIENTIFIC NAME	COMMON NAME	CW	PHYSIOG	AR	IL	IN	IA	KS	MI	MO	MN	ND	NE	OH	OK	ON	SD	WI
Lactuca canadensis	wild lettuce	2	B-Forb	•	1	•	•	•	2	2	•	•	•	2	•	3	•	•
Lactuca ludoviciana	western wild lettuce	5	B-Forb	•	10[E]	X	•	•	2	10[X]	•	•	•	2	•	•	•	•
Lactuca tatarica[14]	western blue lettuce	5	P-Forb	•	☼	•	•	•	10[T]	10[E]	•	•	•	•	•	•	•	•
Lathyrus ochroleucus	pale vetchling	5	P-Forb	•	10[T]	X	•	•	8	•	•	•	•	9[T]	•	8	•	•
Lathyrus palustris	marsh vetchling	-3	P-Forb	•	6	•	•	•	7	10	•	•	•	7	•	6	•	•
Lathyrus venosus	veiny pea	0	P-Forb	•	9	T	•	•	8	8	•	•	•	8[E]	•	8	•	•
Leavenworthia uniflora	Michaux's leavenworthia	4	A-Forb	•	•	E	•	•	•	7	•	•	•	T	•	•	•	•
Lechea intermedia	savanna pinweed	5	P-Forb	•	10[E]	•	T	•	6	7	•	•	•	7[T]	•	7	•	•
Lechea mucronata	hairy pinweed	5	P-Forb	•	7	•	T	•	5	5	•	•	•	7[T]	•	9	•	•
Lechea stricta	bushy pinweed	5	P-Forb	•	8	X	•	•	10[S]	4	•	E	•	•	•	•	•	•
Lechea tenuifolia	slender-leaved pinweed	5	P-Forb	•	6	•	•	•	3	4	•	•	•	8[E]	•	3	•	•
Leersia oryzoides	rice cut grass	-5	P-Grass	•	3	•	•	•	•	•	•	•	•	1	•	•	•	E
Lepidium virginicum	common peppergrass	4	A-Forb	•	0	•	•	•	0	0	•	•	•	1	•	0	•	•
Lespedeza capitata	round-headed bush clover	3	P-Forb	•	4	•	•	•	5	6	•	•	•	6	•	7	•	•
Lespedeza leptostachya[4]	prairie bush clover	5	P-Forb	•	10[E]	T	T	•	•	•	E	•	•	•	•	•	•	E
Lespedeza repens	creeping bush clover	5	P-Forb	•	6	•	S	•	•	4	•	•	•	7	•	•	•	•
Lespedeza stuevei	Stueve's bush clover	5	P-Forb	•	7	•	•	•	•	4	•	•	•	•	•	•	•	•
Lespedeza violacea	violet bush clover	5	P-Forb	•	5	•	•	•	5	4	•	•	•	4	•	10	•	S
Lespedeza virginica	slender bush clover	5	P-Forb	•	5	•	•	•	7	5	•	•	•	2	•	10	•	T
Lesquerella gracilis nuttallii	slender bladderpod	5	A-Forb	•	☼	•	•	•	☼	☼	•	•	•	•	•	•	•	•
Lesquerella ludoviciana	silvery bladderpod	5	P-Forb	•	10[E]	S	E	•	•	•	E	•	•	•	•	•	•	T
Leucospora multifida	obe-wan-conobea	-4	A-Forb	•	3	•	•	•	8	4	•	•	•	8	•	8	•	•
Liatris aspera	rough blazing star	5	P-Forb	•	7	•	•	•	4	6	•	•	•	6	•	10	•	•
Liatris cylindracea	cylindrical blazing star	5	P-Forb	•	8	•	•	•	5	7	•	•	•	8[T]	•	10	•	•

Scientific name	Common name	C	Physiognomy							
Liatris ligulistylis	blazing star	5	P-Forb	•	9		9[S]	•	•	
Liatris mucronata	narrow-leaved gayfeather	5	P-Forb	•		•	10	•	•	
Liatris punctata	dotted blazing star	5	P-Forb	•	☼		10[X] 10[W]	•	•	E
Liatris pycnostachya	prairie blazing star	1	P-Forb	•	6	T	6	•	•	
Liatris spicata	marsh blazing star	0	P-Forb	•	7	W	8 10[X]	8	9[R]	S
Liatris squarrosa	scaly blazing star	5	P-Forb	•	7		5	8[P]	7	
Lilium michiganense	Michigan lily	−1	P-Forb	•	6		5 7	7	8	
Lilium philadelphicum	prairie lily	1	P-Forb	•	10		10	8[T]	7	
Linum medium texanum	small yellow flax	3	P-Forb	•	7	S	7 5	6	8	
Linum rigidum	stiff-stemmed flax	5	A-Forb	☼	☼		☼	☼	10	
Linum sulcatum	grooved yellow flax	5	A-Forb	•	8	R	8[S] 5	8[P]	8	
Liparis loeselii	green twayblade	−4	P-Forb	T	8	W	5 10	9	5	
Lithospermum canescens	hoary puccoon	5	P-Forb	•	6		10 6	7	10	
Lithospermum caroliniense	puccoon	5	P-Forb	•	7		10 6	9[T]	8	
Lithospermum incisum	fringed puccoon	5	P-Forb	•	8	E	10[X] 7		10	
Lobelia cardinalis	cardinal flower	−5	P-Forb	•	6		7 6	7	7	
Lobelia kalmii	bog lobelia	−5	P-Forb	•	10	S	7	9	9	
Lobelia siphilitica	great blue lobelia	−4	P-Forb	•	4		4 4	4	6	
Lobelia spicata	pale spiked lobelia	0	P-Forb	•	5		4 5	6	8	
Lomatium foeniculaceum	hairy parsley	5	P-Forb			E	9			
Lomatium orientale	biscuit root	5	P-Forb			T				
Lotus unifoliatus	Clements' prairie trefoil	5	A-Forb	☼	☼					
Ludwigia alternifolia	seedbox	−5	P-Forb	•	5		8[T] 4	5	10	

[4] Federally designated as Threatened (USFWS 1994).

[14] Including subspecies *oblongifolia* and *pulchella*.

*Indicates nomenclature differs from Kartesz.

†Precedes scientific name cross-referenced in appendix C.

continues

Table A.3. (*Continued*)

SCIENTIFIC NAME	COMMON NAME	CW	PHYSIOG	AR	IL	IN	IA	KS	MI	MO	MN	ND	NE	OH	OK	ON	SD	WI
Ludwigia palustris	water purslane	−5	P-Forb	•	4	•	•	•	4	5	•			4	•	5		•
Ludwigia polycarpa	false loosestrife	−5	P-Forb	•	5	•	•	•	6	6	•	•	•	7	•	8	•	•
Lupinus perennis occidentalis★	wild lupine	5	P-Forb	•	8	T	•		7					10^P	•	10	•	•
Luzula multiflora[15]	wood rush	3	P-Forb	•	5	•	•	•	5	4	•	•	•	5^T	•	6	•	•
Lycopus americanus	common water horehound	−5	P-Forb	•	3	•	•	•	2	4	•	•	•	3	•	4	•	•
Lycopus asper	rough water horehound	−5	P-Forb	•	1	•	•	•	☼	10	•	•	•	☼	•	☼	•	•
Lycopus uniflorus	northern bugle weed	−5	P-Forb	•	7	•	•	•	2	5	•	•	•	3	•	5	•	•
Lygodesmia juncea	skeleton plant	5	P-Forb	☼				•		10^W	•	•	•		•		•	•
Lysimachia ciliata	fringed loosestrife	−3	P-Forb	•	4	•	•	•	4	5	•	•	•	4	•	4	•	•
Lysimachia hybrida	hybrid loosestrife	−5	P-Forb	•	7	•	•	•	10^S	6	•	•	•	6	•		•	•
Lysimachia lanceolata	lance-leaved loosestrife	0	P-Forb	•	6	•	•	•	9	4				8	•			
Lysimachia quadriflora	narrow-leaved loosestrife	−5	P-Forb	•	8	•	•	•	10	8	•	•	•	8	•	10	•	•
Lysimachia terrestris	swamp candles	−5	P-Forb		8	•	•	•	6					6		6		•
Lysimachia thyrsiflora	tufted loosestrife	−5	P-Forb	•	7	•	•	•	6	10^E	•	•	•	6	•	7	•	•
Lythrum alatum	winged loosestrife	−5	P-Forb	•	5	•	•	•	9	6	•	•	•	7	•	5	•	•
†*Machaeranthera pinnatifida*	cutleaf ironplant	5	P-Forb	☼				•			S	•	•		•		•	•
†*Maianthemum stellatum*	starry false Solomon's seal	1	P-Forb	•	5	•	•	•	5	7	•	•	•	5	•	6	•	•
Malus ioensis	Iowa crab	5	Tree	•	3	•	•	•	4	3	•		•		•		•	•
Malvastrum hispidum	false mallow	5	A-Forb	•	5^E		S	•	5^W				•		•			
Manfreda virginica	American aloe	5	P-Forb	•	8	W			7					T	•			
Marshallia caespitosa	Barbara's buttons	5	P-Forb	•					9^S						•			
Melanthium virginicum	bunch flower	−4	P-Forb	•	10^T	E	•	•	7					10^T	•			
Melica nitens	tall melic grass	5	P-Grass	•	7	t	•	•	6	6	T	•		E	•		S	•
†*Mentha canadensis*	wild mint	−5	P-Forb	•	4	•	•	•	3	5	•	•	•	2	•	3	•	•

Scientific name	Common name	Type										
Mentzelia oligosperma	stickleaf	P-Forb	5	•	10	•	•	•	6	•	•	•
†*Mimosa quadrivalvis nuttallii*	sensitive briar	H-Vine	5	•	7	S	•	•	6	•	•	•
Mimulus ringens	monkey flower	P-Forb	−5	•	5	S	•	☼	5	5	5	•
Minuartia michauxii	stiff sandwort	P-Forb	5	•	10	R	S	10	9	5	10^P	6	•
Minuartia patula	slender sandwort	A-Forb	5	•	8^T	•	•	•	7	E	8	•
Mirabilis albida	pale umbrellawort	P-Forb	5	•	☼	•	☼	☼	5	☼	•
Mirabilis hirsuta	hairy umbrellawort	P-Forb	5	•	5^E	☼	☼	☼	3	☼	•
Mirabilis linearis	narrow-leaved umbrellawort	P-Forb	5	•	☼	☼	•	8	•
Mirabilis nyctaginea	wild four o'clock	P-Forb	5	•	☼	☼	☼	☼	0	☼	☼	☼
Monarda citriodora	lemon mint	A-Forb	5	•	☼	•	8	•
Monarda fistulosa	wild bergamot	P-Forb	3	•	4	•	•	2	4	5	6	•
Monarda punctata	spotted bee balm	P-Forb	5	•	5	S	•	4	9	7^E	9	•
Muhlenbergia asperifolia	scratch grass	P-Grass	−3	•	☼	☼	☼	☼	☼	☼	☼	•
Muhlenbergia cuspidata	prairie satin grass	P-Grass	5	•	10	E	•	10^X	10	E	E	•
Muhlenbergia frondosa	common satin grass	P-Grass	−3	•	3	•	•	3	3	3	5	•
Muhlenbergia glabrifloris	smooth satin grass	P-Grass	5	•	7	•	•	7	•
Muhlenbergia glomerata	marsh wild timothy	P-Grass	−4	•	10	•	10	9	7	•
Muhlenbergia mexicana	leafy satin grass	P-Grass	−3	•	4	•	•	3	5	1	•
Muhlenbergia racemosa	upland wild timothy	P-Grass	−3	•	0	•	☼	4	•
Muhlenbergia richardsonis	mat muhly grass	P-Grass	−1	•	10^T	10^T	•
Nassella viridula	green needlegrass	P-Grass	5	•	☼	•	•
Nemastylis geminiflora	celestial lily	P-Forb	5	•	10^W	•
Nemastylis nuttallii	Nuttall's prairie iris	P-Forb	5	•	9^S	•
†*Nothocalais cuspidata*	prairie dandelion	P-Forb	5	•	10^E	10^R	S	S	•

continues

15 Including *Luzula bulbosa*.
*Indicates nomenclature differs from Kartesz.
†Precedes scientific name cross-referenced in appendix C.

Table A.3. (Continued)

SCIENTIFIC NAME	COMMON NAME	CW	PHYSIOG	AR	IL	IN	IA	KS	MI	MO	MN	ND	NE	OH	OK	ON	SD	WI
Nothoscordum bivalve	false garlic	5	P-Forb	•	5	R	•	•		4				T	•	•		•
†*Nuttallanthus canadensis*	blue toadflax	5	A-Forb	•	4	•	•	•	8	3	•		•	8[E]	•	4	•	•
Nuttallanthus texanus	southern blue toadflax	5	A-Forb	•	4			•		3							•	•
Oenothera biennis[16]	common evening primrose	3	B-Forb	•	1	•	•	•	2	0	•	•	•	2	•	0	•	•
Oenothera clelandii	sand evening primrose	5	B-Forb	•	5	•	•	7							•	9		
Oenothera fruticosa s.l.	northern sundrops	5	P-Forb		9	•		7	7	10[S]				5	•	☼		
Oenothera laciniata	ragged evening primrose	3	A-Forb	•	2	•	•	•	3	1	•	T	•	3	•	☼	•	☼
Oenothera linifolia	thread-leaved sundrops	5	A-Forb	•	8			•		4								
Oenothera macrocarpa	Missouri primrose	5	P-Forb		10			•		7					•			
Oenothera nuttallii	white evening primrose	5	P-Forb		☼			•	☼		•	•	•		•		•	☼
Oenothera perennis	small sundrops	0	P-Forb	T	8[E]	T	T	•	5	10[E]	•		•	4	•	6		•
Oenothera pilosella	prairie sundrops	1	P-Forb	•	6	•	•	•	☼	6	S		•	4	•	8		☼
Oenothera rhombipetala	western sand evening primrose	5	B-Forb	•	☼	•	•	•	☼	3	S	T	•		•		•	•
Oenothera speciosa	showy evening primrose	5	P-Forb	•	☼	☼	S	•	•	2				☼	•			
Oenothera triloba	stemless evening primrose	5	A-Forb	•	☼	X	•	•		9[W]			•	X	•			
Onoclea sensibilis	sensitive fern	−3	Crptgm	T	5	•	•	•	2	6	•	T	•	3	•	4	•	S
Onosmodium molle hispidissimum	marbleseed	5	P-Forb	•	5	E	•	•	•	4			•	8[P]	•	8	•	S
Onosmodium molle occidentale	false gromwell	5	P-Forb	•	8	•	•	•		4	•		•		•	•	•	
Onosmodium molle subsetosum	Ozark false gromwell	5	P-Forb	•				•		6								
Ophioglossum engelmannii	glade adder's tongue	4	Crptgm	•	9	R	•	•		6				E	•			
Opuntia fragilis	little prickly pear	5	Shrub		10[E]	•	T	•	10[E]		•	•	•	•	•		•	T
Opuntia humifusa	prickly pear	5	Shrub	•	5	E	•	•	7	4			•	9[P]	•	10[E]	•	•
Opuntia macrorhiza	plains prickly pear	5	Shrub	•	8	•	E	•	10[R]		S				•		•	
Orbexilum onobrychis	French grass	5	P-Forb	•	6	•	E	•	7	7			•	9	•	10		•

Species	C	Common name	Physiognomy													
Orbexilum pedunculatum	5	Sampson's snakeroot	P-Forb	•	6	•	•	•	•	0	7	•	•	8^P	•	•
Orobanche fasciculata	5	clustered broom rape	P-Forb	•	10^E	E	E	S	•	10^T	7	S	•	•	10	T
Orobanche ludoviciana	5	Louisiana broom rape	P-Forb	•	10^E	T	T	S	•	8	10^E	S	T	X	8	S
Orobanche uniflora	5	one-flowered broom rape	P-Forb	•	8	•	•	•	•	8	7	T	•	7	8	S
Orthocarpus luteus	5	owl clover	A-Forb	•	•	•	•	•	•	•	•	•	•	•	•	•
Oxalis dillenii	5	yellow wood sorrel	P-Forb	•	0	•	•	•	•	0	0	•	•	0	0	•
Oxalis violacea	5	violet wood sorrel	P-Forb	•	5	•	•	•	•	10^T	5	•	•	6	6	•
Oxypolis rigidior	-5	cowbane	P-Forb	•	7	•	•	•	•	6	7	•	•	8	8	•
Oxytropis lambertii	4	loco weed	P-Forb	•	•	•	•	•	•	10^W	10^W	•	•	•	9	•
Panicum anceps	-3	beaked panic grass	P-Grass	•	3	•	•	•	•	2	2	•	•	•	7	•
Panicum bicknellii★	5	Bicknell's panic grass	P-Grass	•	•	E	•	•	•	8	8	•	•	8^T	8	•
Panicum boreale★	0	northern panic grass	P-Grass	•	10^E	R	E	E	•	7	7	•	•	8^T	6	•
Panicum clandestinum★	-3	deer tongue grass	P-Grass	•	4	•	•	•	•	3	4	•	•	3	8	•
Panicum depauperatum★	5	starved panic grass	P-Grass	•	5	•	•	•	•	4	4	•	•	9	6	•
Panicum flexile	-4	wiry panic grass	A-Grass	•	7	•	•	•	•	8	4	•	•	4	8	•
†*Panicum lanuginosum implicatum*[17]★	3	slender-stemmed panic grass	P-Grass	•	1	•	•	•	•	3	2	•	•	2	2	•
Panicum lanuginosum lindheimeri★	-1	smooth woolly panic grass	P-Grass	•	4	•	•	•	•	8	3	•	•	2	8	•
Panicum leibergii★	2	prairie panic grass	P-Grass	•	7	T	T	•	•	10^T	9^S	•	•	E	10	•
Panicum linearifolium★	5	slender-leaved panic grass	P-Grass	•	7	•	•	T	•	4	4	•	•	4	6	•
Panicum oligosanthes s.l.★	3	Scribner's panic grass	P-Grass	•	3	•	•	•	•	5	3	•	•	7	7	•
Panicum perlongum★	5	long-stalked panic grass	P-Grass	•	9	•	•	•	•	10	7	•	•	E	10	•
Panicum polyanthes★	5	small-fruited panic grass	P-Grass	•	6	•	•	•	•	10	7	•	•	•	•	•
Panicum praecocius★	5	early-branching panic grass	P-Grass	•	7	•	•	•	•	8	5	•	T	9	9	•
Panicum rigidulum	-3	Munro grass	P-Grass	•	5	•	•	•	•	7	3	•	•	4	9	•

[16] Including *O. stringosa* and *O. villosa*.

[17] Including variety *fasciculatum*.

★Indicates nomenclature differs from Kartesz.

†Precedes scientific name cross-referenced in appendix C.

continues

Table A.3. (Continued)

SCIENTIFIC NAME	COMMON NAME	CW	PHYSIOG	AR	IL	IN	IA	KS	MI	MO	MN	ND	NE	OH	OK	ON	SD	WI
Panicum scoparium★	velvety panic grass	-3	P-Grass	•	9	E	•	•		8				•	•			
Panicum sphaerocarpon★	round-fruited panic grass	3	P-Grass	•	7	•			5	5				4	•	8	•	•
Panicum virgatum	switch grass	-1	P-Grass	•	4	•	•	•	4	4	•	•	•	4	•	6	•	•
Panicum wilcoxianum★	Wilcox's panic grass	5	P-Grass		10	•	•				•	•	•		•		•	S
Parnassia glauca	grass of Parnassus	-5	P-Forb		10	•	•		8		•	•		10	•	8	•	•
Paronychia canadensis	tall forked chickweed	5	A-Forb	•	5	•	•	•	8	4			•	4	•	10	•	•
Paronychia fastigiata	low forked chickweed	5	A-Forb	•	5	•	•	•	8^S	5	S		•	7	•	10	•	•
Parthenium integrifolium	wild quinine	5	P-Forb	•	7	•			6	6	S		•	•	•			T
Parthenium integrifolium hispidum	hairy feverfew	5	P-Forb	•		•				9	E				•			
†Pascopyron smithii	western wheat grass	2	P-Grass	•	☼	☼	•	•	☼	0	•	•	•	☼			•	☼
Paspalum floridanum	Florida bead grass	-3	P-Grass	•	7	•		•		5				☼	•			
Paspalum laeve	smooth lens grass	5	P-Grass	•	2	•		•		2					•			
Paspalum pubiflorum	hairy-flowered bead grass	-3	P-Grass	•	3	•		•		4					•			
†Paspalum setaceum	hairy lens grass	5	P-Grass	•	3	•	•	•	4	3	•		•	3	•	8		
†Pedicularis canadensis	lousewort	2	P-Forb	•	7	•	•	•	10	5	•	•	•	6	•	7	•	•
Pedicularis lanceolata	swamp lousewort	-4	P-Forb	•	9	•	•	•	8	9	•	•	•	8	•	9	•	•
Pediomelum argophyllum	silvery scurfy pea	5	P-Forb		☼		•	•	9^W		•	•	•		•		•	S
Pediomelum esculentum	prairie turnip	5	P-Forb	•			•	•	10		•	•	•		•		•	S
Penstemon albidus	white beard tongue	5	P-Forb				S	•			•	•	•		•			
Penstemon cobaea	showy beard tongue	5	P-Forb	•	☼		S	•	10				•		•			
Penstemon digitalis	foxglove beard tongue	1	P-Forb	•	4	•	•	•	2	4	•		•	3	•	6		•
Penstemon gracilis	slender beard tongue	5	P-Forb	☼	☼	☼	T	10^E			☼	•	•		•		•	
Penstemon grandiflorus	large-flowered beard tongue	5	P-Forb	•	8^E	•	•		10^E		•	•	•		•		•	•
Penstemon hirsutus	hairy beard tongue	5	P-Forb	•	8	•	•		5		•		•	6	•	7	•	S

Scientific name		Physiognomy	Common name												
Penstemon pallidus	5	P-Forb	pale beard tongue	•	6	•	5	4	☼	•			7^T	•	S
Penstemon tubaeflorus★	5	P-Forb	funnelform beard tongue	•	5	X	5	5	•	•			X	•	•
Pentaphylloides floribunda	-3	Shrub	shrubby cinquefoil	•	10	•	10		•	•			10	9	
Phacelia gilioides	5	A-Forb	small-flowered phacelia	•	10	•		3	•	•					•
Phacelia hirsuta	5	A-Forb	hairy phacelia	•		•		4	•	•					•
Phalaris caroliniana	5	A-Grass	May grass	•		•	☼	☼	•	•			☼	•	
Phlox bifida	5	P-Forb	sand phlox	•	7	S	10^T	8	•	•			•	•	S
Phlox glaberrima	-3	P-Forb	marsh phlox	•	6	•		8	•	•		P	•	•	E
Phlox maculata	-5	P-Forb	sweet William phlox	•	10	•	10^T	10^R	•	•		7	☼	•	
Phlox pilosa	1	P-Forb	sand prairie phlox	•	7	•	7	6	•	•		7	9	•	
Phlox pilosa fulgida	-1	P-Forb	prairie phlox	•	7	•	7	6	E	•		7		•	
Phlox pilosa sangamonensis	1	P-Forb	Sangamon phlox	•	10^E	•			•	•				•	
Phyla lanceolata	-5	P-Forb	fog fruit	•	1	•	6	3	•	•		6	8	•	
Physalis heterophylla	5	P-Forb	clammy ground cherry	•	2	•	3	3	•	•		3	3	•	
Physalis longifolia	5	P-Forb	ground cherry	•	☼	•	1	2	•	•		2		•	
Physalis pumila	5	P-Forb	prairie ground cherry	•	5	•	6	6	•	•				•	
Physalis virginiana	5	P-Forb	lance-leaved ground cherry	•	3	•	3	3	•	•		3	8	•	
Physostegia angustifolia	0	P-Forb	false dragonhead	•	7	•		6	•	•				•	
Physostegia virginiana[18]	-3	P-Forb	obedient plant	•	6	•	8	5	•	•		6	8	•	
Plantago aristata	5	A-Forb	bracted plantain	•	1	•	☼	1	•	•		☼	☼	•	
Plantago eriopoda	0	P-Forb	alkali plantain	•	☼	•			•	•				•	
Plantago patagonica	5	A-Forb	Patagonia plantain	•	☼	☼		☼	•	•		E	☼	•	
Plantago pusilla	3	A-Forb	slender plantain	•	3	•		1	•	•				•	
Plantago virginica	4	A-Forb	dwarf plantain	•	1	•	☼	1	•	•		0	☼	•	

continues

[18] Much of the prairie material is referable to subspecies *praemorsa* (=variety *arenaria*).

★Indicates nomenclature differs from Kartesz.

†Precedes scientific name cross-referenced in appendix C.

Table A.3. (Continued)

SCIENTIFIC NAME	COMMON NAME	CW	PHYSIOG	AR	IL	IN	IA	KS	MI	MO	MN	ND	NE	OH	OK	ON	SD	WI
Platanthera ciliaris	orange fringed orchid	-3	P-Forb	•	10[E]	E		•	10[T]	10[E]				10[T]	•	10		
Platanthera clavellata	club-spur orchid	-5	P-Forb	•	10[E]	R	S		6	10[E]	S			8[P]	•	8		•
Platanthera flava	southern rein orchid	-3	P-Forb	•	10[E]	E				10[S]					•			
Platanthera flava herbiola	northern rein orchid	-3	P-Forb		10[E]	W	E	•	10	10[S]	E			6[P]	•	8		T
Platanthera lacera	ragged fringed orchid	-3	P-Forb	•	9	W	S	•	6	10	•			6	•	6		•
Platanthera leucophaea[4]	eastern prairie fringed orchid	-4	P-Forb		10[E]	X	E	•	10[E]	10[X]				10[T]	•	10[R]		E
Platanthera praeclara[4]	western prairie fringed orchid	0	P-Forb			T	T	•	10[E]		E	E	T					
Platanthera psycodes	purple fringed orchid	-3	P-Forb		10[E]	R	T	•	7		•			9[E]		8	•	
Poa arida	plains blue grass	3	P-Grass		☼	☼				10[E]		•	•		•		•	
Poa interior	inland bluegrass	5	P-Grass							10[E]					•		•	•
Poa palustris	marsh blue grass	-4	P-Grass		7	•			3	☼				5	•	5	•	•
Pogonia ophioglossoides	snake-mouth orchid	-5	P-Forb	T	10	W	•	•	10	10[E]	•	•	•	10[T]	•	10	•	•
Polanisia dodecandra trachysperma	large clammy weed	5	A-Forb	•	0		•	•		4			•		•			
Polanisia jamesii	James' clammyweed	5	A-Forb		10[E]	E	E	•			E		•		•			
Polygala incarnata	pink milkwort	4	A-Forb	•	10[E]	E	T	•	10[X]	8			•	T	•	10	•	E
Polygala polygama	bitter milkwort	4	B-Forb	•	7	•	•	•	9	•			•	10[T]	•	9	•	•
Polygala sanguinea	field milkwort	3	A-Forb	•	5	•	•	•	4	5			•	4	•	9	•	•
Polygala senega	Seneca snakeroot	3	P-Forb	•	7	•	•	•	8	6			•	7	•	7	•	•
Polygala verticillata	whorled milkwort	5	A-Forb	•	5	•	•	•	5	4			•	4	•	7	•	•
†*Polygonatum biflorum commutatum*	smooth Solomon's seal	3	P-Forb	•	4	•	•	•	4	4			•	5	•	8	•	•
Polygonella articulata	jointweed	5	A-Forb		9	R			8					8		8		•
Polygonum careyi	Carey's heartsease	-4	A-Forb		10[E]	T	•	•	10[T]	•	E		•	10[X]	•	10	•	•
Polygonum hydropiperoides	mild water pepper	-5	P-Forb	•	4	•	•	•	5	4		T	•	5	•	4	•	•
Polygonum punctatum	dotted smartweed	-5	A-Forb	•	3	•	•	•	5	3		T	•	6	•	4	•	•

Scientific name	Common name		Form										
Polygonum ramosissimum	bushy knotweed	1	A-Forb	•	3	•	7	•	7	•	5	•	8	•
Polygonum tenue	slender knotweed	5	A-Forb	•	5	•	7	•	6	•	6	•	10	•
Polytaenia nuttallii	prairie parsley	5	P-Forb	•	8	E	10^X	E	8	•	8	•	5	•	T
Populus tremuloides	quaking aspen	0	Tree	T	3	•	1	•	10^R	•	2	•	7	•
Potentilla arguta	prairie cinquefoil	4	P-Forb	•	10	•	8	•	10	•	8^E	•	7	•
Potentilla hippiana	woolly cinquefoil	5	P-Forb		☼		☼							•
Potentilla norvegica	rough cinquefoil	0	A-Forb	•	0	•	0	•	0	•	1	•	0	•
Potentilla pensylvanica	gray cinquefoil	5	P-Forb	•	10^T	T	10^T	•	4	•	1	•		
Potentilla rivalis millegrana	brook cinquefoil	–5	P-Forb		10^E	R		E						
Potentilla simplex	common cinquefoil	4	P-Forb	•	3	•	2	•	3	•	1	•	3	•
Prenanthes alba	white lettuce	3	P-Forb	•	5	•	5	•	9	•	5	•	6	•
Prenanthes aspera	rough white lettuce	5	P-Forb	•	8^R	R	8	•	8	•	10^E	E		
Prenanthes racemosa	glaucous white lettuce	–3	P-Forb	•	8	•	10^X	•	8	•	8^P	•	10	•
Prionopsis ciliata	goldenweed	5	A-Forb	☼	☼	☼	☼		2^S					•
Prunella vulgaris lanceolata	self-heal	0	P-Forb	•	1	•	1	•	1	•	0	•	5	•
Prunus americana	wild plum	5	Tree	•	3	•	4	•	4	•	5	•	6	•
Prunus angustifolia	Chickasaw plum	5	Shrub	•	3	•	4	•	4	•	•			
Prunus mexicana	Mexican plum	5	Tree	•	7	•	3	•	3	•	X			
Prunus munsoniana	wild goose plum	5	Tree	T	6	•	3	•	3	•	•			
Prunus pumila	sand cherry	5	Shrub	S	8	•	8	•	8	•	10			
Prunus pumila besseyi	dwarf sand cherry	5	Shrub	S		•		•						
Prunus virginiana	choke cherry	1	Shrub	•	3	•	2	•	3	•	2	•	2	•
Psoralidium lanceolatum	lemon scurfy pea	5	P-Forb	S		•	2	•	3	•	2	•		

continues

---

[4] Federally designated as Threatened (USFWS 1994).

*Indicates nomenclature differs from Kartesz.

[†]Precedes scientific name cross-referenced in appendix C.

Table A.3. (*Continued*)

SCIENTIFIC NAME	COMMON NAME	CW	PHYSIOG	AR	IL	IN	IA	KS	MI	MO	MN	ND	NE	OH	OK	ON	SD	WI
†*Psoralidium tenuiflorum*	scurfy pea	5	P-Forb	•	9	X	•	•		8		T	•		•		•	•
Ptelea trifoliata	hop tree	2	Shrub	•	4	•	•	4		5	☼		•	6	•	9[R]	•	•
Ptilimnium nuttallii	Nuttall's mock bishop's weed	-4	A-Forb	•	7[E]	•		•		4							•	
Pulsatilla patens	pasque flower	5	P-Forb		10		•						•				•	•
Pycnanthemum tenuifolium	slender mountain mint	0	P-Forb	•	4	•	•	6		3			•	3	•	8	•	•
Pycnanthemum verticillatum pilosum	hairy mountain mint	5	P-Forb	•	6	•	•	10[S]		5			•	9[E]	•	10	•	•
Pycnanthemum virginianum	common mountain mint	-4	P-Forb	•	5	•	•	5		6		T	•	3	•	8	•	•
Quercus imbricaria	shingle oak	1	Tree	•	2	•	•	5		3			•	5	•		•	•
Quercus macrocarpa	bur oak	1	Tree	•	5	•	•	5		5			•	6	•	5	•	•
Quercus marilandica	blackjack oak	5	Tree	•	7		•	5		4			•	P	•		•	•
Quercus prinoides	dwarf chestnut oak	4	Tree	•		E	•	7		5			•		•		•	•
Quercus stellata	post oak	4	Tree	•	5	•	•	7		4			•		•		•	•
Ranunculus fascicularis	early buttercup	3	P-Forb	•	5	•	•	10		5			•	8[P]	•	9	•	•
Ranunculus laxicaulis	water plantain spearwort	-5	A-Forb	•	6	E	•	•		7			•		•		•	•
Ranunculus rhomboideus	prairie buttercup	5	P-Forb	•	10[T]	•	•	9[T]					•		•	10	•	•
Ratibida columnifera	long-headed coneflower	5	P-Forb	•	☼	☼		☼		3			•	☼	•	☼	•	☼
Ratibida pinnata	grey-headed coneflower	5	P-Forb	•	4	•	•	4		5			•	7	•	9	•	•
Rhamnus lanceolata	lance-leaved buckthorn	-5	Shrub	•	7	W	•			5			•	6	•		•	S
Rhexia mariana	Maryland meadow beauty	-5	P-Forb	•	10[E]	•	•	10[T]		8			•	6	•		•	
Rhexia mariana interior	meadow beauty	-5	P-Forb	•		W		•		9					•		•	
Rhexia virginica	Virginia meadow beauty	-5	P-Forb	•	10	•	•	9[S]		6			•	8[P]	•	10	•	S
Rhus aromatica	fragrant sumac	5	Shrub	•	4	•	•	7		3			•	4	•	8	•	S
Rhus copallina	winged sumac	5	Shrub	•	2	S	•	3		2	☼		•	6	•	7	•	•
Rhus glabra	smooth sumac	5	Shrub	•	1	•	•	2		1			•	2	•	7	•	•

Scientific name	Common name											
Rhynchosia latifolia	prairie snoutbean	5	P-Forb	•				•				•
Rhynchospora capitellata	clustered beak rush	-5	P-Sedge	10	•	6	7	•	9			•
Rhynchospora globularis	grass beak rush	-3	P-Sedge	10^E	E	10^X	7	•	E			•
Rhynchospora harveyi	Harvey's beak rush	0	P-Sedge	•		10^E		•				•
Rhynchospora macrostachya	horned rush	-5	P-Sedge	R	•	9^S	9	•				•
Rosa arkansana	sunshine rose	5	Shrub	5	•	4	5	•	X	5	•	
Rosa blanda	early wild rose	3	Shrub	4	•	3	6^S	•	8^T	3	•	
Rosa carolina	pasture rose	4	Shrub	4	•	4	4	•	5	6		
Rosa foliosa	white prairie rose	5	Shrub	•				•				
Rosa setigera	prairie rose	2	Shrub	5	•	5^S	4	•	6	5^R		
Rosa woodsii	western wild rose	3	Shrub	•				•				
Rubus allegheniensis	common blackberry	2	Shrub	2	•	1	4	•	1	2		
Rubus flagellaris	common dewberry	4	Shrub	2	•	1	2	•	2	4		
Rubus pensilvanicus	Yankee blackberry	1	Shrub	2	•	2	2	•	2	6		
Rudbeckia fulgida s.l.	orange coneflower	-5	P-Forb	6	•	9^S	7	•	7	☼		
Rudbeckia hirta	black-eyed Susan	3	P-Forb	2	•	1	1	•	3	0		
Rudbeckia missouriensis	Missouri black-eyed Susan	4	P-Forb	10^E	•		6	•	6			
Rudbeckia subtomentosa	sweet black-eyed Susan	-3	P-Forb	5	•		5	•	5			
Rudbeckia triloba	brown-eyed Susan	1	B-Forb	3	•	5	4	S	6	☼		
Ruellia humilis	hairy ruellia	4	P-Forb	3	•	10^T	3	E	•	E		
Rumex hastatulus	sour dock	3	A-Forb	4^E	•		3	•				
Rumex orbiculatus	great water dock	-5	P-Forb	7	•	9	10	•	3	6		
Sabatia angularis	rose gentian	-1	B-Forb	3	•	9^T	4	•	5	9		
Sabatia campestris	prairie rose gentian	3	B-Forb	8^E	S		4	•	3	•		

continues

---

*Indicates nomenclature differs from Kartesz.

†Precedes scientific name cross-referenced in appendix C.

Table A.3. (*Continued*)

SCIENTIFIC NAME	COMMON NAME	CW	PHYSIOG	AR	IL	IN	IA	KS	MI	MO	MN	ND	NE	OH	OK	ON	SD	WI
Salix discolor	pussy willow	-3	Shrub	•	4	•	•	•	1	10^E	•	•	•	3		3	•	•
Salix eriocephala	diamond willow	-3	Tree	•	5	•	•	•	2	5	•	•	•	1		4	•	•
Salix exigua	sandbar willow	-5	Shrub	•	1	•	•	•	1	3	•	•	•	1	•	3	•	•
Salix humilis	prairie willow	3	Shrub	•	5	•	•	•	4	6	•	•	•	4		7	•	•
Salix petiolaris	stalked willow	-5	Shrub	•	6	•	•	•	1	9^E	•	•	•	8^T		3	•	•
Salvia azurea	blue sage	5	P-Forb	•	9	☼	•	•	☼	4	•		•	☼			•	•
Salvia reflexa	Rocky Mountain sage	5	A-Forb	•	☼	☼		•	☼	3	•		•	☼	☼	☼	•	☼
Sanguisorba annua	prairie burnet	5	A-Forb				☼											
Sanguisorba canadensis	American burnet	-4	P-Forb		10^E	E	•		10^T				•	8				•
Sanicula canadensis	Canadian black snakeroot	2	B-Forb	•	4	•	•	•	8	3	S		•	4		7	•	•
Sanicula marilandica	black snakeroot	3	P-Forb		6	•	•	•	4			•	•	5		5	•	•
Sassafras albidum	sassafras	3	Tree	•	2	•	S		5	2				4		6		•
Saxifraga pensylvanica	swamp saxifrage	-3	P-Forb		10	•	•		10				•	6				•
Saxifraga texana	Texas saxifrage	0	P-Forb	•				•		9	•							
Schedonnardus paniculatus	tumble grass	5	P-Grass	•	5		S	•	5	4	S		•				•	•
†*Schizachyrium scoparium*	little bluestem	4	P-Grass	•	5	•	•	•	5	5	•	•	•	6		7	•	•
Scirpus acutus	hard-stemmed bulrush	-5	P-Sedge	•	6	•	•	•	5	7	•	•	•	5		6	•	•
Scirpus atrovirens	dark green rush	-5	P-Sedge	•	4	•	•	•	3	4	•	•	•	2		3	•	•
Scirpus cyperinus	wool grass	-5	P-Sedge	•	5	•	•	•	5	7	•		•	1		4	•	•
Scirpus hallii	Hall's bulrush	-5	A-Sedge	•	10^E	E	S	•	10^E	10								S
Scirpus koilolepis	keeled bulrush	-4	A-Sedge	•	8					9								
Scirpus pendulus	red bulrush	-5	P-Sedge	•	3	•	•	•	3	5	•		•	6		7	•	•
Scirpus tabernaemontani	great bulrush	-5	P-Sedge	•	4	•	•	•	4	5	•	•	•	6		5	•	•
Scleria ciliata	hairy nut rush	0	P-Sedge	•				•		10^S								

continues

Scientific Name	Common Name	C	Physiognomy														
Scleria pauciflora	few-flowered nut rush	3	P-Sedge	•	10	W	•	•	10[E]	8	•	•	10[T]	•	10	•	S
Scleria triglomerata	tall nut rush	0	P-Sedge	•	9		•	•	10[S]	7	•	•	8[P]	•	10	•	
Scrophularia lanceolata	early figwort	2	P-Forb	•	5		•	•	5	10[X]	•	•	5	•	7	•	
Scutellaria parvula	small skullcap	3	P-Forb	•	6	X	•	•	9[T]	4	•	•	•	•	9	•	
Scutellaria parvula australis	southern small skullcap	3	P-Forb	•	6	R	•		5		•						E
Scutellaria parvula leonardii	Leonard's small skullcap	3	P-Forb	•	5		•	•	4		•		•		8	•	
Selaginella eclipes	hidden spikemoss	-4	Crptgm	•	10		•	•	5	8	•	•	9[T]	•	7	•	
Selaginella rupestris	sand club moss	5	Crptgm	•	8	T	S	•	8	9	T	•	10[E]	•	8	•	S
Selenia aurea	golden selenia	5	A-Forb	•	5		•		6		•						
Senecio aureus	golden ragwort	-3	P-Forb	•	5		•	•	5	5	•	•	5	•	7	•	
Senecio congestus	swamp ragwort	-4	A-Forb	•			•	•	10[X]		•						
Senecio integerrimus	western groundsel	0	P-Forb	•							•					•	
Senecio pauperculus	balsam ragwort	-1	P-Forb	•	4		•	•	3	6	•	•	9[T]	•	7	•	
Senecio plattensis	prairie ragwort	4	P-Forb	•	6		•	•	5	6	•	•	5	•	8	•	
Senecio pseudaureus semicordatus	streambank butterweed	-3	P-Forb			S	•		10		S	•	•	•	•	•	S
†*Senna marilandica*	Maryland senna	-3	P-Forb	•	4		•	•	4		•	•	4	•	•	•	
Setaria parviflora	perennial foxtail	0	P-Grass	•	6	E	S	•	6		•	•	☼	•	•	•	
Silene regia	royal catchfly	5	P-Forb	T	9[E]	T	•	•	10[W]		•	•	P	•	•	•	
Silene stellata	starry campion	5	P-Forb	•	6		•	•	10[T]	5	•	•	6	•	•	•	
Silphium integrifolium laeve	western rosinweed	5	P-Forb	•	☼		•				•						
Silphium integrifolium	rosinweed	5	P-Forb	•	5		•	•	10[T]	4	•	•	10[T]	•	7	•	
Silphium laciniatum	compass plant	4	P-Forb	•	5		•	•	9[T]	6	•	•	9[E]	•	3	•	
Silphium perfoliatum	cup plant	-2	P-Forb	•	4		•	•	10[T]	3	•	•	6	•	9	•	

---

*Indicates nomenclature differs from Kartesz.

†Precedes scientific name cross-referenced in appendix C.

Table A.3. (Continued)

SCIENTIFIC NAME	COMMON NAME	CW	PHYSIOG	AR	IL	IN	IA	KS	MI	MO	MN	ND	NE	OH	OK	ON	SD	WI
Silphium terebinthinaceum	prairie dock	1	P-Forb	•	5	•	S		6	5				9		10	•	•
Silphium trifoliatum	whorled rosinweed	5	P-Forb		10^E	•								8				•
Sisyrinchium albidum	common blue-eyed grass	3	P-Forb	•	4	•			7	6				6		9	•	•
Sisyrinchium angustifolium	pointed blue-eyed grass	-2	P-Forb		5	•		•	4	5				4	•	6		•
Sisyrinchium atlanticum	eastern blue-eyed grass	-3	P-Forb	•	10^E	•			9^T	10^R				10^E				
Sisyrinchium campestre	prairie blue-eyed grass	5	P-Forb		6	•	•	•	•	4	•		•	•	•		•	
Sisyrinchium montanum	mountain blue-eyed grass	-1	P-Forb		9^E	E			4		•			10^E		1		•
Sisyrinchium mucronatum	slender blue-eyed grass	-2	P-Forb		9	•			10					10^E		10	•	•
Sium suave	water parsnip	-5	P-Forb	•	5	•	•	•	5	6	•	•	•	5	•	4	•	•
Solidago canadensis gilvocanescens	Canada goldenrod	3	P-Forb		1	•			2	5	•	•	•	1		1	•	
Solidago canadensis scabra	tall goldenrod	3	P-Forb	•	1	•			1	1				1		1	•	•
Solidago gigantea	late goldenrod	-3	P-Forb	•	3	•	•	•	3	4	•	•	•	2	•	4	•	•
Solidago juncea	early goldenrod	5	P-Forb	•	4	•			3	5	•			2		3	•	•
Solidago missouriensis	Missouri goldenrod	5	P-Forb		4	•				4	•	•	•		•		•	
Solidago mollis	soft goldenrod	5	P-Forb								S		•		•		•	
Solidago nemoralis	old-field goldenrod	5	P-Forb	•	3	•	•	•	2	2	•		•	3		2	•	•
Solidago ohioensis	Ohio goldenrod	-5	P-Forb		10	•			8		•			10^P		10	•	•
Solidago petiolaris	downy goldenrod	5	P-Forb	•	8	•	•	•		6			•		•		•	
†*Solidago ptarmicoides*	stiff aster	5	P-Forb	•	9	R			6	9	•		•	10^X		9	•	•
Solidago radula	rough goldenrod	5	P-Forb	•	7	•		•		6			•		•		•	
Solidago riddellii	Riddell's goldenrod	-5	P-Forb	S	7	•			6	10	•	E	•	8	•	10	•	•
Solidago rigida	stiff goldenrod	4	P-Forb	•	4	•	•	•	5	6	•		•	7	•	9	•	•
Solidago rugosa	rough-leaved goldenrod	-1	P-Forb	•	8	•			3	5				3	•	4	•	
Solidago speciosa	showy goldenrod	5	P-Forb	•	7	•	•	•	7	7	•		•	5	•	10	•	•

Scientific name	Common name		Form									
Sorghastrum nutans	Indian grass	2	P-Grass	•	4	•	6	5	•	•	6	6 • 8 • •
Spartina pectinata	prairie cord grass	−4	P-Grass	•	4	•	5	5	•	•	7	7 • 7 • •
Spermolepis divaricata	forked scaleseed	3	A-Forb	•	☼	•		☼	•			
Spermolepis echinata	bristly-fruited spermolepis	5	A-Forb	•	4	•		3	•			
Spermolepis inermis	scaleseed	5	A-Forb	☼	4	☼			•			
Sphaeralcea coccinea	red false mallow	5	P-Forb	•		•		4	•			
Sphenopholis intermedia	slender wedge grass	0	P-Grass	•	5	•	4	6	•	•	5	5 • 6 • •
Sphenopholis obtusata	prairie wedge grass	0	P-Grass	•	5	•	8	5	•	•	7^T	7 • 10 • •
Spiraea alba	meadowsweet	−4	Shrub	•	6	•	4	9^E	•	•	3^X	3 • 3 • •
Spiraea tomentosa	steeple bush	−5	Shrub	•	8	•	5	10^X	•	•	4	4 • 5 • •
Spiranthes cernua	nodding ladies' tresses	−2	P-Forb	•	4	•	4	4	T	•	5	5 • 5 • •
Spiranthes lacera gracilis	slender ladies' tresses	−1	P-Forb	•	8	T	8	6^W	•	•	5	5 • 7 • •
Spiranthes magnicamporum	dune ladies's tresses	−3	P-Forb	•	6	E	S	9	7	•	9^P	9 • 8 • •
Spiranthes tuberosa	little ladies' tresses	5	P-Forb	•	9	W		10	7	•	6	• •
Spiranthes vernalis	spring ladies' tresses	0	P-Forb	•	7^E	R	T		8	•	8	• •
Sporobolus clandestinus	rough rush grass	5	P-Grass	•	6	S	S		5	•		•
Sporobolus compositus	rough dropseed	5	P-Grass	•	3	•	☼	4	•	•	3	3 • 2 • •
Sporobolus cryptandrus	sand dropseed	4	P-Grass	•	4	•	3	5	•	•	8^P	8 • 2 • •
Sporobolus heterolepis	prairie dropseed	4	P-Grass	•	9	•	10^T	7	•	•	T	T • 10 • •
Sporobolus neglectus	small rush grass	5	A-Grass	•	1	•	2	3	•	•	3	3 • 1 • •
Sporobolus vaginiflorus	sheathed rush grass	5	A-Grass	•	0	•	2	2	•	•	5	5 • 1 • •
Stachys palustris	woundwort	−5	P-Forb	•	5	•	5	6	•	•	6	6 • ☼ • •
Stachys tenuifolia	rough hedge nettle	−5	P-Forb	•	5	•	5	5	•	•	4	4 • 7 • •
Stenosiphon linifolius	false gaura	5	B-Forb	•		☼		10^R	•			

continues

---

*Indicates nomenclature differs from Kartesz.

†Precedes scientific name cross-referenced in appendix C.

Table A.3. (Continued)

SCIENTIFIC NAME	COMMON NAME	CW	PHYSIOG	AR	IL	IN	IA	KS	MI	MO	MN	ND	NE	OH	OK	ON	SD	WI
Stillingia sylvatica	queen's delight	5	P-Forb	•											•		•	•
Stipa comata	needle-and-thread	5	P-Grass		☼	X	S	•	☼	8			•	10[T]		•	•	•
Stipa spartea	porcupine grass	5	P-Grass	•	6			•	10	8			•			10	•	•
Strophostyles helvula	trailing wild bean	−1	A-Forb	•	3	•		•	8[S]	2			•	3		8	•	•
Strophostyles leiosperma	small wild bean	5	A-Forb	•	4	T		•		2			•				•	
Stylisma pickeringii	Patterson's bindweed	5	P-Forb	•	9[E]		E			10								
Stylosanthes biflora	pencil flower	5	P-Forb	•	5	•		•		5								
Symphoricarpos occidentalis	wolfberry	5	Shrub		6			4	☼	10[E]	•	•	•		☼	☼	•	S
Symphoricarpos orbiculatus	coralberry	3	Shrub	•	1	•		☼		1	☼		•	6		9	•	
Taenidia integerrima	yellow pimpernel	5	P-Forb	•	7	•		8	8	6			•	6		9		•
Talinum calycinum	rockpink fame flower	5	P-Forb	•	10[E]			•		8								
Talinum parviflorum	prairie fame flower	5	P-Forb		10	T	T	•		10		T	•					
Talinum rugospermum	sand fame flower	5	P-Forb		9	T	E			E	E							S
Tephrosia virginiana	goat's rue	5	P-Forb	•	7	•		10	•	5	S		•	6		10	•	•
Tetraneuris herbacea[4]	lakeside daisy	5	P-Forb		10[E]					S	S			E		10		
Teucrium canadense	germander	−2	P-Forb	•	3	•		4	•	2			•	3		6	•	•
Teucrium canadense occidentale	western germander	−3	P-Forb	•	3	•		4	•	5			•	4		6	•	•
Thalictrum dasycarpum	purple meadow rue	−2	P-Forb	•	5	•		3	•	4			•	7		8	•	•
Thalictrum revolutum	waxy meadow rue	0	P-Forb	•	5	•	E	9[T]	•	5			•	7		9	•	S
Thaspium barbinode	hairy meadow parsnip	5	P-Forb	•	7	•		10	•	6			•	4		9		E
Thaspium trifoliatum aureum	meadow parsnip	5	P-Forb	•	6	•		8	•	6			•	3		9		S
Thelesperma filifolium	fine-leaved thelesperma	5	B-Forb	•	☼	☼		•		10[S]			•				•	
Thelesperma megapotamicum	rayless green thread	5	P-Forb					•		☼	☼		•		•		☼	
Thelypteris palustris pubescens	marsh fern	−5	Crptgm	•	6	•		2	•	10	T	T	•	5	•	5	•	•

Thismia americana	thismia	–5	P-Forb		10^{E}													
Tofieldia glutinosa	false asphodel	–5	P-Forb		10^{T}	R			10		S			10		10		T
Toxicodendron radicans[19]	poison ivy	3	W-Vine	•	1	•	•	•	2	1	•	•	•	1	•	0	•	•
Toxicodendron toxicarium	poison oak	5	W-Vine	•	☼			•		10^{W}					•			
Tradescantia bracteata	long-bracted spiderwort	4	P-Forb	•	7^{E}	☼	•	•	10^{X}	6	•	•	•	•	•		•	•
Tradescantia occidentalis	prairie spiderwort	5	P-Forb	•			•	•			•	•	•		•		•	•
Tradescantia ohiensis	common spiderwort	2	P-Forb	•	3	•	•	•	5	4	S		•	7	•	10		•
Tradescantia tharpii	Tharp's spiderwort	5	P-Forb					•		9					•			
Tradescantia virginiana	Virginia spiderwort	5	P-Forb	•	5	•	S		9^{S}	6				8		☼		
Tragia betonicifolia	noseburn	5	P-Forb	•				•		4					•			
Tragia ramosa	southern noseburn	5	P-Forb	•				•		7^{S}			•		•			
†*Trichostema brachiatum*	false pennyroyal	5	A-Forb	•	7	•	•	•	8^{T}	4	•		•	4	•	9	•	•
Tridens flavus	false redtop	5	P-Grass	•	1	•	•	•	3	1			•	3	•	☼		•
Tridens muticus	slim tridens	5	P-Grass	•				•		10^{R}					•			
Tridens strictus	longspike tridens	3	P-Grass	•	4	•	•	•		5					•			
Trifolium carolinianum	Carolina clover	5	P-Forb	•				•		10^{X}					•			
Trifolium reflexum	buffalo clover	5	A-Forb	•	10^{E}	E	•	•		10^{S}			•	8^{E}	•			
Triglochin maritimum	common bog arrow grass	–5	P-Forb		10	•	T	•	8		•	•	•	9^{T}		8	•	•
Triodanis holzingeri	Holzinger's Venus' looking glass	5	A-Forb	•				•		10			•		•			
Triodanis lamprosperma	shining-seed Venus' looking glass	5	A-Forb	•				•		6					•			
Triodanis leptocarpa	narrow Venus' looking glass	5	A-Forb	•	8		•	•		4	•	•	•		•		•	
†*Triodanis perfoliata*	Venus' looking glass	0	A-Forb	•	2	•	•	•	6	2	•	•	•	3	•	6	•	•

continues

[4] Federally designated as threatened (USFWS 1994).

[19] Including *Toxicodendron rydbergii;* see Swink and Wilhelm (1994), p. 635.

* Indicates nomenclature differs from Kartesz.

† Precedes scientific name cross-referenced in appendix C.

Table A.3. (Continued)

SCIENTIFIC NAME	COMMON NAME	CW	PHYSIOG	AR	IL	IN	IA	KS	MI	MO	MN	ND	NE	OH	OK	ON	SD	WI
Triodanis perfoliata biflora	small Venus' looking glass	5	A-Forb	•	4		•	•		3			•				•	•
Triplasis purpurea	sand grass	5	A-Grass	•	6	•	•	•	6[S]	7	S		•	9[P]	•	8	•	•
Tripsacum dactyloides	gama grass	-1	P-Grass	•	4	W	•	•	☼	5		•	•		•	3	•	•
Ulmus americana	American elm	-2	Tree	•	4	•	•	•	1	4	•	•	•	1	•	6	•	•
Ulmus rubra	slippery elm	0	Tree	•	3	•	S	•	2	3	T	•	•	2	•	10	•	•
Valeriana edulis ciliata	common valerian	-5	P-Forb	•	10	E	S	•	10[T]	0	T	•	•	E	•		•	
Valerianella radiata	beaked corn salad	-1	A-Forb	•	1	•	•	•	0			•	•		•	2		
Verbena bracteata	creeping vervain	3	A-Forb	•	0	•	•	•	☼	☼	•	•	•	•	•		•	•
Verbena hastata	blue vervain	-4	P-Forb	•	3	•	•	•	4	4	•	•	•	4	•	4	•	•
Verbena simplex	narrow-leaved vervain	5	P-Forb	•	4	•	•	•	6	4	S	•	•	5	•	9	•	•
Verbena stricta	hoary vervain	5	P-Forb	•	2	•	•	•	4	3	•	•	•	5	•	7	•	•
Verbesina helianthoides	wingstem	5	P-Forb	•	5	•		•		4			•	•	•			
Vernonia arkansana	great ironweed	0	P-Forb	•	10	•	•	•		6			•		•			
Vernonia baldwinii	western ironweed	5	P-Forb	•	5	•	•	•		3	•	•	•		•		•	
Vernonia fasciculata	common ironweed	-3	P-Forb	•	5	•	•	•	3	6	•		•	7[P]	•		•	•
Vernonia gigantea	tall ironweed	0	P-Forb	•	4	•	•	•	4	5	•			3	•	7		•
Vernonia missurica	Missouri ironweed	-1	P-Forb	•	5	•	•	•	4	4	•	•	•	7[E]	•		•	•
Veronica peregrina	purslane speedwell	5	A-Forb	•	0	•	•	•	0	0	•	•	•	1	•	0	•	•
Veronicastrum virginicum	Culver's root	0	P-Forb	•	6	•	•	•	8	7	•	T	•	9	•	10	•	•
Vicia americana	American vetch	5	H-Vine	•	7	•	•	•	5	8	•	•	•	5	•	9	•	•
Vicia ludoviciana	deer pea vetch	5	A-Forb	•		•	•	•		10			•		•		•	
Viola bicolor	johnny-jump-up	5	A-Forb	•	☼	☼	•	•	8	0	S	•	•	3	•	8	•	•
Viola lanceolata	lance-leaved violet	-5	P-Forb	•	7	•	S	•	8	7	S	•	•	9[P]	•	9	•	•
Viola nephrophylla	northern bog violet	-5	P-Forb	•	8	•	•	•	8		•	•	•	10[E]	•	7	•	•

Scientific name	Common name	C	Form															
Viola nuttallii	yellow prairie violet	5	P-Forb	•	•	•	•	•	•	•	S	•	•					
Viola pedata	bird's foot violet	5	P-Forb	•	•	7	•	•	9	5	•	•	•	9[T]				10[T]
Viola pedatifida	prairie violet	4	P-Forb	•	10	T	•	•	10[T]	10	•	•	•	X				10
Viola primulifolia	primrose violet	-4	P-Forb	•	10[E]	R	•	•				•		8[E]				
Viola sagittata	arrow-leaved violet	-2	P-Forb	•	6	•	•	•	8	7	•	•	•	6				9
Viola soraria	common blue violet	1	P-Forb	•	3	•	•	•	1	2	•	•	•	2				4
Vulpia octoflora	six-weeks fescue	5	A-Grass	•	2	•	•	•	5	2	•	•	•	5				8
Woodsia obtusa	cliff fern	5	Crptgm	•	6	•	•	•	10[T]	5	•	•	•	9				10
Yucca glauca	soapweed	5	Shrub			•	•	•		10[W]								
Zanthoxylum americanum	prickly ash	5	Shrub	•	4	•	•	•	3	4	•	•	•	5				3
Zigadenus elegans	plains white camass	1	P-Forb	•			•	•		10[R]	•	•	•					
Zigadenus elegans glaucus	white camass	-5	P-Forb	•	10[E]	R	•	•	10	10	•	•	•	10[P]				10
Zigadenus nuttallii	death camass	5	P-Forb	•			•	•		10[E]	•	•	•					
Zizia aptera	heart-leaved meadow parsnip	3	P-Forb	•	10	R	•	•	9[T]	7	•	•	•	•				9
Zizia aurea	golden Alexanders	-1	P-Forb	•	6	•	•	•	6	5	•	•	•	7				7
Total Listed				24	102	136	162	12	121	127	68	64	13	191	11	13	11	91
Total Native				735	800	721	760	763	605	825	661	477	649	657	740	529	541	653

*Indicates nomenclature differs from Kartesz.

[†]Precedes scientific name cross-referenced in appendix C

ACKNOWLEDGMENTS

Many biologists contributed to the development of this list or provided specific distributional information. Special thanks are extended to Barbara Andreas, Harvey Ballard, Kim Chapman, Ted Cochrane, Allison Cusick, June Dobberpuhl, Pauline Drobney, Marc Evans, Tom Foti, Craig Freeman, Linda Freid-Ellis, Bob Hamilton, Mike Homoya, Phil Hyatt, Stanley Jones, Jeff Knoop, John Pearson, Mike Penskar, John Taft, Bob Tatina, Ron Tyrl, and George Yatskievych. I am especially grateful to Blane Heumann, Linda Masters, and Gerould Wilhelm for their suggestions and input throughout this project.

SOURCES

Andreas, B. K., and R. W. Lichvar. 1995. *Floristic Index for Establishing Assessment Standards: A Case Study for Northern Ohio.* Technical Report WRP-DE-8. Vicksburg, MS: U.S. Army Corps of Engineers Waterways Experiment Station.

Arkansas Natural Heritage Commission. 1987. "Endangered and Threatened Plants of Arkansas." Unpublished memorandum, Little Rock, Arkansas.

Coffin, B., and L. Pfannmuller, eds. 1988. *Minnesota's Endangered Flora and Fauna.* Minneapolis: University of Minnesota Press.

Eilers, L. J., and D. M. Roosa. 1994. *The Vascular Plants of Iowa.* Iowa City: University of Iowa Press.

Gleason, H. A., and A. Cronquist. 1991. *Manual of Vascular Plants of the Northeastern United States and Adjacent Canada,* 2nd edition. New York, NY: New York Botanical Garden.

Herkert, J. R. 1994. *Endangered and Threatened Species of Illinois: Status and Distribution,* vol. 3—1994 changes to the Illinois list of endangered and threatened species. Springfield: Illinois Endangered Species Protection Board.

Herkert, J. R., ed. 1991. *Endangered and Threatened Species of Illinois: Status and Distribution,* vol. 1—plants. Springfield: Illinois Endangered Species Protection Board.

Herman, K. D., L. A. Masters, M. R. Penskar, A. A. Reznicek, G. S. Wilhelm, and W. W. Brodowicz. 1996. *Floristic Quality Assessment System with Wetland Categories and Computer Application Programs for the State of Michigan.* Lansing: Michigan Department of Natural Resources.

Indiana Department of Natural Resources. 1993. *Indiana's Rare Plants and Animals.* Indianapolis: Indiana Department of Natural Resources.

Iowa Department of Natural Resources. 1994. "Endangered and Threatened Plant and Animal Species." *Iowa Administrative Code.* Des Moines, IA. 13 pp.

Kartesz, J. 1994. *A Synonymized Checklist of the Vascular Flora of the United States, Canada, and Greenland,* 2 vols. Portland, OR: Timber Press.

Ladd, D. 1993. *Coefficients of Conservatism for Missouri Vascular Flora.* St. Louis, MO: Nature Conservancy.

Michigan Natural Features Inventory. 1992. *Michigan's Special Plants.* Lansing, MI: Natural Features Inventory.

Missouri Department of Conservation. 1992. *Rare and Endangered Species Checklist of Missouri.* Jefferson City: Missouri Department of Conservation.

Nebraska Game and Parks Commission. 1992. *Nebraska's Vanishing Species.* Lincoln: Nebraska Game and Parks Commission.

North Dakota Game and Fish Department. 1986. "List of North Dakota's Threatened and Endangered Biota." *North Dakota Outdoors* 49, no. 2:28–32.

Ohio Division of Natural Areas and Preserves. 1994. *Rare Native Ohio Plants: 1994–95 Status List.* Columbus: Ohio Department of Natural Resources.

Oldham, M. J., W. D. Bakowsky, and D. A. Sutherland. 1995. *Floristic Quality Assessment for Southern Ontario.* Peterborough, Ontario: Ontario Ministry of Natural Resources, Natural Heritage Information Centre.

Ontario Ministry of Natural Resources. 1994. *Rare, Threatened, Endangered, Extirpated, or Extinct Species of Ontario.* Peterborough, Ontario: Ontario Ministry of Natural Resources, Terrestrial Ecosystems Branch.

Reed, P. B., Jr. 1988. "National List of Plant Species That Occur in Wetlands: National Summary." *U.S. Fish and Wildlife Service Biological Report* 88, no. 24.

Rollins, R. C. 1993. *The Cruciferae of Continental North America.* Stanford, CA: Stanford University Press.

Swink, F., and G. Wilhelm. 1994. *Plants of the Chicago Region,* 4th edition. Indianapolis: Indiana Academy of Science.

Taft, J. B., G. S. Wilhelm, D. M. Ladd, and L. A. Masters. *Floristic Quality Assessment for Illinois.* Lisle, IL: Morton Arboretum. In preparation.

U.S. Fish and Wildlife Service. 1994. *Endangered and Threatened Wildlife and Plants.* Washington, DC: U.S. Fish and Wildlife Service.

Wilhelm, G. S. 1992. "Technical Comments on the Proposed Revisions to the 1989 Wetland Delineation Manual." *Erigenia* 12:41–50.

Wisconsin Natural Heritage Program. 1993. *Wisconsin Natural Heritage Working Lists.* Madison: Wisconsin Department of Natural Resources.

Appendix B
Terrestrial Vertebrates
of Tallgrass Prairies

Stanley A. Temple

The following table includes all species of terrestrial vertebrates that regularly breed in the tallgrass prairie biome, defined for these purposes as tallgrass regions of Texas, Oklahoma, Kansas, Nebraska, South Dakota, North Dakota, Missouri, Iowa, Minnesota, Illinois, Wisconsin, and Indiana. Animals are arranged phylogenetically. The table excludes migratory species that use the biome only on a temporary basis and extralimital species that are rarely encountered because they are associated primarily with adjacent biomes. The former range of extinct or widely extirpated species is provided. Table and nomenclatural sources include Collins (1990) and Jones and Birney (1988).

Amphibians		
Species	Habitat Requirements	Geographic Range
eastern newt (*Notopthalmus viridescens*)	ponds, still waters	TX, IL, WI, IN, MO, IA
mudpuppy (*Necturus maculosus*)	rivers, streams	MO, IA, IL, WI, MN, ND, IN
tiger salamander (*Ambystoma tigrinum*)	near ponds; savannas, woodlands, grasslands	Throughout biome
plains spadefoot (*Scaphiopus bombifrons*)	sandy soils	OK, KS, NE
Couch's spadefoot (*Scaphiopus couchi*)	friable soils	TX, OK
eastern spadefoot (*Scaphiopus holbrooki*)	friable soils	TX, OK
crawfish frog (*Rana areolata*)	ponds	TX, OK, KS, IA, IL, IN, MO
plains leopard frog (*Rana blairi*)	ponds	TX, OK, KS, NE, IL, IN, IA
bullfrog (*Rana catesbeiana*)	ponds, marshes, lakes, rivers	TX, OK, KS, NE, MO, IA, IL, WI, MN, IN

continues

Amphibians (*Continued*)

Species	Habitat Requirements	Geographic Range
green frog (*Rana clamitans*)	ponds, marshes, streams	TX, OK, KS, NE, MO, IA, IL, WI, MN, IN
pickerel frog (*Rana palustris*)	ponds, streams, marshes	TX, IA, WI, MN, OK, IL, IN
southern leopard frog (*Rana sphenocephala*)	ponds, streams, marshes	TX, OK, KS, MO, IL, IN
northern leopard frog (*Rana pipiens*)	wet meadows	IL, IA, MN, WI, ND, SD, NE, IN
eastern narrowmouth toad (*Gastrophryne carolinensis*)	ponds	TX, OK, MO, IL
Great Plains narrowmouth toad (*Gastrophyrne olivacea*)	ponds, marshes	TX, OK, KS, NE
American toad (*Bufo americanus*)	ponds, marshes	OK, KS, NE, IA, IL, MN, ND, SD, IN, WI
Great Plains toad (*Bufo cognatus*)	ponds, floodplains	TX, OK, KS, NE, IA, MN, ND, SD
green toad (*Bufo debilis*)	ponds	TX, OK, KS
Canadian toad (*Bufo hemiophyrs*)	ponds	ND, SD, MN
Houston toad (*Bufo houstonensis*)	ponds	TX
Texas toad (*Bufo speciosus*)	ponds, sandy soils	TX
Gulf Coast toad (*Bufo valliceps*)	ponds	TX
Woodhouse's toad (*Bufo woodhousii*)	ponds	TX, OK, KS, NE, MO, IL, IN
northern cricket frog (*Acris crepitans*)	ponds, streams	TX, IN, OK, KS, NE, MO, IL, IA, WI
gray tree frog (*Hyla chrysocelis* and *H. versicolor*)	savanna	IL, IA, MO, WI, NE, KS
spotted chorus frog (*Pseudacris clarkii*)	ponds	TX, OK, KS
Strecker's chorus frog (*Pseudacris streckeri*)	ponds	TX, OK, IL, MO
western chorus frog (*Pseudacris triseriata*)	marshes	Throughout biome
white-lipped frog (*Leptodactylus labialis*)	wet areas	TX

Reptiles

Species	Habitat Requirements	Geographic Range
American alligator (*Alligator mississippiensis*)	Water	TX
snapping turtle (*Chelydra serpentina*)	Water	Throughout biome

Species	Habitat Requirements	Geographic Range
alligator snapping turtle (*Macroclemys temmincki*)	Water	TX, OK
eastern mud turtle (*Kinosternon subrubrum*)	Water	OK, TX
yellow mud turtle (*Kinosternon flavescens*)	Sand-bottomed ponds	IL, IA, MO
common musk turtle (*Sternotherus odoratus*)	Water	TX, OK, IL, IA, WI
river cooter (*Pseudemys concinna*)	Water	TX, OK, MO, IL
Texas river cooter (*Pseudemys texana*)	Water	TX
painted turtle (*Chrysemys picta*)	Water	KS, NE, MO, IL, IA, WI, MN, ND, SD, IN
red-eared slider (*Trachemys scripta*)	Water	TX, OK, KS, MO, IL, IN
chicken turtle (*Dierochelys reticularia*)	Water	TX
Blanding's turtle (*Emydoidea blandingii*)	Marshes	IL, WI, MN, NE, IN
map turtle (*Graptemys geographica*)	Water	OK, IL, KS, WI, MN, IA
Mississippi map turtle (*Graptemys kohni*)	Water	TX, OK, KS, MO, IL
false map turtle (*Graptemys pseudogeographica*)	Water	OK, KS, MO, IA, IL, WI, IN
eastern box turtle (*Terrapene carolina*)	Moist areas in woods	TX, OK, KS, MO, IL, IN
ornate box turtle (*Terrapene ornata*)	Friable soils	TX, OK, KS, NE, IA, IL, WI, MN, SD, IN
Berlandier's tortoise (*Gopherus berlandieri*)	Sandy soils	TX
smooth softshell (*Apalone mutica*)	Water	TX, OK, KS, NE, IA, IL, WI, MN, IN
spiny softshell (*Apalone spinifera*)	Water	TX, OK, KS, NE, IA, IL, WI, MO, SD, MN
spot-tailed earless lizard (*Holbrookia lacerata*)	Friable soils	TX
lesser earless lizard (*Holbrookia maculata*)	Friable soils	TX, OK, KS, NE
Texas horned lizard (*Phrynosoma cornutum*)	Friable soils	TX, OK, KS
eastern fence lizard (*Sceloporus undulatus*)	Open grassland	TX, OK, KS, NE, SD, MO, IL
western slender glass lizard (*Ophisaurus attenuatus*)	Dry friable soils	TX, OK, KS, MO, IL, IA, WI, IN

continues

Species	Habitat Requirements	Geographic Range
six-lined racerunner (*Cnemidophorus sexlineatus*)	Dry areas	TX, OK, KS, NE, MO, IA, IL, WI, SD, IN
Great Plains skink (*Eumeces obsoletus*)	Moist areas	TX, OK, KS, NE, MO
prairie skink (*Eumeces septentrionalis*)	Moist areas	TX, OK, KS, NE, IA, WI, MN, ND, SD
four-lined skink (*Eumeces tetragrammus*)	Dry areas	TX
Texas blind snake (*Leptotyphlops dulcis*)	Dry areas	TX, OK, KS
glossy snake (*Arizona elegans*)	Dry areas	TX, OK, KS
worm snake (*Carphophis amoenus*)	Moist areas	OK, KS, MO, IA, WI, IL
Kirtland's snake (*Clonophis kirtlandii*)	Moist areas	IL, IN
racer (*Coluber constrictor*)	Diverse areas	Throughout biome
black-striped snake (*Coniophanes imperialis*)	Dry areas	TX
ringneck snake (*Diadophis punctatus*)	Moist areas	TX, OK, KS, NE, MO, IL, WI, MN, SD, IA
indigo snake (*Drymarchon corais*)	Dry areas	TX
fox snake (*Elaphe vulpina*)	Prairie, savanna	NE, IA, IL, WI, IN, MN
western hognose snake (*Heterodon nasicus*)	Friable soils	TX, OK, KS, NE, IA, MN, ND, SD, IL
eastern hognose snake (*Heterodon platirhinos*)	Friable soils	TX, OK, KS, MO, NE, IA, IL, WI, MN, SD, IL
prairie kingsnake (*Lampropeltis calligaster*)	Rocky areas; tallgrass prairie	TX, OK, KS, MO, IA, IL, IN
common kingsnake (*Lampropeltis getula*)	Diverse areas	TX, OK, MO, IA, KS, IL
milk snake (*Lampropeltis triangulum*)	Diverse areas	TX, OK, KS, NE, MO, IL, IA, WI, IN
coachwhip (*Masticophis flagellum*)	Dry areas	TX, OK, KS, MO
green water snake (*Nerodia cyclopion*)	Water	TX, MO, IL
plainbelly water snake (*Nerodia erythrogaster*)	Water	TX, OK, KS, MO, IL, IA
southern water snake (*Nerodia fasciata*)	Water	TX, OK, MO, IA
diamond back water snake (*Nerodia rhombifer*)	Water	TX, MO, IL, IA, OK, KS
northern water snake (*Nerodia sipedon*)	Ponds, streams	OK, KS, NE, MO, IA, IL, WI, MN, IN

Species	Habitat Requirements	Geographic Range
smooth green snake (*Opheodrys vernalis*)	Moist areas	MO, IA, IL, WI, MN, ND, SD, NE
bull snake (*Pituophis melanolenens*)	Dry, friable soils	TX, OK, KS, NE, MO, IA, IL, IN, WI, MN, SD
Graham's crayfish snake (*Regina grahamii*)	Prairie marshes	TX, OK, KS, NE, MO, IA, IL
ground snake (*Sonora semiannulata*)	Dry friable soils	TX, OK, KS, MO
brown snake (*Storeria dekayi*)	Moist areas	TX, IN, OK, KS, MO, IA, IL, WI, MN
flat-headed snake (*Tantilla gracilis*)	Rocky areas	TX, OK, KS, MO
checkered garter snake (*Thamnophis marcianus*)	Dry areas	TX, OK, KS
western ribbon snake (*Thamnophis proximus*)	Marshes, ponds	TX, OK, KS, NE, MO, IA, IL, WI, IN
plains garter snake (*Thamnophis radix*)	Moist areas, mesic prairie	KS, NE, MO, IA, IL, WI, MN, ND, SD
common garter snake (*Thamophis sirtalis*)	Moist areas, bluffs	Throughout biome
lined snake (*Tropidoclonion lineatum*)	Dry or rocky grassland	TX, OK, KS, NE, MO, IA, IL
western diamondback rattlesnake (*Crotalus atrox*)	Dry areas	TX, OK
timber rattlesnake (*Crotalus horridus*)	Rocky areas	TX, OK, KS, IA, IL, WI, MN
massasauga (*Sisturus catenatus*)	Wet areas	TX, OK, MO, IN, NE, KS, IL, WI, IA
pigmy rattlesnake (*Sisturus miliarius*)	Wet areas	TX, OK, MO

Birds

Species	Habitat Requirements	Geographic Range
Clark's grebe (*Aechmophorus clarkii*)	Water	MN, ND, SD
western grebe (*Aechmophorus occid*)	Water	WI, MN, ND, SD, IA
red-necked grebe (*Podiceps grisegena*)	Water	MN, WI, ND, SD
horned grebe (*Podiceps auritus*)	Water	MN, ND, WS
eared grebe (*Podiceps nigricollis*)	Water	IA, MN, ND, SD
pied-billed grebe (*Podilymbus podiceps*)	Water	IL, WI, IA, MN, ND, SD, NE, KS, MO, IN
American white pelican (*Pelecanus erythrorhynchos*)	Water	WI, MN, ND, SD

continues

Species	Habitat Requirements	Geographic Range
double-crested cormorant (*Phalacrocorax auritus*)	Water	IA, IL, WI, MN, ND, SD, NE, KS, OK
least bittern (*Ixobrychus exilis*)	Marshes	Throughout biome
American bittern (*Botaurus lentiginosus*)	Marshes	Throughout biome
sandhill crane (*Grus canadensis*)	Wet areas	WI, MN, IL, IA, IN
trumpeter swan (*Cygnus buccinator*)	Water	WI, MN, SD
Canada goose (*Branta canadensis*)	Water	OK, KS, NE, IA, IL, WI, MN, ND, SD, MO, IN
mallard (*Anas platyrhynchos*)	Water	Throughout biome
mottled duck (*Anas fulvigula*)	Water	TX
gadwall (*Anas strepera*)	Water	KS, NE, IA, WI, MN, ND, SD, MO, IL
American widgeon (*Anas americana*)	Water	MN, ND, SD, NE, IA, WS
northern pintail (*Anas acuta*)	Water	KS, NE, MO, IA, IL, WI, MN, ND, SD
northern shoveler (*Anas clypeata*)	Water	KS, NE, MO, IA, IL, WI, ND, SD, MN, IN
blue-winged teal (*Anas discors*)	Water	OK, KS, NE, MO, IA, IL, WI, ND, SD, MN, IL
ruddy duck (*Oxyura jamaicensis*)	Water	KS, NE, IA, WI, MN, ND, SD, IL, IN
canvasback (*Aythya valisineria*)	Water	MN, ND, SD, IA
redhead (*Aythya americana*)	Water	WI, MN, NE, IA, ND, SD, IN
lesser scaup (*Aythya affinis*)	Water	IA, WI, MN, ND, SD, NE
king rail (*Rallus elegans*)	Marshes	Throughout biome
Virginia rail (*Rallus limicola*)	Marshes	Throughout biome
sora (*Porzana carolina*)	Marshes	KS, NE, MO, IA, IL, WI, MN, ND, SD, IN
yellow rail (*Coturnicops noveboracensis*)	Marshes	WI, MN, ND, SD
common moorhen (*Gallinula chloropus*)	Marshes, water	OK, MO, IA, IL, WI, MN, SD, IN
American coot (*Fulica americana*)	Marshes	Throughout biome

Species	Habitat Requirements	Geographic Range
American avocet (*Recurvirostra americana*)	Shallow water	MN, ND, SD, WS
piping plover (*Charadrius melodus*)	Sandy shore	MN, ND, IN
killdeer (*Charadrius vociferus*)	Diverse areas	Throughout biome
marbled godwit (*Limosa fedoa*)	Near water	MN, ND
willet (*Catoptrophorus semipalmatus*)	Marshes	MN, ND, SD
spotted sandpiper (*Actitis macularia*)	Near water	KS, ND, MO, IN, IA, IL, WI, MN, ND, SD, IN
Wilson's phalarope (*Phalaropus tricolor*)	Shallow water	MN, ND, SD, IA, WS
common snipe (*Gallinago gallinago*)	Marshes	IA, IL, WI, MN, ND, SD, IN
upland sandpiper (*Bartramia longicauda*)	Open areas	Throughout biome
Franklin's gull (*Larus pipixcan*)	Water	MN, ND, SD, IA
ring-billed gull (*Larus delawarensis*)	Water	MN, WI, ND, SD, NE
common tern (*Sterna hirundo*)	Water	WI, MN, ND, SD, IL
Forster's tern (*Sterna forsteri*)	Water	WI, MN, ND, SD, IL
black tern (*Chlidonias niger*)	Water	KS, NE, IA, IL, WI, MN, ND, SD, IN
turkey vulture (*Cathartes aura*)	Diverse areas	Throughout biome
black vulture (*Coragyps atratus*)	Diverse areas	TX, OK, IL, MO, IN
Mississippi kite (*Ictinia mississippiensis*)	Near trees	TX, OK, KS, MO, IL
northern harrier (*Circus cyaneus*)	Wet areas	OK, KS, NE, MO, IA, IL, WI, MN, ND, SD, IN
red-tailed hawk (*Buteo jamaicensis*)	Near trees	Throughout biome
Swainson's hawk (*Buteo swainsoni*)	Near trees	TX, OK, KS, NE, SD, ND, MN, IA, IL, MO
white-tailed hawk (*Buteo albicaudatus*)	Near trees	TX
crested caracara (*Polyborus plancus*)	Dry areas, trees	TX
American kestrel (*Falco sparverius*)	Near trees	Throughout biome

continues

Species	Habitat Requirements	Geographic Range
greater prairie-chicken (*Tympanuchus cupido*)	Open areas	Rare throughout biome
sharp-tailed grouse (*Tympanuchus phasianellus*)	Brushy areas	NE, IA, WI, MN, ND, SD
northern bobwhite (*Colinus virginianus*)	Brushy areas	TX, OK, KS, NE, MO, IL, WI, MN, SD, IA, IN
mourning dove (*Zenaida macroura*)	Diverse areas	Throughout biome
common ground-dove (*Columbina passerina*)	Brushy areas	TX
grouse-billed ani (*Crotophaga sulcirostris*)	Near trees	TX
short-eared owl (*Asio flammeus*)	Near marshes	KS, NE, MO, IA, IL, WI, MN, ND, SD, IN
great horned owl (*Bubo virginianus*)	Near trees	Throughout biome
burrowing owl (*Athene cunicularia*)	Near prairie dogs	TX, OK, KS, NE, IA, MN, ND, SD
common nighthawk (*Chordeiles minor*)	Diverse areas	Throughout biome
lesser nighthawk (*Chordeiles acutipennis*)	Near water	TX
chimney swift (*Chaetura pelagica*)	Near buildings	Throughout biome
eastern kingbird (*Tyrannus tyrannus*)	Near brush	Throughout biome
western kingbird (*Tyrannus verticalis*)	Near brush	TX, OK, KS, NE, IA, MN, ND, SD
scissor-tailed flycatcher (*Tyrannus forficatus*)	Near brush	TX, OK, KS, NE, MO, IA
horned lark (*Eremophila alpestris*)	Sparse vegetation	Throughout biome
tree swallow (*Tachycineta bicolor*)	Near water	MO, NE, IA, IL, WI, MN, ND, SD, IN
bank swallow (*Riparia riparia*)	Dirt banks	KS, MO, NE, IA, IL, WI, MN, ND, SD, IN
cliff swallow (*Hirundo pyrrhonota*)	Cliff-like sites	Throughout biome
barn swallow (*Hirundo rustica*)	Cliff-like sites	Throughout biome
black-billed magpie (*Pica pica*)	Near trees	OK, KS, NE, SD, ND, MN
American crow (*Corvus brachynchos*)	Near trees	Throughout biome
marsh wren (*Cistothorus palustris*)	Marshes	Throughout biome

Species	Habitat Requirements	Geographic Range
sedge wren (*Cistothorus platensis*)	Marshes	KS, NE, MO, IA, IL, WI, MN, ND, SD, IN
eastern bluebird (*Sialia sialis*)	Near trees	Throughout biome
loggerhead shrike (*Lanius ludovicianus*)	Near brush	Throughout biome
Sprague's pipit (*Anthus spragueii*)	Open areas	MN, ND, SD
yellow warbler (*Dendroica petechia*)	Near wet brushy areas	OK, KS, NE, MO, IA, IL, WI, MN, ND, SD, IN
indigo bunting (*Passerina cyanea*)	Near edges	Throughout biome
grasshopper sparrow (*Ammodramus sarannarum*)	Open areas	Throughout biome
Baird's sparrow (*Ammodramus bairdii*)	Open areas	ND
Henslow's sparrow (*Ammodramus henslowii*)	Wet areas	KS, NE, MO, IA, IL, WI, MN, SD, IN
LeConte's sparrow (*Ammodramus leconteii*)	Wet areas	WI, MN, ND
sharp-tailed sparrow (*Ammodramus candacutus*)	Near water	MN, ND
vesper sparrow (*Pooecetes gramineus*)	Open areas	NE, MO, IA, IL, WI, MN, ND, SD, IN
Savannah sparrow (*Passerculus sandwichensis*)	Open areas	NE, MO, IA, IL, WI, MN, ND, SD, IN
song sparrow (*Melospiza melodica*)	Brushy areas	MO, NE, IA, IL, WI, MN, ND, SD, IN
swamp sparrow (*Melospiza georgiana*)	Marshes	IA, IL, WI, IN, MN, ND, SD
lark sparrow (*Chondestes grammacus*)	Diverse areas	Throughout biome
Cassin's sparrow (*Aimophila cassinii*)	Dry areas	TX, OK
field sparrow (*Spizella posilla*)	Brushy areas	Throughout biome
chipping sparrow (*Spizella passerina*)	Near woody edges	Throughout biome
clay-colored sparrow (*Spizella pallida*)	Brushy areas	NE, IA, WI, MN, ND, SD, IL
chestnut-collared longspur (*Calcarius ornatus*)	Moist areas	MN, ND, SD
dickcissel (*Spiza americana*)	Open areas	Throughout biome
lark bunting (*Calamospia melanocorys*)	Dry areas	KS, NE, ND, SD, MN, MO

continues

Species	Habitat Requirements	Geographic Range
bobolink (*Dolichonyx oryzivorus*)	Moist areas	NE, IA, IL, WI, MN, ND, SD, IN
eastern meadowlark (*Sturnella magna*)	Open areas	TX, OK, KS, MO, NE, IA, WI, MN, IL, IN
western meadowlark (*Sturnella neglecta*)	Open areas	TX, OK, KS, NE, IA, IL, WI, MN, ND, SD, IN
yellow-headed blackbird (*Xanthocephalus xanthocephalus*)	Marshes	KS, NE, MO, IA, IL, WI, MN, ND, SD, IN
red-winged blackbird (*Agelaius phoeniceus*)	Marshes	Throughout biome
Brewer's blackbird (*Euphagus cyanocephalus*)	Open areas	IA, IL, WI, MN, ND, SD
brown-headed cowbird (*Molothrus ater*)	Diverse areas	Throughout biome
bronzed cowbird (*Molothrus aeneus*)	Diverse areas	TX
common grackle (*Quiscalus quiscula*)	Diverse areas	Throughout biome
great-tailed grackle (*Quiscalus mexicanus*)	Wet areas	TX, OK, KS
American goldfinch (*Carduelis tristis*)	Brushy areas	Throughout biome

Mammals

Species	Habitat Requirements	Geographic Range
Virginia opossum (*Didelphis virginiana*)	Brush areas	TX, IN, OK, KS, NE, MO, IA, IL, WI, MN, SD
arctic shrew (*Sorex arcticus*)	Wet areas	WI, MN, ND
masked shrew (*Sorex cinereus*)	Moist areas	NE, IA, IL, WI, MN, IN, ND, SD
pygmy shrew (*Sorex hoyi*)	Diverse areas	ND, SD, MN, IA, WI, IL, IN
southeastern shrew (*Sorex longirostris*)	Moist diverse areas	IL, IN(?)
water shrew (*Sorex palustris*)	wet areas	MN, WI, ND(?)
northern short-tailed shrew (*Blarina brevicauda*)	Diverse grasslands	ND, SD, NE, MN, IA, MO, WI, IL, IN
southern short-tailed shrew (*Blarina carolinensis*)	Diverse grasslands	IA, NE, KS, MO, OK, TX
Elliot's short-tailed shrew (*Blarina hylophaga*)	Diverse grasslands	NE, IA, IL, MO, KS
least shrew (*Cryptotis parva*)	Moist areas	TX, IN, OK, KS, NE, MO, IA, IL, WI, MN, SD
eastern mole (*Scalopus aquaticus*)	Well-drained soils	TX, IN, OK, KS, NE, MO, IA, IL, MN, SD
little brown myotis (*Myotis lucifugus*)	Near roost sites	MO, IA, IL, WI, MN, ND, SD, IN

Species	Habitat Requirements	Geographic Range
northern myotis (*Myotis septentrionalis*)	Diverse areas	ND, SD, NE, KS, OK, MN, IA, MO, WI, IL, IN
silver-haired bat (*Lasionycteris noctivagans*)	Diverse areas	Throughout biome
eastern pipistrelle (*Pipistrellus subflavus*)	Areas with moist rock formations	NE, KS, OK, TX, MN, IA, MO, WI, IL, IN
big brown bat (*Eptesice fuscus*)	Near roost sites	Throughout biome
red bat (*Lasiurus borealis*)	Diverse areas with trees	Throughout biome
hoary bat (*Lasiurus cinereus*)	Diverse areas with conifers	Throughout biome
evening bat (*Nycticeius humeralis*)	Diverse areas with trees	NE, KS, OK, TX, IA, MO, IL, IN
Brazilian free-tailed bat (*Tadarida brasiliensis*)	Near roost sites	TX, OK
nine-banded armadillo (*Dasypus novemcinctus*)	Well-drained soils	TX, OK
eastern cottontail (*Sylvilagus floridanus*)	Near brush	Throughout biome
white-tailed jackrabbit (*Lepus townsendii*)	Open areas	KS, NE, IA, WI, MN, ND, SD
black-tailed jackrabbit (*Lepus californicus*)	Open areas	TX, OK, KS, NE, MO, SD
woodchuck (*Marmota monax*)	Near woods	KS, NE, MO, IA, IL, WI, MN, ND, SD
Richardson's ground squirrel (*Spermophilus richardsonii*)	Open areas	MN, ND, SD, IA
thirteen-lined ground squirrel (*Spermophilus tridecemlineatus*)	Open areas	Throughout biome
Mexican ground squirrel (*Spermophilus mexicanus*)	Dry areas	TX
Franklin's ground squirrel (*Spermophilus franklinii*)	Near brush	KS, NE, MO, IA, IL, WI, MN, ND, SD, IN
northern pocket gopher (*Thomomys talpoides*)	Diverse grasslands	ND, SD, MN, NE
plains pocket gopher (*Geomys bursarius*)	Well-drained soils	Throughout biome
Texas pocket gopher (*Geomys personatus*)	Well-drained soils	TX
plains pocket mouse (*Perognathus flavescens*)	Well-drained soils	KS, NE, IA, MN, ND, SD
beaver (*Castor canadensis*)	Riparian areas	Throughout biome
hispid pocket mouse (*Perognathus hispidus*)	Sparse vegetation	TX, OK, KS, NE

continues

Species	Habitat Requirements	Geographic Range
marsh rice rat (*Oryzomys palustris*)	Wet areas	TX, IL, OK
plains harvest mouse (*Reithrodontomys montanus*)	Open areas	TX, OK, KS, NE
eastern harvest mouse (*Reithrodontomys humulis*)	Near brush	TX, OK
western harvest mouse (*Reithrodontomys megalotis*)	Open areas	NE, IA, IL, WI, MN, SD, ND, KS, OK
fulvous harvest mouse (*Reithrodontomys fulvescens*)	Dry areas	TX, OK
white-footed mouse (*Peromyscus leucopus*)	Bush and riparian areas	Throughout biome
deer mouse (*Peromyscus maniculatus*)	Near brush; open areas	Throughout biome
northern pygmy mouse (*Baiomys taylori*)	Open areas	TX
northern grasshopper mouse (*Onychomys leucogaster*)	Dry areas, weedy and disturbed	TX, OK, KS, NE, IA, MN, ND, SD
hispid cotton rat (*Sigmodon hispidus*)	Open areas	TX, IA, OK, KS, NE
meadow vole (*Microtus pennsylvanicus*)	Diverse areas, especially grasslands	NE, MO, IA, IL, WI, MN, ND, SD, IN
prairie vole (*Microtus ochrogaster*)	Open areas	OK, KS, NE, MO, IA, IL, WI, MN, ND, SD, IN
muskrat (*Ondatra zibethicus*)	Marshes	Throughout biome
southern bog lemming (*Synaptomys cooperi*)	Moist areas	KS, MO, IA, IL, WI, MN, ND, SD, IN
meadow jumping mouse (*Zapus hudsonius*)	Moist areas or grassy fields	NE, MO, IA, IL, WI, MN, ND, SD, IN
coyote (*Canis latrans*)	Diverse areas	Throughout biome
gray wolf (*Canis lupus*)	Diverse areas	Extirpated throughout biome
red wolf (*Canis rufus*)	Diverse areas	TX
red fox (*Vulpes vulpes*)	Diverse areas	Throughout biome
swift fox (*Vulpes velox*)	Open areas	KS, NE, IA(?), MN(?), ND, SD
gray fox (*Urocyon cinereoargenteus*)	Near wooded areas	Throughout biome
raccoon (*Procyon lotor*)	Near water	Throughout biome
short-tailed weasel, ermine (*Mustela erminea*)	Diverse areas	WI, MN, ND, SD, IA
least weasel (*Mustela nivalis*)	Diverse areas	IA, IL, WI, MN, ND, SD, IN, MO, KS
long-tailed weasel (*Mustela frenata*)	Diverse areas	Throughout biome
mink (*Mustela vison*)	Near water	Throughout biome
badger (*Taxidea taxus*)	Open areas	Throughout biome

Species	Habitat Requirements	Geographic Range
eastern spotted skunk (*Spilogale putorius*)	Near woods	TX, WI, OK, KS, NE, MO, IA, MN, SD, ND
striped skunk (*Mephitis mephitis*)	Diverse areas	Throughout biome
collared peccary (*Dicotyles tajacu*)	Diverse areas	TX
river otter (*Lutra canadensis*)	Riparian areas	Originally throughout; extirpated and reintroduced
mountain lion (*Felis concolor*)	Diverse areas	Extirpated; occasional reports
bobcat (*Felis rufus*)	Diverse areas	Throughout biome
elk (*Cervus elaphus*)	Diverse areas	Extirpated throughout biome, reintroduced in northwestern MN
mule deer (*Odocoileus hemionus*)	Diverse, open areas	Stragglers in MN, IA, ND, SD, NE
white-tailed deer (*Odocoileus virginianus*)	Near woods, brush	Throughout biome
bison (*Bison bison*)	Open areas	Extirpated throughout biome

SOURCES

Collins, J.T. 1990. *Standard Common and Current Scientific Names for North American Amphibians and Reptiles.* Lawrence, KS: Society for the Study of Amphibians and Reptiles Herpetological Circular No. 19.

Jones, J.K., Jr., and E.C. Birney. 1988. *Handbook of Mammals of the North-Central States.* Minneapolis: University of Minnesota Press.

Risser, P.G., E.C. Birney, H.D. Blocker, et al. 1981. *The True Prairie Ecosystem,* vol. 16. Stroudsburg, PA: Hutchinson Ross Publishing.

Appendix C
Cross References
for Plant Names

Table C.1. Scientific Names of Plants Mentioned in the Text

Common Name	Scientific Name
alum root	*Heuchera richardsonii* and *H. americana*
anemone, rue	†*Thalictrum thalictroides*
ash, green	*Fraxinus pennsylvanica*
aspen, quaking	*Populus tremuloides*
aster, azure	†*Aster oolentangiensis*
aster, false	†*Boltonia asteroides*
aster, flax-leaved	†*Ionactis linariifolius*
aster, heath	*Aster ericoides*
aster, New England	*Aster novae-angliae*
aster, smooth blue	*Aster laevis*
aster, stiff	†*Solidago ptarmicoides*
asters	*Aster* spp.
avens, white	*Geum canadense*
basswood	*Tilia americana*
beard tongues	*Penstemon* spp.
beech	*Fagus grandifolia*
beech, blue	*Carpinus caroliniana*
bergamot, wild	*Monarda fistulosa*
black-eyed Susan	*Rudbeckia hirta*
black-eyed Susan, Missouri	*Rudbeckia missouriensis*
black-eyed Susan, sweet	*Rudbeckia subtomentosa*
blazing star, cylindrical	*Liatris cylindracea*
blazing star, marsh	*Liatris spicata*
blazing star, prairie	*Liatris pycnostachya*
blazing star, rough	*Liatris aspera*
blazing stars	*Liatris* spp.
bloodroot	*Sanguinaria canadensis*
blue-eyed grass, prairie	*Sisyrinchium campestre*
bluegrass	*Poa* spp.

---

*Indicates nomenclature differs from Kartesz.

†Precedes scientific names cross-referenced in table C.2.

Table C.1. (*Continued*)

Common Name	Scientific Name
bluegrass, Canada	*Poa compressa*
bluegrass, Kentucky	*Poa pratensis*
bluestem, big	*Andropogon gerardii*
bluestem, little	†*Schizachyrium scoparium*
briars	*Rubus* spp.
brome, smooth	*Bromus inermis*
broom rape, clustered	*Orobanche fasciculata*
buckthorn, common	*Rhamnus cathartica*
buckthorn, Dahurian	*Rhamnus davurica*
buckthorn, glossy	*Rhamnus frangula*★
bundleflowers	*Desmanthus* spp.
burdock	*Arctium* spp.
bush clover, round-headed	*Lespedeza capitata*
cardinal flower	*Lobelia cardinalis*
cherry, black	*Prunus serotina*
cinquefoil, common	*Potentilla simplex*
cinquefoils	*Potentilla* spp.
clover, Korean bush	*Kummerowia stipulacea*
clover, purple prairie	†*Dalea purpurea*
clover, red	*Trifolium pratense*
clover, white	*Trifolium repens*
clover, white prairie	†*Dalea candida*
clover, white sweet	*Melilotus alba*★
clover, yellow sweet	*Melilotus officinalis*
clovers, prairie	*Dalea* spp.
columbine	*Aquilegia canadensis*
compass plant	*Silphium laciniatum*
coneflower, grey-headed	*Ratibida pinnata*
coneflower, long-headed	*Ratibida columnifera*
coneflower, narrow-leaved	*Echinacea angustifolia*
coneflower, pale purple	*Echinacea pallida*
coneflower, purple	*Echinacea purpurea*
coreopsis	*Coreopsis* spp.
coreopsis, prairie	*Coreopsis palmata*
cottonwood	*Populus deltoides*
Culver's root	*Veronicastrum virginicum*
daisy	*Leucanthemum vulgare*
dandelion	*Taraxacum officinale*
dewberry, common	*Rubus flagellaris*
dock, prairie	*Silphium terebinthinaceum*
dogwood, gray	*Cornus racemosa*
dogwood, rough-leaved	*Cornus drummondii*
dropseed, prairie	*Sporobolus heterolepis*

Table C.1. (*Continued*)

Common Name	Scientific Name
dropseed, tall	*Sporobolus compositus*
elder, box	*Acer negundo*
elm, Americam	*Ulmus americana*
elm, winged	*Ulmus alata*
false foxglove, eared	†*Agalinis auriculata*
fern, bracken	*Pteridium aquilinum*
fescue, meadow	*Festuca pratensis* and/or *F. arundinacea*
fleabane	*Erigeron* spp.
fleabane, annual	*Erigeron annuus*
fleabane, daisy	*Erigeron strigosus*
foxtails	*Setaria* spp.
gentians	*Gentiana* spp.
geranium, wild	*Geranium maculatum*
golden Alexanders	*Zizia aurea*
golden glow	*Rudbeckia laciniata*
goldenrod, Canada	*Solidago canadensis*
goldenrod, early	*Solidago juncea*
goldenrod, grass-leaved	†*Euthamia graminifolia*
goldenrod, Missouri	*Solidago missouriensis*
goldenrod, stiff	*Solidago rigida*
goldenrod, tall	*Solidago canadensis scabra*
goldenrods	*Solidago* spp.
grama, blue	*Bouteloua gracilis*
grama, side-oats	*Bouteloua curtipendula*
grama grasses	*Bouteloua* spp.
grass, blue joint	*Calamagrostis canadensis*
grass, Indian	*Sorghastrum nutans*
grass, Johnson	*Sorghum halepense*
grass, June	†*Koeleria macrantha*
grass, porcupine	*Stipa spartea*
grass, prairie cord	*Spartina pectinata*
grass, prairie panic	*Panicum leibergii* ★
grass, quack	*Elytrigia repens*
grass, reed canary	*Phalaris arundinacea*
grass, switch	*Panicum virgatum*
grass, thickspike wheat	†*Elymus lanceolatus*
grass, tufted hair	*Deschampsia cespitosa*
grass, western wheat	†*Pascopyron smithii*
grasses, brome	*Bromus* spp.
grasses, needle	*Stipa* spp.
hazel or hazelnut	*Corylus americana*
honeysuckle, Amur	*Lonicera maackii*
honeysuckle, belle	*Lonicera* × *bella*

continues

★Indicates nomenclature differs from Kartesz.

†Precedes scientific names cross-referenced in table C.2.

Table C.1. (*Continued*)

Common Name	Scientific Name
honeysuckle, Japanese	*Lonicera japonica*
honeysuckle, Morrow's	*Lonicera morrowii*
honeysuckle, Tartarian	*Lonicera tatarica*
hornbeam, hop	*Ostrya virginiana*
horseweed	*Conyza canadensis*
Indian plantain, prairie	*Arnoglossum plantagineum*
indigo bush	*Amorpha fruticosa*
indigos, wild	*Baptisia* spp.
iris, blue flag	*Iris virginica shrevei*
ivy, poison	*Toxicodendron radicans*
knapweed, spotted	†*Centaurea biebersteinii*
lead plant	*Amorpha canescens*
lily, prairie	*Lilium philadelphicum*
locust, black	*Robinia pseudoacacia*
loosestrife, purple	*Lythrum salicaria*
lupines	*Lupinus* spp.
maple, black	*Acer nigrum*
maple, sugar	*Acer saccharum*
marigold, tall swamp	*Bidens coronata*
Mayapple	*Podophyllum peltatum*
milkweed, common	*Asclepias syriaca*
milkweed, swamp	*Asclepias incarnata*
milkweed, whorled	*Asclepias verticillata*
mustard, garlic	*Alliaria petiolata*
mustards	*Cruciferae*
nettle, horse	*Solanum carolinense*
nightshade, enchanter's	*Circaea lutetiana* ssp. *canadensis*
oak, black	*Quercus velutina*
oak, blackjack	*Quercus marilandica*
oak, bur	*Quercus macrocarpa*
oak, northern pin	*Quercus ellipsoidalis*
oak, pin	*Quercus palustris*
oak, post	*Quercus stellata*
oak, red	*Quercus rubra*
oak, swamp white	*Quercus bicolor*
oak, white	*Quercus alba*
oats, wild	*Avena fatua*
olive, autumn	*Elaeagnus umbellata*
onion, nodding wild	*Allium cernuum*
orchid, prairie fringed	*Platanthera leucophaea* and *P. praeclara*
parsley, hedge	*Torilis arvensis* and *T. nodosa*
parsnip, heart-leaved meadow	*Zizia aptera*
parsnip, wild	*Pastinaca sativa*

Table C.1. (*Continued*)

Common Name	Scientific Name
pasque flower	*Pulsatilla patens*
pea, partridge	†*Chamaecrista fasciculata*
pea, veiny	*Lathyrus venosus*
peppervine	*Ampelopsis arborea*
phloxes	*Phlox* spp.
pigweeds	*Amaranthus* spp.
poplar, white	*Populus alba*
prairie smoke	*Geum triflorum*
puccoons	*Lithospermum* spp.
Queen Anne's lace	*Daucus carota*
quinine, wild	*Parthenium integrifolium*
ragweed, common	*Ambrosia artemisiifolia*
rattlesnake master	*Eryngium yuccifolium*
redtop	*Agrostis gigantea* (formerly *A. alba*)
rose, multiflora	*Rosa multiflora*
roses	*Rosa* spp.
rye, Canada wild	*Elymus canadensis*
sedge, common wood	*Carex blanda*
sedges	*Cyperaceae,* esp. *Carex* spp.
self-heal	*Prunella vulgaris lanceolata*
senna, Maryland	†*Senna marilandica*
shooting star	*Dodecatheon meadia*
smartweeds	*Polygonum* spp.
snakeroot, Seneca	*Polygala senega*
snakeroot, white	†*Ageratina altissima*
sneezeweed	*Helenium autumnale*
spiderworts	*Tradescantia* spp.
spurge, flowering	*Euphorbia corollata*
spurge, leafy	*Euphorbia esula*
strawberry, wild	*Fragaria virginiana*
sumac, smooth	*Rhus glabra*
sumac, winged	*Rhus copallina*
sunflower, false	*Heliopsis helianthoides*
sunflower, Maximilian	*Helianthus maximiliani*
sunflower, showy	†*Helianthus pauciflorus*
sunflowers	*Helianthus* spp.
tea, New Jersey	*Ceanothus americanus*
teasel	*Dipsacus* spp.
teasel, common	†*Dipsacus fullonum* ssp. *sylvestris*
teasel, cut-leaved	*Dipsacus laciniatus*
thistle, Canada	*Cirsium arvense*
thistle, prairie	*Cirsium hillii*
thistles	*Cirsium* spp.

*Indicates nomenclature differs from Kartesz.

†Precedes scientific names cross-referenced in table C.2.

continues

Table C.1. (*Continued*)

Common Name	Scientific Name
tick trefoils	*Desmodium* spp.
tickseeds	*Bidens* spp.
timothy	*Phleum pratense*
toadflax, false	†*Comandra umbellata*
vervain, blue	*Verbena hastata*
vetch, Canadian milk	*Astragalus canadensis*
vetch, crown	*Coronilla varia*
violet, bird's foot	*Viola pedata*
violet, prairie	*Viola pedatifida*
violets	*Viola* spp.
walnut, black	*Juglans nigra*
willow, prairie	*Salix humilis*
wood sorrel, violet	*Oxalis violacea*
yarrow	*Achillea millefolium*

★Indicates nomenclature differs from Kartesz.

†Precedes scientific names cross-referenced in table C.2.

Table C.2.

Scientific Names Synonymized

This list includes synonyms commonly used for plants listed in the tables found in this book. A "K" following the name indicates that this is the name used in Kartesz (*A Synonymized Checklist of the Vascular Flora of the United States, Canada, and Greenland*, 2 vols., Timber Press, Portland, OR, 1994), which is the nomenclatural system used throughout this book. Synonyms followed by "G&C" are those used in Gleason and Cronquist (*Manual of Vascular Plants of the Northeastern United States and Adjacent Canada*, 2nd edition, New York Botanical Garden, Bronx, New York, 1991). Synonyms that are commonly used in a variety of plant guides but that do not follow either of the above nomenclatural systems have been included without referencing a source.

Agalinis auriculata (K) = *Tomanthera auriculata*

Agalinis purpurea (K) = *Gerardia purpurea*

Agalinis tenuifolia (K) = *Gerardia tenuifolia*

Ageratina altissima (K) = *Eupatorium rugosum* (G&C)

Agoseris cuspidata, see *Nothocalais cuspidata* (K)

Agropyron repens, see *Elytrigia repens* (K)

Agropyron smithii, see *Pascopyron smithii* (K)

Agropyron trachycaulum, see *Elymus trachycaulus* (K)

Allium burdickii (K) = *Allium tricoccum burdickii* (G&C)

Allium tricoccum burdickii (G&C), see *Allium burdickii* (K)

Ambrosia coronopifolia (K) = *Ambrosia psilostachya* (G&C)

Ambrosia psilostachya (G&C), see *Ambrosia coronopifolia* (K)

Andropogon scoparius, see *Schizachyrium scoparium* (K)

Anemonella thalictroides (G&C), see *Thalictrum thalictroides* (K)

Arenaria lateriflora (G&C), see *Moehringia lateriflora* (K)

Arisaema atrorubens, see *Arisaema triphyllum* (K)

Arisaema triphyllum (K) = *Arisaema atrorubens*

Arnoglossum atriplicifolium (K) = *Cacalia atriplicifolia* (G&C)

Arnoglossum plantagineum (K) = *Cacalia plantaginea* (G&C), *C. tuberosa*

Artemisia campestris caudata (K) = *Artemisia caudata*

Artemisia caudata, see *Artemisia campestris caudata* (K)

Aster azureus, see *Aster oolentangiensis* (K)

Aster cordifolius sagittifolius (K) = *Aster sagittifolius* (G&C)

Aster lanceolatus (K) = *Aster simplex*

Aster linariifolius (G&C), see *Ionactis linariifolius* (K)

Aster oolentangiensis (K) = *Aster azureus*

Aster ptarmicoides, see *Solidago ptarmicoides* (K)

Aster sagittifolius (G&C), see *Aster cordifolius sagittifolius* (K)

continues

Table C.2. (*Continued*)

Aster simplex, see *Aster lanceolatus* (K)

Aureolaria grandiflora (K) = *Gerardia grandiflora*

Baptisia alba macrophylla (K) = *Baptisia lactea* (G&C), *B. leucantha*

Baptisia bracteata (G&C), see *Baptisia bracteata leucophaea* (K)

Baptisia bracteata leucophaea (K) = *Baptisia bracteata* (G&C), *B. leucophaea*

Baptisia lactea (G&C), see *Baptisia alba macrophylla* (K)

Baptisia leucantha, see *Baptisia alba macrophylla* (K)

Baptisia leucophaea, see *Baptisia bracteata leucophaea* (K)

Besseya bullii (K) = *Wulfenia bullii*

Boltonia asteroides (K) = *Boltonia latisquama recognita*

Boltonia latisquama recognita, see *Boltonia asteroides* (K)

Brickellia eupatorioides (K) = *Kuhnia eupatorioides* (G&C)

Bromus pubescens (K) = *Bromus purgans*

Bromus purgans, see *Bromus pubescens* (K)

Cacalia atriplicifolia (G&C), see *Arnoglossum atriplicifolium* (K)

Cacalia plantaginea (G&C), see *Arnoglossum plantagineum* (K)

Cacalia tuberosa, see *Arnoglossum plantagineum* (K)

Calopogon pulchellus, see *Calopogon tuberosus* (K)

Calopogon tuberosus (K) = *Calopogon pulchellus*

Calystegia spithamaea (K) = *Convolvulus spithamaeus*

Campanula americana (G&C), see *Campanulastrum americanum* (K)

Campanulastrum americanum (K) = *Campanula americana* (G&C)

Cardamine concatenata (K) = *Dentaria laciniata*

Carex complanata hirsuta (G&C), see *Carex hirsutella* (K)

Carex hirsutella (K) = *Carex complanata hirsuta* (G&C)

Carex lanuginosa, see *Carex pellita*★

Carex pellita★ = *Carex lanuginosa*

Cassia fasciculata, see *Chamaecrista fasciculata* (K)

Cassia hebecarpa, see *Senna hebecarpa* (K)

Cassia marilandica, see *Senna marilandica* (K)

Caulophyllum giganteum (K) = *Caulophyllum thalictroides* (G&C)

Caulophyllum thalictroides (G&C), see *Caulophyllum giganteum* (K)

Ceanothus herbaceus (K) = *Ceanothus ovatus*

Ceanothus ovatus, see *Ceanothus herbaceus* (K)

Centaurea biebersteinii (K) = *Centaurea maculosa* (G&C)

Centaurea maculosa (G&C), see *Centaurea biebersteinii* (K)

Chamaecrista fasciculata (K) = *Cassia fasciculata*

Chenopodium gigantospermum, see *Chenopodium simplex* (K)

Chenopodium hybridum, see *Chenopodium simplex* (K)

Chenopodium simplex (K) = *Chenopodium hybridum*, *C. gigantospermum*

Comandra richardsiana, see *Comandra umbellata* (K)

Table C.2. (*Continued*)

Comandra umbellata (K) = *Comandra richardsiana*

Convolvulus spithamaeus, see *Calystegia spithamaea* (K)

Dalea candida (K) = *Petalostemum candidum*

Dalea purpurea (K) = *Petalostemum purpureum*

Dasistoma macrophylla (K) = *Seymeria macrophylla*

Dentaria laciniata, see *Cardamine concatenata* (K)

Dipsacus fullonum ssp. *sylvestris* (K) = *Dipsacus sylvestris* (G&C)

Dipsacus sylvestris (G&C), see *Dipsacus fullonum* ssp. *sylvestris* (K)

Elymus hystrix (K) = *Hystrix patula*

Elymus lanceolatus ssp. *lanceolatus* (K) = *Elytrigia dasystachya* (G&C)

Elymus trachycaulus (K) = *Agropyron trachycaulum*

Elytrigia dasystachya (G&C), see *Elymus lanceolatus* ssp. *lanceolatus* (K)

Elytrigia repens (K) = *Agropyron repens*

Elytrigia smithii (G&C), see *Pascopyron smithii* (K)

Enemion biternatum (K) = *Isopyrum biternatum* (G&C)

Euonymus atropurpureus (G&C), see *Evonymus atropurpurea* (K)

Euonymus obovatus (G&C), see *Evonymus obovata* (K)

Eupatorium rugosum (G&C), see *Ageratina altissima* (K)

Eustoma grandiflorum, see *Eustoma russellianum* (K)

Eustoma russellianum (K) = *Eustoma grandiflorum*

Euthamia graminifolia (K) = *Solidago graminifolia*

Evonymus atropurpurea (K) = *Euonymus atropurpureus* (G&C)

Evonymus obovata (K) = *Euonymus obovatus* (G&C)

Festuca obtusa, see *Festuca subverticillata* (K)

Festuca subverticillata (K) = *Festuca obtusa*

Gaura biennis pitcheri (G&C), see *Gaura longiflora* (K)

Gaura longiflora (K) = *Gaura biennis pitcheri* (G&C)

Gentiana alba (K) = *Gentiana flavida* (G&C)

Gentiana crinita, see *Gentianopsis crinita* (K)

Gentiana flavida (G&C), see *Gentiana alba* (K)

Gentiana quinquefolia, see *Gentianella quinquefolia* (K)

Gentianella quinquefolia (K) = *Gentiana quinquefolia*

Gentianopsis crinita (K) = *Gentiana crinita*

Gerardia grandiflora, see *Aureolaria grandiflora* (K)

Gerardia purpurea, see *Agalinis purpurea* (K)

Gerardia tenuifolia, see *Agalinis tenuifolia* (K)

Helianthus laetiflorus, see *Helianthus pauciflorus* (K)

Helianthus pauciflorus (K) = *Helianthus laetiflorus, H. rigidus*

Helianthus rigidus, see *Helianthus pauciflorus* (K)

Hepatica acutiloba (G&C), see *Hepatica nobilis acuta* (K)

Hepatica nobilis acuta (K) = *Hepatica acutiloba* (G&C)

★ Indicates nomenclature differs from Kartesz.

continues

Table C.2. (*Continued*)

Heracleum lanatum (G&C), see *Heracleum maximum* (K)

Heracleum maximum (K) = *Heracleum lanatum* (G&C)

Hypericum ascyron (K) = *Hypericum pyramidatum* (G&C)

Hypericum pyramidatum (G&C), see *Hypericum ascyron* (K)

Hystrix patula, see *Elymus hystrix* (K)

Ionactis linariifolius (K) = *Aster linariifolius* (G&C)

Isanthus brachiatus (G&C), see *Trichostema brachiatum* (K)

Isopyrum biternatum (G&C), see *Enemion biternatum* (K)

Koeleria cristata, see *Koeleria macrantha* (K)

Koeleria macrantha (K) = *Koelaria pyramidata* (G&C), *K. cristata*

Koeleria pyramidata (G&C), see *Koeleria macrantha* (K)

Kuhnia eupatorioides (G&C), see *Brickellia eupatorioides* (K)

Kummerowia stipulacea (K) = *Lespedeza stipulacea* (G&C)

Lespedeza stipulacea (G&C), see *Kummerowia stipulacea* (K)

Linaria canadensis (G&C), see *Nuttallanthus canadensis* (K)

Lonicera prolifera (G&C), see *Lonicera reticulata* (K)

Lonicera reticulata (K) = *Lonicera prolifera* (G&C)

Maianthemum racemosum (K) = *Smilacina racemosa* (G&C)

Maianthemum stellatum (K) = *Smilacina stellata* (G&C)

Mentha arvensis villosa (G&C), see *Mentha canadensis* (K)

Mentha canadensis (K) = *Mentha arvensis villosa* (G&C)

Microseris cuspidata (G&C), see *Nothocalais cuspidata* (K)

Mimosa quadrivalvis nuttallii (K) = *Schrankia nuttallii, S. uncinata*

Moehringia lateriflora (K) = *Arenaria lateriflora* (G&C)

Nothocalais cuspidata (K) = *Microseris cuspidata* (G&C), *Agoseris cuspidata*

Nuttallanthus canadensis (K) = *Linaria canadensis* (G&C)

Panicum implicatum, see *Panicum lanuginosum implicatum*★

Panicum lanuginosum implicatum★ = *Panicum implicatum*

Pascopyron smithii (K) = *Elytrigia smithii* (G&C), *Agropyron smithii*

Paspalum ciliatifolium, see *Paspalum setaceum* (K)

Paspalum setaceum (K) = *Paspalum ciliatifolium*

Petalostemum candidum, see *Dalea candida* (K)

Petalostemum purpureum, see *Dalea purpurea* (K)

Polygonatum biflorum commutatum (K) = *Polygonatum canaliculatum*

Polygonatum canaliculatum, see *Polygonatum biflorum commutatum* (K)

Psoralea tenuiflora, see *Psoralidium tenuiflorum* (K)

Psoralidium tenuiflorum (K) = *Psoralea tenuiflora*

Ranunculus hispidus nitidus (K) = *Ranunculus septentrionalis*

Ranunculus septentrionalis, see *Ranunculus hispidus nitidus* (K)

Samolus floribundus (G&C), see *Samolus valerandi* ssp. *parviflorus* (K)

Samolus parviflorus, see *Samolus valerandi* ssp. *parviflorus* (K)

Table C.2. (*Continued*)

Samolus valerandi ssp. parviflorus (K) = *Samolus floribundus* (G&C), *S. parviflorus*

Schizachyrium scoparium (K) = *Andropogon scoparius*

Schrankia nuttallii, see *Mimosa quadrivalvis nuttallii* (K)

Schrankia uncinata, see *Mimosa quadrivalvis nuttallii* (K)

Senna hebecarpa (K) = *Cassia hebecarpa*

Senna marilandica (K) = *Cassia marilandica*

Seymeria macrophylla, see *Dasistoma macrophylla* (K)

Smilacina racemosa (G&C), see *Maianthemum racemosum* (K)

Smilacina stellata (G&C), see *Maianthemum stellatum* (K)

Solidago graminifolia, see *Euthamia graminifolia* (K)

Solidago ptarmicoides (K) = *Aster ptarmicoides*

Specularia perfoliata, see *Triodanis perfoliata* (K)

Thalictrum thalictroides (K) = *Anemonella thalictroides* (G&C)

Tomanthera auriculata, see *Agalinis auriculata* (K)

Trichostema brachiatum (K) = *Isanthus brachiatus* (G&C)

Triodanis perfoliata (K) = *Specularia perfoliata*

Wulfenia bullii, see *Besseya bullii* (K)

★ Indicates nomenclature differs from Kartesz.

Appendix D
Publications on Natural
Communities of the Tallgrass Region

The following references classify and detail the composition, structure, and processes of tallgrass prairie, savanna, woodland, and wetland communities. Additional reference lists for many of these and related topics can be found in the bibliographies contained within these publications. Some of these references may be hard to find, but all are available in college libraries, through interlibrary loan, or through state natural resources departments. Copies of some can be obtained by writing to the listed addresses or to the publisher. Theses are available at the school where they were written.

General References

Botts, P., A. Haney, K. Holland, S. Packard, eds. 1994. *Midwest Oak Ecosystems Recovery Plan (September 1994),* a published report of the Nature Conservancy, Illinois Field Office, Chicago, IL. (Available from U.S. Environmental Protection Agency, Great Lakes National Program Office, 77 W. Jackson Blvd., Chicago, IL 60604.)

> A consensus document that includes many useful local species lists such as "Plants and Animals of Sand Savannas of Indiana" and "Savanna and Woodland Birds of Illinois," as well as plant and animal species lists for savannas and oak woodlands of the Midwest.

Collins, S.L., and L.L. Wallace, eds. 1990. *Fire in North American Tallgrass Prairies.* Norman: University of Oklahoma Press.

> An introduction by a variety of authors to fire in tallgrass prairies. The effect of fire on the biota, including plant reproduction and seedling establishment, small mammals, below-ground processes, and community structure, is reviewed. Historical, ecosystem, and landscape processes are also highlighted.

Curtis, John T. 1959. *The Vegetation of Wisconsin: An Ordination of Plant Communities.* Madison: University of Wisconsin Press.

> Far and away the best summary of the composition and ecology of the natural communities of the tallgrass region. Although specific to Wisconsin, it is well worth study by any restorationist, particularly those in Minnesota, Iowa, Illinois, Indiana, and Michigan. Includes extensive lists of the principal species of major prairie, savanna, and wetland types. Dry woodlands are treated as "Xeric Forest." Mesic and wet woodlands did not survive well at the time of Curtis's studies and were not included.

Fralish, J.S., R.C. Anderson, J.E. Ebinger, and R. Szafoni, eds. 1994. *Proceedings of the North American Conference on Barrens and Savanna,* October 15-16, 1994, Illinois State University, Normal, Illinois. Printed by the U.S. Environmental Protection Agency. (Available at some conservation agencies and science libraries.)

> A wide-ranging collection of articles on savannas and barrens, including the history and nature of savannas, policy and planning issues in savanna conservation, savanna fauna, regional variation in savanna and barrens, and restoration and management.

Grossman, D., K. Goodin, and C. Reuss, eds. 1944. In *Rare Plant Communities of the Conterminous United States, An Initial Survey,* prepared for the U.S. Fish and Wildlife Service by the Nature Conservancy, 1815 N. Lynn Street, Arlington, Virginia 22209.

> Describes many of the known rare plant communities of the lower forty-eight states of the U.S. Since midwestern prairie, savanna, and woodland communities are rare, most of them are covered in this book. A system of vegetation classification is used that emphasizes vegetation structure and a combination of dominant and characteristic species. Includes for each community a short list of diagnostic species and a "conservation rank," which reflects rarity.

Leach, Mark, and Laurel Ross, eds. *Midwest Oak Ecosystem Recovery Plan: A Call to Action,* September 1995. (Available from the U.S. Environmental Protection Agency, Great Lakes National Program Office, 77 W. Jackson Blvd., Chicago, IL 60604.)

> Good overview of the still poorly understood oak savannas and woodlands, with an excellent bibliography. Discussion of vegetation classification by Don Faber-Langendoen. Sample conservation and recovery plans for three midwestern oak savanna and woodland types (northern bur oak openings, northern black oak barrens, and northern white oak–bur oak woodlands). Lists plant indicator species of recoverable oak savannas and open oak woodlands.

Morgan, J.P., D.R. Collicutt, and J.D. Durant. 1995. *Restoring Canada's Native Prairies: A Practical Manual.* Prairie Habitats, P.O. Box 1, Argyle, Manitoba, Canada R0C 0B0.

> Covers all five Canadian provinces that contain (or historically contained) prairie: Alberta, British Columbia, Manitoba, Ontario, and Saskatchewan. A full-

color guide to obtaining and processing seed, preparing sites, and managing restored prairies. Includes species lists for each province broken down by prairie type. Written for an audience ranging from schoolchildren to professional resource managers.

Risser, P.G., E.C. Birney, H.D. Blocker, S.W. May, W.J. Parton, and J.A. Wiens. 1981. *The True Prairie Ecosystem*. US/IBP Synthesis Series No. 16. Stroudsburg, PA: Hutchinson Ross Publishing Company.

> A compilation of studies from tallgrass prairie sites in the central United States.

Swink, F.S., and G.S. Wilhelm. 1994. *Plants of the Chicago Region*. Indianapolis: Indiana Academy of Science.

> Summarizes composition and dynamics for natural communities in southeast Wisconsin, northeast Illinois, northwest Indiana, and southwest Michigan. Provides an authoritative introduction to floristic quality assessment in this region and includes coefficients of conservatism for all species treated. Of more than regional significance; especially valuable for its lists of plant species' associates and habitats.

Weaver, J.E. 1954. *North American Prairie*. Lincoln, Nebraska: Johnsen Publishing Company.

> The classic study of the midwestern tallgrass prairie, focusing mostly on the area west of the Mississippi.

References for States and Provinces

Arkansas

Shepherd, B. ed. 1984. *Arkansas's Natural Heritage*. Little Rock, AR: August House.

> Provides a good introduction to Arkansas natural communities including an overview of rare plants, animals, plant communities, and aquatic ecosystems. The bibliography provides the best available references to further readings.

Illinois

Taft, J.B., G.S. Wilhelm, D.M. Ladd, and L.A. Masters. 1996. "Floristic Quality Assessment for Illinois." *Erigenia* 15, no. 1.

> Method and application of assessing floristic quality using the plant species present in an area. It includes a checklist of plant species known from Illinois, with the scientific name, common name, coefficient of conservatism, wetness category, nativity, and physiognomy.

White, J. 1978. *Technical Report: Illinois Natural Areas Inventory*. Illinois Department of Conservation, Lincoln Tower Plaza, 524 S. Second Street, Springfield, IL 62701.

> Good information on many types of prairies, wetlands, savannas, barrens, flatwoods, and other ecosystem types (including short lists of dominant and characteristic species). Woodlands are lumped with forest.

Indiana

Homoya, M.A., D.B. Abrell, J.R. Aldrich, and T. W. Post. 1985. "The Natural Regions of Indiana." *Proceedings of the Indiana Academy of Science* 94:245–268.

> Maps the natural regions of the state and then describes the natural communities within each region. Lists the species restricted to those regions and lists both indicator species for natural communities and threatened and endangered species present.

Iowa

Delong, K.T., and C. Hooper. 1996 "A Potential Understory Flora for Oak Savanna in Iowa." *Journal of the Iowa Academy of Science* 103: 9–28.

> Lengthy discussion of midwestern savannas. Comprehensive listing of 252 plant species potentially found in Iowa oak savannas, including notes for each species on abundance, habitat caraciteristics, and presence in comparable sites in Illinois, Wisconsin, and Minnesota.

Eilers, L.J., and D.M. Roosa. 1994. *The Vascular Plants of Iowa*. Iowa City: University of Iowa Press.

> Presents a comprehensive list of plant species occurring in Iowa with information on nativeness, habitat, and range. This book also includes a summary of plant community types in Iowa including short lists of characteristic species for each community. Landform and other maps associated with plant community types are included. An extensive bibliography cites in-depth floristic and natural history studies of specific regions and community types.

Howe, R.W., M.J. Huston, W.P. Pusateri, R.H. Laushman, and W.E. Shennum. 1984. *An Inventory of Significant Natural Areas in Iowa*. Iowa Natural Areas Inventory, Iowa Conservation Commission, Department of Natural Resources, Wallace State Office Building, Des Moines, IA 50319.

> Presents descriptions of and a key to natural communities in Iowa. Natural communities are related to landforms of Iowa. Habitats of rare plants and animals are noted.

Mutel, C.F. 1989. *Fragile Giants: A Natural History of the Loess Hills*. Iowa City: University of Iowa Press.

> Comprehensive guide to the natural features and human-induced alterations of western Iowa's and northwestern Missouri's Loess Hills, which (in Iowa) include the state's largest remaining prairies.

Kansas

Kuchler, A.W. 1974. "A New Vegetation Map of Kansas." *Ecology* 55:586–604.

> The best technical reference for Kansas. This publication provides both a map

(unfortunately now out of print) and specific descriptions of the sixteen major plant communities in Kansas including lists of species for those communities.

Reichman, O.J. 1987. *Konza Prairie: A Tallgrass Natural History.* Lawrence: University of Kansas Press.

> Provides a specific description of Konza Prairie, one type of prairie in Kansas. Written for a general audience, it gives a good description of the Flint Hills, the largest remaining region of tallgrass prairie in North America.

Manitoba

Scoggan, H.J. 1957. *Flora of Manitoba.* Bulletin 140 of Biological Series 47, Department of Northern Affairs and Natural Resources, National Museum of Canada, Ottawa, Ontario.

> A technical guide (no pictures) to the plants of Manitoba. A good source for earlier plant records and species ranges.

Teller, J.T., ed. 1984. *Natural Heritage of Manitoba.* Winnipeg, Manitoba: Manitoba Museum of Man and Nature.

> An introduction to the vegetation, geology, soils, and natural and cultural history of Manitoba. Well-illustrated survey of Manitoba's historical landscape.

Michigan

Chapman, K.A. 1984. "An Ecological Investigation of Native Grassland in Southern Lower Michigan." M.S. thesis, Western Michigan University, Kalamazoo, Michigan.

> Vegetation samples of most of Michigan's prairies compared with one another using ordination and classified into prairie types. Good historical descriptions of prairies and savannas.

Herman, K.D., L.A. Masters, M.R. Penskar, A.A. Resnicek, G.S. Wilhelm, and W.W. Brodowicz. 1996. *Floristic Quality Assessment System with Wetland Categories and Computer Application Programs for the State of Michigan.* Michigan Department of Natural Resources, Wildlife Division, Natural Heritage Program, Box 30028, Lansing, MI 48909.

> Method and application of assessing floristic quality using the plant species present in an area from remnant natural areas to wetland mitigation projects. It includes a checklist of plant species known from Michigan, with the scientific name, common name, coefficient of conservatism, wetness category, nativity, and physiognomy. Also included is a computer program useful in the application of the system.

Minnesota

Eggers, S.D., and D.M. Reed. 1987. *Wetland Plants and Plant Communities of Minnesota and Wisconsin.* U.S. Army Corps of Engineers,

North Central District, 1421 U.S. Post Office and Custom House, 180 E. Kellogg Boulevard, St. Paul, MN 55101.

Categorizes natural and disrupted wetlands in Minnesota and Wisconsin into fifteen plant communities, with descriptions and color photos.

Minnesota Natural Heritage Program. 1993. *Minnesota's Native Vegetation: A Key to Natural Communities.* Version 1.5, Biological Report 20, Minnesota Department of Natural Resources, 500 Lafayette Road, St. Paul, MN 55155.

A descriptive key to the fifty-five natural communities presently recognized in Minnesota. The text for each community type includes general information on structure, dominant and typical species, and ecology. Appendices list common plants for the prairies and wetland communities recognized in the key.

Wovcha, D.S., B.C. Delaney, and G.E. Nordquist. 1995. *Minnesota's St. Croix River Valley and Anoka Sandplain: A Guide to Native Habitats.* Minneapolis: University of Minnesota Press.

Provides a landscape history and descriptions of the present natural communities of the St. Croix River Valley and Anoka Sand Plain region of east central Minnesota. Each natural community description contains a fact sheet with information on structure as well as distribution and lists of common, characteristic, and rare plant and animal species. Because this region spans Minnesota's three major biomes, the book provides detailed information on thirty-nine of the fifty-five communities presently recognized in the state.

Missouri

Ladd, D.M. 1993. *Coefficients of Conservatism for Missouri Vascular Flora.* The Nature Conservancy, 2800 S. Brentwood Boulevard, St. Louis, MO 63144.

Method and application of assessing floristic quality using the plant species present in an area. A checklist of plant species known from Missouri, with the scientific name, common name, coefficient of conservatism, wetness category, nativity, and physiognomy, is included.

Nelson, P.W. 1987. *The Terrestrial Natural Communities of Missouri: A Guide to Missouri's Presettlement Landscape.* The Missouri Natural Areas Committee, Missouri Department of Natural Resources, P.O. Box 176, and Missouri Department of Conservation, P.O. Box 180, Jefferson City, MO 65102.

Gives an overview of Missouri's six major terrestrial communities, with detailed descriptions of eighty individual communities including maps showing where the community generally occurred in presettlement times and where it can be seen today. Lists a few characteristic dominant and restricted species for each community. Also included are photographs, charts, illustrations, and keys.

Nebraska

Kaul, R.B., and S.B. Rolfsmeier. 1993. *Native Vegetation Map of Nebraska.* Geological Survey, Conservation and Survey Division, University of Nebraska, Lincoln, NE 68588.

> A large map depicting the major presettlement plant communities of Nebraska with their various subtypes. Includes a written description of each community along with a list of dominant species and a short statement about the status (present condition and abundance) as well as the location of existing remnants.

Weaver, J.E. 1965. *Native Vegetation of Nebraska.* Lincoln: University of Nebraska Press.

> Covers tallgrass prairie types in great detail. Very good species lists for lowland and upland prairies. Less detailed descriptions of forest types. A whole chapter on the forbs of upland prairies. A good reference on soils. Many black-and-white photos.

North Dakota

Stewart, R.K., and H.A. Kantrud. 1972. *Vegetation of Prairie Potholes, North Dakota, in Relation to Quality of Water and Other Environmental Factors.* United States Geological Survey Professional Paper 585-D, Washington, DC.

Ohio

Anderson, D.M. 1982. *The Plant Communities of Ohio: A Preliminary Classification and Description.* Ohio Department of Natural Resources, Division of Natural Areas and Preserves, Fountain Square, Columbus, OH 43224.

> Moves beyond Gordon (see below) in breaking down communities into much finer gradations (e.g., the various types of oak woods and forest as well as many different types of Ohio prairie such as little bluestem prairies, etc.). Based on extensive fieldwork.

Andreas, B.K., and R.W. Lichvar. 1995. *Floristic Index for Establishing Assessment Standards: A Case Study for Northern Ohio.* Technical Report WRP-DE-8. Vicksburg, MS: U.S. Army Corps of Engineers Waterways Experiment Station.

> Includes the method and application of assessing floristic quality using the plant species present in an area. It includes a checklist of plant species known from thirty-one counties in northern Ohio, with the scientific name, family, coefficient of conservatism, nativity, and rarity status.

Gordon, Robert B. 1969. "The Natural Vegetation of Ohio in Pioneer Days." *Bulletin of the Ohio Biological Survey,* New Series, 3, no. 2:1–113.

> Color map of presettlement vegetation of Ohio. Text includes descriptions of major community types with species lists and indicator species for each.

Stuckey, Ronald L., and Karen J. Reese, eds. 1981. *The Prairie Penin-sula—in the "Shadow" of Transeau: Proceedings of the Sixth North American Prairie Conference,* August 12–17, 1978, Ohio State University, Columbus, Ohio. Ohio Biological Survey Biological Notes No. 15.

> Papers often dealing with specific features of Ohio—prairie sites, soils, glacial features, etc. Good species lists for Ohio prairies.

Oklahoma

Blair, W.F., and T.H. Hubbell. 1938. "The Biotic Districts of Oklahoma." *American Midland Naturalist* 20:425–454.

> Describes eleven biotic districts and includes a map of their distribution in the state. Descriptions of each biotic district consider physiography, geology, climate, and principal plant associations with lists of dominant species.

Bruner, W.E. 1931. "The Vegetation of Oklahoma." *Ecological Monographs* 1:100–188.

> Discusses major plant communities within the deciduous forest and grassland formation of Oklahoma. Dominant plant species in each community type are listed. Map of the state's major biotic provinces.

Duck, L.G., and J.B. Fletcher. 1945. *A Survey of the Game and Fur-Bearing Animals of Oklahoma.* Department of Wildlife Conservation, 1801 N. Lincoln, P.O. Box 53465, Oklahoma City, OK 73152.

> Although the title suggests otherwise, this publication devotes most of its attention to describing the plant communities across Oklahoma. The authors created a multicolored map of vegetation types in the state while touring by automobile in the 1940s.

Rice, E.L., and W.T. Penfound. 1959. "The Upland Forests of Oklahoma." *Ecology* 40:592–608.

> A thorough analysis and description of woody species composition in upland forests. The majority of stands analyzed were cross timbers or oak savanna.

Ontario

Bakowsky, W.D. 1988. "The Phytosociology of Midwestern Savanna in the Carolinian Region of Southern Ontario." M.S. thesis, Department of Botany, University of Toronto.

> Lists species in order of decreasing prevalence for four tallgrass savanna types (wet-mesic, mesic, dry-mesic, and dry).

Faber-Langendoen, D., and P. F. Maycock. 1994. "Vegetation Analysis of Tallgrass Prairie in Southern Ontario." In *Proceedings: 13th North American Prairie Conference,* R.G. Wickett, P.D. Lewis, A. Woodliffe, and P. Pratt, eds. Windsor, Ontario: Department of Parks and Recreation.

Lists most prevalent prairie in fire-moisture segments. Reviews relationship of prairies to moisture and soil type.

Oldham, M.J., W.D. Bakowsky, and D.A. Sutherland. 1995. *Floristic Quality Assessment for Southern Ontario*. Natural Heritage Information Centre, Ontario Ministry of Natural Resources, P.O. Box 700, Peterborough, Ontario, Canada K97 8M5.

Includes the method and application of assessing floristic quality using the plant species present in an area. It includes a checklist of plant species known from southern Ontario, with the scientific name, common name, coefficient of conservatism, wetness category, nativity, and physiognomy.

South Dakota

Barnes, P.W., and L.L. Tieszen. 1978. *A Phytosociological Study of 14 Selected Communities at the Samuel H. Ordway Prairie*. Data report to the Nature Conservancy, Midwest Office, 1313 5th Street SE, Minneapolis, MN 55414.

Hansen, P.L., and G.R. Hoffman. 1988. *The Vegetation of the Grand River / Cedar River, Sioux, and Ashland Districts of the Custer National Forest: A Habitat Type Classification*. General Technical Report RM-157. Washington, DC: USDA Forest Service.

A habitat-type classification of eight grassland types found on U.S. Forest Service land in northwestern South Dakota and southeastern Montana. Includes a dichotomous key to these vegetation types, photos of the different types, plot locations, site characteristics, and tables of phytosociological data (species cover, frequency, and tree-size classes). Also includes a discussion of each habitat type, methods of sampling, and successional relationships.

Texas

Correll, D.S., and M.C. Johnston. 1979. *Manual of Vascular Plants of Texas*. Dallas: University of Texas at Dallas.

A guide to the flora of Texas that describes the ten ecological areas of the state and mentions their characteristic species.

Wisconsin

Curtis, J.T. 1959. *The Vegetation of Wisconsin: An Ordination of Plant Communities*. Madison: University of Wisconsin Press.

Describes origin and ecology of plant community types including forests, prairies, savannas, shrublands, and wetlands. Lists most prevalent species for most types in five moisture-based segments (wet, wet-mesic, mesic, dry-mesic, and dry).

Wisconsin Department of Natural Resources. 1995. *Plant Species Composition of Wisconsin Prairies, An Aid to Selecting Species for Plantings and Restorations Based upon University of Wisconsin–Madison Plant Ecology Laboratory Data.* Technical Bulletin No. 188. Wisconsin Department of Natural Resources, Box 7921, Madison, WI 53707.

Provides guidance on species selection, seeding rates, and seeding ratios for Wisconsin.

Appendix E
Sources of Seeds and Equipment

Buying Local Seed

There is no easy way to find the best sources of local seed. Often the best information comes by word of mouth, if you can find a network of knowledgeable people. Nature centers, state parks, universities, and conservation organizations are good places to start your search. Another source is the many people who write up their restoration results in the journal *Restoration and Management Notes*.

As you search for reliable sources of native seed, keep in mind that not all people in the business will have the same standards as you. Definitions vary and miscommunication is common. Some buyers have paid extra for local seed only to find that the seed was not as local as believed. It is hard to verify dealers' assurances regarding the source of their seed. A seed-seller's reputation is important, and many sellers have excellent reputations. Ask around.

The following questions and comments will help you assess seed dealers and their products:

- *Are the nursery's seeds of local genotype, i.e., does the nursery wild-collect from within a certain range (both within and outside of the nursery's home state)?*

   If your restoration plan calls for seeds to be from within a certain distance of the restoration site, you need to know where your seed comes from. Nurseries that sell plants should also be able to tell you the source of their seed. This should be relatively simple for them to do for both wild-collected seed and nursery-propagated seed (see third question below). Seed ranges will vary by species, so you need to check for each species you order.

- *Does the nursery sell seed that has been purchased from wholesalers or other dealers, and if so, does it know the collection range of those materials? Are those "bought-in" seeds kept separate from other stock?*

    Knowing which dealer the seed came from is not enough to determine a seed's origin; you need to know the collection range to determine its suitability for your site. If the nursery does not have that information, it should be able to refer you to the original dealer.

- *Does the nursery sell seeds that are field-grown and harvested as opposed to wild-collected? What is the origin of the seeds used to plant those fields?*

    Many nurseries are mass-producing seeds due to economies of scale. They should know the origin of the seeds used to plant their fields, and in particular, they should know whether the seed planted into those fields was wild-collected or harvested from an existing field. The concern here is the "distance" (in generations) of the seeds from the wild; some research has shown that with each generation removed from the wild state, genotypes become more conditioned to the "easy life" of a field, where competition for resources is minimal. These genotypes may result in plants that are less hardy when planted in a wild condition such as a restoration.

- *Does the nursery sell inoculant?*

    Legume seeds require *rhizobium* inoculant for successful germination. If the nursery sells legume seeds without supplying inoculant (or at least informing you of the necessity for inoculant), you should be concerned about the qualifications of the nursery.

A regional list of purveyors of local native seeds and nursery plants is maintained by the National Wildflower Research Center, 2600 FM 973 North, Austin, TX 78725–4201 (512–929–3600).

The following list contains the best overall clearinghouses for sources of local seed in each state. Those agencies with asterisks can provide you with lists of local seed sources. These lists vary in their standards and inclusiveness. In the center of the tallgrass region there will be many more options to choose among. Asking questions like the above will help you decide on the relative merits of the available options. Agencies without asterisks do not necessarily provide lists of seed sources but may have general restoration suggestions or give some sources verbally. The best approach with these agencies is often to seek out the individual most knowledgeable about restoration.

ILLINOIS
*Division of Natural Heritage, Illinois Department of Natural Resources, 524 S. 2nd Street, Springfield, IL 62701–1787 (217–785–8774, fax 217–785–8277).

INDIANA
*Division of Nature Preserves, Indiana Department of Natural Resources, 402 W. Washington Street, Room W267, Indianapolis, IN 46204 (317–232–4052, fax 317–233–0133).
*Pigeon River Fish and Wildlife Area, P.O. Box 71, Mongo, IN 46771 (219–367–2164, fax 219–367–2043).

IOWA
*Ecological Services, Iowa Department of Natural Resources, Wallace State Office Building, Des Moines, IA 50319 (515–281–3891, fax 515–281–6794).
*U.S. Fish & Wildlife Service, Walnut Creek National Wildlife Refuge, P.O. Box 399, Prairie City, IA 50228 (515–994–2415, fax 515–994–2104).

KANSAS
*The Land Institute, 2440 E. Water Well Road, Salina, KS 67401 (913–823–5376, fax 913–823–8728).

MICHIGAN
*Natural Heritage Program, Michigan Department of Natural Resources, Attn. Stewardship and Natural Areas, P.O. Box 30444, Lansing, MI 48909–7944 (517–373–1263, fax 517–373–6705).

MINNESOTA
*State Scientific and Natural Areas Program, Minnesota Department of Natural Resources, Box 7, 500 Lafayette Street, St. Paul, MN 55155 (612–296–3344, fax 612–297–4961).

MISSOURI
*Natural History Division, Missouri Department of Conservation, P.O. Box 180, Jefferson City, MO 65102–0180 (314–751–4115, fax 314–526–5582; e-mail: smitht2@mail.conservation.state.mo.us).

NEBRASKA
Prairie Plains Resource Institute, 1307 L Street, Aurora, NE 68818–2126 (402–694–5535).

NORTH DAKOTA
Natural Heritage Program, North Dakota Parks and Recreation, 1835
    Bismarck Expressway, Bismarck, ND 58504 (701–328–5368, fax
    701–328–5363).

OHIO
Division of Natural Areas and Preserves, Ohio Department of Natural
    Resources, 1889 Fountain Square Court, Columbus, OH 43224
    (614–265–6468, fax 614–267–3096).
*Hamilton County Park District, 10245 Winton Road, Cincinnati, OH
    45231, (513–521–7275, fax 513–521–2606).
The Nature Conservancy, Northwest Ohio Lake Plain Office, 10420
    Old State Line Road, Swanton, OH 43558 (419–867–1521, fax
    419–867–1521).

OKLAHOMA
*Tall Grass Prairie Preserve, The Nature Conservancy, P.O. Box 458,
    Pawhuska, OK 74056 (918–287–4803, fax 918–287–1296).

SOUTH DAKOTA
Natural Heritage Program, South Dakota Game, Fish, and Parks Depart-
    ment, 523 E. Capital Avenue, Pierre, SD 57501 (605–773–4227;
    e-mail: daveo@gfp.state.sd.us).

TEXAS
*National Wildflower Research Center, 2600 FM 973 North, Austin,
    TX 78725–4201 (512–929–3600).
*Native Plant Society of Texas, P.O. Box 891, Georgetown, TX 78627
    (512–863–9685, fax 512–869–0393).

WISCONSIN
Wisconsin Department of Natural Resources, Bureau of Endangered
    Resources, P.O. Box 7921, Madison, WI 53707 (608–267–5066,
    fax 608–267–3579; e-mail: kearns@dnr.state.wi.us).

Buying Restoration Equipment and Seed Supplies

Not long ago tools used in the infant discipline of restoration were hand-
built original devices or modifications of machines designed for some
other purpose. More recently, however, restoration has discovered its
kindred disciplines of forestry and agriculture. As it has learned
techniques from them, it has borrowed their equipment. Thus suppliers
of equipment such as "Farm and Fleet" and "Forestry Suppliers" have

become as familiar to many restorationists as the miscellaneous home-made contraptions that still do much of restoration's daily work.

The list below contains the major suppliers of equipment and supplies as well as addresses for much of the specialized equipment described earlier in this book.

GENERAL SUPPLIERS

Aside from your nearest farm supplies dealer (a particularly good source for locating inexpensive bulk herbicide and people who do contract tractor work), the most comprehensive sources of restoration and monitoring supplies are the big forestry equipment retailers. Their catalogs brim with everything from fire swatters and meter tapes to herbicide sprayers and bulldozer attachments.

Forestry Suppliers, P.O. Box 8397, Jackson, MS 39284–8397 (800–647–5368, fax 800–543–4203).

Ben Meadows Company, 3589 Broad Street, Atlanta, GA 30341 (800–241–6401, fax 800–628–2068).

INOCULANT

For live *Rhizobium* bacteria, which are usually essential when planting legumes: Liphatech, 3101 W. Tester Avenue, Milwaukee, WI 53209 (414–462–7600).

FANNING MILLS AND CLEANING SCREENS

Bount Agri/Industrial Corporation, 805 S. Decker Drive, P.O. Box 256, Bluffton, IN 46714 (219–824–3400).

Crippen Manufacturing Company, Alma, MI 48801 (517–463–2119 or 800–248–8318).

Hance Corporation, 235 E. Broadway, Westerville, OH 43081 (614–882–7400).

Kaltenberg Seed Farms, 5506 Hwy. 19, Waunakee, WI (608–251–5880).

NASCO, 901 Janesville Avenue, Fort Atkinson, WI 53538–0901 (414–563–2446).

Seedburo Equipment Company, 1022 W. Jackson Boulevard, Chicago, IL 60607–2990 (312–738–3700 or 800–284–5779).

HARVESTING AND COLLECTING EQUIPMENT

Ag-Renewal, Inc., 1710 Airport Road, Weatherford, OK 73096 (405–772–7059 or 800–658–1446, fax 405–772–6887). Woodward Flail-Vac seed stripper, pneumatic seed shucker.

Environmental Survey Consulting, 4602 Placid Place, Austin, TX 78731 (512–458–8531). Grin Reaper.

Prairie Habitats, Box 1, Argyle, MB, Canada R0C 0B0 (204–467–9371, fax 204–467–5004). Seed strippers.

HAMMERMILLS
Winona Attrition Mill Company, 1009 W. 5th Street, Winona, MN (507–452–2716).

SEED DRILLS AND GRASS PLANTERS
Ag-Renewal, Inc., 1710 Airport Road, Weatherford, OK 73096 (405–772–7059 or 800–658–1446, fax 405–772–6887).
Brillion Iron Works, 200 Park Avenue, Brillion, WI 54110 (414–756–2121).
Truax Company, Inc., 3609 Vera Cruz Avenue, Minneapolis, MN 55422 (612–537–6639).

SEED TESTING LABS
Plant Industries Division, Missouri Seed Control Lab, Missouri Department of Agriculture, P.O. Box 630, Jefferson City, MO 65102 (314–715–4340).
Hulsey Seed Laboratory, Inc., P.O. Box 132, Decatur, GA 30031 (404–294–5450).
Ark-Mo Commercial Seed Lab, P.O. Box 9, Route 2, Lee Town Road, Pea Ridge, AR 71751 (501–451–1703).
Seed Testing of America, 950 Boston Avenue, Longmont, OH 80501 (303–651–6417).

Appendix F
Restoration Contacts

Restoration Organizations

Natural Areas Association, 108 Fox Street, Mukwonago, WI 53149 (414–363–5500)
A nonprofit organization of professional and active workers in natural area identification, preservation, protection, management, and research. Aims to provide a medium of exchange and coordination and to advance the public understanding and appreciation of natural areas and other elements of natural diversity.
Publication: *Natural Areas Journal*

Society for Conservation Biology, Department of Wildlife Ecology, University of Wisconsin, Madison, WI 53706 (608–263–6827)
A professional society dedicated to providing the scientific information and expertise required to protect the world's biological diversity. Incorporated as a tax-exempt scientific organization, the society has an international advisory council and a board composed of scholars, government personnel, administrators, and representatives from scientific and conservation organizations.
Publication: *Conservation Biology*

Society for Ecological Restoration, University of Wisconsin–Madison Arboretum, 1207 Seminole Highway, Madison, WI 53711 (608–262–9547)
Created to promote the development of ecological restoration both as a discipline and as a model for a healthy relationship with nature, and to raise awareness of the value and limitations of restoration as a conservation strategy.
Publications: *Ecological Restoration; Restoration and Management Notes; SER News*

Society of Wetland Scientists, 810 E. 10th Street, P.O. Box 1897, Lawrence, KS 66044 (913–843–1221)
Publication: *Wetlands, the Journal of the Society of Wetland Scientists*

The Nature Conservancy, 1815 North Lynn Street, Arlington, VA 22209 (703–841–5300) The mission of the Nature Conservancy is to preserve plants, animals, and natural communities that represent the diversity of life on earth by protecting the lands and waters they need to survive.
Publication: *The Nature Conservancy*

World Wide Web Sites

Dr. Virginia Kline's Teaching Collection (video images of plants)
gopher://gopher.adp.wisc.edu:70/11/.data/.bot/.veg/.list

Grand Prairie Friends
http://www.prairienet.org/community/clubs/gpf/homepage.html

Iowa Prairie Network Homepage
http://www.netins.net/showcase/bluestem/ipnapp.htm

Northern Prairie Science Center
http://npsc.nbs.gov

Tallgrass Prairie in Illinois (Illinois Natural History Survey)
http://www.prairienet.org/tallgrass/

The Konza Prairie
http://climate.konza.edu/region.html

Where the Buffalo roam (Fermilab)
http://www.fnal.gov/ecology.html

Contributors

Author *Roger C. Anderson* is distinguished professor of plant ecology in the Department of Biological Sciences at Illinois State University, Normal, Illinois. He has been the director of the University of Wisconsin–Madison Arboretum and served as a member of the Illinois Nature Preserves Commission for six years. He serves on the editorial board of the journal *Restoration Ecology*. Dr. Anderson has written nearly fifty articles and three book chapters on aspects of the ecology of tallgrass prairies.

Author *Steven I. Apfelbaum* is senior ecologist and president of Applied Ecological Services, Inc., in Brodhead, Wisconsin. He has been active in thousands of research and restoration projects involving savanna, prairie, wetlands, and other ecological systems throughout the United States and Canada.

Author *Brian J. Bader* is the native plant propagation specialist at the University of Wisconsin–Madison Arboretum. He has been working with native plant propagation and prairie restoration since the early 1980s. Prior to coming to the UW Arboretum, he directed native plant production activities at a commercial wildflower nursery.

Author *Victoria J. Byre* is a curatorial assistant at the Oklahoma Museum of Natural History in Norman, Oklahoma, and a contract biologist for the Nature Conservancy. During the past twenty years, she has been involved in the management and monitoring of breeding-bird communities throughout the Midwest. Currently, she is working with least terns and black-capped vireos.

Author *Richard R. Clinebell II* is a doctoral candidate in the Department of Biology at St. Louis University, where he is studying pollination biology of prairie pentstemons. He holds bachelor's degrees in biology and applied mathematics and master's degrees in biology and statistics.

He has harvested prairie seed for twenty-three consecutive years and has grown prairie plants during most of that time.

Author *Neil Diboll* is a consulting ecologist and president of Prairie Nursery of Westfield, Wisconsin. Since 1982, his work has focused on restoring native plant communities and providing plants, seeds, and technical information to the public. His goal is to help individuals and organizations to understand and apply ecological principles to further the preservation, management, and restoration of North American ecosystems.

Chapter editor and author *Dave Egan* is associate editor of *Restoration and Management Notes* at the University of Wisconsin Arboretum. When not wordsmithing or working as a consultant on prairie restoration projects, he can be found canoeing the waters of the Wisconsin River or collecting seeds along the roadsides near his rural home.

Author *Fred Faessler* is a senior staff member with Applied Ecological Services, Inc., and Taylor Creek Restoration Nurseries, both located in Brodhead, Wisconsin. He is creatively involved in the design, fabrication, and testing of seed harvesting and cleaning equipment.

Author *William R. Jordan III* is the founding editor of the journal *Restoration and Management Notes* and a founding member of the Society for Ecological Restoration. He is the author of the forthcoming book *Sunflower Forest: Ecological Restoration and the New Communion with Nature*, among other publications. Since 1977 he has worked at the University of Wisconsin–Madison Arboretum, where he is in charge of publications.

Author *Virginia M. Kline* received her doctorate in plant ecology from the University of Wisconsin. As arboretum ecologist, she has been responsible for planning and evaluating the management of the Arboretum's one thousand acres of prairie, savanna, wetland, and forest for nearly two decades. She coordinates research at the Arboretum and has published numerous scientific papers and lay articles related to ecological restoration.

Appendix author *Douglas Ladd* is director of science and stewardship for the Missouri Chapter of the Nature Conservancy. He works extensively with midwestern prairies and woodlands, where he places special emphasis on vegetation monitoring and assessment and on fire-vegetation interrelationships. His most recent publication is the book *Tallgrass Prairie Wildflowers*.

Author *David Mahler* is a partner with Environmental Survey Consulting, a firm that carries out habitat restoration work in Central Texas, as well as naturalistic rockwork, native landscaping, wetland creations, and erosion-control projects. He is the inventor of the Grin Reaper, a native-seed harvester that ESC manufactures and sells.

Author *Linda A. Masters* is a restoration ecologist at Conservation Design Forum in Naperville, Illinois, where she is involved in restoration and development of restoration performance standards. She has developed computer programs for assimilation and analysis of monitoring data, which emphasize floristic quality and physiognomic changes.

Author *Kenneth S. Mierzwa* is a senior ecologist and project manager with TAMS Consultants, Inc., in Chicago, Illinois, where he is involved in a variety of endangered-species research studies, ecological inventories, and wetland restoration plans. He is especially interested in the metapopulation dynamics of amphibians within natural areas and restoration sites.

Author *R. Michael Miller* is soil ecologist in the Environmental Research Division at Argonne National Laboratory. He has over twenty years of experience in reclamation and restoration ecology. His recent investigations have focused on the role of mycorrhizal fungi as facilitators in the restoration process, especially their role in pedogenesis. This research is being conducted in both tallgrass prairie and tropical montane ecosystems.

Author *John P. Morgan* is co-owner and manager of Prairie Habitats, Canada's first prairie restoration company. He holds an honors degree in zoology and a master's degree in natural resources management from the University of Manitoba. He has a strong love of prairies and has received national recognition for his pioneering work on prairie restoration in Canada. He is co-author of *Restoring Canada's Native Prairies—A Practical Manual*.

Volume editor and author *Cornelia F. Mutel* has authored books on the natural history of the Loess Hills (*Fragile Giants*) and Colorado (*Grassland to Glacier*). A historian of science at the University of Iowa's Institute for Hydraulic Research, she has attempted to foster healthy and sustainable interactions with the natural environment through these and other books and publications, as well as through her position as consulting editor for the University of Iowa Press's natural history publications.

Artist *Paul W. Nelson* is director of the Natural Resource Management Program, Missouri Department of Natural Resources, Division of State Parks, in Jefferson City, Missouri. He authored *The Terrestrial Natural Communities of Missouri*, has illustrated many botanical guides, and has worked extensively in restoring midwestern savannas, glades, and prairies. Despite considerable skepticism and resistance from other restorationists, he initiated savanna and woodland restoration through prescribed burning in the early 1980s. Today the practice is applied to thousands of wooded Missouri acres.

Artist *John Norton* is a freelance scientific and nature illustrator and cartoonist in Annapolis, Maryland, who has illustrated several biology textbooks, field guides, and booklets on many diverse topics.

Volume editor and author *Stephen Packard* is director of science and stewardship for the Illinois Chapter of the Nature Conservancy and research associate in the Department of Botany at the Field Museum of Natural History in Chicago. He co-convened the first Midwest Savanna Conference and proposed and co-authored the first Midwest Oak Ecosystems Recovery Plan. He began his restoration career in 1977 as a volunteer with the North Branch Prairie Project; he is currently steward of one of the project's twelve restoration sites, the ninety-acre Somme Prairie Grove.

Author *Wayne R. Pauly* is naturalist for Dane County Parks in Madison, Wisconsin. He works with over a thousand volunteers who help manage the county's natural areas, and who collect, clean, and plant thirty to forty acres of prairie flowers each year.

Author *James A. Reinartz* is senior scientist and resident biologist-manager of the University of Wisconsin–Milwaukee Field Station. He has worked on the ecological genetics, population biology, and ecology of rare plants and applied these studies to the development of recovery programs. His research also includes wetland ecology and the study of applied natural area management and restoration.

Author *Laurel M. Ross* has coordinated the work of the Volunteer Stewardship Network for the Illinois Chapter of the Nature Conservancy. She is currently director of the Conservancy's conservation programs in northeastern Illinois (Chicago Wilderness) and a volunteer steward with the North Branch Prairie Project, specializing in seed harvest. She counts among her favorite recent projects Prairie University, the Mighty Acorns (youth stewardship volunteers), and the Orchid Recovery Project.

Author *Peter Schramm* pioneered prairie restoration procedures at Knox College, where he is now emeritus professor of biology. He applies his thirty-one years of work in prairie restoration and prairie vertebrate studies to his commercial prairie planting business (Peter Schramm–Prairie Restorations), through which he plants twenty-five to thirty prairies a year in Illinois, Iowa, and Missouri, specializing in drilled, high-density forb mosaic prairies.

Author *Mary Kay Solecki* is a natural areas preservation specialist with the Illinois Nature Preserves Commission. She has been active in prairie and savanna restoration for over eight years.

Author *James F. Steffen* is an ecologist at the Chicago Botanic Garden in Glencoe, Illinois, where he is working on the restoration of oak savannas and woodlands. He holds a master's degree in environmental science from the University of Wisconsin–Green Bay.

Author *Allen A. Steuter* is director of science and stewardship for the Nebraska Chapter of the Nature Conservancy. He directs the management of the 54,000-acre Niobrara Valley Preserve. He holds a Ph.D. in range science from Texas Tech University in Lubbock. He is the author or co-author of over thirty technical papers, most of which focus on the fire and grazing ecology of Great Plains grasslands. With his family, he owns and operates a ranch in the Nebraska Sandhills.

Author *Douglas J. Taron* has been co-steward at Bluff Spring Fen near his home in Elgin, Illinois, since 1982. Since 1989, he has been volunteer coordinator for the Illinois Butterfly Monitoring Network. He holds a Ph.D. in biochemistry from Northwestern University and is employed by Vysis, Inc., of Downers Grove, Illinois, where he researches the use of DNA probes for cancer diagnostics.

Appendix author *Stanley A. Temple* is the Beers–Bascom professor in conservation in the Department of Wildlife Ecology, University of Wisconsin– Madison. He has been president of the Society of Conservation Biology and chair of the Wisconsin Chapter of the Nature Conservancy. He has restored a tallgrass prairie remnant on his farm in rural Wisconsin.

Author *Gerould S. Wilhelm* is the principal environmental scientist at Conservation Design Forum in Naperville, Illinois. He holds a Ph.D. in botany from Southern Illinois University, Carbondale. He is co-author, with Floyd Swink, of the book *Plants of the Chicago Region,* and currently is an SER board member and editor of *Erigenia*. His interests include the floristics and ecology of the lichens and vascular plants of the Midwest, and the restoration of their habitats.

Index